Nirali's New Series

CONCISE STUDY SERIES

COMPUTER NETWORK TECHNOLOGY

For
T.E. SEMESTER – I
THIRD YEAR DEGREE COURSES
IN INFORMATION TECHNOLOGY

As Per New Revised Syllabus of UoP, 2014

NN SAKHARE
M. E. (Computer Networks)
Lecturer, Comp. Engg. Dept.
Vishwakarma Institute of
Information Technology (VIIT),
Kondhwa, Pune.

DS GAIKWAD
M. E. (Computer)
Assistant Professor,
Comp. Engg. Dept.
NBN Sinhgad School of Engineering
Ambegoan, Pune.

ND LAMBE
M. E. (Computer)
Assistant Professor, Comp. Engg. Dept.
NBN Sinhgad School of Engineering
Ambegaon, Pune

AM BAGUL
M. E. (Computer)
Assistant Professor, Comp. Engg. Dept.
NBN Sinhgad School of Engineering
Ambegaon, Pune

NIRALI PRAKASHAN
ADVANCEMENT OF KNOWLEDGE

N 3181

COMPUTER NETWORK TECHNOLOGY (T.E. I T)   ISBN 978-93-5164-145-2

First Edition	:	August 2014
©	:	Author

The text of this publication, or any part thereof, should not be reproduced or transmitted in any form or stored in any computer storage system or device for distribution including photocopy, recording, taping or information retrieval system or reproduced on any disc, tape, perforated media or other information storage device etc., without the written permission of Authors with whom the rights are reserved. Breach of this condition is liable for legal action. Every effort has been made to avoid errors or omissions in this publication. In spite of this, errors may have crept in. Any mistake, error or discrepancy so noted and shall be brought to our notice shall be taken care of in the next edition. It is notified that neither the publisher nor the authors or seller shall be responsible for any damage or loss of action to any one, of any kind, in any manner, therefrom.

Published By :

NIRALI PRAKASHAN
Abhyudaya Pragati, 1312, Shivaji Nagar,
Off J.M. Road, PUNE - 411005
Tel - (020) 25512336/37/39, Fax - (020) 25511379
Email : niralipune@pragationline.com

Printed By :

REPRO INDIA LTD
Mumbai.

DISTRIBUTION CENTRES
PUNE

Nirali Prakashan
119, Budhwar Peth, Jogeshwari Mandir Lane
Pune 411002, Maharashtra
Tel : (020) 2445 2044, 66022708, Fax : (020) 2445 1538
Email : bookorder@pragationline.com

Nirali Prakashan
S. No. 28/25, Dhyari,
Near Pari Company, Pune 411041
Tel : (022) 24690204 Fax : (020) 24690316
Email : dhyari@pragationline.com
bookorder@pragationline.com

MUMBAI
Nirali Prakashan
385, S.V.P. Road, Rasdhara Co-op. Hsg. Society Ltd.,
Girgaum, Mumbai 400004, Maharashtra
Tel : (022) 2385 6339 / 2386 9976, Fax : (022) 2386 9976
Email : niralimumbai@pragationline.com

DISTRIBUTION BRANCHES

NAGPUR
Pratibha Book Distributors
Above Maratha Mandir, Shop No. 3, First Floor,
Rani Jhanshi Square, Sitabuldi, Nagpur 440012,
Maharashtra, Tel : (0712) 254 7129

BENGALURU
Pragati Book House
House No. 1, Sanjeevappa Lane, Avenue Road Cross,
Opp. Rice Church, Bengaluru - 560002.
Tel : (080) 64513344, 64513355,
Mob : 9880582331, 9845021552
Email:bharatsavla@yahoo.com

JALGAON
Nirali Prakashan
34, V. V. Golani Market, Navi Peth, Jalgaon 425001,
Maharashtra, Tel : (0257) 222 0395
Mob : 94234 91860

KOLHAPUR
Nirali Prakashan
New Mahadvar Road,
Kedar Plaza, 1st Floor Opp. IDBI Bank
Kolhapur 416 012, Maharashtra. Mob : 9855046155

CHENNAI
Pragati Books
9/1, Montieth Road, Behind Taas Mahal, Egmore,
Chennai 600008 Tamil Nadu, Tel : (044) 6518 3535,
Mob : 94440 01782 / 98450 21552 / 98805 82331, Email : bharatsavla@yahoo.com

RETAIL OUTLETS
PUNE

Pragati Book Centre
157, Budhwar Peth, Opp. Ratan Talkies,
Pune 411002, Maharashtra
Tel : (020) 2445 8887 / 6602 2707, Fax : (020) 2445 8887

Pragati Book Centre
Amber Chamber, 28/A, Budhwar Peth,
Appa Balwant Chowk, Pune : 411002, Maharashtra,
Tel : (020) 20240335 / 66281669
Email : pbcpune@pragationline.com

Pragati Book Centre
676/B, Budhwar Peth, Opp. Jogeshwari Mandir,
Pune 411002, Maharashtra
Tel : (020) 6601 7784 / 6602 0855

PBC Book Sellers & Stationers
152, Budhwar Peth, Pune 411002, Maharashtra
Tel : (020) 2445 2254 / 6609 2463

MUMBAI
Pragati Book Corner
Indira Niwas, 111 - A, Bhavani Shankar Road, Dadar (W), Mumbai 400028, Maharashtra
Tel : (022) 2422 3526 / 6662 5254, Email : pbcmumbai@pragationline.com

www.pragationline.com   info@pragationline.com

PREFACE

It gives us immense pleasure to present this book **'Computer Network Technology'** to the students of Third Year Degree Course in Information Technology of the University of Pune.

As per New Revised Examination Scheme which has been implemented from this academic year, In-semester assessment carries 30 Marks, over first three units and End Semester Examination carries 70 Marks over entire syllabus of which First Three Units will carry 20 Marks and Units 4, 5, 6 will carry 50 Marks.

We would like to extend our sincere thanks to **Management of VIIT (BRACT) and STES, Dr. Mrs. Karkare (Principal VIIT), Dr. SD Markande (Principal NBNSSOE), Dr. Sakhare (Head, Comp. Dept, VIIT)** and **Dr. R. S. Prasad Sir (Head, Comp. Dept, NBN SSOE)** for their untiring support in our work.

The objectives of this text are :

Unit I Covers : Network Layer

Unit II Covers : Transport Layer

Unit III Covers : Application Layer

Unit IV Covers : Wireless Lans, Pans and Mans

Unit V Covers : AD-HOC Networks and Sensor Networks

Unit VI Covers : Routing in Sensor Networks and Recent Trends

Publication of this book in such a short period required a very dedicated and active co-operation from the publisher, Shri Dineshbhai Furia, Shri Jignesh Furia and Shri M. P. Munde and team Mrs. Anita Kulkarni, Mrs. Pratibha Bele and Mrs. Roshan Shaikh, Miss Sarika Shinde.

The frontiers of knowledge are boundless and fathomless. Any suggestions and feedback shall be appreciated and acknowledged.

August 2014   **Authors**

Pune

Dear Students,

It gives us great pleasure to introduce a New Series "**C**oncise **S**tudy **S**eries" for Second Year Engineering students. These "**CSS**" books are written by Experienced and Eminent Professors of respective subjects.

The specialty of this new Series "**CSS**" is that it:

- Covers full syllabus of University of Pune.
- Contains Matter written in Simple and Lucid language.
- Includes "To the Point" Topics and well arranged articles.
- Includes Most Likely Questions.
- Includes Previous Years University Question Papers.
- Available in all leading stores at Affordable Price.

Happy Studying and Best of Luck!!!

Nirali Prakashan

SYLLABUS

Unit - I : Network Layer   6 Hours
Packet Switching, Virtual Circuits, Datagram, Routing Algorithms: Optimality Principle, Shortest path routing- Dijkstra'sAlgorithms, Distance Vector, Routing, Link State Routing, Counting to infinity problem, RIP, OSPF, BGP, IP Addressing IPv4, IP Address Classes, Subnetting, CIDR/Supernetting, IP Fragmentation, ARP, DHCP, RARP, ICMP, IPv6.

Unit – II : Transport Layer   6 Hours
Transport layer duties and functionalities, application expectations and IP delivery semantics, Reliability at transport layer Vs. reliability at the Link Layer?
UDP : UDP functionality, UDP Header;
TCP : TCP Features, byte-stream, Connection-oriented, TCP Header Format, 2-way, 3-way Handshake, TCP State Diagram, TCP Sliding Window, Congestion Control Algorithms, Leaky Bucket, Token Bucket, Congestion Avoidance, RTT estimation , TCP Tahoe, Fast Retransmit, Fast Recovery, UNIX Socketsm, Congestion Avoidance, RTT Estimation , TCP Tahoe, Fast Retransmit, Fast Recovery, UNIX Sockets, Timer Management, Performance issue (concepts like: Throughput, Delay, Bandwidth Utilization, Error Rate, Congestion and Network Reliability).

Unit - III : Application Layer   6 Hours
Client/Server Model, Telnet Domain Name System, File Transfer protocol: FTP, TFTP, HyperText Transfer Protocol POP3, IMAP, SMTP, E-mail, MIME, Simple Network Management Protocol

Unit – IV : Wireless Lans, Pans And Mans   6 Hours
Introduction (Infrastructure and Ad-hoc Networks), Comparison of Wireless Networks in ISM Band Fundamentals of WLAN – technical issues, Network Architecture, IEEE 802.11- physical layer, Mac Layer Mechanism, CSMA/CA, Bluetooth - Specification, Transport Layer, Middleware Protocol Group, Bluetooth Profiles, IEEE 802.16 –differences between IEEE 802.11 and 802.16, Physical Layer, Data Link Layer.

Unit - V : Ad-Hoc Networks And Sensor Networks   6 Hours
Introduction to MANETs, Sensor Networks, Operating Environment Constraints, Protocols supported by Wireless Networks, Applications of Sensor Networks, Sensor Node Architecture (hardware components), Sensor Network Architectures (Concept of sink and source, Topologies, Design Principles), Radio Propagation and Propagation Impairments, MAC Protocol: Fundamentals, STEM, S-MAC, LEACH, IEEE 802.15.4

Unit – VI : Routing In Sensor Networks And Recent Trends   6 Hours
Routing in MANET : AODV, DSDV, DSR,
Naming and Addressing in WSN : Basic concepts, MAC address, Distributed assignment of locally unique addresses, Content-based and geographic addressing, Routing in Sensor Networks : Challenges and design issues. Routing Protocols for WSNs: Flooding, SPIN, PEGASIS, Directed Diffusion, Geographic Routing Recent Trends (References web, no formal text) Software Defined Networking, Wi-FiOffloads, 100G Ethernet and its variants
Internet of Things (IoT) and Web of Things, Bring your own Device (BYOD)

CONTENTS

UNT I : Network Layer — 1.1-1.70

- 1.1 Introduction — 1.1
  - 1.1.1 Packet Switching (Store and Forward) — 1.1
  - 1.1.2 Virtual Circuit — 1.1
  - 1.1.3 Implementation of Connection Oriented Service — 1.2
  - 1.1.4 Implementation of Connectionless Service — 1.2
  - 1.1.5 Comparison of Virtual Circuit and Datagram Subnets — 1.3
- 1.2 Packet Switching — 1.3
- 1.3 Datagram Routing Algorithms — 1.6
  - 1.3.1 Optimality Principle — 1.6
- 1.4 Static Routing Algorithms (Non-Adaptive) — 1.8
  - 1.4.1 Shortest Path Routing — 1.8
  - 1.4.2 Flooding — 1.11
  - 1.4.3 Flow Based Routing — 1.11
- 1.5 Dynamic Routing Algorithms (Adaptive) — 1.12
  - 1.5.1 Distance Vector Routing — 1.12
  - 1.5.2 Link State Routing — 1.15
  - 1.5.3 Routing Information Protocol — 1.18
  - 1.5.4 Open Shortest Path First (OSPF) — 1.23
  - 1.5.5 Border Gateway Protocol (BGP) — 1.29
- 1.6 Internet Protocol (IP) — 1.32
  - 1.6.1 IP Header — 1.32
  - 1.6.2 ID Address — 1.35
  - 1.6.3 Network Address — 1.37
  - 1.6.4 Globally Routable (Public) and Private Network IP Addresses — 1.39
  - 1.6.5 IPv4 Limitations — 1.41
- 1.7 Subnetting In IP — 1.41
  - 1.7.1 Subnet Masks — 1.42
- 1.8 Supernetting — 1.46
  - 1.8.1 Classless Interdomain — 1.46
- 1.9 Introduction — 1.50
  - 1.9.1 Address Resolution Protocol (ARP) — 1.51
  - 1.9.2 Reverse Address Resolution Protocol (RARP) — 1.55
  - 1.9.3 Internet Control Message Protocol — 1.56
- 1.10 IPv6 (Internet Protocol Version 6) — 1.59
  - 1.10.1 IPv6 Addresses — 1.60
  - 1.10.2 IPv6 Header — 1.62
  - 1.10.3 IPv4 Vs IPv6 Header — 1.63
  - 1.10.4 Difference Between IPv4 and IPv6 — 1.64
- 1.11 Dynamic Host Configuration Protocol (DHCP) — 1.64
- • Questions — 1.68

UNIT II : Transport Layer — 2.1-2.44

- 2.0 Introduction — 2.1
- 2.1 Transport Layer Duties — 2.2
- 2.2 Transport Layer Services to Upper Layer — 2.2
  - 2.2.1 Advantage of Transport Layer — 2.3
  - 2.2.2 Quality of Service (Qos) — 2.4

2.3	Transport Service Premitives		2.5
2.4	The Internet Transport Protocol		2.7
	2.4.1	User Datagram Protocol (UDP)	2.7
	2.4.2	Transmission Control Protocol (TCP)	2.10
	2.4.3	TCP Congestion Control	2.24
	2.4.4	TCP Timer Management	2.27
2.5	Congestion Control Algorithms		2.30
	2.5.1	Leaky Bucker	2.31
	2.5.2	Token Bucket	2.32
2.6	Congestion Avoidance		2.33
	2.6.1	RTT Estimation	2.33
	2.6.2	Retransmission	2.33
	2.6.3	TCP Tahoe	2.34
	2.6.4	Fast Recovery	2.34
2.7	Socket		2.35
2.8	Berkeley Socket Premitives		2.37
2.9	Steps in Socket Programming		2.38
2.10	Performance Issues		2.40
	2.10.1	Throught	2.43
	2.10.2	Delay	2.43
	2.10.3	Network Reliability	2.43
•	Questions		2.44

UNIT III : Application Layer — 3.1 -3.50

3.1	Client Server Model		3.1
	3.1.1	Server	3.1
	3.1.2	Client	3.1
3.2	Telnet		3.1
	3.2.1	Introduction	3.1
	3.2.2	Telnet Model	3.2
	3.2.3	Options	3.2
	3.2.4	Telnet Commands	3.4
	3.2.5	Telnet for Client/Server Applications	3.5
	3.2.6	Telnet and Security	3.5
3.3	Hyper Text Transport Protocol (HTTP)		3.5
	3.3.1	Types of HTTP Messages	3.6
	3.3.2	HTTP is Statelss Protocl	3.10
	3.3.3	HTTP Connections Types	3.11
	3.3.4	Cookies	3.11
3.4	World Wide Web (WWW)		3.13
	3.4.1	Browser Architecture	3.14
	3.4.2	Categories of Web Documents	3.14
3.5	Hypertext Markup Language		3.15
	3.5.1	Web Page Structure	3.16
	3.5.2	Some Common HTML Tags	3.17
	3.5.3	Dynamic Documents	3.17
	3.5.4	Common Gateway Interface (CGI)	3.18
	3.5.5	Active Documents	3.19

3.6	File Transfer Protocol (FTP)		3.19
	3.6.1	Control Connection	3.21
	3.6.2	Data Connections	3.21
	3.6.3	Communication Over Control Connection	3.22
	3.6.4	Communication Over Data Connection	3.23
	3.6.5	File Transfer	3.24
	3.6.6	FTP Commands	3.24
3.7	Trivial File Transfer Protocol (TFTP)		3.26
	3.7.1	TFTP Operation	3.26
	3.7.2	Modes of TFTP	3.27
	3.7.3	Uses	3.27
	3.7.4	Disadvantages of TFTP	3.27
	3.7.5	Comparison of FTP and TFTP	3.27
3.8	Simple Mail Transfer Protocol		3.27
	3.8.1	Commands and Responses	3.28
	3.8.2	Working	3.30
3.9	Post Office Protocol (POP)		3.31
	3.9.1	POP3	3.31
	3.9.2	Limitations of POP3 Protocol	3.32
3.10	Internet Mail Access Protocol (IMAP4)		3.33
	3.10.1	Comparison of IMAP and POP3	3.33
3.11	Multipurpose Internet Mail Extensions (Mime)		3.33
3.12	Domain Name System		3.35
	3.12.1	Working on DNS	3.35
	3.12.2	Domain Name Space	3.35
	3.12.3	Fully Qualified Domain Names	3.37
	3.12.4	Partially Qualified Domain Names	3.37
	3.12.5	Domain	3.37
	3.12.6	Domain Name Servers	3.37
	3.12.7	Zone	3.38
	3.12.8	Root Server	3.39
	3.12.9	Primary and Secondary Servers	3.39
	3.12.10	Resolution	3.39
	3.12.11	DNS Messages	3.42
3.13	Resource Records (RR)		3.44
3.14	Simple Network Management Protocol (SNMP)		3.44
	3.14.1	Concept	3.44
	3.14.2	SNMpv3 Defines Eight Types of Packets	3.46
•	Questions		3.47
UNIT IV : Wireless Lans, Pans and Mans			**4.1-4.48**
4.1	Infrastructure and AD HOC Networks		4.1
	4.1.1	Ad-hoc (Peer-to-Peer) Network	4.1
	4.1.2	How Client Join BSS or Infrastructure Wireless Network ?	4.2
4.2	Comparison of Wireless Networks in ISM Band		4.3
4.3	Fundamentals of Wireless Lan		4.7
4.4	Architecture of Wireless Network		4.9
4.5	DSS Services		4.11
4.6	SS Services		4.12

4.7	The 802.11 Protocol Stack		4.13
	4.7.1	Physical Layer	4.13
	4.7.2	Medium Access Layer	4.13
4.8	Bluetooth		4.17
	4.8.1	Architecture	4.18
	4.8.2	The Bluetooth Protocol Stack	4.19
	4.8.3	Bluetooth Frame Structure	4.21
	4.8.4	Advantages of Bluetooth	4.21
4.9	Bluetooth Specification		4.22
	4.9.1	Radio Specifications	4.22
	4.9.2	Baseband Specification	4.23
4.10	Bluetooth Profiles		4.35
	4.10.1	Synchronization	4.36
	4.10.2	File Transfer	4.37
	4.10.3	Object Push	4.37
4.11	Difference Between 802.11 and 802.16		4.37
	4.11.1	Physical Layer of 802.11. G	4.40
	4.11.2	PHY Frames	4.40
	4.11.3	Medium Access Control of 802.11 G	4.42
•	Questions		4.48
UNIT V : AD HOC Networks and Sensor Networks			**5.1-5.40**
5.1	Introduction to Manet		5.1
5.2	Introduction to Wireless Sensor Network (WSN)		5.3
	5.2.1	Context of Sensor Networks	5.5
	5.2.2	Unique Features of Sensor Network	5.6
5.3	Operating Environment Constraints		5.7
	5.3.1	Need of Operating Environment Constraints	5.7
	5.3.2	Programming Paradigms and Application Programming Interfaces	5.8
	5.3.3	Interfaces to the Operating System	5.9
	5.3.4	Structure of Operating Environment and Protocol Stack	5.10
	5.3.5	Dynamic Energy and Power Management	5.11
5.4	Protocols Supported by Wireless Networks		5.11
5.5	Applications of Sensor Networks		5.13
5.6	Sensor Node Architecture		5.16
	5.6.1	Hardware Components	5.16
5.7	Sensor Network Architecture		5.19
	5.7.1	Design Factors and Requirements	5.20
5.8	Radio Propagation and Propagation Impairments		5.23
5.9	Medium Access Control (MAC) Protocol		5.30
	5.9.1	Fundamentals of MAC Protocol	5.30
	5.9.2	Requirements and Design Constraints for Wireless MAC Protocol	5.30
	5.9.3	Important Classes of MAC Protocols	5.31
5.10	Sparse Topology and Energy Management (STEM)		5.33
5.11	S-MAC		5.34
5.12	Low Energy Adaptive Clustering Hierarchy (Leach) Protocol)		5.36
5.13	IEEE 802.15.4		5.37
	5.13.1	Network Architecture and Types on Nodes	5.38
	5.13.2	Superframe Structure	5.38

	5.13.3	GTS Management	5.39
	5.13.4	Data Transfer Procedures	5.39
	Questions		5.40

UNIT VI : Routing in Sensor Network and Recent Trends   6.1-6.42

6.1	Routing Protocols in Manet		6.1
6.2	Naming and Addressing in WSN		6.9
	6.2.1	Use of Addresses and Names in (Sensor) Networks	6.9
	6.2.2	Uniqueness of Addresses	6.10
	6.2.3	Address Management Tasks	6.10
	6.2.4	Assignment of MAC Addresses	6.11
	6.2.5	Distributed Assignment of Locally Unique Address	6.11
	6.2.6	Content-Based and Geographic Addressing	6.13
6.3	Routing in Sensor Networks : Challenges and Design Issues		6.15
	6.3.1	Network Characteristics and Design Objectives	6.16
6.4	Routing Protocols		6.20
	6.4.1	Flooding	6.20
	6.4.2	Sensor Protocols for Information via Negotiations (SPIN)	6.21
	6.4.3	Power-Efficient Gathering in Sensor Information Systems (PEGASIS)	6.22
	6.4.4	Directed Diffusion	6.23
	6.4.5	Geographic Routing	6.23
6.5	Recent Trends in WSN		6.25
	6.5.1	Software Defined Networks (SDN)	6.25
	6.5.2	Wi-Fi Offloads	6.27
	6.5.3	100 G Ethernet and its Variants	6.30
	6.5.4	Internet of Things and Web of Things	6.32
	6.5.5	Web of Things	6.35
	6.5.6	Bring Your Own Device	6.38
	•	Questions	6.42
		Important Points	I.P.1 – I.P. 8
		Appendix A	A. 1 to A. 20

Unit - I

NETWORK LAYER

1.1 INTRODUCTION

- Any large network in the world contains many computers and routers.
- If you draw the network on paper, it will look like graph.
- In this graph, there are number of possible paths from one computer to another via number of intermediate routers.
- Network layer is concerned with getting packets from the source all the way to the destination.
- It is responsible for path selection from source machine to the destination machine; this function clearly contrasts with that of data link layer which has the more modest goal of just moving frames from one end of the wire to the other.

For path selection (often called as routing), it has some sophisticated algorithms which we will discuss in this chapter. Based on these algorithms we have some network layer protocols.

1.1.1 Packet Switching (Store and Forward)

- In this mechanism, the source host, with a packet to send, transmits it to the nearest router.
- The packet is stored on that router until it has fully arrived.
- After full arrival of the packet the checksum for the packet is verified and after the checksum verification the packet is forwarded to the next router.
- This process gets repeated until the packet is reached to the destination host. This mechanism is called as store and forward packet switching.

1.1.2 Virtual Circuit

- The idea behind virtual circuit is to route every packet on the same path after setting up connection between source and destination.
- After using the connection when the connection is released, the virtual circuit also gets terminated.
- With connection-oriented service, each packet carries an identifier telling which virtual circuit it belongs to, and this identifier is called as Virtual Circuit Identifier (VCI).
- Every virtual circuit has its own identifier associated with it.
- With a connection-oriented service, the user has to pay for the length (i.e. the duration for which the user is using the connection. In case of telephone system, we have to pay more when we talk for more time) of his connection. Usually, this will involve a fixed start up fee.

- Now, if the user intends to send a constant stream of data down the line, he is given a reliable service for as long as he wants.
- However, if the user wants to send only a packet or two packets of data - now the cost of setting up the connection greatly overpowers the cost of sending that one or two packet.
- Consider also the case where the user wishes to send a packet once every 3 minutes. In a connection-oriented service, the line will thus be idle for the majority of the time, thus wasting bandwidth. So, connection-oriented services seem to be useful only when the user wishes to send a constant stream of data.

1.1.3 Implementation of Connection Oriented Service

- A connection oriented service is one in which the user is given a "reliable" end to end connection.
- For communication, the user requests a connection with the help of network layer protocol at the remote site before sending the data packet.
- When the connection is established, a sequence of packets from source to destination can be send one after another.
- In this case, packets are sent **on the same path in sequential order.**
- A packet is logically connected to the packet travelling before it and to the packet travelling after it.
- When all packets of the message have been delivered, the connection is terminated.
- A telephone call is the classic example of a connection oriented service. In this service, the decision about the route for a sequence of packets with some source and destination addresses can be made only once, when the connection is established. After that the route is never changed runtime.

1.1.4 Implementation of Connectionless Service

- In a connectionless service, the network layer protocol treats each packet independently, with each packet having no relationship to any other packet.
- The packets in the message may or may not travel the same path to their destination. In connectionless service, the decision about the route of packet is made individually by each router. IP (internet protocol) is connectionless protocol; which provides connectionless service.
- Connectionless service is similar to the postal system. A letter is sent, that is, put in the post box. It then comes in the "postal network" where it gets bounced around and hopefully will leave the network in the correct place, that is, in the addressee's letter box. We can never be totally sure that the letter will arrive, but we know that there is a high probability that it will, and so we place our trust in the postal network.
- In the connectionless service, the packets are frequently called as 'datagrams' and the subnet is called as datagram subnet.

1.1.5 Comparison of Virtual Circuit and Datagram Subnets

Here is the comparison of Virtual-circuit and datagram subnets

Issue	Datagram subnet	Virtual-circuit subnet
Circuit Setup	Not needed.	Needed.
Addressing	Each packet contains full source and destination address.	Each packet contains a virtual circuit (VC) number.
State Information	Router do not hold state information about connection.	Each VC requires router table space per connection.
Routing	Each packet is routed independently.	Route is chosen when VC is set up; all packets follow it.
Effect of router failure	None, except for packets lost during the crash.	All VCs that passed through the failed router are terminated.
Quality of service	It is difficult to maintain quality of service.	Comparatively easy to maintain the quality of service than datagram subnet, if enough resources are allocated in advance for each VC.
Congestion control	It is difficult to handle congestion control.	Easy if enough resources can be allocated in advance for each VC.

1.2 PACKET SWITCHING

- Packet switching is similar to message switching which is using short messages.
- Any message exceeding a network-defined maximum length is broken up into shorter units, known as packets, for transmission; the packets, each with an associated header, are then transmitted individually through the network.
- The fundamental difference in packet communication is that the data is formed into packets with a predefined header format and well-known "idle" patterns which are used to occupy the link when there is no data to be communicated.
- Packet network equipment discards the "idle" patterns between packets and processes the entire packet as one piece of data.
- The equipment examines the Packet Header Information (PCI) and then either removes the header (in an end system) or forwards the packet to another system.
- If the outgoing link is not available, then the packet is placed in a queue until the link becomes free.
- A packet network is formed by links which connect packet network equipment.

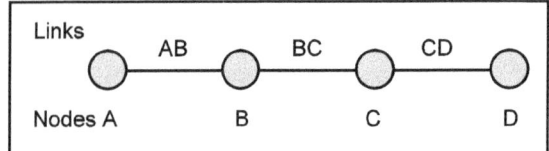

Fig. 1.1 : Communication Between A and D using Circuits which are Shared Using Packet Switching

(The message in this case has been broken into three parts labelled 1-3.)

There are two important benefits from packet switching :

- The first and most important benefit is that since packets are short, the communication links between the nodes are only allocated to transferring a single message for a short period of time while transmitting each packet. Longer messages require a series of packets to be sent, but do not require the link to be dedicated between the transmission of each packet. The implication is that packets belonging to other messages may be sent between the packets of the message being sent from A to D. This provides a much fairer sharing of the resources of each of the links.

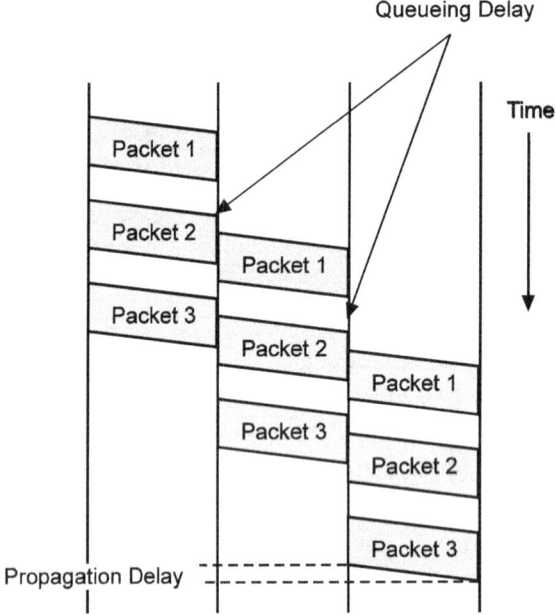

Fig. 1.2 : Packet-switched Communication Between Systems A and D

1. Another benefit of packet switching is known as "pipelining". Pipelining is visible in the Fig. 1.1. At the time, packet 1 is sent from B to C, packet 2 is sent from A to B; packet 1 is sent from C to D while packet 2 is sent from B to C, and packet 3 is sent from A to B, and so forth. This simultaneous use of communication links represents a gain in efficiency; the total delay for transmission across a packet network may be considerably less than for message switching, despite the inclusion of a header in each packet rather than in each message.

Circuit Switching Versus Packet Switching :
Circuit switching and packet switching differ in many respects :
- To start with, circuit switching requires that a circuit be set up end to end before communication begins. Packet switching does not require an advance setup. The first packet can be sent as soon as it is available.
- The result of connection setup with circuit switching is the reservation of bandwidth all the way from source to destination. All packets follow this path. Among other properties, having all packets follow the same path means that they can not arrive out of order. With packet switching there is no path, so different packets can follow different paths, depending on the network conditions at the time they are sent. They may arrive out of order.
- Packet switching is more fault tolerant (it handles the fault better) than circuit switching. In fact, that is why it has invented. If the switch goes down, all the circuits using it are terminated and no more traffic can be sent on any of them. With packet switching, packets can be routed around dead switches.
- In case of circuit switching path set up is done in advance with the corresponding bandwidth reservation. If bandwidth is reserved, then when packet arrives, it can be sent out immediately over the reserved bandwidth. With packet switching no bandwidth is reserved, so packets may have to wait their turn to be forwarded.
- If a circuit has been reserved for a particular user and there is no traffic to send, the bandwidth of the circuit is wasted. It cannot be used for other traffic. Packet switching does not waste bandwidth and thus it is more efficient.
- Packet switching uses store and forward mechanism. A packet gets stored in the router's memory, and then after applying routing algorithm, it is routed to the next router, due to that it adds delay while transmitting the packet.
- Here is a comparison of circuit switched and packet switched networks.

Item	Circuit switched	Packet switched
Call setup	Required	Not needed
Dedicated Physical Path	Yes	No
Each packet follows same route	Yes	No
Packets arrive in order	Yes	No
Is a switch crash fatal	Yes	No
Bandwidth available	Fixed	Dynamic
Time of possible congestion	At setup time	On every packet
Bandwidth wastage	Yes	No
Store and forward transmission	No	Yes

- Two distinct techniques are used in data communications to transfer data. Each has its own advantages and disadvantages. They are the connection-oriented method and the connectionless method.

1.3 DATAGRAM ROUTING ALGORITHMS

An internet is a combination of networks connected by routers. When datagram goes from source to destination, it will probably pass through many routers until it reaches the router attached to the destination network.

A router receives a packet from a network and passes it to another network. It is usually attached to several networks. When it receives a packet, to which network should it pass the packet ? The decision is based on optimization, i.e. which of the pathway is the optimum pathway ?

- **Routing** is the process of finding a path from source machine to the destination machine in the network.
- **The routing algorithm** is the part of network layer software which is responsible for deciding on which output line an incoming packet should be transmitted.
- If the subnet is datagram subnet, then this decision must be made every time for every incoming packet as the best route might be different than that of the last time.
- If the subnet is virtual circuit subnet, routing decisions are made only when a new virtual circuit is being setup. After that data packets just follow the previously established route.
- The latter case is sometimes called as **"Session Routing"** because the route remains same for entire user session.
- Regardless of whether routes are chosen independently for each packet or only when new connections are established. There are certain properties that are desirable in a routing algorithm :
- Correctness and simplicity hardly requires any comment, but the need of robustness may be less obvious at first.
- Once a major network comes in existence it may be expected to run continuously for many years without systemwise failures. During that period there will be hardware and software failures.
- The routing algorithm should be able to cope up with the changes in the topology and traffic without requiring all jobs in all hosts to be broadest and the network to be rebooted every time when some router crashes.

1.3.1 Optimality Principle

- General statement about optimal routes without regard to topology or traffic: "If router J is on the optimal path from router I to router K , then the optimal path from J to K also falls along the same route"

- The general statement about optimal routes without regard to network topology or traffic. This statement is known as the optimality principle.
- It states that if router J is on the optimal path from router I to router K, then the optimal path from J to K also falls along the same route. To see this, call the part of the route from I to Jr1 and the rest of the route r2.
- If a route better than r2 existed from J to K, it could be concatenated with r1 to improve the route from I to K, contradicting our statement that r1r2 is optimal. As a direct consequence of the optimality principle, we can see that the set of optimal routes from all sources to a given destination form a tree rooted at the destination.
- Such a tree is called a sink tree and is illustrated in Fig. 3-6, where the distance metric is the number of hops. Note that a sink tree is not necessarily unique; other trees with the same path lengths may exist. The goal of all routing algorithms is to discover and use the sink trees for all routers.

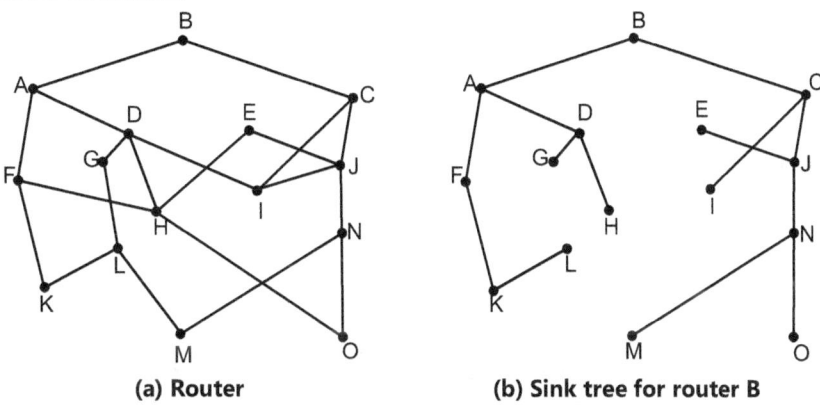

(a) Router   **(b) Sink tree for router B**

Fig. 1.3

- Since a sink tree is indeed a tree, it does not contain any loops, so each packet will be delivered within a finite and bounded number of hops. In practice, life is not quite this easy.
- Links and routers can go down and come back up during operation, so different routers may have different ideas about the current topology. Also, we have quietly finessed the issue of whether each router has to individually acquire the information on which to base its sink tree computation or whether this information is collected by some other means.

Datagram Routing algorithms are grouped into two major classes :

1. Adaptive Algorithms
2. Non-adaptive Algorithms

1. Adaptive Algorithms :

- Adaptive algorithms, in contrast, change their routing decisions to reflect the changes in the technology, and usually the traffic as well.

- Adaptive algorithms differ in where they get information (e.g. locally, from adjacent routers, or from all routers), when they change the routes (e.g. every ΔT seconds, when the load changes or when the topology changes), and what metric is used for optimization (e.g. distance, number of hopes, or estimated transit time).
- Adaptive algorithms are categorized into the following types :
    (i) Distance vector routing
    (ii) Link state routing
    (iii) Broadcast routing
    (iv) Multicast routing
    (v) Hierarchical routing

(i) Non-adaptive Algorithms :
- These algorithms do not base their routing decisions on measurement and estimates of the current traffic and topology.
- Instead, the choice of route to use to get from I to J (for all I and J) is computed in advance.
- This procedure is sometimes called as static routing.
- Following are the non-adaptive algorithms :
    (i) Shortest path routing
    (ii) Flooding
    (iii) Flow-based routing

1.4 STATIC ROUTING ALGORITHMS (NON-ADAPTIVE)

- Before doing the study of actual routing process, the idea is to build the graph of the subnet, with each node of the graph representing a router and each arc of the graph representing a communication line (link).
- To choose a route between a given pair of routers, the algorithm just finds the shortest path between them on the graph.

1.4.1 Shortest Path Routing

- One way of measuring path length is number of hopes.
- Another way is geographic distance in kilometeres.

Many other techniques, beside hopes and physical distance are also possible. e.g. each arc could be labelled with mean queuing and transmission delay for some standard test packet as determined by hour test runs. With this graph labeling, the shortest path is the fastest path rather than the path with the fewest arc or kilometeres.

- In general case, the labels on the arcs could be computed as a function of the 1. distance, 2. bandwidth, 3. average 4. traffic, 5. communication cost, 6. mean queue length, 7. measured delay and other factors.

- The algorithm uses various parameters that have been stated above and computes the shortest path based on any one or combination of above parameters.

Dijkstra's shortest path algorithm :

Let G = (V, E) be a simple graph. Let a and z be any two vertices of the graph. Suppose L(x) denotes the label of the vertex x which represents the **length of the shortest path from** the vertex a to the vertex x. w_{ij} denotes the weight of the edge e_{ij} = (v_i, v_j).

Step 1 : Let P = dp where P is the set of those vertices which have permanent labels and T = {all vertices of the graph G}

Set L (a) = 0, L(x) = ∞ ∀ x ∈ T and x ≠ a

Step 2 : Select the vertex v in T which has the smallest label. This label is called the permanent label of v.

Also set P = P ∪ { v } and T = T − { v }. If v = z, then L (z) is the length of the shortest path from the vertex a to z and stop.

Step 3 : If v ≠ z, then revise the labels of vertices of T i.e. **the vertices which do not have permanent labels**. The new label of a vertex x in T is given by

$$L(x) = \min \{ \text{old } L(x), L(v) + w(v, x) \}$$

where w(v, x) is the weight of the edge joining the vertex v and x.

If there is no direct edge joining v and x then take w (v, x) = ∞ .

Step 4 : Repeat steps 2 and 3 until z gets the permanent label.

SOLVED EXAMPLE

Example 1.1 : For the following graph shown in Fig. 1.4 (a), find the shortest path using Dijkstra's algorithm.

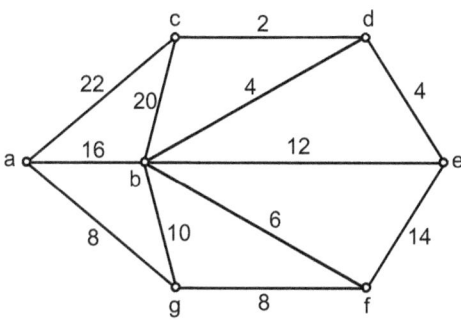

Fig. 1.4 (a)

Solution : According to the algorithm, the shortest path from a to e can be calculated as follows :

(1)   P = dp,   T = { a, b, c, d, e, f, g }

   L (a) = 0,   L(x) = ∞ ∀ x ∈ T, x ≠ a

(2) V = a, the permanent label of a = 0.

P = {a}, T = { b, c, d, e, f, g}
L (b) = min (∞, 0 + 16) = 16
L (c) = min (∞, 0 + 22) = 22
L (d) = min (∞, 0 + ∞) = ∞
L (e) = min (∞, 0 + ∞) = ∞
L (f) = min (∞, 0 + ∞) = ∞
L (g) = min (∞, 0 + 8) = 8

(3) V = g, the permanent label of g = 8.
P = (a, g), T = { b, c, d, e, f}
L (b) = min (16, 8 + 10) = 16
L (c) = min (22, 8 + ∞) = 22
L (d) = min (∞, 8 + ∞) = ∞
L (e) = min (∞, 8 + ∞) = ∞
L (f) = min (∞, 8 + 8) = 16

(4) V = b, the permanent label of b is 16.
P = { a, g, b }, T = { c, d, e, f }
L (c) = min (22, 16 + 20) = 22
L (d) = min (∞, 16 + 4) = 20
L (e) = min (∞, 16 + 12) = 28
L (f) = min (16, 16 + 6) = 16

(5) V = f, the permanent label of f is 16.
P = { a, g, b, f }, T = { c, d, e }
L (c) = min (22, 16 + ∞) = 22
L (d) = min (20, 16 + ∞) = 20
L (e) = min (28, 16 + 14) = 28

(6) V = d, the permanent label of d is 20.
P = { a, g, b, f, d }, T = { c, e }
L (c) = min (22, 20 + 2) = 22
L (e) = min (28, 20 + 4) = 24

(7) V = c, the permanent label of c is 22.
P = { a, g, b, f, d, c }, T = { e }
L (e) = min (24, 22 + ∞) = 24

(8) V = e, the permanent label of e is 24.

Hence, the length of shortest path from a to e is 24.

The shortest path from a to e is abde which is shown below.

1.4.2 Flooding

In this algorithm, every incoming packet is sent out on every outgoing line except the one it arrived on. The problem with flooding is that it generates vast number of duplicate packets unless some measures are taken to control this process. One such measure is to have a hop counter contained in the header of each packet, which is decremented at each hop. When the value of hop counter becomes zero, the packet is discarded from the network. Ideally this hop counter is initialized to the length of the path from source to destination. If the sender does not know the maximum length of the path then sender can initialize the counter to the worst case, namely, the full diameter of the subnet. Another technique is keep track of which packets have been flooded, and then avoids sending them out a second time.

Selective Flooding :

In this algorithm the router do not send every incoming packet out on every line, it sends the packet only on those lines that are going approximately in the right direction.

Where to use ?

Flooding algorithms are used in that application which requires very high robustness. So it can be used prominently in the military applications as well as distributed database applications.

1.4.3 Flow Based Routing

The algorithms studied so far takes only the topology into account, they do not consider the load. Flow based routing algorithm deals both with topology and load (network traffic).

In the Fig. 1.5 considering that there is a huge traffic from A to B. In that situation if we route some more traffic to C from A through B, then obviously there is a lot of scope for the congestion to take place. Also the network performance might get degraded due to that, so it is always better to follow a different path than this. So traffic is sent from A to C not through B but through G, E, F nodes.

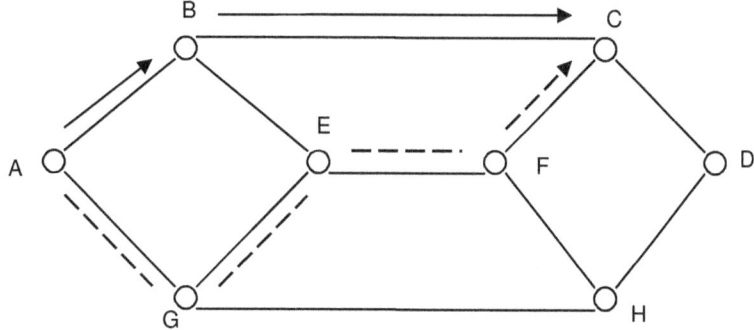

Fig. 1.5

It is possible to optimize the routing by analyzing the data flow mathematically.

The mathematical analysis is based on the idea that for a given line if the capacity and the average data flow are known, then it is possible to calculate the mean packet delay using the "Queuing theory".

1.5 DYNAMIC ROUTING ALGORITHMS (ADAPTIVE)

1.5.1 Distance Vector Routing

- In distance vector routing, the least cost route between any two nodes is the route with minimum distance.
- In this algorithm, each node (router) maintains a vector table of minimum distance to every node.
- The table at each node also guides the packets to the desired node by showing the next stop in the route (next-hop routing).
- Fig. 1.7 shows a system of five nodes with their corresponding tables. The table for node A shows how we can reach any node from this node. For example, our least cost to reach node E is 6 and the corresponding route passes through C.

Initialization :

- In Fig. 1.6, each node knows how to reach any other node and the cost.
- At the beginning, however, this is not the case. Each node can know only this distance between itself and the immediate neighbors, those directly connected to it.

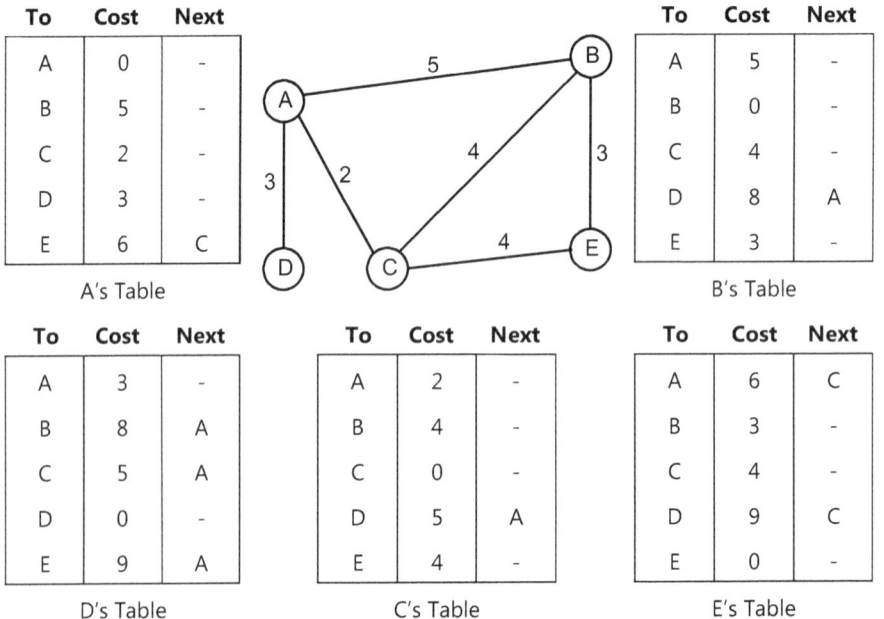

Fig. 1.6 : Distance Vector Routing Table

- So for the moment, we assume that each node can send a message to the immediate neighbors and find the distance between itself and these neighbors.
- Following Fig. 1.7 shows the initial tables for each node. The distance for any entry that is not a neighbor is marked as infinite (unreachable).

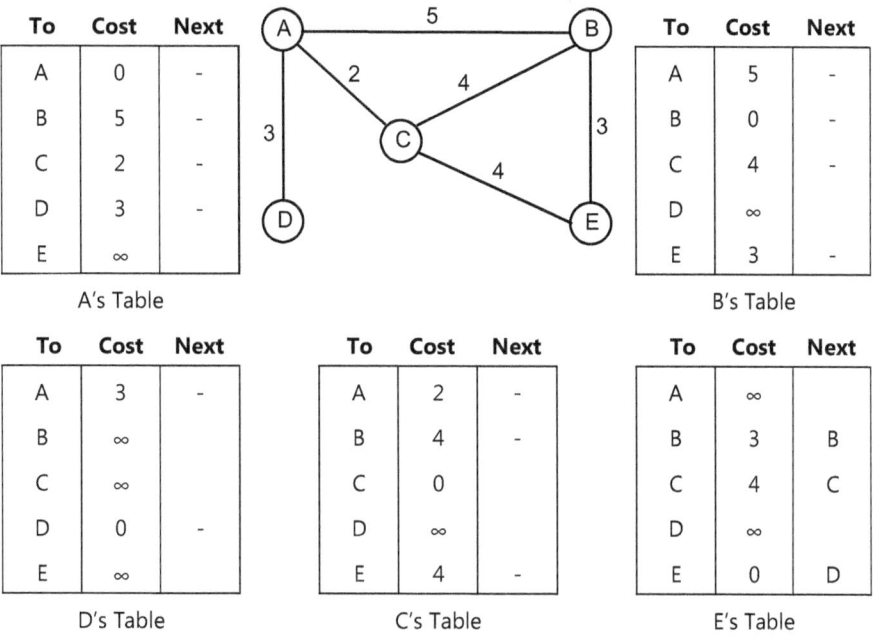

Fig. 1.7 : Initialization of Tables in Distance Vector Routing

Sharing :

- The whole idea of distance vector routing is sharing of information between the neighbors.
- Although node A does not know about node E, node C does. So if node C shares routing table with A, node A can also know how to reach node E.
- On the other hand, node C does not know how to reach node D, but node A does. If node A shares its routing table with node C, node C also knows how to reach node D. In other words, node A and C as immediate neighbors, can improve their routing tables if they help each other.
- Still there is a problem. How much of the table must be shared with each neighbor ? The best solution for each node is to send its entire table to the neighbor and let the neighbor decide what part to use and what to discard. However, the third column of the table is not useful to the neighbor. When the neighbor receives the table, this column needs to be replaced with the sender's name. A node therefore can send only first two columns of its table to any neighbor. In other words, sharing here means only sharing of first two columns.

Updating :

- When a node receives a two column table from a neighbor, it needs to update its routing table. Updating takes three steps :

1.1. The receiving node needs to add the cost between itself and the sending node to each value in the second column. The logic is clear. If node C claims that its distance to destination is x miles, and the distance between A and C is y miles, then the distance between A and that destination I via C, is x + y miles.

2.2. The receiving node needs to add the name of the sending node to each row as the third column if the receiving node uses the information from any row. The sending node is the next node in the route.

3.3. The receiving node needs to compare each row of its old table with the corresponding row of the modified version of the received table.

a.(a) If the next node entry is different, the receiving node chooses the row with the smaller cost. If there is a tie, the old one is kept.

b.(b) If the next node entry is the same, the receiving node chooses the new row. For example, if node C has previously advertised a route to node X with distance 3. Suppose that now there is no path between C and X; node C now advertises this route with the distance of infinity. Node a must not ignore this value even though its old entry is smaller. The old route does not exist any more. The new route has the distance of infinity.

Following Fig. 1.8 shows how node A updates its routing table after receiving the partial table from node C.

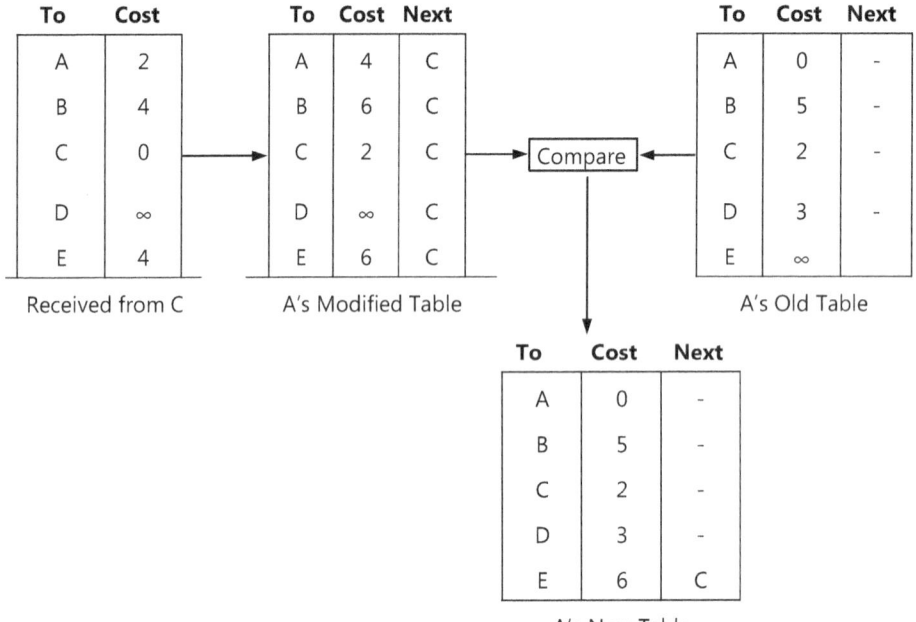

Fig. 1.8 : Updating in Distance Vector Routing

There are several points that we need to emphasize here :
- First, as we know from mathematics, when we add any number to infinity, the result is still infinity.
- Second, the modified table shows how to reach A from A via C. If A needs to reach itself via C, it needs to go to C and then come back, a distance of 4.
- Third, the only benefit from this updating of node A is the last entry, how to reach E (distance of infinity); now it knows that cost is 6 via C.
- Each node can update its table using the tables received from other nodes. In short period of time, if there is no change in the network itself, such as a failure in a link, all nodes reach a stable condition in which the content of the table remains the same.

When to share vector tables ?
- The table is sent both periodically and when there is a change in the table. Nodes send its routing table, normally every 30 seconds in a periodic update.

1.5.2 Link State Routing

- Distance vector routing was used in the APRANET until 1979, when it was replaced by link state routing. Two primary problems caused its failure.
- Since the delay metric was queue length, it did not take line bandwidth into account when choosing routes.
- Initially, all the lines were 56 kbps, so line bandwidth was not an issue, but after some line had been upgraded to 230 kbps and others to 1.54 Mbps, not taking bandwidth into account was major problem. Ofcourse, it would have been possible to change the delay metric to factor in line bandwidth.
- The algorithm often took too long to converge even with tricks like split horizon.
- Due to that, it was replaced by an entirely new algorithm which is now called as link state routing.
- The idea behind link state routing is simple and can be stated as five parts. Each router must :
- Discover its neighbors and learn their network addresses.
- Measure the delay or cost to each of its neighbor.
- Construct a packet telling all it has just learned.
- Send this packet to all other routers.
- Compute the shortest path to every other router.
- In effect the complete topology and all delay are experimentally measured and distributed to every router. Then to find the shortest path to every other router Dijkstra's algorithm is used by considering the five steps described below :

1. **Learning about the neighbors :**
   When a router is booted, its first task is to learn who are its neighbors. It accomplishes this properly by sending a special **HELLO packet** on each point to point line. The router

on the other end is expected to send back a reply telling who it is. These names must be globally unique.

2. **Measuring Line Cost :**

   The link state routing algorithm requires each router to know for at least has a reasonable estimate, of the delay to each of its neighbors. The most direct way to determine this delay is to send a special ECHO packet over the line that the other side is required to send back immediate. By measuring the round trip time and dividing it by two, the sending router can get a reasonable estimate of the delay. For even better results the test can be conducted several times and the average is used.

3. **Building Link State Packets :**

   Once the information needed for the exchange has been collected the next step for each router is to build packet containing all the data. The packet starts with the identity of the sender, followed by a sequence number and age, and list of neighbors. For each neighbors, the delay to that neighbor is given. An example subnet is given in Fig. 1.8 (a) with delays shown in the lines. The corresponding link state packets for all six routes are shown in Fig. 1.8 (b).

Limitations :

Count to Infinity Problem :

- The core of the count-to-infinity problem is that if A tells B that it has a path somewhere, there is no way for B to know if the path has B as a part of it.
- To see the problem clearly, imagine a subnet connected like A-B-C-D-E-F, and let the metric between the routers be "number of jumps".
- Now suppose that A goes down (out of order). In the vector-update-process B notices that its once very short route of 1 to A is down - B does not receive the vector update from A.
- The problem is, B also gets an update from C, and C is still not aware of the fact that A is down - so it tells B that A is only two jumps from it, which is false.
- This slowly propagates through the network until it reaches infinity.

Explanation of Count to Infinity Problem :

Consider that we are having four routers L-M-N-O-P as shown in the Fig. 1.9 given below :

- Initially consider that router L is down. So from the point of all routers, it is at a distance of ∞.
- When L comes into network, other routers get this information through the vector exchange table.
- At the first vector exchange, router M gets the information that router L is one hop away from it and is at left hand side.

- Accordingly router L updates its table. Refer Fig. 1.8 (a) (i).

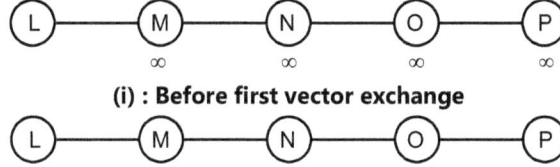

(i) : Before first vector exchange

(ii) : After first vector exchange

Fig. 1.9 (a)

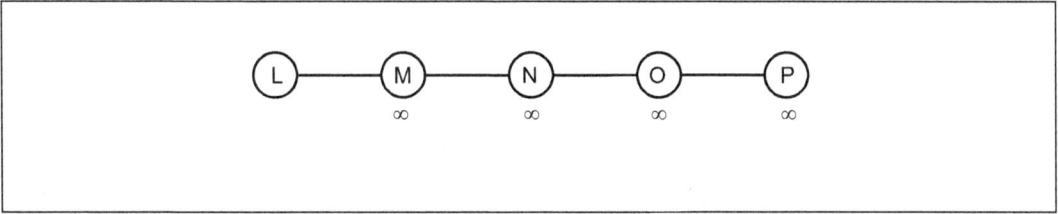

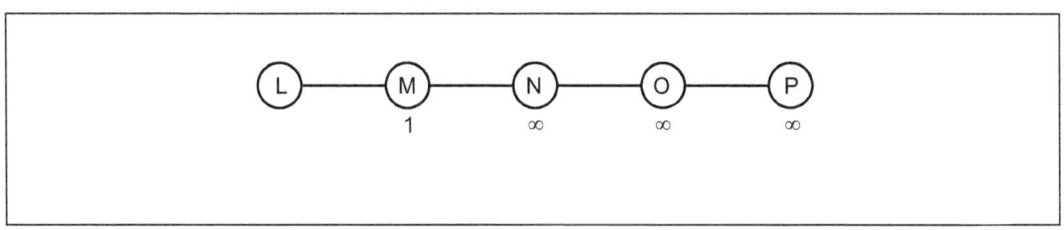

- At the second vector exchange, router N comes to know about router L that, router L is two hops away from it. Based on this, router N updates its routing table. Thus finally all routers will get the information about router L's presence on the network. Refer Fig. 1.9 (b).

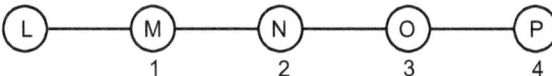

- Now, if router L goes down suddenly due to any hardware problem.
- Now after that, the next vector exchange will tell router M that there is no direct path from L to M, but there is a path to router L from router M through router N (because still router N is not aware that router L is down, so it is maintaining its old routing table).
- As router L is 2 hops away from router N, so now by this vector exchange, router L will be 3 hops away from router M (this is absolutely wrong). This is shown in Fig. 1.9 (c).

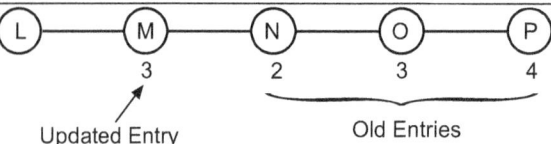

Updated Entry   Old Entries

- On second exchange, router N comes to know that, both its neighbour M and N claim to have a path of length 3 to router L. So it picks one of them at random and makes its new distance to L as 4. This is shown in Fig. 1.9 (d).

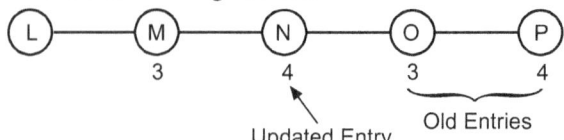

Updated Entry   Old Entries

Fig. 1.9

- In the same way, other routers keep updating their tables after every exchange.
- Finally after many exchanges, we will get ∞ distance of router L in the routing tables of router M, N, O and P.
- The conclusion of the entire process is that bad news propagate slowly. And this is a count-to-infinity problem.
- One can overcome this problem by using split horizon algorithm.

1.5.3 Routing Information Protocol

- This is an intradomain (interior) routing protocol used inside an Autonomous system (AS).
- It is very simple protocol based on Distance Vector Routing mechanism.
- Typical format of routing table is shown in the table given below :

Destination Network Address field	Hop Count field	Next Router field

- First column consists of destination networks address.
- The Hop Count Field the number of Hops that are required to reach the destination using shortest path algorithms.
- Next router field column contains the address of the next router to which the packet is to be delivered.

Example of a domain using RIP :

- Fig. 1.10 shows an autonomous system with seven networks and four routers.
- The table of each router is also shown. Let's look at the routing table of R1.
- The table has seven entries to show how to reach each network in the autonomous system.

- Router 1 is directly connected to networks 130.10.0.0 and 130.11.0.0, which means that there are no Next router entries for these two networks.
- To send a packet to one of the three networks at the far left, router R1 needs to deliver the packet to router R2.
- The next router entry for these three networks is the interface of router R2 with IP address 130.10.0.1.
- To send a packet to the two networks at the far right, router R1 needs to send the packet to the interface of router R4 with IP address 130.11.0.1.
- Similarly, one can give explanations of other routing tables given in the following figure.

Initializing Routing Table :
- When router is added to a network, it initializes its routing table.
- Such a table consists of only the directly attached networks and the hop counts. The next hop field which identifies the next router is empty.
- When RIP messages are received, each routing table is updated using RIP updating algorithm.

RIP advertisement :
- The routing table is updated very frequently, when the host machine gets a RIP response message from the neighbouring routers.
- In RIP, routing updates are exchanged between neighbours approximately every 30 seconds using Routing Response Message.
- These routing response messages are also known as RIP advertisements.

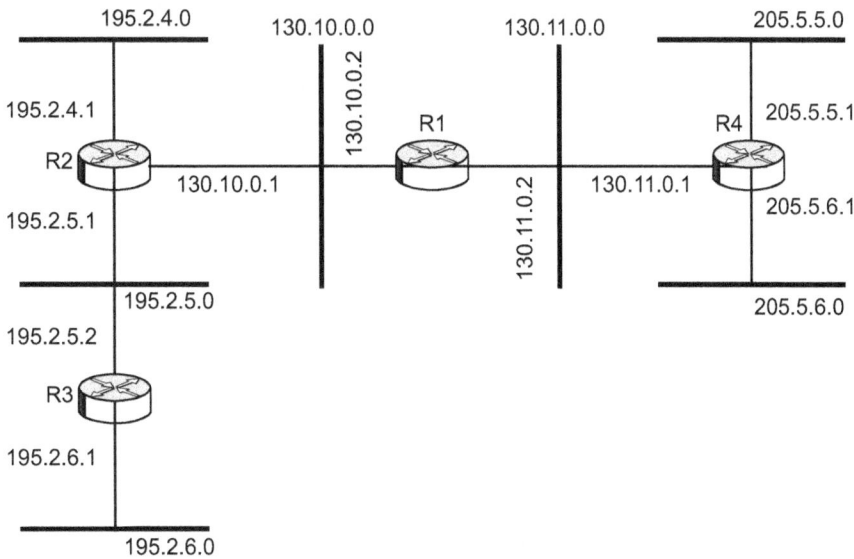

Dest.	Hop	Next	Dest.	Hop	Next	Dest.	Hop	Next	Dest.	Hop	Next
130.10.0.0	1	——	130.10.0.0	1	——	130.10.0.0	2	195.2.5.1	130.10.0.0	2	130.11.0.2
130.11.0.0	1	——	130.11.0.0	2	130.10.0.2	130.11.0.0	3	195.2.5.1	130.11.0.0	1	——
195.2.4.0	2	130.10.0.1	195.2.4.0	1	——	195.2.4.0	2	195.2.5.1	195.2.4.0	3	130.11.0.2
195.2.5.0	2	130.10.0.1	195.2.5.0	1	——	195.2.5.0	1	——	195.2.5.0	3	130.11.0.2
195.2.6.0	3	130.10.0.1	195.2.6.0	2	195.2.5.2	195.2.6.0	1	——	195.2.6.0	4	130.11.0.2
205.5.5.0	2	130.11.0.1	205.5.5.0	3	130.10.0.2	205.5.5.0	4	195.2.5.1	205.5.5.0	1	——
205.5.6.0	2	130.11.0.1	205.5.6.0	3	130.10.0.2	205.5.6.0	4	195.2.5.1	205.5.6.0	1	——
R1 Table			R2 Table			R3 Table			R4 Table		

Fig. 1.10 : Example of Domain using RIP

RIP message format (RIPv1) :

- The format of RIP version 1 message is shown in Fig. 1.11.
  Following are the fields of RIP message :
- **Command :** This is 8 bit field. It specifies the type of the message : (1) Request and (2) Response.
- **Version :** This 8 bit field defines a version. There are two versions of RIP message.
- **Family :** This 16 bit field defines the family of the protocol used. For TCP/IP protocol the value is 2.
- **IP Address :** The address field defines the IP address of the specific entry.
- **Metric :** This 32-bit field defines the hop count from the advertising router to the destination network. This value is between 1 to 15 for valid route and 16 for unreachable route.

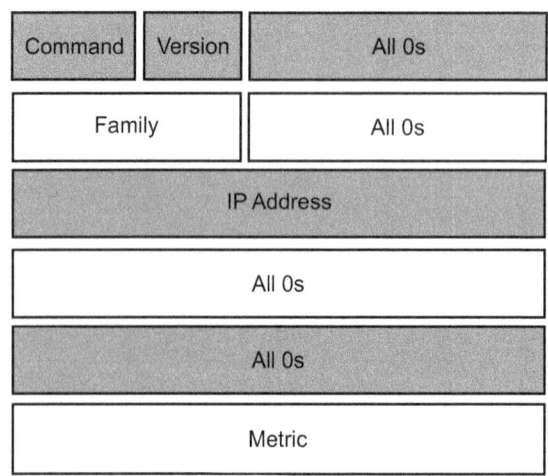

Fig. 1.11 : RIP Message Format (RIPv1)

Requests and Responses :

RIP has two types of messages :

1.1. Request message :
- A request message is sent by a router that has just come up or by a router that has some timeout entries.
- A request can ask about specific entries or all entries. (Fig. 1.12)

2.2. Response message :
- Response can be either solicited or unsolicited. A solicited response is sent only in answer to a request.
- An unsolicited response, on the other hand, is sent periodically, every 30 seconds or when there is a change in the routing table.

Timers in RIP :

RIP uses three timers :

1) Periodic Timer :
- It controls advertising and regular update messages. Although the protocol specifies that this timer must be set to 30 seconds, the working model uses a random number between 25 and 35 seconds.
- It is count down timer; when 0 is reached, the update message is sent, and the timer is randomly set once again.

2) Expiration Timer :
- It governs the validity of the route.
- When router receives update information for a route, expiration timer is set to 180 sec for that particular route.
- Every time a new update for a particular route is received, the timer is reset.
- In normal situations it occurs after every 30 seconds.
- If there is a problem on an internet and no update is received within the allotted 180 seconds, the route is considered as expired which means the destination is unreachable.
- Every route has its own expiration timer.
    3. **Garbage Collection Timer :** This timer is used to remove the routing information from the table when the route becomes invalid. When this timer becomes zero, the route is washed out from the routing table.

RIP Version 2 :

RIPv2 was designed to overcome some of the shortcomings of RIPv1. The designers of version2 have only replaced those fields in version 1 that were filled with 0s by some new fields.

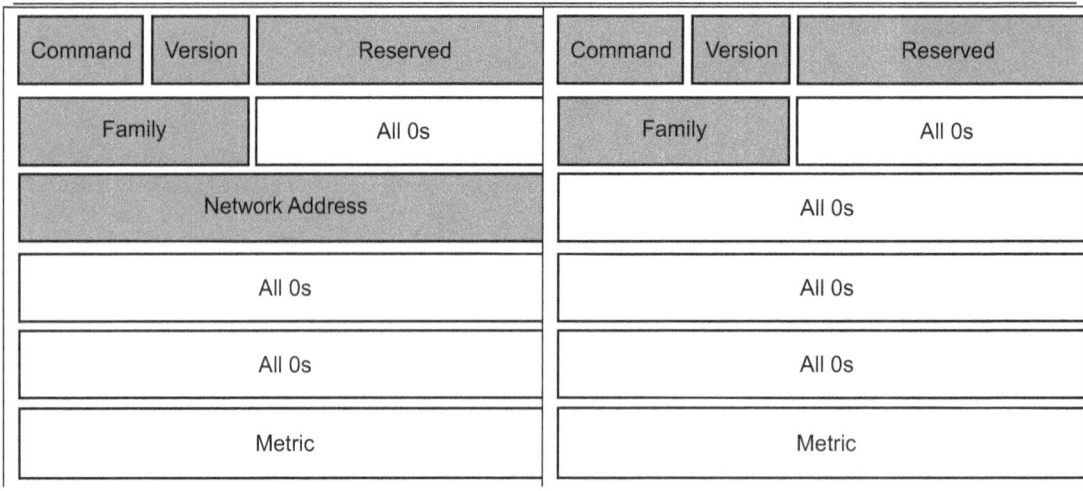

(a) Request for some   (b) Request for all

Fig. 1.12 : Request Messages

Message format for RIPv2 :

The message format is shown in the following Fig. 1.13.

The new fields that are not present in RIPv1 are :

- **Route Tag :** This field carries information such as autonomous system number.
- **Subnet Mask :** It is 4 byte field that carries the subnet mask. This means that RIP2 supports classless addressing and CIDR.
- **Next-Hop Address :** This field shows the address of the next hop.

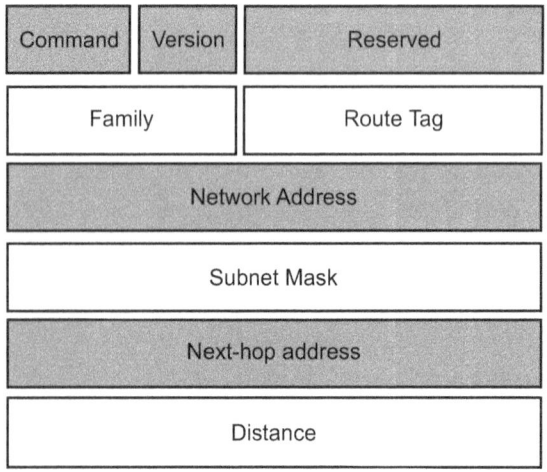

Fig. 1.13 : RIPv2

RIPv1 Vs RIPv2 :

RIPv1	RIPv2
• Uses distance vector routing algorithm.	• Uses distance vector routing algorithm.
• Maximum hop count is 15. If it exceeds 15, it means that destination is unreachable.	• Maximum hop count is 15. If it exceeds 15, it means that destination is unreachable.
• Uses Classful addressing mechanism.	• Uses Classless addressing mechanism.
• No support for Variable length subnet masks (VLSM).	• Supports VLSM.
• No support for discontiguous networks.	• Support for discontiguous networks.

1.5.4 Open Shortest Path First (OSPF)

- It is an intradomain/interior routing protocol based on link state routing. Its domain is an autonomous system.
- For handling routing efficiently, OSPF divides an autonomous system into '**Areas**'.

What is Area ?

- An area is a collection of networks, hosts and routers within a specific autonomous system.
- An autonomous system can be divided into many different areas. All the networks inside an area must be connected.
- Normally two types of routers are used in the autonomous system :

1. Area Border Routers :

- These are the special routers used at the border of the area.
- These routers summarize the information about its area and send it to other areas.

2. Backbone Routers inside backbone area :

- Among the areas inside the autonomous system, there is a special area called as backbone area.
- All of the areas inside an autonomous system must be connected to the backbone. In short, backbone works as primary area and the other areas work as secondary areas.
- The routers inside the backbone area are called as backbone routers.
- Backbone router can also be an area border router.
- In case, if some problem occurs and the connectivity between the backbone and the area is broken, virtual link between the routers must be created by the administrator to allow continuity of functions of the backbone as the primary area.
- Each area has area identification. The area identification of backbone is zero. Following Fig. 1.14 shows an autonomous system and its areas.

OSPF Versus RIP :

- In earlier days, the most popular routing protocol was RIP. But it was only good when the network is small.

- It has some limitations which could problem in large networks. Comparison between RIP Vs OSPF is given below.

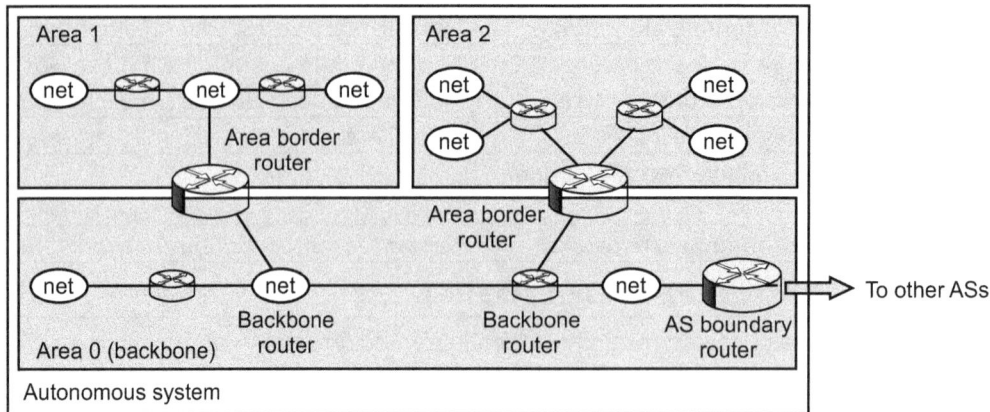

Fig. 1.14 : Areas in Autonomous System

RIP :
- RIP has limited HOP counts. It is 15. If a RIP Network spans more than 15 HOPS, it is considered as unreachable. In short network diameter is 15 hops.
- RIP doesn't support for variable length subnet masks (VLSM).
- Periodic update of routing table consumes lots of bandwidth especially on WAN clouds.
- RIP converges slower than OSPF does.
- RIP Network is a FLAT network. Here no concept of Autonomous systems, Areas, Boundaries and Summarization.
- RIP does not support multipath routing.
- It doesn't support authentication.

OSPF :
- No limitations on the HOP count. Possibly network diameter is 65535 hops.
- Can use VLSM.
- Converges quickly.
- Can divide into Areas. This will help us to use summarization.
- Allows Authentication.
- It uses Dijkstra's algorithm (SPF algorithm).
- Reducing the usage of BW, by sending triggered updates to announce the Network changes.
- Sending periodic updates on long intervals.
- OSPF supports multipath routing.
- Rather than exchanging node (and network) reachability information, OSPF routers exchange link state information.

- Unlike RIP, OSPF doesn't send any routing updates on periodic intervals. It will only send triggered updates. It means every time it doesn't send full routing table to its neighbors. Whenever any changes in network, like new router added or a router removed from the network, it will send information about that particular network to its neighbor.

Features of OSPF :
1. **Type of service :** Depending on the requirement and the nature of the application, it can provide different services to different routes. e.g. high throughput can be selected for one class of service, while minimum delivery delay is more critical for some other applications.
2. **Load balancing :** When multiple routes are available to a particular destination, traffic can be distributed on the routes so as to balance the traffic load. No path will carry a very high traffic and no path will carry very low traffic. Traffic will be distributed evenly.
3. **Subdivision of autonomous system :** Autonomous systems are further divided into smaller areas, which is always better from network administration point of view.
4. **Security :** Routing information exchanges between the routers are authenticated. Malicious transmissions from foreign routers are discarded.
5. **Special features to support LAN environment :** Although the relationships between routers are maintained on a logical link basis, link state transmissions are minimized by the architecture.
6. **OSPF is an open specification :** It means, anyone can implement this standard without paying royalties.
7. **OSPF area :** An area is a collection of networks, hosts and routers within a specific autonomous system. The topology of area is hidden from rest of the autonomous system. This technique reduces the storage of routing traffic information on a specific router.

Metric :
- OSPF protocol allows the administrator to assign a cost, called the metric, to each route.
- A metric can be based on type of service (minimum delay, maximum throughput, and so on).
- As a matter of fact a router can have multiple routing tables, each based on different type of service.

Types of Links :
In OSPF terminology, a connection is called as link. There are four types of links/connections available in OSPF.
  (i) Point to point
  (ii) Transient
  (iii) Stub

(iv) Virtual

1. **Point to point link :**
   - A point to point link connects two routers without any other host or router in between.
   - Graphically, routers are represented by nodes and the link is represented by bidirectional edge connecting the nodes.

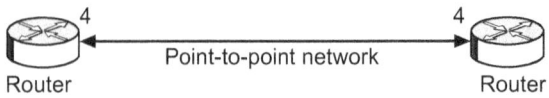

Fig. 1.15 : Point to Point Link

2. **Transient Link :**
   - Transient link is a network with several routers attached to it.
   - The data can enter and exit through any of the router.
   - All LANs and some WANs with two or more routers are of this type.

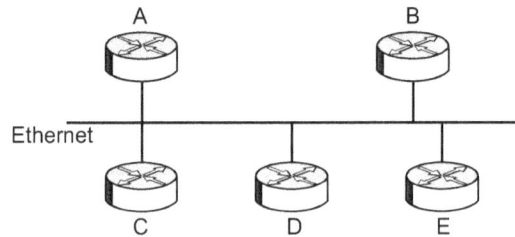

(a) Transient Network

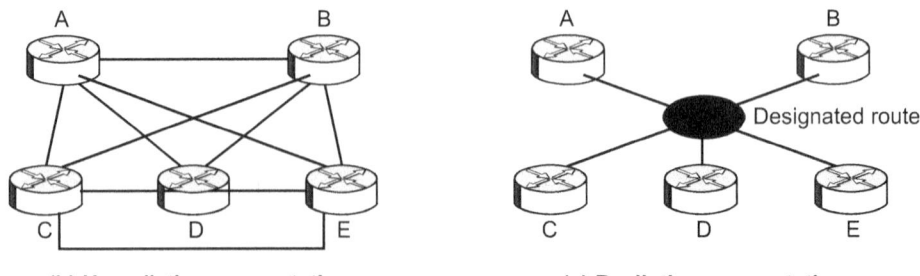

(b) Unrealistic representation   (c) Realistic representation

Fig. 1.16 : Transient Link

3. **Stub Link :**
   - A stub link is a network that is connected to only one router.
   - Data packets enter and exit the network through this single router.
   - This is a special case of transient network.

(a) Stubnetwork   (b) Representation

Fig. 1.17 : Stub Link

4. **Virtual Link :**
   - When the link between two routers is broken, the administration may create a virtual link between them using a longer path that probably goes through several routers.

OSPF packets :

OSPF uses five different types of packets as shown in the following figure given below :

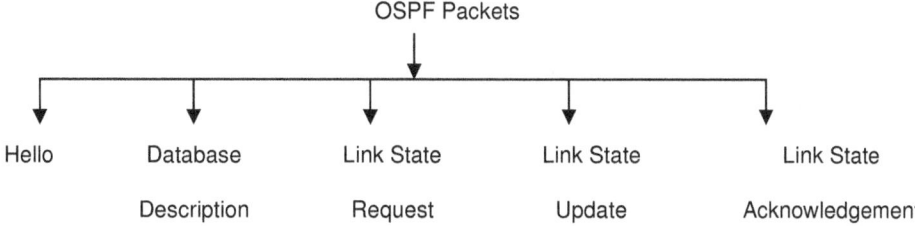

Fig. 1.18 : Types of OSPF packets

The most important type of OSPF packet is Link State Update that itself has five different kinds which are as follows :

1. Router Link
2. Network Link
3. Summary Link to Network
4. Summary Link to Autonomous System boundary router
5. External Link.

Common Header of OSPF packet :

All OSPF packets have the same common header as shown in the following figure. Let's take some more information about it.

Fields of OSPF Header are as follows :

(1) **Version :** It defines the version of OSPF protocol. Currently it is version 2.

(2) **Type :** It defines the type of the packet. We have five types as defined earlier.

(3) **Message Length :** It defines the total length of the message including header.

(4) **Source Router IP address :** It defines an IP address of the router that sends the packet.

(5) **Area Identification :** It defines the area within which the routing takes place.

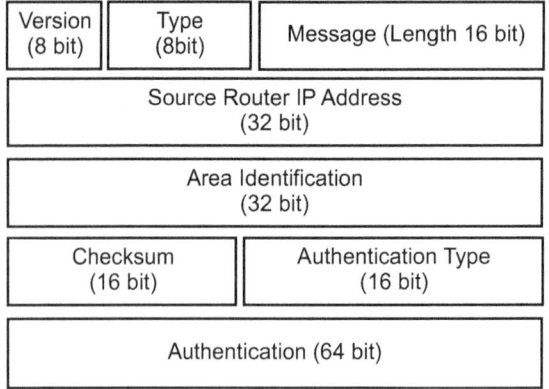

Fig. 1.19 : OSPF Header

(6) **Checksum :** This field is used for error detection on the entire packet excluding the authentication type and authentication data field.

(7) **Authentication Type :** It defines the authentication protocol used in this area. At this time, two types of authentication are defined : 0 for none and 1 for password.

(8) **Authentication :** This 64-bit field is the actual value of the authentication data. If authentication type is 0, this field is filled with 0s. If authentication type is 1, this field carries an eight-character password.

Link State Update Packet :
- It is the most important type of OSPF packet.
- It is the heart of OSPF operation.
- It is used by the router to advertise the states of its links.
- Each link state update packet may contain several different Link State Advertisements (LSAs) which are explained below :

Link State Advertisements (LSAs) :

As stated above there are five different types of Link State Advertisements (LSA) which are as follows :

1. Router Link LSA
2. Network Link LSA
3. Summary Link to Network LSA
4. Summary Link to Autonomous System boundary router LSA
5. External Link LSA

A short description of each LSA is given below :

1. **Router Link LSA :**
   - The router generates router link advertisement for the area too which it belongs.
   - This advertisement describes the collected states of router's links to the area.

- This advertisement also tells that whether the router is an area border router or it is an Autonomous System boundary router.

2. **Network Link LSA :**
   - This advertisement is originated by the designated router for the transit network.
   - It gives the information about all OSPF routers fully adjacent to the designated router.

3. **Summary Link LSA :**
   - Summary link advertisement describes a single route to a destination.
   - The destinations described are external to the area but internal to the autonomous system.
   - Some condensing of the routing information occurs when creating these summary link state advertisements.

4. **Summary Link to Autonomous System Boundary Router LSA :**
   - These are similar to summary link advertisement except they describe routes to Autonomous system boundary routers.

5. **External Link LSA :**
   - These describe the routes external to the autonomous systems.

1.5.5 Border Gateway Protocol (BGP)

- It is an exterior/interdomain protocol.
- The purpose of exterior gateway protocol is to enable two different Autonomous Systems (AS) to exchange routing information so that IP traffic can flow across the autonomous system border.
- BGP was developed for use in conjunction with internets that employ the TCP/IP protocol suite.
- BGP is based on the routing method called as "Vector path routing".
- BGP is interdomain routing protocol that is used to exchange network reachability information among BGP routers (BGP speakers).
- Each BGP speaker establishes a connection with one or more BGP speakers (routers).
- Two routers are considered to be neighbours, if they are attached to the same subnetwork.
- If two routers are in different autonomous systems, they may wish to exchange routing information.
- BGP performs three functional procedures :

(1) Neighbour acquisition :
- These procedure are used to exchange the routing information between two routers in different autonomous systems.
- To perform neighbour acquisition, one router sends an open message to another.

- If target router accepts the message, it returns a keepalive message in response.

(2) Neighbour reachability :
- Once a neighbour relationship is established, the neighbour reachability procedure is used to maintain the relationship.
- Both sides' needs to be assured that the other side still exists and is still engaged in the neighbour relationship.
- For this purpose both routers send keepalive messages to each other.

(3) Network reachability :
- Both sides router maintains a database of the subnetworks that can reach and the preferred route for reaching the subnetworks.
- If the database changes, router issues an update message that is broadcast to all other routers implementing BGP.
- By broadcasting this update message, all the BGP routers can build up and maintain routing information.
- BGP connections inside an autonomous system are called as internal BGP and BGP connections between different autonomous systems are called as external BGP.

BGP Messages :
- BGP has four different types of messages : Open, Update, Keepalive and Notification (Refer following figure).

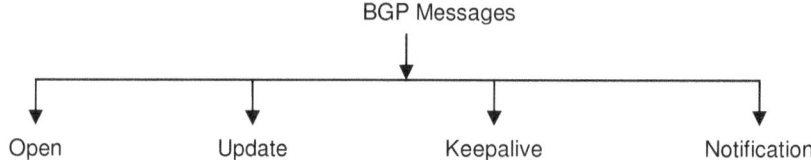

Fig. 1.20 : Types of BGP Messages

- **Open Message :** To create a neighbourhood relationship, a router running BGP opens a connection with a neighbour and sends an open message. If neighbour accepts the neighbourhood relationship, it responds with a *keep-alive* message, which means that a relationship has been established between the two routers.
- **Update message :** The update message is the heart of BGP protocol. It is used by a router to withdraw destinations that have been advertised previously, announce a route to a new destination, or do both. Note that BGP can withdraw several destinations that were advertised before, but it can only advertise one new destination in a single update message.
- **Keep Alive Message :** Routers running BGP protocols exchange keep-alive messages regularly to tell each other that they are alive.

- **Notification Message :** A notification message is sent by a router whenever an error condition is detected or a router wants to close a connection.

Packet Format :
- All the BGP packets (messages) share the same common header. The fields of this header are as follows : (Refer Fig. 1.21).
1. **Marker :** The 16 byte marker field is reserved for authentication. The sender may insert value in this field that would be used as part of an authentication mechanism to enable the recipient to verify the identity of the sender.

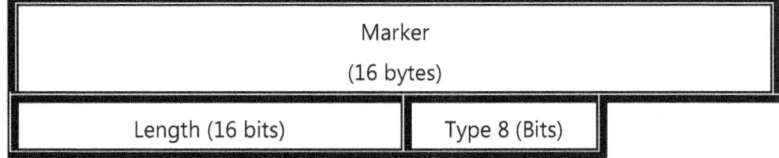

Fig. 1.21 : BGP Header Format

2. **Length :** This 2 byte field defines the length of the total message including the header.
3. **Type :** This field indicates the type of the message, which we have already seen.

BGP Operation :
- To acquire a neighbour, a router first opens a TCP connection to the neighbour router of interest.
- It then sends the open message. The message identifies the AS to which the sender belongs and provides the IP address of the router.
- It also includes a hold timer parameter. The hold timer defines the maximum number of seconds that can elapse until one of the parties receive a keepalive or update message from the other.
- If a router does not receive one of these messages during the hold time period, it considers the other party dead.
- The KEEPALIVE messages are exchanged often enough as to not cause the hold timer to expire.
- The recommended time between successive KEEPALIVE messages is one-third of the hold time interval.
- This value ensures that, the KEEPALIVE message arrive at the receiving router almost always before the hold timer expires, even if the transmission delay of TCP is variable.
- If hold time is zero, then KEEPALIVE messages will not be send.
- When a BGP router detects an error, the router sends a NOTIFICATION message and then closes the TCP connection.
- After the connection is established, BGP peers exchange routing information by using the UPDATE message.

- The UPDATE message may contain three pieces of information : (1) Unfeasible Routes (2) Path Attributes and (3) Network Layer Reachability Information.
- An UPDATE message can advertise a single route and withdraw a list of routes.
- UPDATE messages are used to construct a graph of AS connectivity. It also withdraws multiple unfeasible routes.
- A BGP router uses Network Layer Reachability Information (NLRI), the total path attribute length and the path attributes to advertise a route.

The NLRI field contains a list of IP address prefixed that can be reached by the route.

1.6 INTERNET PROTOCOL (IP)

- Internet protocol is responsible for routing the data packets between the source machine and destination machine.
- It is simple, connectionless internetworking protocol.
- It does not give guarantee of reliable data transmission between source and destination.
- IP relies on protocols in other layers to establish the connection if connection oriented services is required, as well as to provide error detection and error recovery.
- Each IP datagram is handled independently and each one can follow a different route to the destination. So there is always a possibility of receiving the packets out of order at the destination.
- IP relies on ICMP protocol to report errors in the processing of datagrams and provide additional administrative and status message.

1.6.1 IP Header

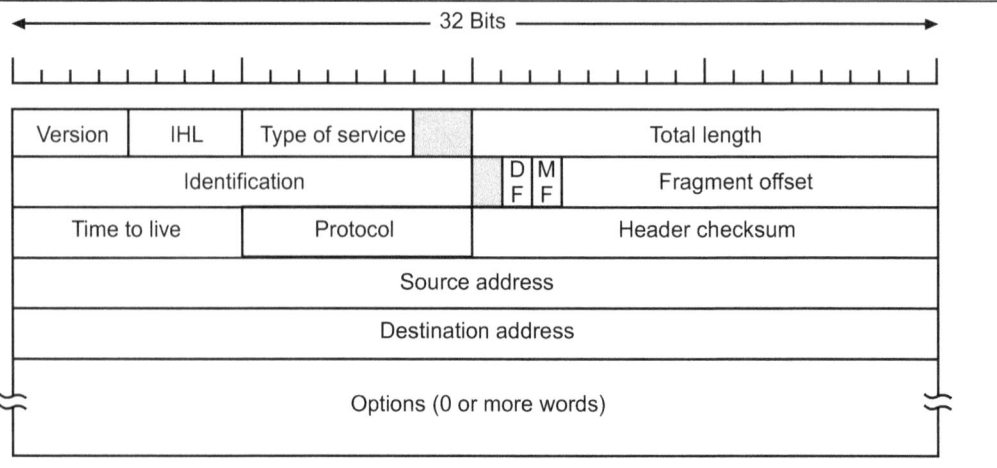

Fig. 1.22 : IP Header

- An IP datagram consists of a header part and a data part. The header has a 20-byte fixed part and a variable length optional part. The header format is shown in Fig. 1.22.

  Various fields of IP header are as follows:

- **Version :** The Version field keeps track of which version of the protocol the datagram belongs to. Currently there are two versions of IP protocol, IPV4 and IPV6.
- **Header Length :** This is 4 bit field. It contains the length of the header expressed in 4 bytes. The size of header without including the Options field is 20 bytes.
- **Type of Service :** This is 8 bit field contains a combination of 1-bit flags that can be used to request delay, throughput and reliability parameters.
- **Total Length :** This 16 bit field contains the total length of IP datagram. The total length includes the length of header as well as the data field. The maximum length is 65535 bytes.
- **Identifier :** It helps the destination host to determine, to which datagram the newly arrived fragment belongs to. All the fragments of the datagram contain the same identification number.
- **DF flag (Don't Fragment) :** It is 1 bit field. DF stands for do not fragment. If destination is incapable of putting the fragments of the datagram, back together that time DF flag is set to 1. It instructs the router for not doing fragments of the datagram.
- **MF (More Fragments) :** This is 1 bit field. MF stands for more fragments. All fragments except the last one has this bit set. It is needed to know the destination that all fragments of the datagram are arrived.
- **Fragment Offset :**

This is 13 bit field, shows the relative position of this fragment with respect to the whole datagram.

- It is the offset of the data in the original datagram measured in units of 8 bytes.
- Fig. 1.22 shows the datagram of 4000 bytes fragmented into 3 fragments.
- The bytes in the original datagram are numbered from 0 to 3999. In that the first fragment carries bytes from 0 to 1399. The offset for this datagram is 0/8 = 0.
- The second fragment carries bytes 1400 to 2799; the offset value for this fragment is 1400/8 = 175.
- Finally, the third fragment carries bytes 2800 to 3999. The offset value for this fragment is 2800/8 = 350.
- Remember that the value of the offset is measured in units of 8 bytes. This is done because the length of the offset field is 13 bits long and can not represent the sequence of bytes greater than 8191 (because 2^{13} = 8192).
- This forces hosts or routers that fragment datagrams, to choose the size of each fragment so that the first byte number is divisible by 8.

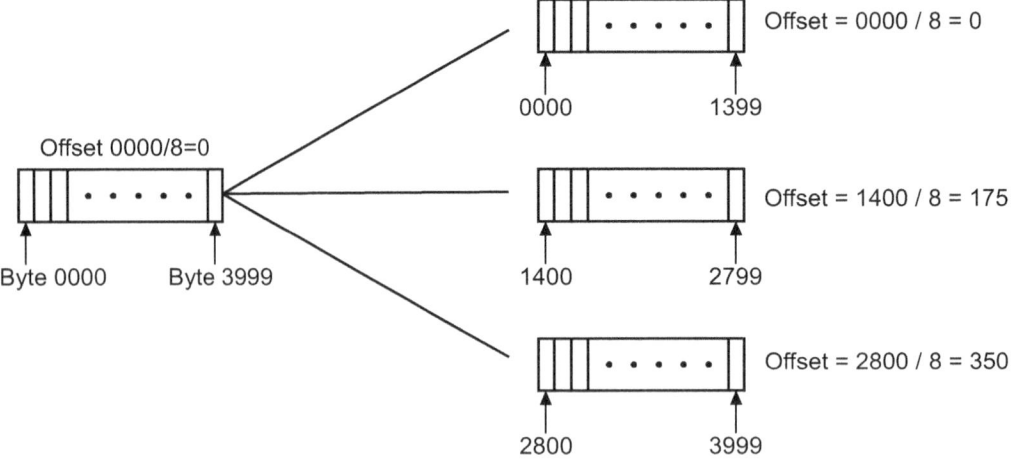

Fig. 1.23 : Fragmentation Example

- **Time to live :**
  - This field is used as counter, which is used to limit packet lifetimes.
  - If the maximum lifetime is 255, the counter is decremented on visiting each hop.
  - When the counter becomes zero, the packet is discarded from the network.
- **Protocol :**
  - This 8 bit field defines the higher-level protocol that uses the service of the IP layer.
  - An IP datagram can encapsulate the data from several higher level protocols such as TCP, UDP, ICMP and IGMP.
  - This field specifies the final destination protocol to which the IP datagram should be delivered.
  - The value of this field for different higher level protocols (in network as well as transport layer protocols) is shown in the 1.1 table.

Table 1.1 : Protocols

Value	Protocol
1	ICMP
2	IGMP
6	TCP
17	UDP
89	OSPF

- **Header Checksum :** This field verifies the header only. This field is used to detect the error in the header.
- **Source address :**
  - This 32 bit field defines the IP address of the source.

- This field must remain unchanged during the time the IP datagram travels from the source host to the destination host.
- **Destination Address :**
  - This 32 bit field defines the IP address of the destination.
  - This field must remain unchanged during the time the IP datagram travels from the source host to the destination host.
- **Options :** Allows IP to support various options, such as security.

1.6.2 IP Address

- Every host and router on the Internet has an IP address, which encodes its network number and host number.
- The combination is unique : in principle, no two machines on the Internet have the same IP address.
- All IP addresses are 32 bits long and are used in the Source address and Destination address fields of IP packets.
- 32 bits of IP address are divided into 4 parts, containing 8 bits in each part.
- There are three methods of depicting IP address :
    1. **Dotted decimal** as in 11.15.10.23
    2. **Binary** as in 00001100.10101000.00001101.00100101
    3. **Hexadecimal** as in 8B.39.C2.43
- It is important to note that an IP address does not actually refer to a host. It really refers to a network interface, so if a host is on two networks (e.g. gateways can be on two networks as they may contain two network interface cards), it must have two IP addresses. However, in practice, most hosts are on one network and thus have one IP address.
- IP address is a structured or hierarchical address. It contains two main parts (1) Network address and (2) Host address (refer Fig. 1.24). The network addresses uniquely addresses each network.
- Every machine on same network shares that network address as a part of its IP address.
- In the IP address 137.57.30.57, 137.57 is network address and 30.57 is host address (refer Fig. 1.23 Class B IP address format).

1.6.2.1 Classes of IP Address

- From several decades, IP addresses were divided into the five categories listed below.
- This allocation is called as **classful addressing.**
- IP addresses are classified into 5 types as given below :
    1. Class A
    2. Class B

3. Class C
4. Class D
5. Class E

Following table shows the ranges of IP address belonging to the five classes.

Class	Staring IP	Ending IP
Class A	1.0.0.0	127.255.255.255
Class B	128.0.0.0	191.255.255.255
Class C	192.0.0.0	223.255.255.255
Class D	224.0.0.0	239.255.255.255
Class E	240.0.0.0	255.255.255.255

The formats for all the classes of IP address are given in the following figure.

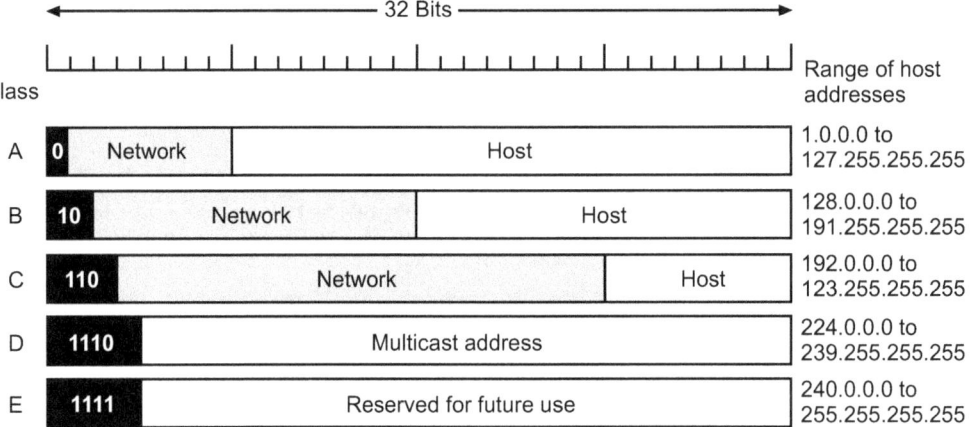

Fig. 1.24 : IP Address Formats

Significance of Leading Bits of Network Address :

See the figure given below. When the router wants to make the routing process fast, router only observes the leading bits (i.e. 0, 10, 110, 1110 and 1111). By reading only these first bits it takes the decision of routing.

Special purpose IP address and function of these addresses are listed below.

1. Network address with all zeros :

   00000000. 00000000. 00000000. 00000000

   This address is used for the current network or host

2. Network address with all 1's :

   11111111. 11111111. 11111111. 11111111

   Interpreted as broadcast address to all hosts on the network.

3. 127.XX.YY.ZZ : reserved for loop-back tests.

4. 0.0.0.0 : Used by the host at booting time, but it is not used afterwards.

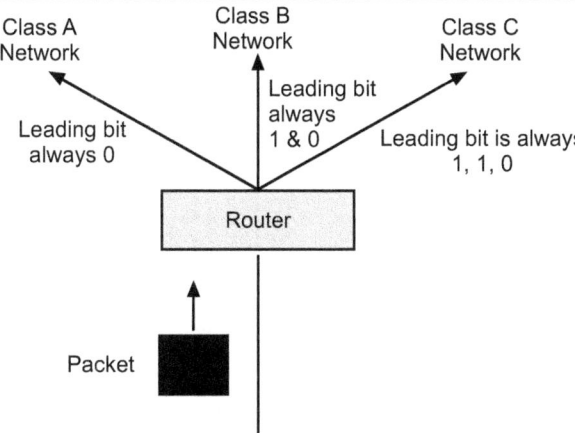

Fig. 1.25 : Leading Bits of Network Address

1.6.3 Network Address

Following figures shows the examples of Class A, B and Class C type of network addresses.

Example of Class-A Network address :

- As per previous discussion the range of Class-A network addresses is from 1.0.0.0 to 127.255.255.255.
- By referring Fig. 1.24 one can easily say that, Class-A IP address contains 8 bits of network id and remaining 24 bits gives the Host Id.
- Now observe the following figure, in which the example of Class-A network is given.

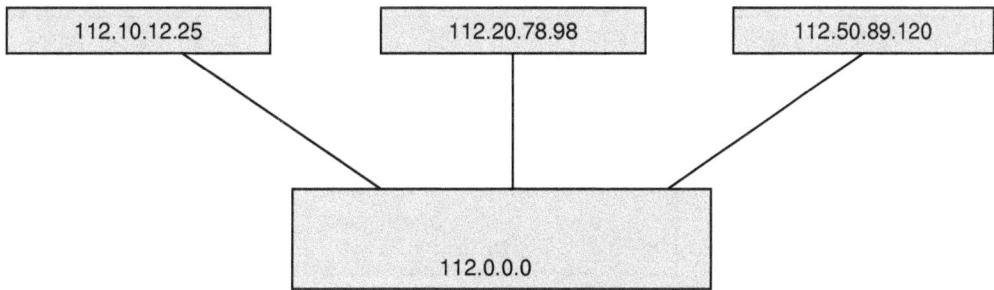

Fig. 1.26 : Class-A Network Address

Note : *Here network address in this example is 112.0.0.0. The value of first octet (Network ID) remains same for all the hosts inside the network. That's why the host addresses are 112.10.12.25, 112.20.78.98 and 112.50.89.120.*

Example of Class-B Network address :

- As per previous discussion the range of Class-B network addresses is from 128.0.0.0 to 191.255.255.255.

- By referring Fig. 1.24 one can easily say that, Class-B IP address contains 16 bits of network id and remaining 16 bits gives the Host Id.
- Now observe the following figure, in which the example of Class-B network is given.

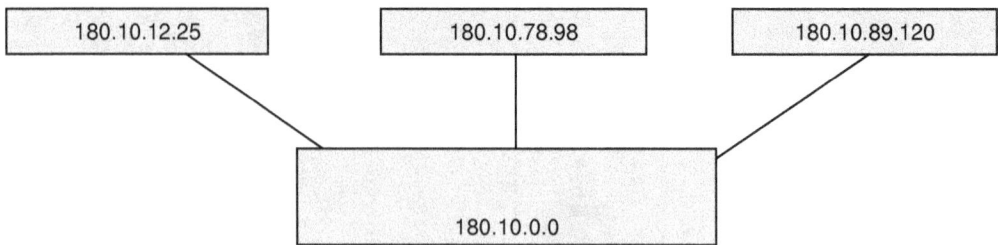

Fig. 1.27 : Class-B Network Address

Note : *Here network address in this example is 180.10.0.0. The value of first 2 octets (Network ID) remains same for all the hosts inside the network. That's why the host addresses are 180.10.12.25, 180.10.78.98 and 180.10.89.120.*

Example of Class-C Network address :

- As per previous discussion the range of Class-C network addresses is from 192.0.0.0 to 223.255.255.255
- By referring Fig. 1.24 one can easily say that, Class-C IP address contains 24 bits of network id and remaining 8 bits gives the Host Id
- Now observe the following Fig. 1.28 in which the example of Class-C network is given.

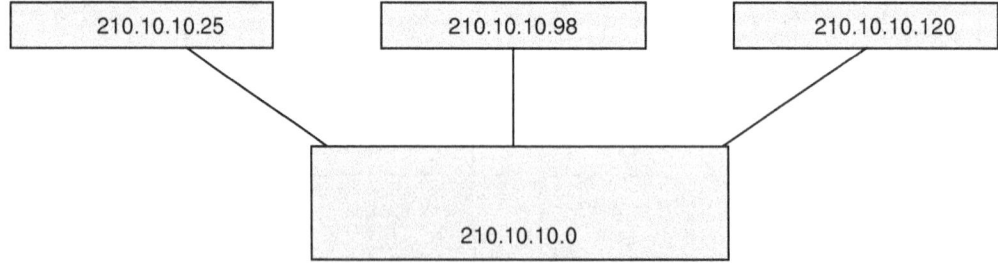

Fig. 1.28 : Class-C Network Address

Note : *Here network address in this example is 210.10.10.0. The value of first 3 octets (Network ID) remains same for all the hosts inside the network. That's why the host addresses are 210.10.10.25, 210.10.10.98 and 210.10.10.120.*

Problem :

From the IP address 222.151.210.34, find out its class, Network ID and Host ID.

Solution :

The first octet value is 222. As it is 222, then by referring Fig. 1.24, one can easily say that it is Class-C IP address. In class C IP address, first 24 bits represents the Network ID, and last 8 bits represents the Host ID.

So accordingly, we can say that the network id is 222.151.210 and host id is 34.

1.6.4 Globally Routable (Public) and Private Network IP Addresses

- There are two types of IP addresses :
    (i) Globally routable (included in the routing tables on the Internet), and
    (ii) Those which have been set aside for private networks.
- It is generally recommended that organizations use IP addresses from the blocks of private network addresses for hosts that require IP connectivity within their company network, but do not require external connections to the global Internet.
- The system with non-routable (private) IP addresses was introduced to help prevent a future shortage of IP addresses due to the explosive growth of the Internet.
- Because addresses belonging to these address blocks are not routed through the Internet routing system, the same numbers can be used at the same time by many different organizations.
- The three blocks of IP addresses which have been reserved for private networks are :

    10.0.0.0   -   10.255.255.255   (24-bit block/Class A)
    172.16.0.0   -   172.31.255.255   (20-bit block/Class B)
    192.168.0.0   -   192.168.255.255   (16-bit block/Class C)

- There are no official rules for when to use which of the three private network IP address blocks, but generally the one of the most suitable size is used. For obvious reasons there is no need to use 10.x.x.x if it is unthinkable that your LAN will ever grow to more than 254 hosts.
- Hosts with private network IP addresses cannot communicate directly with the Internet, because the Internet refuses to receive and transmit data with such origin or destination address.
- For a host with a private network IP address to be allowed to communicate with the Internet, it must have its data stream to the Internet handled by an intermediary host, which can act as an 'Internet representative' for the private host.

The intermediary host must have ways to relay data between the global Internet and the host on the private network. Therefore it must have a globally routable IP address that it uses when communicating with the Internet and a private network IP address that is uses for communication with the private host.

- There are a number of different types of intermediary hosts that fit this description. The most common types of intermediary hosts are proxy servers.
- Public IP address of the proxy server is the identity of the organizations private network on the internet. By using this IP, organization's private network communicates with the internet.
- NAT (network address translation mechanism is used for conversion between the proxy server's private IP address to public IP address.
- Using private network IP addresses also gives a company a measure of security.
- Globally routable IP addresses are advertised in the routing tables on the Internet, making the system vulnerable to hackers.
- When private IP network addresses are used, however, the intermediary host (such as a proxy server) will work as a barrier against unwanted visits from the Internet.
- The current version of IP, IP version 4, defines a 32-bit address, which means that there are only 2^{32} (4,294,967,296) addresses available globally.

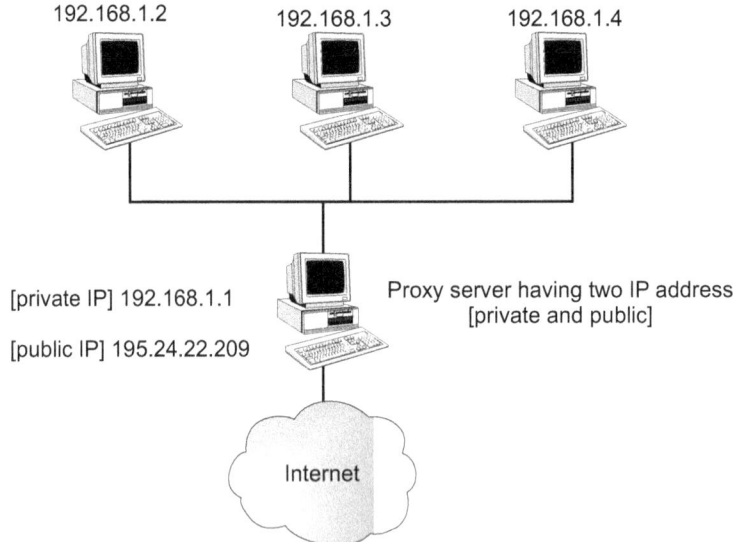

Fig. 1.29 : A Proxy Server Translating Private Network IP Addresses to Globally Routable IP Addresses

- Over the past few years, the number of available IP addresses on the Internet has started to run out, as the number of companies and people wishing to go on-line has exploded.
- As a consequence, a new generation of IP addresses (IPv6) is currently in the works. The current IP system will not become obsolete overnight; however, as the two systems will coexist for some time after the new version has been implemented.

1.6.5 IPv4 Limitations

Following are the major limitations of IPv4 addresses :
- **Shortage of IP addresses :** IPv4 uses a 32 bit address, which generate 2^{32} (4 billion) possible addresses. Now a day's network is growing exponentially. Due to that IP addresses are getting tremendously consumed. So the unique addresses are becoming inadequate.
- **Auto-configuration and mobility :** New technologies (mobile equipment, wireless network) are emerging and its use is quickly becoming common. There is no automatic way to automatically configure this kind of equipment in the network.
- **Security :** The security option in IPv4 is optional, so it is not possible to keep all the data secure while it's routing through the network.
- **Support for real time applications :** Services such as transmission of real time audio and video are becoming common nowadays. IPv4 does not provide ways for managing and reserving bandwidth for such real time transmissions.

1.7 SUBNETTING IN IP

In the previous section, you learned how to define and find the valid host ranges used in a Class A, Class B, and Class C network address by turning the host bits all off and then all on. However, you were defining only one network. What happens if you wanted to take one network address and create six networks from it ? You would have to perform what is called subnetting, which allows you to take one larger network and break it into many smaller networks.

There are many reasons to perform subnetting. Some of the benefits of subnetting include the following :

1. **Reduced network traffic :** We all appreciate less traffic of any kind. Networks are no different. Without trusty routers, packet traffic could grind the entire network down to a near standstill. With routers, most traffic will stay on the local network; only packets destined for other networks will pass through the router. Routers create broadcast domains. The smaller broadcast domains you create the less network traffic on that network segment.
2. **Optimized network performance :** This is a result of reduced network traffic.
3. **Simplified management :** It is easier to identify and isolate network problems in a group of smaller connected networks than within one gigantic network.
4. **Facilitated spanning of large geographical distances :** Because WAN links are considerably slower and more expensive than LAN links, a single large network that spans long distances can create problems in every arena listed above. Connecting multiple smaller networks makes the system more efficient.

1.7.1 Subnet Masks

For the subnet address scheme to work, every machine on the network must know which part of the host address will be used as the subnet address. This is accomplished by assigning a *subnet mask* to each machine. This is a 32-bit value that allows the recipient of IP packets to distinguish the network ID portion of the IP address from the host ID portion of the IP address.

- The network administrator creates a 32-bit subnet mask composed of 1s and 0s.
- The 1s in the subnet mask represent the positions that refer to the network or subnet addresses.
- Not all networks need subnets, meaning they use the default subnet mask. This is basically the same as saying that a network doesn't have a subnet address.
- Table 1.2 shows the default subnet masks for Classes A, B, and C. These cannot change. In other words, you cannot make a Class B subnet mask as 255.0.0.0. The host will read such an address as invalid and typically won't even let you type it in.

Table 1.2

Class	Format	Default Subnet Mask
A	Net.Host.Host.Host	255.0.0.0
B	Net.Net.Host.Host	255.255.0.0
C	Net.Net.Net.Host	255.255.255.0

Contiguous versus Non-contiguous Subnet Mask :

In the early days of subnetting, a noncontiguous subnet mask might have been used. By noncontiguous we mean a series of bits that is not a string of 1s followed by a string of 0s, but a mixture of 0s and 1s. Today, however, only contiguous masks (a series of 1s followed by a series of 0s) are used.

SOLVED EXAMPLES

Example 1.2 :

What is the subnet address if the destination address is 200.45.34.56 and subnet mask is 255.255.240.0 ?

Solution : To find the subnet address AND the given IP address and corresponding subnet mask are as shown in the following figure.

From below figure the subnet address is 200.45.32.0

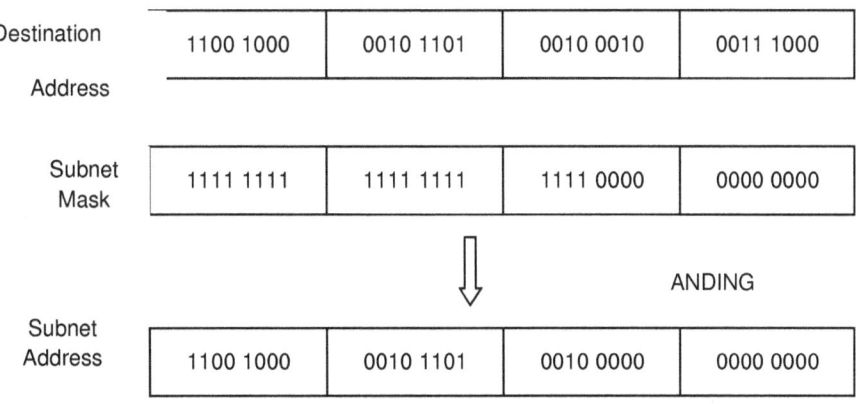

Fig. 1.30

Example 1.3 :
Find the subnet address and the host id for the following :

Sr. No.	IP address	Mask
1.	120.14.22.16	255.255.128.0
2.	140.11.36.22	255.255.255.0
3.	141.181.14.16	255.255.224.0
4.	200.34.22.156	255.255.255.240

Solution :

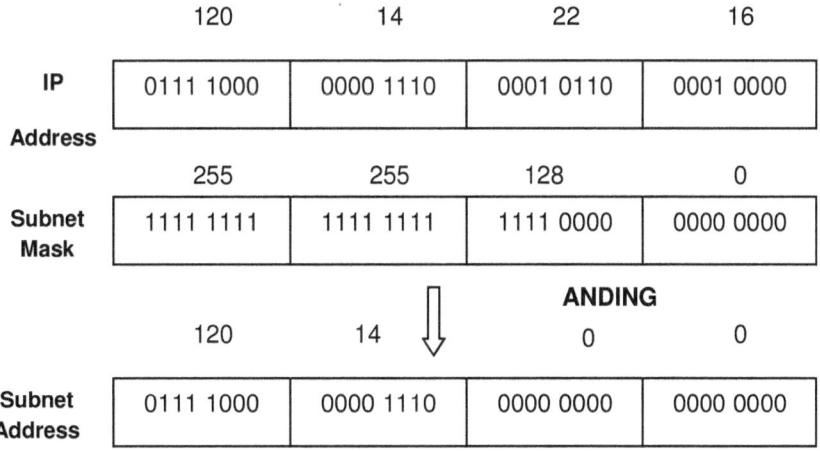

Fig. 1.31

From Fig. 1.30 the subnet address is 120.14.0.0. Similarly we can find other subnet addresses. For calculating the host id of the above subnet address, examine the first octet. It is 120, which is between 0 and 127. Hence this is class A network (refer Fig. 1.24). For class A network, only the first byte/octet corresponds to the net id and remaining 3 bytes correspond to the host id.

So the host id is 14.0.0. Similarly we can solve the other problems.

Example 1.4

For a given class C network 195.188.65.0 design equal subnets in such a way that each subnet has atleast 60 nodes.   **[May 2006, 8 Marks]**

Solution : Structure of class C network is:

Net.Net.Net.Host

In class C network, 3 bytes are reserved for network id and one byte is for host id.

We have to design equal subnets such that atleast 60 nodes should be there.

In order to identify 60 nodes, we will require 6 bits (as $2^6=64$). So out of 8 bits of the last octet, last 6 bits will be used for 64 hosts, so remaining (first) 2 bits will be used for subnetting. In that 2 bits four ($2^2 = 4$) equal subnets can be created.

Example 1.5 :

A network on the internet has a subnet mask of 255.255.240.0. What is the maximum number of hosts it can handle ?

[May 2007, 6 Marks]

Solution : Structure of class B network is :

Net.Net.Host.Host

The given subnet mask is 255.255.240.0, which is shown in the following figure.

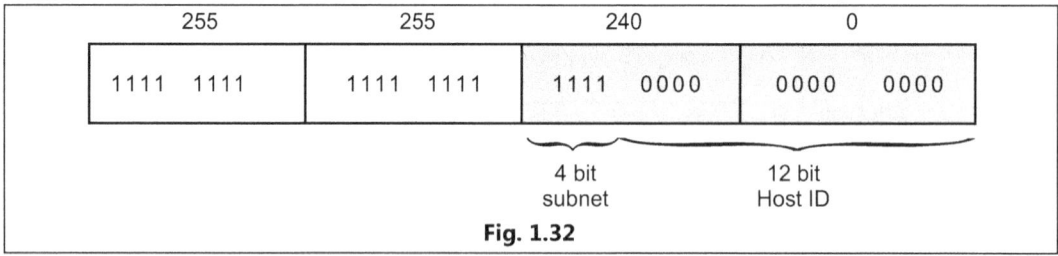

Fig. 1.32

By referring Fig., we can say that each subnet can have 2^{12} = 4096 number of hosts.

Problem 1.6 : The IP address of a host on class C network is 198.123.46.237. Four networks are allowed for this subnet mask. So what is the subnet mask?

[May 2002, 8Marks]

Solution : Class C's default subnet mask is :

Net.Net.Net.Host

For having 4 subnets, we will require 2 bits ($2^2 = 4$).

Hence the default mask and subnet mask are shown in the following Fig. 1.33.

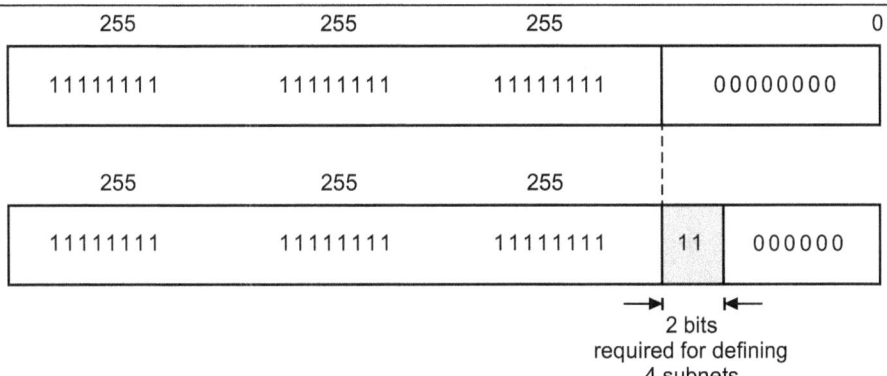

Fig. 1.33

So the required subnet mask is 255.255.255.192

Problem 1.6 :

The Company has granted a site address 201.70.64.0. The company needs 6 subnets. Design these subnets. **[May 2004, 8 Marks]**

Solution : The class C's default subnet mask is :

Net.Net.Net.Host

As per the need of 6 subnets, we will require 3 bits for representing 6 subnets. ($2^3 = 8$ we don't choose 2 bits because $2^2 = 4$ that is less than 6 subnets).

From this the binary form of subnet mask is given in the following Fig..

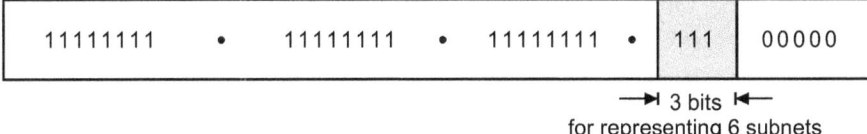

Fig. 1.34

For having 6 subnets, we have to generate 6 combinations from the 3 bits, which are as follows :

Combination	Subnet Number
000	1
001	2
010	3
011	4
100	5
101	6

With respect to all these subnets (refer Fig. 1.33) the remaining 5 bits of the last octet (host id), will give 25 = 32 host id for each subnet. So various addresses of 6 subnets are shown in the following table.

Subnet Number	Addresses
1.	201.70.64.0 To 201.70.64.31
2.	201.70.64.32 To 201.70.64.63
3.	201.70.64.64 To 201.70.64.95
4.	201.70.64.96 To 201.70.64.127
5.	201.70.64.128 To 201.70.64.159
6.	201.70.64.160 To 201.70.64.191

1.8 SUPERNETTING

- Although class A and B addresses are almost exhausted, class C addresses are still available.
- However the size of class C block with a maximum number of 256 addresses may not satisfy the needs of an organization.
- Even a mid size organization may need more addresses.
- One solution to this problem is supernetting.
- In supernetting, an organization can combine several class C blocks to create a larger range of addresses.
- In other words, several networks are combined to create a supernetwork.
- By doing this, an organization can apply for a set of class C blocks instead of just one.
- For example, an organization that needs 1000 addresses can be granted four class C blocks. The organization can then use these addresses in one supernetwork as shown in the following figure.

1.8.1 Classless Interdomain

- CIDR was invented several years ago to keep the internet from running out of IP addresses.
- The "classful" system of allocating IP addresses can be very wasteful; anyone who could reasonably show a need for more than 254 host addresses was given a Class B address block of 65533 host addresses.
- Even more wasteful were companies and organizations that were allocated Class A address blocks, which contain over 16 million host addresses! Only a tiny percentage of the allocated Class A and Class B address space has ever been actually assigned to a host computer on the Internet.
- People realized that addresses could be conserved if the class system is eliminated.

- By accurately allocating only the amount of address space that was actually needed, the address space crisis could be avoided for many years.

1.8.1.1 What is CIDR ?

- The old Classfull IP Addressing scheme is provided for Class A, B and C networks :

Class type	Starting bits for the first octet	How many networks per Class ?	How many hosts per network ?	Range of the first octet	
Class A	0	126	$(2^{24}) - 2 = \sim 16$ Million	1-126	127 = Loopback
Class B	10	$2^{14} = 16384$	$(2^{16}) - 2 = \sim 65000$	128-191	
Class C	110	$2^{21} = \sim 2$ Million	$(2^{8}) - 2 = 254$	192-223	
Class D	1110	-	-	224-239	
Class E	1111	-	-	240-255	

- The default Subnet Masks for these networks are :

Class type	Number of bits used for the Network ID	Number of bits used for the Host ID	Default Subnet Mask
Class A	8	24	255.0.0.0
Class B	16	16	255.255.0.0
Class C	24	8	255.255.255.0

- The problem with such a scheme is that we are bound to the blocks of IP addresses and if we don't need all of them (for example if a small company would need 100 computers they would still have to use a class C network).
- The inefficiencies are mainly in the block assignments. You get a class C network and use only a hundred of those. That means there are suddenly 154 unused and unavailable addresses.
- On the bigger scale some investigations have indicated that while we are running out of address blocks to assign only a very small percentage of the total addresses are being used (less than 10%).

- Of course these networks could be subnetted on a local level, but that would only be good for our local networks, not for the Internet traffic.
- With the expansion of smaller networks the routing table sizes are increasing rapidly. The capacity is being overtaxed.
- One method of solving the problem is to use subnetting. Another is to have all the smaller networks use the privately assigned address space and use proxies.
- One more efficient and new scheme that has been developed for this purpose is called CIDR.

1.8.1.2 How does CIDR work ? How does it differ from Classfull IP Addressing ?

- The class system is being replaced with a prefix anywhere from 13 to 27 bits which serves as a generalized network prefix.
- Thus a new IP address might look like this 192.168.255.48/25. The first 25 bit in the address are used to identify the network, while the remaining 7 bits are used to identify the host.
- Instead of using the old Classfull IP Addressing scheme where the previous IP address was identified as a class C IP address (the first octet is in the range of 192 to 223) and thus we would be forced to use the remaining last octet (the last 8 bits) as the Host ID, we will now use only the last 7 bits as the Host ID and thus have 25 bits for the Network ID instead of the old 24 bits.
- CIDR blocks and number of Host IDs per segment :

CIDR Block	Number of Network ID bits	Number of Host ID bits	Total number of Host addresses per segment = (2 ^# of Host ID bits)	Number of usable Host addresses per segment = (2 ^# of Host ID bits)-2
/27	27	5	32	30
/26	26	6	64	62
/25	25	7	128	126
/24	24	8	256	254
/23	23	9	512	510
/22	22	10	1,024	1,022
/21	21	11	2,048	2,046

CIDR Block	Number of Network ID bits	Number of Host ID bits	Total number of Host addresses per segment = (2 ^# of Host ID bits)	Number of usable Host addresses per segment = (2 ^# of Host ID bits)-2
				(Contd.)
/20	20	12	4,096	4,094
/19	19	13	8,192	8,190
/18	18	14	16,384	16,382
/17	17	15	32,768	32,766
/16	16	16	65,536	65,534
/15	15	17	131,072	131,070
/14	14	18	262,144	262,142
/13	13	19	524,288	524,286

1.8.1.3 How can I calculate the Subnet Mask from a CIDR-type address ?

- It's simpler than you think. You need to write down the number of bits that are in the CIDR notation (in Binary notation), divide them into 4 octets, and convert them to decimal notation.

For example:

- CIDR address: 212.43.43.33/27
    1. Write down 27 bits as 1 (one), and the rest (5) as 0 (zero):
        11111111111111111111111111100000
    2. Divide them into 4 octets:
        11111111.11111111.11111111.11100000
    3. Convert to decimal:
        255.255.255.224

Bingo!

Remember that class A networks are followed by a /8, class B networks are followed by a /16, and class C networks are followed by a /24. This will make life easier for you.

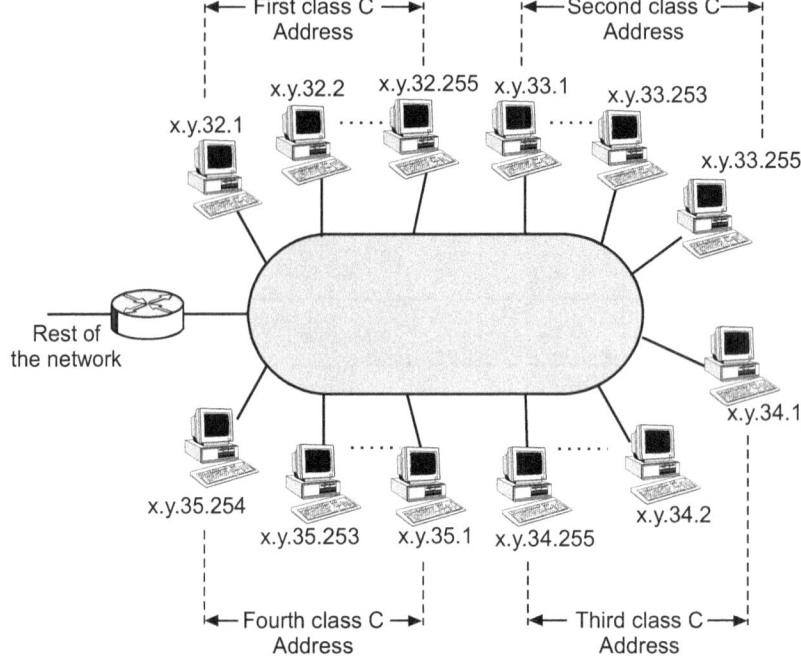

Fig. 1.35 : A Supernetwork

1.9 INTRODUCTION

- Network layer is the third layer in the OSI model. It deals with routing the packets on the internet.
- For packet routing there are certain protocols on the network layer, out of that
    - ICMP
    - IGMP
    - IP
    - ARP
    - RARP
    - DHCP

  are some of the most important protocols.
- The main protocol in Network layer is IP (Internet Protocol). It is responsible for the source to destination delivery of the data packet; during this operation it needs the services of other protocols.
- IP needs ICMP, ARP, and RARP for some specific functions while doing the routing operation.
- Due to that the functionalities of each protocol have been discussed in this unit.

1.9.1 Address Resolution Protocol (ARP)

- Every machine on the Internet has one (or more) IP addresses; but these addresses cannot actually be used for sending packets because the data link layer hardware does not understand Internet addresses (IP addresses).
- Every machine on the network contains an Ethernet card and every Ethernet card is equipped with a 48-bit Ethernet address (also called as MAC address). These Ethernet addresses are the unique addresses worldwide.
- The Ethernet card can send and receive frames based on 48-bit Ethernet addresses. They know nothing at all about 32-bit IP addresses.

How do IP addresses get mapped onto data link layer addresses, such as Ethernet (MAC) ?

Consider Fig. 1.36, here we have two Ethernets, one in the Computer Science Department with IP address 192.31.65.0 and one in Electrical Engineering, with IP address 192.31.63.0. These are connected by a campus backbone ring (e.g., FDDI) with IP address 192.31.60.0. Each machine on an Ethernet has a unique Ethernet address, labeled *E1* through *E6*, and each machine on the FDDI ring has an FDDI address, labeled *F1* through *F3*.

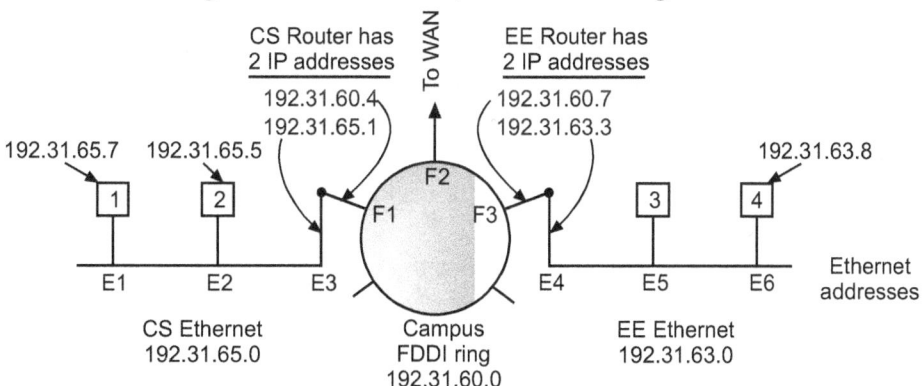

Fig. 1.36 : Interconnected Networks

If machine in Computer Science Dept. (host 1) wants to send a packet to another machine in Computer Science Dept (host 2), then following sequence of events will take place :

- The upper layer software on host 1 builds a packet with 192.31.65.5 as a Destination address and gives it to the IP software to transmit.
- The IP software can look at the address and see that the destination is on its own network, but it needs some way to find the destination's Ethernet address.

Solution to problem : Host 1 will output a broadcast packet onto the Ethernet asking: Who owns IP address 192.31.65.5 ?

- The broadcast packet will arrive at every machine on Ethernet 192.31.65.0, and each one will check its IP address with the destination IP address field of the broadcast packet.

- Host 2 alone finds that the destination IP address of the packet is same as its own IP address, so Host 2 will accept the packet and it will respond Host 1 with its Ethernet address (*E2*). In this way host 1 learns that IP address 192.31.65.5 is on the host with Ethernet address *E2*.
- The protocol used for asking this question and getting the reply is called **ARP** (**Address Resolution Protocol**). Almost every machine on the Internet runs it.

Now, if machine in Computer Science Dept. (host 1) wants to send a packet to another machine in Electrical Engineering Dept (host 4), then following sequence of events will take place :

- Look at Fig. 1.36 again, only this time host 1 (192.31.65.7) wants to send a packet to host 4 (192.31.63.8).
- **Using ARP will fail because host 4 will not be visible in the broadcasting mechanism as routers do not forward Ethernet-level broadcasts.**
- There are two solutions. First, the Computer Science router could be configured to respond to ARP requests for network 192.31.63.0 (and possibly other local networks).
- In this case, host 1 will make an ARP cache entry of (192.31.63.8, E3) and happily send all traffic for host 4 to the local router. This solution is called **proxy ARP**.
- The second solution is to have host 1 immediately see that the destination is on a remote network and just send all such traffic to a default Ethernet address that handles all remote traffic, in this case *E3*. This solution does not require having the CS router know which remote networks it is serving.
- Either way, what happens is that host 1 packs the IP packet into the payload field of an Ethernet frame addressed to *E3*.
- When the Computer Science router gets the Ethernet frame, it removes the IP packet from the payload field and looks up the IP address in its routing tables.
- It discovers that packets for network 192.31.63.0 are supposed to go to router 192.31.60.7.
- If it does not already know the FDDI address of 192.31.60.7, it broadcasts an ARP packet onto the ring and learns that its ring address is *F3*. It then inserts the packet into the payload field of an FDDI frame addressed to *F3* and puts it on the ring.
- At the Electrical Engineering router, the FDDI driver removes the packet from the payload field and gives it to the IP software, which sees that it needs to send the packet to 192.31.63.8.
- If this IP address is not in its ARP cache, it broadcasts an ARP request on the Electrical Engineering Ethernet and learns that the destination address is *E6*, so it builds an Ethernet frame addressed to *E6*, puts the packet in the payload field, and sends it over the Ethernet.
- When the Ethernet frame arrives at host 4, the packet is extracted from the frame and passed to the IP software for processing.

1.9.1.1 Packet Format of ARP Packet

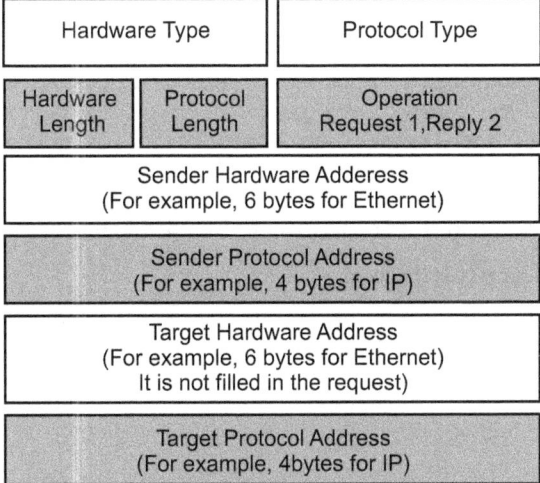

Fig. 1.37 : ARP Packet Format

Various fields in the ARP packet are as follows :

- **Hardware Type :** It is 16 bit field which specifies the type of the network on which ARP is running. e.g. Ethernet is given the type 1. ARP can be used on any physical network.
- **Protocol Type :** This is 16 bit field defining the protocol. For example, the value of this field for IPV4 protocol is 0800_{16}. ARP can be used with any higher level protocol.
- **Hardware Length :** This is 8 bit field defining the length of the physical address in bytes. For example, for Ethernet the value is 6 (as Ethernet address is 48 bits - 6 bytes).
- **Protocol Length :** This is the 8 bit field defining the length of logical address in bytes. For example, for IPV4 protocol the value is 4 (as IP address is 32 bits - 4 bytes)
- **Operation :** This is 16 bit field defining the type of the packet. Two packet types are defined : 1. ARP request, 2. ARP reply.
- **Sender Hardware Address :** This is a variable length field defining the logical address of the sender. For IP protocol, this field is 4 bytes long.
- **Target Hardware Address :** This is a variable length field defining the physical address of the target. For example, for Ethernet this field is 6 bytes long.
- **Target Protocol Address :** This is a variable length field defining the logical address of the target. For IPV4 protocol this field is 4 bytes long.

1.9.1.2 ARP Packet Encapsulation

- An ARP packet is encapsulated directly into a data link frame. For example, in the following figure, ARP packet is encapsulated in Ethernet frame.
- Note that the type field indicates that the data carried by the frame is ARP packet.

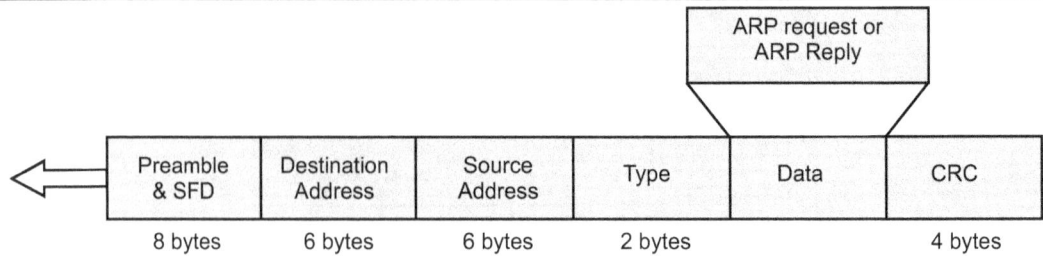

Fig. 1.38 : Encapsulation of ARP packet

1.9.1.3 ARP Functions on Internet

Let's see how ARP functions on a typical internet. First we describe the steps involved. Then we discuss the four cases in which the host or router needs to use ARP.

Steps Involved :

These are the steps involved in an ARP process. Refer Fig. 1.39.

1. The sender knows the IP address of the target. We will see how the sender obtains this shortly.
2. IP asks ARP to create an ARP message, filling in the sender's physical address, the sender IP address and the target IP address. The target physical address field is filled with zeros.
3. The message is passed to data link layer where it is encapsulated in a frame using the physical address of the sender as the source address and the physical broadcast address as the destination address.
4. Every host or router receives the frame. Because the frame contains a broadcast destination address, all stations remove the message and pass it to ARP. All machines except the one targeted drop the packet. The target machine recognizes the IP address.
5. The target machine replies with the ARP reply message that contains its physical address. The message is unicast.
6. The sender receives the reply message. It now knows the physical address of the target machine.
7. The IP datagram, which carries data for the target machine, is now encapsulated in a frame and is unicast to the destination.

ARP services are used in following four different cases :

i. The sender is a host and wants to send the packet to another host on the same network.
ii. The sender is a host and wants to send the packet to another host on another network.
iii. The sender is a router that has received a datagram destined for a host on another network.

iv. The sender is a router that has received a datagram destined for a host on same network.

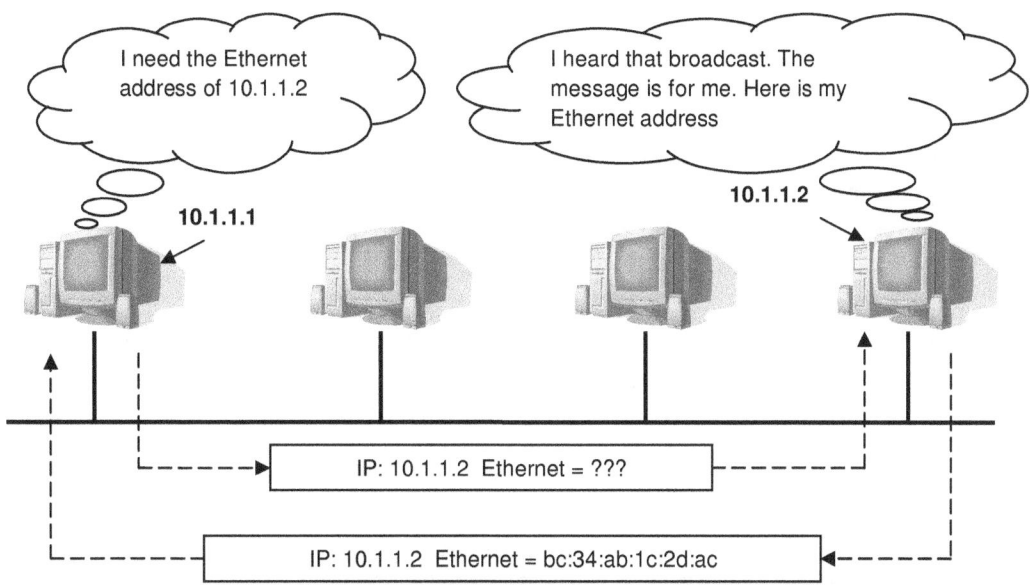

Fig. 1.39 : Local ARP broadcast

1.9.2 Reverse Address Resolution Protocol (RARP)

- If ARP maps IP address to MAC (Ethernet) address. RARP performs reverse operation and maps MAC (Ethernet) address to IP address.
- For mapping MAC (Ethernet) address to its corresponding IP address, reverse address resolution protocol is used.
- Diskless clients depend on another host or server for booting from which they retrieve a network boot file. Each network boot file is named according to the IP address of each client. To request the correct network boot file, each client uses RARP to obtain its IP address at boot time.
- This protocol allows a newly-booted workstation to broadcast its Ethernet address and say : My 48-bit Ethernet address is 14.04.05.18.01.25. Does anyone out there know my IP address ? The RARP server sees this request, looks up the Ethernet address in its configuration files, and sends back the corresponding IP address.
- A disadvantage of RARP is that it uses a destination address of all 1s (limited broadcasting) to reach the RARP server.
- However, such broadcasts are not forwarded by routers, so a **RARP server is needed on each network**.

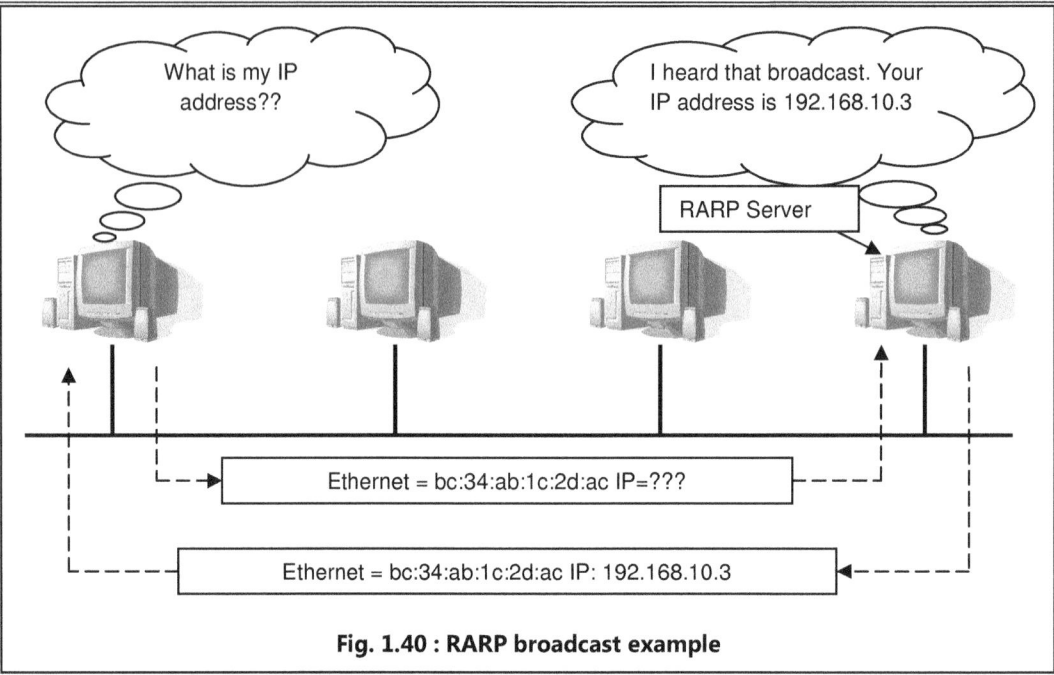

Fig. 1.40 : RARP broadcast example

1.9.3 INTERNET CONTROL MESSAGE PROTOCOL

- Internet protocol has two deficiencies :
  1. Lack of error control
  2. Lack of assistance mechanism
- Internet control message protocol (ICMP) allows routers to send error or control messages to other routers or hosts.
- ICMP provides a communication between the internet protocol software on one machine and internet protocol software on another.
- Technically, ICMP is an error reporting mechanism; it provides a power to the routers that encounter an error, to make aware to the original source about the error.
- ICMP messages are not passed directly to the data link layer as it would be expected, instead the messages are first encapsulated into the IP datagram's just as TCP and UDP segments are carried as IP datagram's. This two level encapsulation process is shown in the following figure.
- ICMP sends messages by encapsulating them in IP packets and setting the headers protocol field to 1.
- The sole function of ICMP is to report the problems and not to correct them.

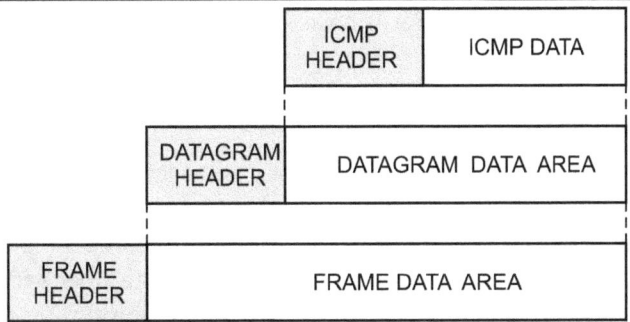

Fig. 1.41 : Two levels of ICMP encapsulation

- Responsibility of error correction lies with sender. ICMP can send the messages only to the source, not to an intermediate router because the datagram carries only the addresses of the original sender and the final destination.
- Following Fig. 1.43 shows ICMP message format.

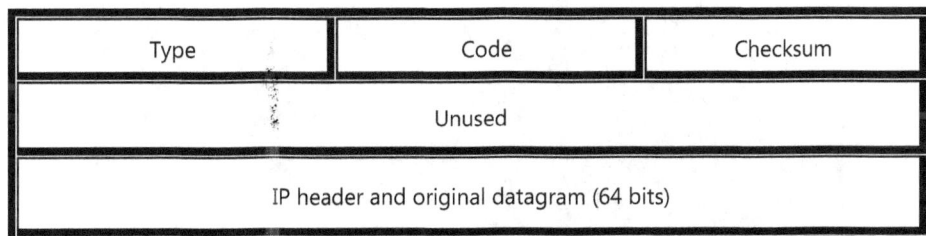

Fig. 1.42 : ICMP Message Format

Following are the fields in ICMP message format :

1. **Type :** Size of this field is 8 bit. This field is used to identify the type of ICMP message. i.e. whether the message is error reporting or it is a query message
2. **Code :** Size is 8 bit. It provides the information or parameter of message type.
3. **Checksum :** Size is 16 bits. It is checksum of entire ICMP message.

- Applications like PING and traceroute makes use of the ICMP messages.

1.9.3.1 Types of ICMP Messages

- Broadly ICMP messages are divided into two categories :
    1. Error reporting messages
    2. Query messages

(1) Error reporting messages :

- Error reporting is one of the major tasks of ICMP. As Internet Protocol (IP) is unreliable, so it does not worry about error checking and error reporting.

- Due to that ICMP comes into existence, even though ICMP reports the errors but it does not have the ability of error correcting.
- It only detects the errors and left the correction process to the higher level protocols (such as transport layer protocols).
- When ICMP founds errors, it gives the information about the errors back to the source host, which has generated ICMP packets. For example, consider a simple example of ping command. If the user tries to ping to some destination, then it receives the appropriate feedback of whether the destination host is reachable or not. See the following screenshot, where the destination host is not reachable. Ping sends 4 ICMP packets and as destination host is not reachable, all packets get lost.

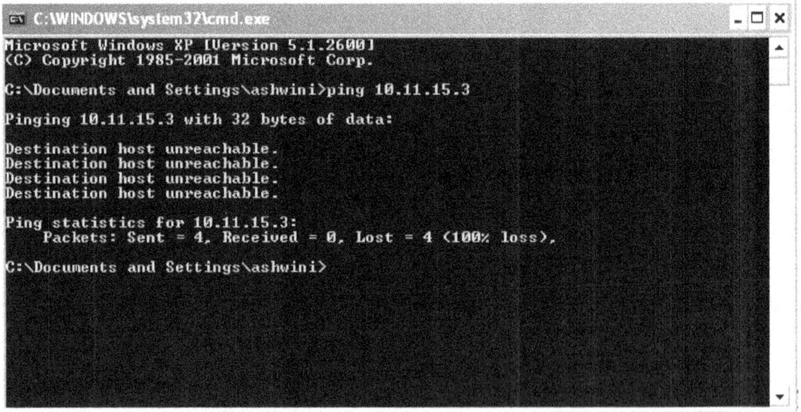

Fig. 1.43 : Ping Command

- ICMP can handle following errors :

  (a) Destination Unreachable : Whenever the packet is not forwarded to destination due to some problems (destination not available or link to destination has been damaged) then ICMP sends destination host unreachable message back to the source machine. (Refer the above example of PING utility).

  (b) Source quench : This is the mechanism for detecting the congestion in the network. If the network is congested, source quench messages aware the source about the congestion and also ask the source to reduce its outgoing flow, which can help in reducing the network congestion.

  (c) Time exceeded : This message can be generated in two cases :
  - If router receives a datagram with a 0 in the TTL field then it discards that datagram and sends a time exceeded message back to the original source.
  - If all the fragments which make up a message do not arrive at the destination host within a certain time limit then time exceeded message is sent back.

(d) **Parameter problem :** When there is a problem in the header part of the datagram, then the router or the host discards such datagram from the network and send a parameter problem message back to the sender of that datagram.

(e) **Redirection :**
- If a router or host wants to send a packet to the host on another network then it should know the IP address of the next router.
- The routers and hosts must have a routing table to find the address of the next router and the routing table must have to be updated constantly.
- For such an updating, the ICMP sends a redirection message back to its host.

(2) Query Messages :
- An ICMP message does the network diagnosis using query messages.
- Query messages contain following messages :
    (a) **Echo request and reply :** It contains Echo request and Echo reply messages. The work of these messages is to check whether two systems can communicate with each other.
    (b) **Time stamp request and reply :** It is used to find out the RTT (Round Trip Time) needed for the datagram to travel between the specific source host and the destination host. Also it can be used for clock synchronization purpose between source and destination machines.
    (c) **Address mask request and reply :** When the source machine knows its IP address but does not know its bifurcation into network address, subnet address, host identifier and network identifier, then it can send the message of address mask to the nearby router. The router then gives the address mask reply by specifying the bifurcation.
    (d) **Router solicitation and advertisement :** A host wants to send data to a host on another network, for that it must know the address of the routers connected to its network. For that the host broadcast a router solicitation message. The routers receiving this message send the routing information using router advertisement message.

1.10 IPv6 (INTERNET PROTOCOL VERSION 6)

Due to the limitations of IPv4, IPv6 comes into existence. This is next-generation internet protocol and had many advantages on the previously existing version of Internet protocol (IPv4). These are listed below :

1. **Larger address space :**
   - An IPv6 address is 128 bits long (compared to IPv4, IPv6 address is very long because IPv4 address was only of 32 bits).

- So total number of addresses generated using IPv6 is 2^{128}.

2. **Better Header Format :**
   - IPv6 uses a new header format in which options are separated from the base header and inserted when needed, between base header and upper layer data.
   - This simplifies and speeds up the routing process because most of the options do not need to be checked by routers.

3. **New options :**
   - IPv6 has new options to allow additional functionalities.

4. **Allowance for extension :**
   - IPv6 is designed to allow the extension of the protocol if required by new technologies or applications.

5. **Support for resource allocation :**
   - In IPv6, the type of service field has been removed, but a mechanism (called flow label) has been added to enable the source to request special handling of packet.
   - This mechanism can be used to support traffic such as real time audio and video.

6. **Support for more security :**
   - The encryption and authentication options in IPv6 provide confidentiality and integrity of the packet.

7. **Plug and Play :**
   - IPv6 includes plug and play in the standard specification. It therefore must be easier for novice user to connect their machines to network, it will be done automatically.

8. **Clearer specification :**
   - IPv6 follows good practices of IPv4, and rejects its minor problems.

1.10.1 IPv6 Addresses

An IPv6 address consists of 16 bytes (octets); it is 128 bits long. Refer Fig. 1.45.

Hexadecimal Colon Notation :
- To make addresses more readable, IPv6 specifies hexadecimal colon notation.
- In this notation, 128 bits are divided into eight sections, each of 2 bytes in length.
- Two bytes in hexadecimal notation require four hexadecimal digits.
- Therefore, the address consists of 32 hexadecimal digits, with every four digits separated by a colon.

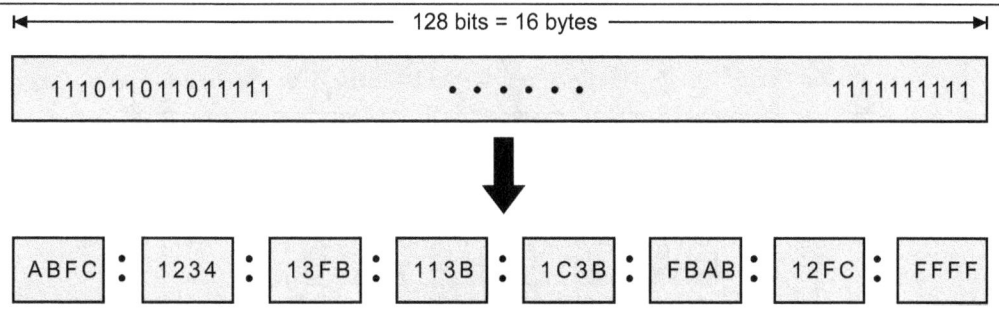

Fig. 1.44 : IPv6 address

Abbreviation :

- Although, IP addresses in hexadecimal format are very long, many of the digits are zeros, in this case we can abbreviate the address.
- The leading zeros of the section (four digits between two colons) can be omitted. Only leading zeros can be dropped, not the trailing zeros (Refer Fig. 1.42).

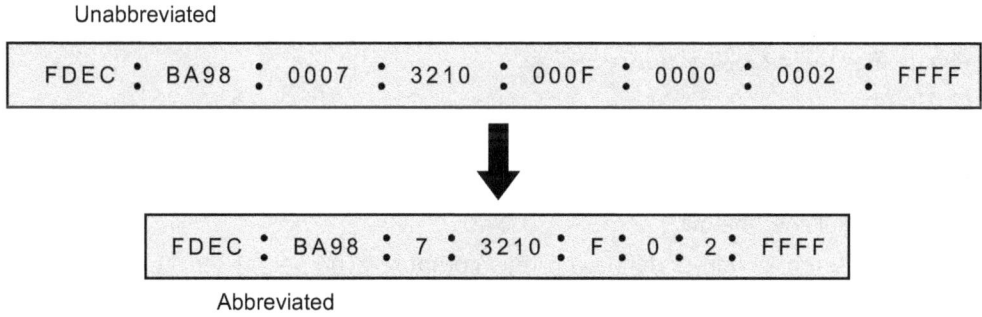

Fig. 1.45 : Abbreviated Address

- Using this form of abbreviation, 0074 can be written as 74, 000F as F, and 0000 as 0. Note that 3200 can not be abbreviated.
- Further abbreviation is possible, if there are consecutive sections consisting of zeros only.
- We can remove the zeros altogether and replace them with double semicolon. Refer Fig. 1.47. Note that this type of abbreviation is allowed only once per address. If there are two runs of zero sections, only one of them can be abbreviated.
- Re-expansion of the abbreviated address is very simple: align the unabbreviated portions and insert zeros to get the original expanded address.

Abbreviated

```
ABFC : 0 : 0 : 0 : 0 : BBFF : 0 : FFFF
```

```
ABFC :: BBFF : 0 : FFFF
```
More abbreviated

Fig. 1.46 : Abbreviated Address with Consecutive Zeros

CIDR Notations :

IPv6 allows classless addressing and CIDR notation. For example, following Fig. 1.48 shows how we can define a prefix of 60 bits using CIDR.

```
ABFC :: BBFF : 0 : FFFF/60
```

Fig. 1.47 : CIDR Address

Categories of Addresses :

IPv6 defines three types of addresses :

1. Unicast
2. Anycast
3. Multicast

These are explained below.

1. **Unicast :** A unicast address defines a single computer. The packet sent to unicast address must be delivered to that specific computer.
2. **Anycast :**
   - It defines a group of computers with addresses that have the same prefix. For example, all computers connected to the same physical network share the same prefix address.
   - A packet sent to an anycast address must be delivered to exactly one of the members of the group – the closest or the most easily accessible.
3. **Multicast :** It defines a group of computers. The packet sent to a multicast address must be delivered to each member of the group.

1.10.2 IPv6 Header

Fig. 1.49 shows the base header of IPv6 having fixed length of 40 octets, consisting of following fields.

- **Version :** Size is 4 bits. It specifies the internet protocol version number. For IPv6 it is 6.
- **Priority (Traffic class) :** Size is 4 bits. It defines the priority of the packet with respect to traffic congestion.

- **Flow label :** The flow label is 3 byte field that is designed to provide special handling for a particular flow of data. It may be used by a host to label those packets for which it is requesting special handling by routers within a network.

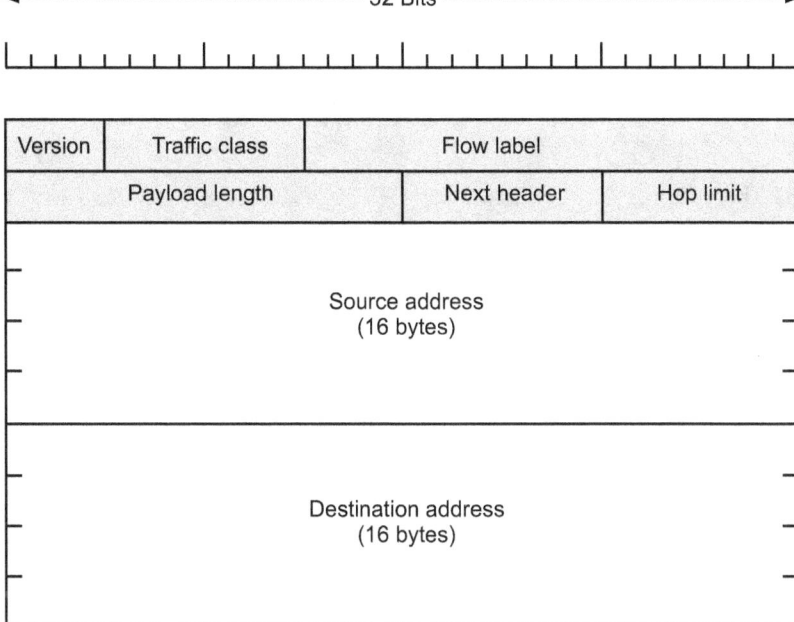

Fig. 1.48 : IPv6 header format

- **Payload length :** It is 16 it is field. It defines the total length of IP datagram including the base header.
- **Next header :** It is a 8 bits field. It identifies the type of header immediately following IPv6 header.
- **Hop Limit :** This is 8 bits field; it serves the same purpose as the TTL field in IPv4.
- **Source Address :** Source address is 128 bits field. It identifies the original source of the datagram.
- **Destination Address :** Destination address is a 128 bits field. It identifies the destination of the datagram.

1.10.3 IPv4 Vs IPv6 Header

1. The header length field is eliminated in IPv6 because the length of the header is fixed in this version.
2. The service type field is eliminated in IPv6. The priority and flow label fields together take over the function of the service type field.
3. The total length is eliminated in IPv6 and replaced by the payload length field.
4. The identification, flag and offset fields are eliminated from the base header in IPv6. They are included in the fragmentation extension header.

5. The TTL field is called Hop Limit in IPv6.
6. The protocol field is replaced by the next header field.
7. The header checksum is eliminated because the checksum is provided by upper layer protocols; it is therefore not needed at this level.
8. The option fields in IPv4 are implemented as extension headers in IPv6.

1.10.4 Difference Between IPv4 and IPv6

IPv4	IPv6
• It is 32 bit source and destination addresses	• It is 128 bit source and destination addresses.
• There are maximum 2^{32} IP addresses.	• There are maximum 2^{128} IP addresses.
• IPv4 addresses are written by dotted decimal notation. e.g. 10.15.11.23	• IPv6 addresses are written in hexadecimal colon notation. e.g. FADB:A2B2:A453:1212:AAB3:ADBD:BBCC:1234
• Basic length of IPv4 header is 20 bytes (excluding option field)	• Length of IPv6 header is 40 bytes.
• IPv4 header has a checksum.	• It has no header checksum.
• Security is optional parameter.	• It has been designed to satisfy the growing and expanded need for network security.
• Headers include option field.	• No option field is present in the basic header. All optional data is moved to extension header.
• IPsec support is optional.	• IPsec support is compulsory.
• Manual or DHCP configuration is required.	• Gets automatically configured, no need of manual and DHCP configuration.

1.11 DYNAMIC HOST CONFIGURATION PROTOCOL (DHCP)

- BOOTP is not a dynamic configuration protocol.
- When client requests its IP address, BOOTP server consults a table that matches the physical address of the client with its IP address.
- This implies that the binding between the IP address and the physical address of the client already exists. The binding is predetermined.

- As BOOTP is static configuration protocol, it can not assign temporary IP address to the host; also it can not handle the situation when the host moves from one physical network to the other.
- To remove the limitations of BOOTP, DHCP protocol comes into existence, where DHCP provides static and dynamic address allocation that can be manual or automatic.
- DHCP is backward compatible with BOOTP, which means a host running the BOOTP client can request a static address from a DHCP server.

Dynamic Address Allocation :
- DHCP database contains a pool of available IP addresses. This database makes DHCP dynamic.
- When a DHCP client requests a temporary IP address, DHCP server goes to the pool of available IP addresses and assigns an IP address for negotiable period of time.
- When DHCP client send a request to a DHCP server, the server first checks its static database.
- If an entry with the requested physical address exists in the static database, the permanent IP address of the client is returned.
- On the other hand, if the entry does not exist in the static database, the server selects an IP address from the available pool, assigns the IP address to the client, and adds the entry to the dynamic database.
- The dynamic aspect of DHCP is needed when the host moves from network to network or is connected and disconnected from the network.
- DHCP provides temporary IP address for a limited period of time.
- The address assigned from the pool is temporary addresses. The DHCP server issues a lease for a specific period of time.
- When the lease is expired, the client must either stop using the IP address or renew the lease.
- The server has a choice to agree or disagree with the renewal. If the server disagrees, the client stops using the address.

Packet Format :
- As discussed previously, we know that DHCP is backward compatible with BOOTP.
- To make it backward compatible, the designers of DHCP have decided to use almost the same packet format as that of BOOTP protocol.
- They have only added one bit flag to the packet. However, for allowing different interaction with the server, extra options have been added to the option field. (Refer following figure).

The fields are described below :
- **Operation code :** This 8 bit field defines the type of BOOTP packet : (1) Request or (2) Reply.
- **Hardware type :** This 8 bit field defines the type of physical network. For Ethernet the value is 1.

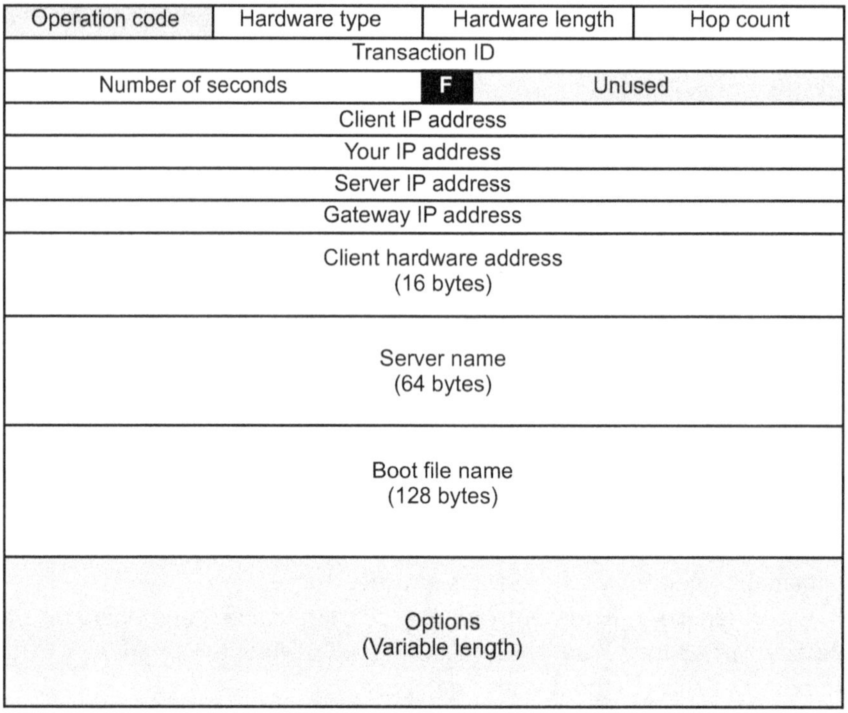

Operation code	Hardware type	Hardware length	Hop count
Transaction ID			
Number of seconds		F	Unused
Client IP address			
Your IP address			
Server IP address			
Gateway IP address			
Client hardware address (16 bytes)			
Server name (64 bytes)			
Boot file name (128 bytes)			
Options (Variable length)			

Fig. 1.49 : DHCP packet

- **Hardware length :** This 8 bit field defines the length of physical address in bytes. For example, for Ethernet the value is 6.
- **Hop count :** This 8 bit field defines the maximum number of hops the packet can travel.
- **Transaction ID :** This is a 4 byte field carrying an integer. This is set by the client and used to match reply with the request.
- **Number of seconds :** This is a 16 bit field that indicates the number of seconds elapsed since the time the client started to boot.
- **Flag :** Server uses this field to specify the client that it is a forced broadcast reply. For unicast reply to the client, the destination IP address of the IP packet is the address assigned to the client. If the client does not know its IP address, it discards the packet. But if the IP datagram is broadcast, every host will receive and process the broadcast message.
- **Client IP address :** This is a 4 byte field that contains the client IP address. If client does not have this information, this field has a value of 0.

- **Your IP address :** This is a 4 byte field that contains the client IP address. It is filled by the server at the request of the client.
- **Server IP address :** This is a 4 byte field that contains the server IP address. It is filled by the server in a reply message.
- **Gateway IP address :** This is a 4 byte field that contains the router IP address. It is filled by the server in a reply message.
- **Client Hardware address :** This is the physical address of the client.
- **Server name :** This is an optional 64 byte field, filled by the server in reply packet.
- **Boot filename :** This is an optional 128 byte field that can be filled by the server in a reply packet. It contains the full pathname of the boot file. The client can use this path to retrieve other booting information.
- **Options :** Several options have been added to the list of options. The option field in DHCP can be upto 312 bytes. Options for DHCP are shown in the following table.

Value	Value
1. DHCPDISCOVER	5. DHCPACK
2. DHCPOFFER	6. DHCPNACK
3. DHCPREQUEST	7. DHCPRELEASE
4. DHCPDECLINE	

DHCP Transition States :
- Refer the DHCP transition diagram given in the Fig. 1.51.
- At start, DHCP client is in the initializing state. The client broadcasts a DHCPDISCOVER message (it is a request message with DHCPDISCOVER option).
- After DHCPDISCOVER message, client goes into the selecting state, where server offers an IP address to the client by generating DHCPOFFER message.
- The server that sends DHCPOFFER locks the offered IP address so that it is not available for any other client within the lease duration.
- After accepting DHCPOFFER message from the DHCP server, client generates a DHCPREQUEST message for the DHCP server and goes to the requesting state.
- If the client does not receive DHCPOFFER message, it tries for four more times, each with time span of 2 seconds. Even though if the client did not get a reply, the client sleeps for 5 minutes before trying again.

- In the requesting state, client receives DHCPACK message when the server creates binding between client's physical address and its IP address. After receipt of DHCPACK, the client goes into the bound state.
- In bound state, client can use the IP address until the lease expires. When 50% of the lease period is reached, the client sends another DHCPREQUEST to ask for renewal. It then goes to renewing state. In the bound state client can also cancel the lease and go to the initializing state.
- Client remains in the renewing state until it receives DHCPACK. If it does not receive DHCPACK and 87.5% of lease time expires, the client goes to rebinding state.
- In rebinding state, if client receives DHCPACK, it goes to the bound state and resets the timer; else it goes to initializing state when the lease gets expired.

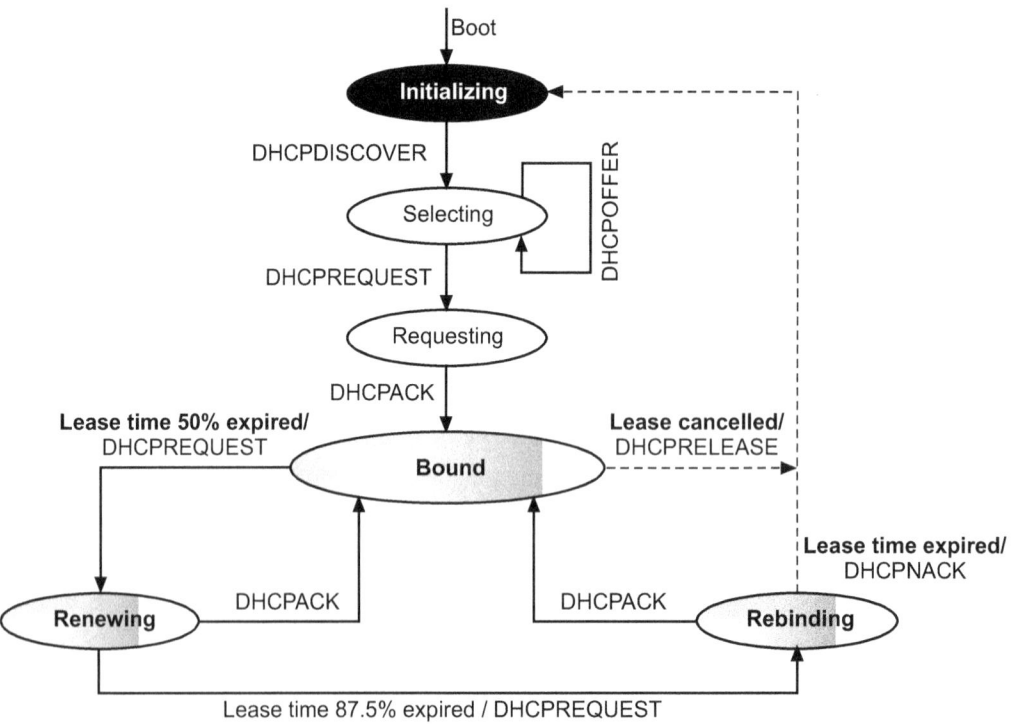

Fig. 1.50 : DHCP Transition Diagram

QUESTIONS

1. Explain the IP header.
2. Explain the purpose of ICMP protocol.

3. Write a short note on ARP and RARP protocol.
4. Explain IGMP.
5. Name different protocols in network layer.
6. Explain the concept of Unicast routing.
7. What are the limitations of IPv4 ?
8. What are the advantages of IPv6 ?
9. Compare IPv4 and IPv6.
10. What is CIDR ?
11. How does CIDR work ? How does it differ from Classfull IP Addressing ?
12. What is routing information protocol (RIP) ?
13. Compare OSPF and RIF.
14. Explain different features of OSPF.
15. Write a short note on OSPF header.
16. Explain BGP protocol.
17. What are the different types of BGP messages ?
18. Explain the BGP operation.
19. What is multicast routing ?
20. Explain IGMP.
21. Write a short note on Multiprotocol Label Switching (MPLS) ?
22. What is Virtual LAN (VLAN) ?
23. Explain the concept of Bootstrap (BOOTP) protocol.
24. Why do we need BOOTP ?
25. Explain BOOTP packet format.
26. Explain the concept of Dynamic Host configuration protocol ? Why it is required ?
27. What are the different classes of IP address ? Also specify the range of each class of IP address.
28. Explain IPv6 header format.
29. What is IP subletting ?
30. Write a short note on subnet masks.
31. What is super netting ? Why it is required ?
32. What do you mean by private IP address? Why they are required ?
33. Explain RIP message format.
34. Explain the types of RIP messages.

35. Compare packet switching and circuit switching.
36. Why layered protocol is used in network model ?
37. For a given class-C network 195.188.65.0 design the equal subnets in such a way that each subnet has at least 60 nodes.
38. Write a short note on : IPv6
39. What is DHCP ? What are its advantages ? Explain various messages used in DHCP ?
40. Compare between BOOTP and DHCP host configuration protocols.
41. Assume that Wi-Fi network is available in the organization. How can one connect laptop to the sever by using DHCP protocol ?
42. IPv6 uses 16-byte addresses. If a block of 1 million addresses is allocated every picosecond, how long will be the addresses last ?
43. What is the purpose of ARP and RARP protocols ? What is the size of ethernet frame carrying an ARP packet as well as RARP packet ?
44. For a given class-C network, design 4 equal subnets having minimum 50 nodes in each subnetwork.

    Explain BOOTP and DHCP in detail.
45. How DHCP protocol assign the addresses dynamically ? Explain stepwise procedure carried out by DHCP server and DHCP client.
46. For a given class B network 144.155.0.0 with default subnet mask, how can you divide it into 8 equal subnets ? How many hosts can be accommodated in each sub-network ?
47. Explain BOOTP and DHCP in detail.
48. What is fragmentation ? Explain how it is supported in IPv4 and IPv6.
49. Consider any class-C network with default subnet mask. How many actual hosts can be connected in that network ? Divide that network into 4 equal subnets. What is the new subnet mask ? How many hosts can be connected in each subnet ?
50. Explain and compare DHCP and BOOTP.

Unit - II

TRANSPORT LAYER

2.0 INTRODUCTION

- The Network layer protocols are largely concerned with finding a path through the network from a source host to a destination host.
- The Network layer doesn't provide an interface for application processes.
- Above the Network layer is the Transport layer. The Transport layer provides an application process interface for actually connecting one process to another via the underlying network.
- The goal of the Transport layer is application processes should communicate without needing to consider the network technology.
- The Transport layer is an important layer in the protocol stack and perhaps the only layer seen by the ordinary users of the network. It is like a outer skin of the network which hides all the organs and functions of the network.

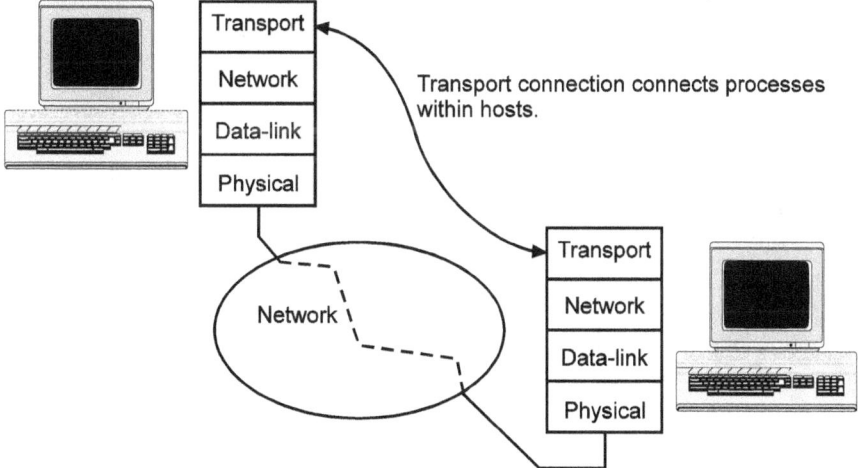

Fig. 2.1 : Transport Layer

- Its main task is to provide reliable connection from a network application running on a source computer to its corresponding application running on the destination computer.
- The connection could be both connectionless and connection-oriented. The OSI model specifies the Transport layer as providing only connection-oriented services. In TCP/IP standards, the Transport layer has provision for both connectionless and connection-oriented services.

2.1 TRANSPORT LAYER DUTIES

- The basic duties of the transport layer is to accept data/message from the application (such as email application) which is running on the application layer.
- Transport layer then splits the received data/message into smaller units if needed.
- It then passes these smaller data units (TPDU) to the network layer and ensures that the pieces all arrive correctly at the other end. But before sending the data units to network layer, transport layer adds transport layer header in front of each data unit.
- Transport layer header prominently contains source & destination port numbers as well as sequence numbers.
- The transport layer is a true end-to-end layer, all the way from the source to the destination.
- In other words, a program on the source machine carries on a conversation with a similar program on the destination machine, using the message headers and control messages.
- Transport layer provides end to end flow control and error control.

2.2 TRANSPORT LAYER SERVICES TO UPPER LAYER

- The ultimate goal of the transport layer is to provide efficient, reliable, and cost-effective service to its users.
- To achieve this goal, the transport layer takes help of the services provided by the network layer.
- The hardware and/or software within the transport layer that does the work is called the **transport entity**.

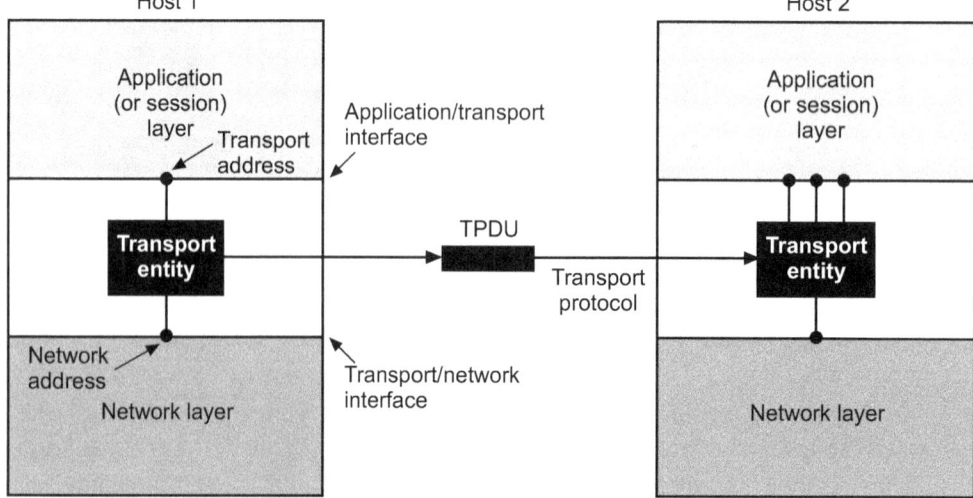

Fig. 2.2 : The relation between network, transport, and application layers

- The transport entity can be located in the operating system kernel, in a separate user process, in a library package bound into network applications, or conceivably on the network interface card.
- The (logical) relationship of the network, transport, and application layers is illustrated in Fig. 2.2.

Similar to the network services, transport layer also contains two types of transport service.

1. **Connectionless :** It is very much similar to the connectionless network service.
2. **Connection Oriented :**
   a. The connection-oriented transport service is similar to the connection-oriented network service in many ways.
   b. In both cases, connections have three phases :
      - Establishment,
      - Data transfer and
      - Release.

   Addressing and flow control are also similar in both layers.

If the transport layer service is so similar to the network layer service, why are there two distinct layers ?

1. The transport code runs completely on the users' machines, but the network layer mostly runs on the routers.
2. The users have no real control over the network layer, so they cannot solve the problem of poor service by using better routers or putting more error handling in the data link layer.
3. The only possibility is to put on top of the network layer another layer that improves the quality of the service.
4. If, in a connection-oriented subnet, a transport entity is informed halfway through a long transmission so that its network connection has been abruptly terminated, with no indication of what has happened to the data currently in transit, it can set up a new network connection to the remote transport entity.
5. Using this new network connection, it can send a query to its peer asking which data arrived and which did not, and then pick up from where it left off.
6. In essence, the existence of the transport layer makes it possible for the transport service to be more reliable than the underlying network service.
7. Lost packets and garbled data can be detected and compensated for by the transport layer.

2.2.1 Advantage of Transport Layer

Thanks to the transport layer, application programmers can write code according to a standard set of primitives and have these programs work on a wide variety of networks, without having to worry about dealing with different subnet interfaces and unreliable transmission.

2.2.2 Quality of Service (QoS)

1. Quality of service provided by Network layer is out of our control.
2. Network layer involves routers across the Internet, which we do not *own* (the carriers own them).
3. If routers or the routing mechanism is faulty, it can result in introducing errors in the data and packet lost.
4. To deal with such poor service, we can't change Network layer as we don't *own* those machines.
5. Our only option is to put a further layer on top of Network layer and try to improve quality of service.
6. Transport layer tries to provide reliable service to Application layer. Transport service can be more reliable than underlying Network service. Unreliability of Network service is hidden from higher layer.
7. For improving quality of service, following parameters play an important role
    - **Connection Establishment Delay :** Generally for establishing the connection, the source does a request to the destination host; destination host gives acknowledgement to the source. If the acknowledgement is positive, the connection gets established. So some time goes from the moment of requesting the connection till the instant at which connection is confirmed. This time difference is called as connection establishment delay. This delay should be as small as possible.
    - **Transit Delay :** This is the time difference between, the instant at which the message is sent by the transport user on the source machine and the instant when it is received by the transport user at the destination machine.
    - **Protection :** Normally, intruders monitor the network traffic. So it is better to send the data securely. For sending the data in secure manner, some data protection mechanisms are required.
    - **Residual Error Ratio :** It is the ratio of number of lost or garbled messages to the total message sent out on the network.
    - **Priority :** Priority is associated with every network connection, which shows that some connections are more important than the other. It plays very important role in case of congestion control. During congestion, the higher priority connections get service before the lower one.
    - **Throughput :** It is nothing but number of data bytes transferred per second. Every connection has different throughput value associated with it.

- **Resilience :** Due to some hardware/software problem or due to congestion, the transport layer spontaneously terminates a connection. The resilience parameter gives the probability of such a termination.

2.3 TRANSPORT SERVICE PREMITIVES

- To allow users to access the transport service, the transport layer provides a transport service interface.
- Each transport service has its own interface.
- The transport service is similar to the network service with some important differences. The main difference is that the network service is intended to model the service offered by real networks. Real networks can lose packets, so the network service is generally unreliable.
- The (connection-oriented) transport service, in contrast, is reliable. Of course, real networks are not error-free, but that is precisely the purpose of the transport layer to provide a reliable service on top of an unreliable network.
- See the following table for getting the exact idea of transport services. It lists five important primitives of simple transport service. These primitives also plays a crucial role in the socket programming that we are going to study in next section of this unit.

Primitive	Packet sent	Meaning
LISTEN	(none)	Block until some process tries to connect
CONNECT	CONNECTION REQ.	Activity attempt to establish a connection
SEND	DATA	Send information
RECEIVE	(none)	Block until a DATA packet arrives
DISCONNECT	DISCONNECTION REQ.	This side wants to release the connection

Practically to see how these primitives might be used, consider an application with a server and a number of remote clients.

1. First, the server executes a LISTEN primitive, that block the server until a client sends CONNECT request.
2. When a client wants to talk to the server, it executes a CONNECT primitive. While establishing connection with server, transport entity blocks the caller/client. The connection request message (TPDU), encapsulated in the payload field of the packet is sent to servers transport entity. In short, client's CONNECT call causes a CONNECTION REQUEST TPDU to be sent to the server

3. When it arrives, the transport entity checks to see that the server is blocked on a LISTEN (i.e., server is interested in handling requests). It then unblocks the server and sends a CONNECTION ACCEPTED TPDU back to the client.
4. When this TPDU arrives, the client is unblocked and the connection is established.
5. Data can now be exchanged using the SEND and RECEIVE primitives. The data exchange in network layer is more complicated than that of transport layer.
6. During transport layer, every packet that is sent has to be acknowledged.
7. The acknowledgement process is carried out by transport entities using network layer protocols.
8. Transport entities have to take care of timers and retransmissions.
9. To the transport layer users, a connection is like a reliable bit pipe in which sender stuffs bits at one end and they magically appear at the other end. It hides the complexity.
10. When a connection is not needed, it must be released to free up table space within the two transport entities.

Disconnection has Two Variants :
- Asymmetric and
- Symmetric.

In the asymmetric variant, either transport user can issue a DISCONNECT primitive, which results in a DISCONNECT TPDU being sent to the remote transport entity. Upon arrival, the connection is released.

Transport Protocol Data Unit (TPDU) ?
- Refer Fig. 2.3
- TPDUs are used to send message from source transport entity to destination transport entity.
- Thus, TPDUs (exchanged by the transport layer) reside in packets (exchanged by the network layer).
- Packet resides in frames (exchanged by the data link layer).
- When a frame arrives, the data link layer processes the frame header and passes the contents of the frame payload field to the network entity.
- The network entity processes the packet header and passes the contents of the packet payload to the transport entity.

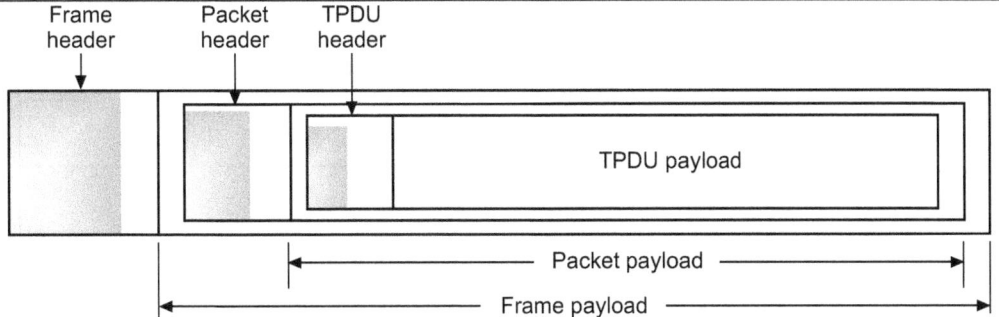

Fig. 2.3 : Nesting of TPDUs, packets, and frames

2.4 THE INTERNET TRANSPORT PROTOCOL

The Internet has two main protocols in the transport layer, a connectionless and a connection-oriented protocol. The connectionless protocol is UDP (user datagram protocol) and connection-oriented protocol is TCP (transmission control protocol).

2.4.1 User Datagram Protocol (UDP)

- It is a connectionless, unreliable transport protocol.
- UDP provides a way for applications to send encapsulated IP datagram's without having to establish a connection.
- UDP transmits segments consisting of an 8-byte header followed by the payload. The data segment sent using the UDP protocol is called as datagram.
- It serves as intermediary between the application programs and network operations.
- It helps in process to process communication; it uses port numbers to accomplish this task.
- Another responsibility is to provide control mechanism at transport layer.
- It performs very limited error checking.
- It does not contain flow control and acknowledgement mechanism for the received packets.
- It is very simple protocol with a minimum overhead. If process wants to send a small message and does not care much about the reliability, it can use UDP.

2.4.1.1 User Datagram

UDP packets, called user datagrams, have a fixed size header of 8 bytes. Following Fig. 2.4 shows the format of a user datagram header.

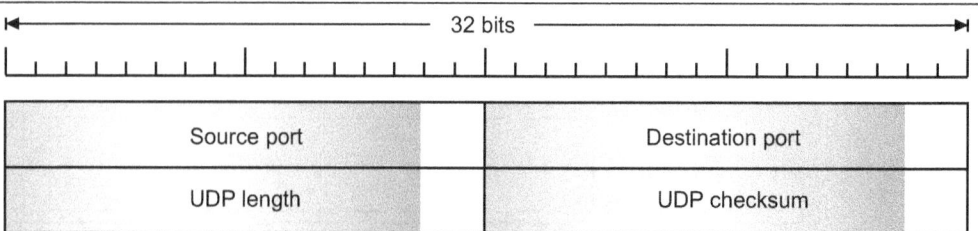

Fig. 2.4 : User datagram header format

The fields are as follows :

Source Port Number :
- This is the port number used by the process running on source host.
- It is 16 bit long, which means that port number can range from 0 to 65,535.
- If the source host is the client (a client sending a request), the port number, in most cases is an ephemeral port number requested by the process and chosen by the UDP software running on the source host.
- If source host is server (a server sending a response), the port number, in most cases is a well-known port number.

Destination Port Number :
- This is a port number used by the process running on the destination host.
- It is also 16 bit long.
- If destination host is the server, the port number in most cases, is a well-known port.
- If destination host is a client, the port number in most cases is ephemeral port number. In this case, server copies the ephemeral port number it has received in the request packet.

UDP Length :
- This is a 2 byte (16 bit) field that defines the total length of user datagram (i.e. header + data).
- The 16 bit can define total length of 0 to 65,535 bytes. However the total length needs to be much less because an UDP user datagram is stored in an IP datagram with the total length of 65535 bytes.
- The length field in a UDP user datagram is actually not necessary.
- A user datagram is encapsulated in an IP datagram. There is a field in the IP datagram that defines the total length. There is another field in the IP datagram that defines the length of the header. So after subtracting the value of second field from the first, we can find out the length of UDP datagram that is encapsulated in an IP datagram.

$$UDP\ length = IP\ length - IP\ header's\ length$$

- However, the designers of the UDP protocol felt that it was more efficient for the destination UDP to calculate the length of the data from the information provided in the UDP user datagram rather than asking the IP software to supply this information. Also, we should remember that when the IP software delivers the UDP user datagram to the UDP layer, it has already dropped the IP header.

UDP Checksum :
- This field is used to detect errors over the entire user datagram (header + data). UDP checksum calculation involves three sections : the pseudoheader, the UDP header and data coming from the application layer. (Pseudoheader is a part of the header of IP packet in which user datagram is to be encapsulated.)

2.4.1.2 Encapsulation and Decapsulation

To send a message from one process to another, the UDP protocol encapsulates and decapsulates messages (see Fig. 2.5).

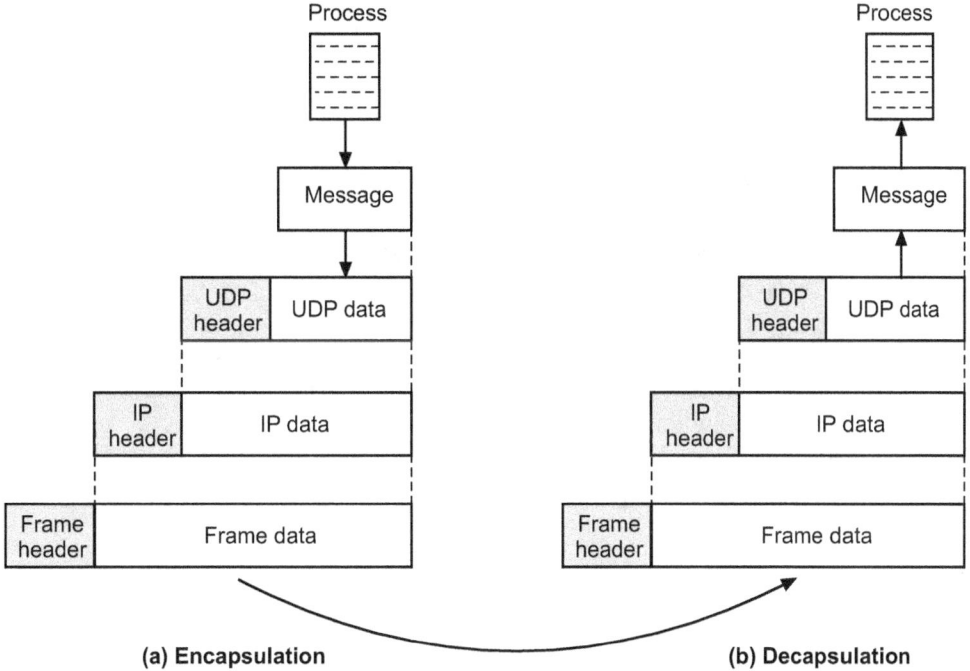

(a) Encapsulation (b) Decapsulation

Fig. 2.5 : Encapsulation and Decapsulation

Encapsulation
- When a process has a message to send through UDP, it passes the message to UDP alongwith a pair of socket addresses and length of data.
- UDP receives the data and adds the UDP header.
- UDP then passes the user datagram to IP with socket addresses.

- IP adds its own header, using the value 17 in the protocol field, indicating that the data has come from the UDP protocol.
- The IP datagram is then passed to the data link layer.
- Data link layer then receives the IP datagram, adds its own header and passes it to the physical layer.
- The physical layer encodes the bits into electrical or optical signals and sends it to the remote machine.

Decapsulation :
- When message arrives at the destination host, the physical layer decodes the signals into bits and passes it to the data link layer.
- The data link layer uses the header (and trailer) to check the data.
- If there is no error, the header and trailer are dropped and datagram is passed to IP.
- The IP software does its own checking.
- If there is no error, the header is dropped and the user datagram is passed to UDP.
- UDP uses the checksum to check the entire user datagram. If there is no error, the header is dropped and the application data along with the sender socket address is passed to the process.
- The sender socket address is passed to the process in case it needs to respond to the message received.

2.4.2 Transmission Control Protocol (TCP)

- TCP is a connection oriented, reliable transport protocol.
- It lies between application layer and network layer and serves as intermediary between application programs and network operation.
- TCP provides a way for applications to send encapsulated IP packets by establishing a connection.
- It uses flow and error control mechanisms in the transport layer.
- It helps in process to process communication; it uses port numbers to accomplish this task.
- It is a full duplex protocol, meaning that each TCP connection supports a pair of byte streams, one flowing in each direction.
- TCP also implements a congestion-control mechanism.

2.4.2.1 Introduction to TCP
- TCP (Transmission Control Protocol) was specifically designed to provide a reliable end-to-end delivery of data over an unreliable internetwork.

- An internetwork differs from a single network because different parts may have wildly different topologies, protocols, bandwidths, delays, packet sizes, and other parameters.
- TCP was designed to dynamically adapt to properties of the internetwork and to be robust to face many kinds of failures.
- The reliability mechanism of TCP allows devices to deal with lost, delayed, or duplicate packets.
- The IP layer gives no guarantee that datagram's will be delivered properly, so by using the timeout mechanism; the lost packets are detected and then retransmitted.
- Datagrams may arrive in the wrong order; so it is up to TCP to reassemble them into messages in the proper sequence.
- Following are some of the services offered by TCP to the processes at the application layer
    1. Stream delivery service
    2. Full Duplex service
    3. Connection oriented service
    4. Reliable service

2.4.2.2 TCP Services

1. Stream Delivery Service

- TCP is stream-oriented protocol.
- It allows sending and receiving process to send and accept data as a stream of bytes.
- TCP creates an environment, in which an imaginary "tube" connects the sending and receiving process. This tube carries their data across the internet.
- This imaginary environment is shown in Fig. 2.6, where sender's process writes a stream of bytes on the tube at one end and the receiver's process reads the stream of bytes from the other end.

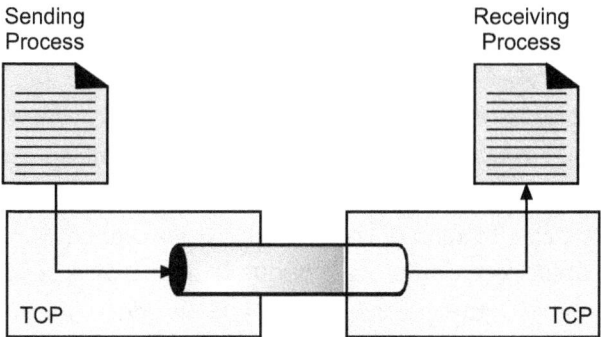

Fig. 2.6 : Stream Delivery

- Because the sending and receiving processes may not read or write the data at the same speed, TCP needs buffer storage.
- Hence, TCP contains two buffers :
  1. Sending buffer and
  2. Receiving buffer

  used at sender and receiver side process respectively.
- These buffers can be implemented by using a circular array of 1 byte locations as shown in Fig. 2.7. For simplicity we have shown buffers of smaller size. Practically, the buffers are much larger than this.

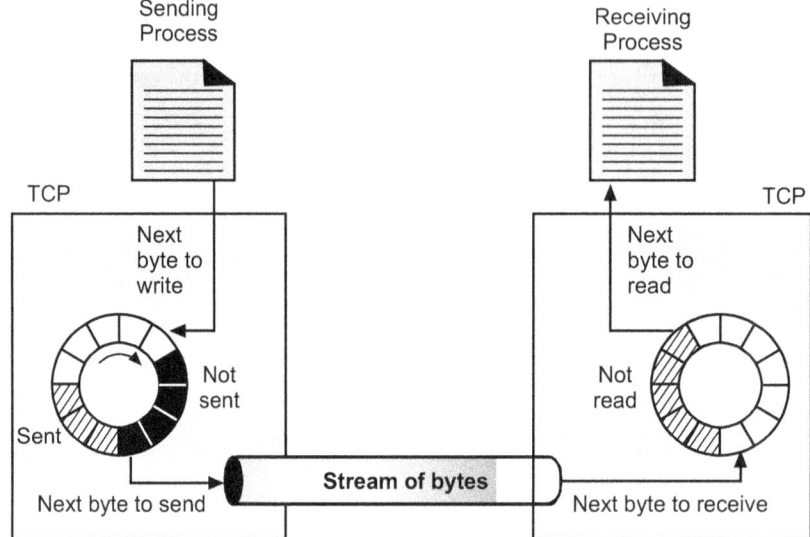

Fig. 2.7 : Sending and receiving buffer

- Fig. 2.7 shows data movement in one direction. At the sending site, the buffer contains three types of compartments.
  - The white section contains empty compartments, which can be filled by the sending process.
  - The area holds bytes that have been sent but not yet acknowledged.
  - TCP keeps these bytes in the buffer until it receives the acknowledgement.
  - The black area contains bytes to be sent by the sending TCP process.
  - TCP may be able to send only part of this black section. This could be due to the slowness of the receiving process or due to the network congestion problem.
  - When the bytes in the gray section are acknowledged, the chambers become free and get available for use to the sending process.
  - At receiver side, the circular buffer is divided into two areas (white and gray).

- The white area contains empty compartments, to be filled by bytes, received from the network.
- The gray area contains received bytes that can be read by the receiving process. Once the byte is read by the receiving process, the compartment is freed and added to the pool of empty compartments.
- Buffering is used to handle the difference between the speed of data transmission and data reception. But only buffering is not enough, we need one more step before we can send the data.
- IP layer, as a service provider for TCP, needs to send data in packets, not as a stream of bytes.
- At transport layer, TCP groups the number of bytes together into a packet called as a segment; TCP adds a header to each segment and delivers the segment to the IP layer for transmission.
- The segments are encapsulated in an IP datagram and then transmitted.

2. Full Duplex Communication Service :
- TCP provides full duplex service, when data can flow in both directions at the same time.
- Each TCP then have a sending and receiving buffer and segments in both directions.

3. Connection Oriented Service :
- TCP is a connection oriented protocol.
- When one process at site A wants to send and receive data from another process at site B, following things take place :
    - The two TCPs establish a connection between them.
    - Data are exchanged in both the directions.
    - The connection is terminated.
- Note that the connection is virtual and not the physical.

4. Reliable Service

TCP is reliable transport protocol. It uses acknowledgement mechanism to check the safe and sound arrival of the data.

2.4.2.3 The TCP Service Model

- TCP service is obtained by both the sender and receiver creating end points, called sockets.
- Each socket has a socket number (address) consisting of the IP address of the host and a 16-bit number local to that host, called a port.
- A port is the TCP name for a TSAP. For obtaining TCP service, a connection must be explicitly established between a socket on the sending machine and a socket on the receiving machine.

- Two or more connections may terminate at the same socket. Connections are identified by the socket identifiers at both ends, that is, (*socket1*, *socket2*). No virtual circuit numbers or other identifiers are used.
- See the listing of socket calls in the table given below :

Primitive	Meaning
SOCKET	Create a new communication end point
BIND	Attach a local address to a socket
LISTEN	Announce willingness to accept connections
ACCEPT	Block the caller until a connection attempt arrives
CONNECT	Actively attempt to establish a connection
SEND	Send some data over the connection
RECEIVE	Receive some data from the connection
CLOSE	Release the connection

- Port numbers below 1024 are called "well-known ports" and are reserved for standard services. For example, any process wishing to establish a connection to a host to transfer a file using FTP can connect to the destination host's port 21 to contact its FTP daemon.
- All TCP connections are full duplex and point-to-point. Full duplex means that traffic can go in both directions at the same time.
- Point-to-point means that each connection has exactly two end points.
- TCP does not support multicasting or broadcasting.
- A TCP connection is a byte stream, not a message stream.
- When an application passes data to TCP, TCP may send it immediately or buffer it.
- However, sometimes, the application really wants the data to be sent immediately. To force data out, applications can use the PUSH flag, which tells TCP not to delay the transmission.
- **Urgent Data :**
  - In this case, if the sending application puts some control information in the data stream and gives it to TCP along with the URGENT flag, this event causes TCP to stop accumulating data and transmit everything it has for that connection immediately.
  - When the urgent data is reached at the destination, the receiving application is interrupted, so it can stop whatever it was doing and read the data stream to find the urgent data.
  - The end of the urgent data is marked so the application knows when it is over.
  - The start of the urgent data is not marked. It is up to the application to figure it out.

2.4.2.4 The TCP Protocol

- The sending and receiving TCP entities exchange data in the form of segments.
- A TCP segment consists of a fixed 20-byte header (plus an optional part) followed by zero or more data bytes.
- The TCP software decides how big segments should be.
- It can accumulate data from several writes into one segment or can split data from one write over multiple segments.
- Two limits restrict the segment size.
   1. Each segment, including the TCP header, must fit in the 65,515-byte IP payload.
   2. Each network has a maximum transfer unit, or MTU, and each segment must fit in the MTU.
- The basic protocol used by TCP entities is the sliding window protocol.
- When a sender transmits a segment, it also starts a timer. When the segment arrives at the destination, the receiving TCP entity sends back a segment (with data if any exist, otherwise without data) bearing an acknowledgement number equal to the next sequence number of the segment it expects to receive. If the sender's timer goes off before the acknowledgement is received, the sender transmits the segment again.

Following Problems can Occur During Transmission of Segments :

- Segments can arrive out of order.
- Segments can be delayed in the transit.

TCP must be prepared to deal with these problems and solve them in an efficient way. A considerable amount of effort has gone into optimizing the performance of TCP. A number of the algorithms used by many TCP implementations will be discussed later.

2.4.2.5 The TCP Segment Header

- See Fig. 2.10 of TCP header.
- TCP protocol has fixed 20 byte header.
- This header is followed by the optional field, and which is further followed by the data part.
- Data part is also optional. Segments without any data are legal and are commonly used for acknowledgements and control messages.

2.4.2.6 TCP Protocol Operation

TCP protocol operations may be divided into three phases :

1. Connections must be properly established in a multi-step handshake process (connection establishment) before entering the data transfer phase.
2. Then data transfer takes place.
3. After data transmission is completed, the connection termination closes established virtual circuits and releases all allocated resources.

A TCP connection is managed by an operating system through a programming interface that represents the local end-point for communications called as the Internet socket.

1. **TCP Connection Establishment :**
   - For establishing a connection, the server, passively waits for an incoming connection by executing the LISTEN and ACCEPT primitives.
   - The other side, say, the client, executes a CONNECT primitive, specifying the IP address and port to which it wants to connect.
   - The CONNECT primitive sends a TCP segment with the SYN bit 1 and ACK bit 0 and waits for a response.
   - When this segment arrives at the destination, the TCP entity there checks to see if there is a process that has done a LISTEN on the port given in the Destination port field. If not, it sends a reply with the *RST* bit on to reject the connection.
   - If some process is listening to the port, that process is given the incoming TCP segment. It can then either accept or reject the connection.
   - After acceptance of the segment, an acknowledgement segment is sent back. The sequence of TCP segments sent in normal is shown in Fig. 2.8 (a).

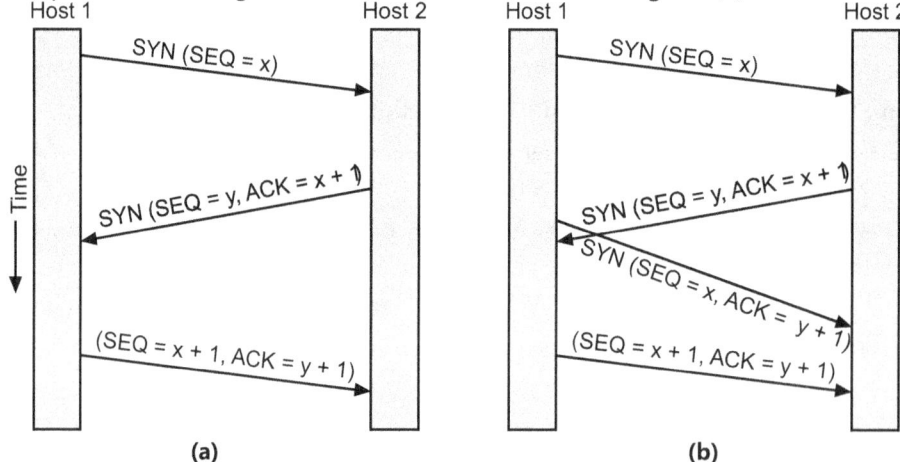

Fig. 2.8 : (a) TCP connection establishment in the normal case,
(b) Call collision

   - If two hosts simultaneously attempt to establish a connection between the same two sockets, the sequence of events is as illustrated in Fig. 2.8 (b).
   - The result of these events is that just one connection is established, not two because connections are identified by their end points.

2. **TCP Connection Release :**
   - To release a connection, either party can send a TCP segment with the FIN bit set, which means that it has no more data to transmit.
   - When the *FIN* is acknowledged, that direction is shut down for new data. Data may continue to flow indefinitely in the other direction, however.

- When both directions have been shut down, the connection is released.
- Four TCP segments are needed to release the connection : one FIN and one ACK for each direction.

2.4.2.7 TCP Connection Management

- 11 steps required for establishing and releasing connections can be represented in a finite state machine.
- In each state, certain events are legal. When a legal event happens, some action may be taken. If some other event happens, an error is reported. Following table shows the states used in the TCP connection management of finite state machine.

State	Description
CLOSE	No connection is active or pending
LISTEN	The server is waiting for an incoming call
SYN RCVD	A connection request has arrived; wait for ACK
SYN SENT	The application has started to open a connection
ESTABLISHED	The normal data transfer state
FIN WAIT 1	The application has said it is finished
FIN WAIT 2	The other side has agreed to release
TIMED WAIT	Wait for all packets to die off
CLOSING	Both sides have tried to close simultaneously
CLOSE WAIT	The other side has initiated a release
LAST ACK	Wait for all packets to die off

- Initially, each connection starts in the CLOSED state.
- It leaves that state when it does either a passive open (LISTEN), or an active open (CONNECT).
- If the other side does the opposite one (it means that, if the connection state is LISTEN and other side gives a CONNECT call or vice versa) a connection is established and the connection state becomes ESTABLISHED.
- Connection release can be initiated by either side. When it is complete, the state returns to CLOSED.
- The finite state machine shown in Fig. 2.9.

Each transition is labelled by the event causing it and the action resulting from it, separated by a slash.

- One can best understand the diagram by first following the path of a client (the heavy solid line), and then later following the path of a server (the heavy dashed line).
- When an application program on the client machine issues a CONNECT request, the local TCP entity creates a connection record, marks it as being in the SYN SENT state, and sends a SYN segment.
- When the SYN+ACK arrive, TCP sends the final *ACK* of the three-way handshake and switches into the ESTABLISHED state. Data can now be sent and received.

- When an application is finished, it executes a CLOSE primitive, due to the local TCP entity send a FIN segment and wait for the corresponding *ACK* (dashed box marked active close). When the *ACK* arrives, a transition is made to state FIN WAIT 2 and one direction of the connection is now closed.

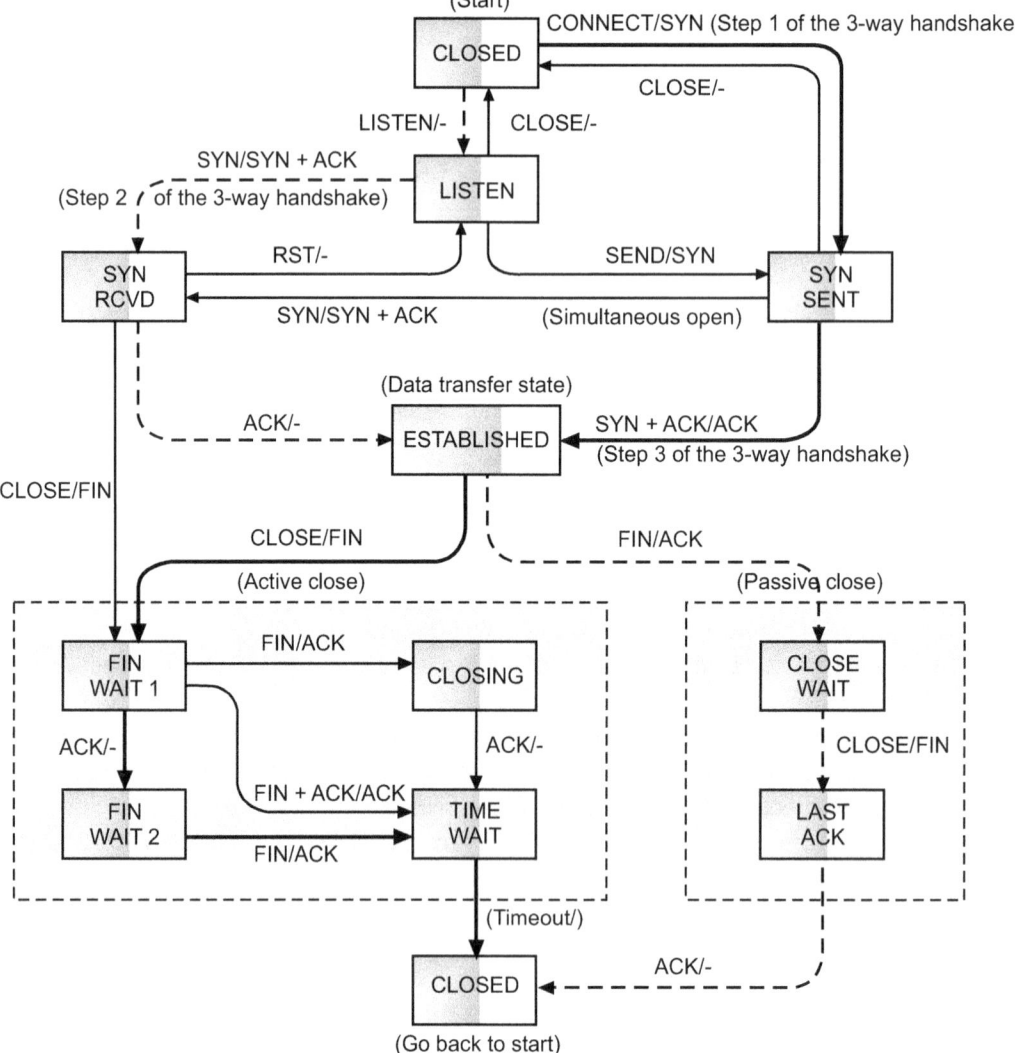

Note :
    The heavy solid line is the normal path for a client.
    The heavy dashed line is the normal path for a server.
    The light lines are unusual events.
        Fig. 2.9 : TCP connection management finite state machine

- When the other side closes, too, a FIN comes in, which is acknowledged. Now both sides are closed, but TCP waits a time equal to the maximum packet lifetime to guarantee that all packets from the connection have died off, just in case the acknowledgement was lost. When the timer goes off, TCP deletes the connection record.
- Now let us examine connection management from the server's viewpoint. The server does a LISTEN and settles down to see who turns up.
- When a SYN comes in, it is acknowledged and the server goes to the SYN RCVD state. When the server's SYN is itself acknowledged, the three-way handshake is complete and the server goes to the ESTABLISHED state. Data transfer can now occur.
- When the client is done, it does a CLOSE, which causes a FIN to arrive at the server (dashed box marked passive close). The server is then signaled. When it, too, does a CLOSE, a FIN is sent to the client. When the client's acknowledgement shows up, the server releases the connection and deletes the connection record.

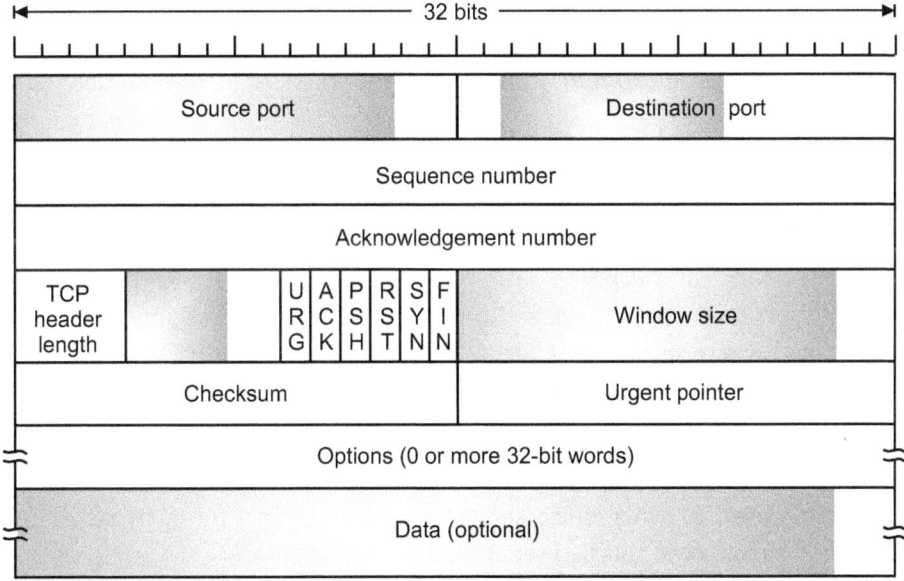

Fig. 2.10 : TCP header

Fields of TCP header :
- **Source Port :** 16 bits.
- **Destination Port :** 16 bits
  - The *Source port* and Destination port fields identify the local end points of the connection.
  - The source and destination end points together identify the connection.

- **Sequence number :** 32 bits – has a dual role :
  - If the SYN flag is set, then this is the initial sequence number. The sequence number of the actual first data byte (and the acknowledged number in the corresponding ACK) will then be this sequence number plus 1.
  - If the SYN flag is clear, then this is the accumulated sequence number of the first data byte of this packet for the current session.
- **Acknowledgement Number :** It specifies the next data byte that is expected.
- **TCP Header length :**
  - The TCP header length tells how many 32-bit words are contained in the TCP header.
  - This information is needed because the Options field which is the part of TCP header is of variable length, due to that the TCP header also becomes of variable length.
- Next 6 bit field is unused.
- 1 Bit Flags : There are 6 one bit flags which are given below.
  1. URG is set to 1 if the Urgent pointer field is in use. The Urgent pointer is used to indicate a byte offset from the current sequence number at which urgent data are to be found.
  2. The ACK bit is set to 1 to indicate that the Acknowledgement number is valid. If ACK is 0, the segment does not contain an acknowledgement so the Acknowledgement number field is ignored.
  3. The PSH bit indicates PUSHed data. This bit requests the receiver to deliver the data to the application upon arrival and not store the data in the buffer until a full buffer signal has been received.
  4. The RST bit is used to reset a connection that has become confused due to a host crash or some other reason. In general, if you get a segment with the RST bit on, you have a problem in your hands.
  5. SYN bit is used to synchronize sequence numbers. Only the first packet sent from each end should have this flag set.
  6. The FIN bit is used to release a connection. It specifies that the sender has no more data to transmit.
- **Window Size :** The size of the window, which specifies the number of bytes that the sender/receiver is currently willing to send/receive.
- **Checksum :** A *Checksum* is also provided for extra reliability. It checksums the header, the data, and the conceptual pseudo header as shown in Fig. 2.11.

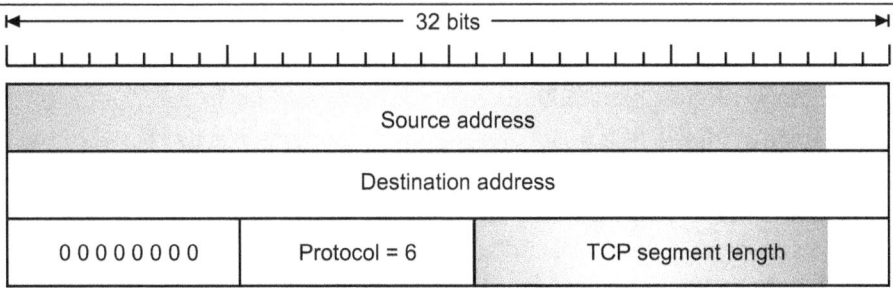

Fig. 2.11 : Pseudo header

- **Option :** The Options field provides a way to add extra facilities not covered by the regular header such as Maximum Segment Size, Window scale factor, Timestamp and many more. Now days some of the options are obsolete.

2.4.2.8 TCP Transmission Policy

- See Fig. 2.12 of window management in TCP.
- From Fig. 2.12, when sender sends data, the receiver gives acknowledgement to the received data.

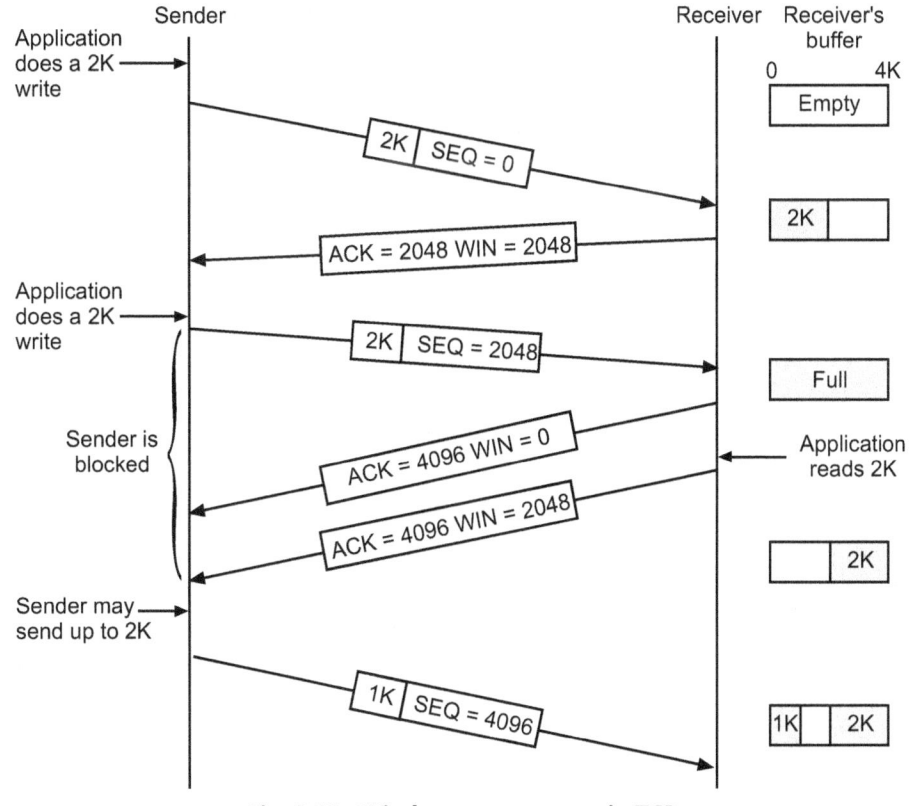

Fig. 2.12 : Window management in TCP

- But while giving the acknowledgement, it also tells the sender about the current size of receiver window (refer Fig. 2.12).
- Suppose the receiver has a 4096-byte buffer, as shown in Fig. 2.12.
- If the sender transmits a 2048-byte segment that is correctly received, the receiver will acknowledge the segment.
- However, since it now has only 2048 bytes of buffer space (until the application removes some data from the buffer), it will advertise a window size of 2048 for the next byte expected.
- Now the sender transmits another 2048 bytes. Now consider the scenario at the receiver side buffer.
- Previously the buffer was having data of 2048 bytes, and now once again sender has sent the same amount of data. So, as the buffers capacity is of 4096 bytes, it gets full.
- In this situation, when the receiver sends the acknowledgement back to the server, that time (as the receiver side buffer if full) it advertises its window size as 0 bytes.
- Now the sender must stop until the application process on the receiving host removes some data from the buffer.
- When the receiver's application reads/consumes the 2048 byte of data, it advertises the window size as 2048 bytes (which is the free space of receiver buffer).
- That time server gets unblocked, and it starts sending the data once again, till it gets the receiver window having non-zero byte size.
- When the window is 0, the sender may not normally send segments.
- But sender can send the segments with two exceptions.
  - Urgent data may be sent, for example, to allow the user to kill the process running on the remote machine.
  - The sender may send a 1-byte segment to make the receiver re-announce the next byte expected and window size.
- The TCP standard explicitly provides this option to prevent deadlock if a window announcement ever gets lost.
- Senders are not required to transmit data as soon as it comes from the application.
- Neither are receivers required to send acknowledgements as soon as possible.
- For example, when the first 2 kb of data came in, sender transport entity, knowing that it had a 4 kb receiver window available, then it is completely correct to buffer the data until another 2 kb came in, so that the total size of transmitting segment will be 4 kb (as that of the size of receiving window). This freedom can be further used to improve performance.
- This is used to reduce the usage of the system. Another way to reduce the system uses has been stated in the Nagle's Algorithm.

Nagle's Algorithm :
- When data come into the sender one byte at a time, just send the first byte and buffer all the rest until the outstanding byte is acknowledged.
- Then send all the buffered characters in one TCP segment and start buffering again until they are all acknowledged.
- Nagle's algorithm is widely used by TCP implementations, but there are times when it is better to avoid it.
- For example, when an X Windows application is being run over the Internet, mouse movements have to be sent to the remote computer. (The X Window system is the windowing system used on most UNIX systems.) Gathering them up to send in bursts makes the mouse cursor move inconsistently, which can irritate the users.
- So it is better to send each mouse movement separately, but that degrades the TCP performance.

Silly Window Syndrome :
- Another problem that can degrade TCP performance is the silly window syndrome.
- The main reason of this problem is sender sends the data in larger blocks, but the receiver side application reads the data one byte at a time. Refer Fig. 2.13.
- Initially, the buffer on the receiving side is full and the sender knows this as the receiver send the window of size 0 with the acknowledgement after the successful data reception.
- Then the receiver's application reads one character from the buffer. Due to this receiver sends a window update to the sender saying that you can send 1 byte of data.
- Then the sender sends 1 byte.
- The buffer is now full, so the receiver acknowledges the 1-byte segment with advertising the window size equal to 0. This process gets repeated forever.
- Clark's solution is used to prevent the receiver from sending a window update for 1 byte.
- Instead it is forced to wait until it has a sufficient amount of buffer space available at the receiver side.
- Specifically, the receiver should not send a window update until it can handle the maximum segment size that it has advertised at the time of connection establishment or until its buffer is half empty, whichever is smaller.
- By not sending tiny segments, sender can also help to improve the performance. Instead, it should try to wait until it has accumulated enough space in the window to send a full segment or at least one containing half of the receiver's buffer size.
- Nagle's algorithm and Clark's solution to the silly window syndrome are opposite.

- o Nagle was trying to solve the problem caused by the sending application delivering data to TCP a byte at a time.
- o Clark was trying to solve the problem of the receiving application sucking the data up from TCP a byte at a time.

Both solutions are valid and can work together. The goal is for the sender not to send small segments and the receiver not to ask for them.

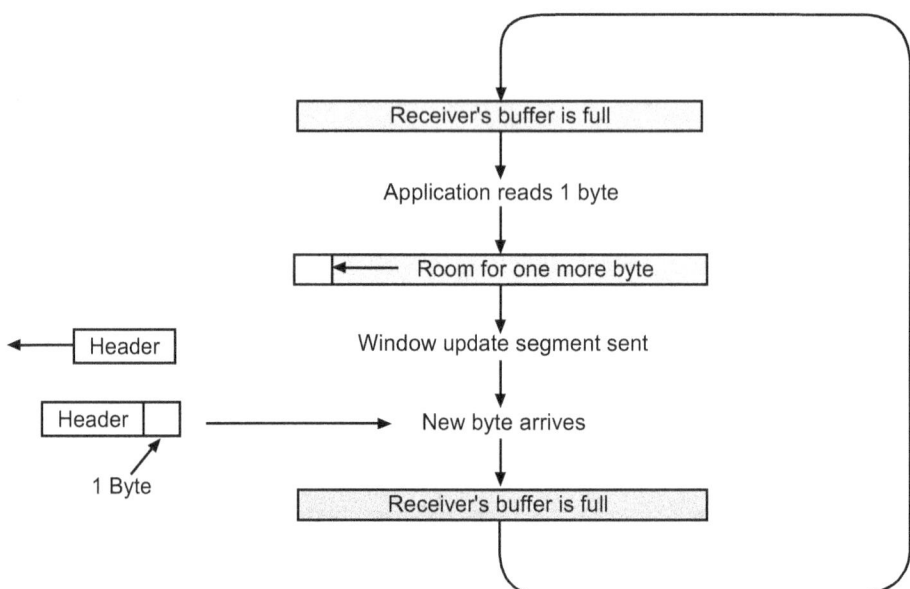

Fig. 2.13 : Silly window syndrome

2.4.3 TCP Congestion Control

- Congestion occurs, when the load offered to any network is more than it can handle.
- The basic principal of congestion control is, do not inject more packets into the network until the old one is delivered properly.
- There are mostly two approaches to solve the problem of congestion :
1. **Proactive Approach :** In this technique the congestion control algorithm tries to avoid the congestion from occurring.
2. **Reactive Approach :** In this technique once the congestion takes place in the network, then efforts are taken to reduce it.
    - In this section we will discuss algorithms that have been developed to deal with congestion.

- Along with the network layer, transport layer also tries to manage congestion; because the real solution to congestion is to slow down the data rate and that can only be done by the transport layer.
- The first step in managing congestion is detecting it. In the old days, detecting congestion was difficult.
- Before discussing how TCP reacts to congestion, we will first see how to try to prevent congestion from occurring in the first place (congestion avoidance mechanism).
- When a connection is established, a suitable window size has to be chosen. The receiver can specify a window based on its buffer size. If the sender sticks to this window size, problems will not occur due to buffer overflow at the receiving end, but they may still occur due to internal congestion within the network.
- For solving the problem of congestion on the internet, it is important to understand the two potential problems :
  - network capacity and
  - receiver capacity

  And to deal each of the problem separately.
- To do so, each sender maintains two windows : the window the receiver has granted and a second window, the congestion window. In Transmission Control Protocol (TCP), the congestion window, also called the TCP receive window, determines the number of bytes that can be outstanding at any time.

2.4.3.1 Slow Start Algorithm

- When a connection is established, the sender initializes the congestion window to the size of the maximum segment in use on the connection.
- It then sends one maximum segment. If this segment is acknowledged before the timer goes off, it adds one segment's worth of bytes to the congestion window to make it two maximum size segments and sends two segments.
- As each of these segments is acknowledged, the congestion window is increased by one maximum segment size.
- When the congestion window is *n* segments, if all *n* are acknowledged on time, the congestion window is increased by the byte count corresponding to *n* segments. In effect, each burst acknowledged doubles the congestion window.
- Until timeout occurs or the receiver's window is reached, the size of congestion window increases exponentially.
- In short, it tells that if bursts of size, say, 512, 1024, 2048, and 4096 bytes work fine but a burst of 8192 bytes gives a timeout, the congestion window should be set to 4096 to avoid congestion.

- As long as the congestion window remains at 4096, no traffic bursts longer than 4096 will be sent, no matter how much the size of receiver window is.
- Even though this algorithm is called slow start, but it is not slow at all. It is exponential in nature.

2.4.3.2 Internet Congestion Control Algorithm

- Now let's see the effect of one more parameter known as Threshold on the congestion mechanism.
    - Assume that initially threshold value is of 64 kB. When a timeout occurs during data transmission, the threshold is set to half of the current congestion window, and the congestion window is reset to one maximum segment.
    - Slow start is then used to determine what the network can handle, except that exponential growth stops when the threshold is hit.
    - From that point on, successful transmissions grow the congestion window linearly (by one maximum segment for each burst).
    - In effect, this algorithm is guessing that it is probably acceptable to cut the congestion window in half, and then it gradually works its way up from there.
    - See Fig. 2.14. Initially, the congestion window was 64 kB, but a timeout occurred, so the threshold is set to 32 kB and the congestion window to 1 kB for transmission number 0.

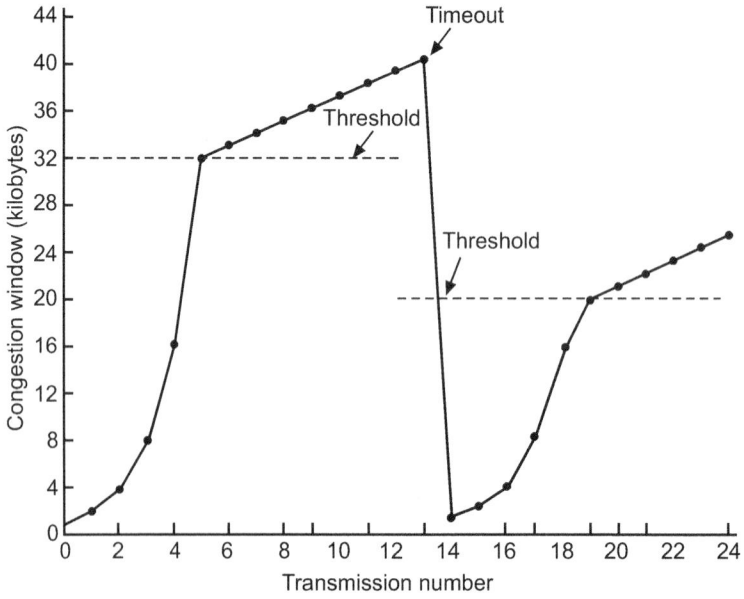

Fig. 2.14 : An example of the Internet congestion algorithm

- The congestion window then grows exponentially until it hits the threshold (32 kB). From there, it starts growing linearly.
- At Transmission number 13 timeout occurred once again. The threshold is set to half the current window (by now 40 kB, so half is 20 kB), and slow start is initiated all over again.
- When the acknowledgements from transmission 14 start coming in, then for first four acknowledgements congestion window gets doubled, but after that, growth becomes linear again as it reaches to the threshold value (of 20 kB).
- If no timeout occurs in the future, the congestion window will continue to grow till the size of receiver's window, once the size of receiver's window is reached, the congestion window stops growing.

2.4.4 TCP Timer Management

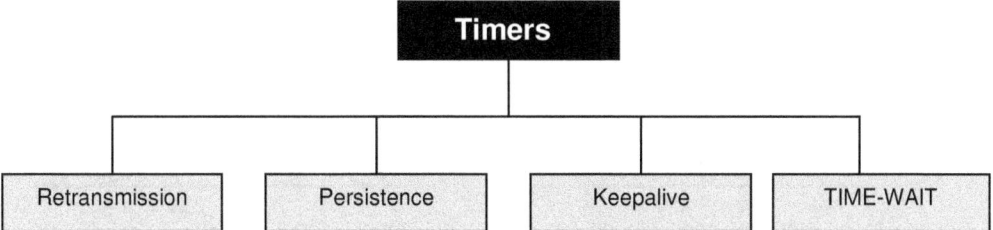

Fig. 2.15 : TCP Timers

- TCP uses multiple timers (at least conceptually) to do its work.
- The most important of these is the retransmission timer.
- When a segment is sent, a retransmission timer is started.
- If the segment is acknowledged before the timer expires, the timer is stopped.
- If, on the other hand, the timer goes off before the acknowledgement comes in, the segment is retransmitted (and the timer started again).

How long should the timeout interval be ?
- This problem is much more difficult to solve in the transport layer than that of data link layer protocol.
- The timeout interval should be enough long such that as soon as the acknowledgement is received to the sender, the timer should be go off as shown in Fig. 2.16 (a).
- Normally the acknowledgements are rarely delayed in data link layer, the absence of an acknowledgement at the expected time generally means either the frame or the acknowledgement has been lost.
- Lots of factors decide the performance of the network, so it is very difficult to calculate the round trip time to the destination.

- If the timeout is set too short, say, *T1* in Fig. 2.16 (b), unnecessary retransmissions will occur, filling the Internet with useless packets.
- If it is set too long, (e.g. *T2*), performance will suffer due to the long retransmission delay whenever a packet is lost.
- The best solution on this problem is to use a highly dynamic algorithm that constantly adjusts the timeout interval, based on continuous measurements of network performance.

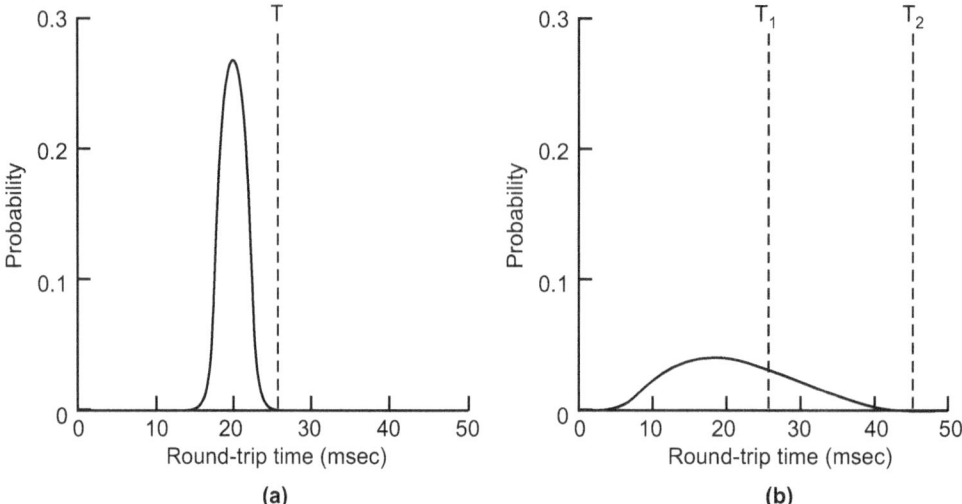

Fig. 2.16 : Probability density of acknowledgement arrival times in
(a) The data link layer, (b) For TCP

2.4.4.1 Jacobson Algorithm of Timeout Interval

- For each connection, TCP maintains a variable called RTT that is the best current estimate of the round-trip time (RTT) to the destination.
- When a segment is sent, a timer is started, to see how long the acknowledgement takes and to trigger a retransmission if it takes too long.
- If the acknowledgement gets back before the timer goes off, TCP measures how long the acknowledgement took (say M). It then updates *RTT* according to the formula;

$$RTT = \alpha\, RTT + (1 - \alpha)\, M$$

where α is a smoothing factor. Typically $\alpha = 7/8$.

- For a given good value of *RTT*, choosing a suitable retransmission timeout is not an easy task.
- By studying all these facts, Jacobson proposed a new smoothing factor that has been given below;

$$D = \alpha\, D + (1 - \alpha)\, |\, RTT - M\,|$$

- And the corresponding timeout is calculated by

  Time out = 4D + RTT
- One problem that occurs with the dynamic estimation of *RTT* is what to do when a segment times out and is sent again ?
- The solution to this problem is "don't update *RTT* on any segments that have been retransmitted. Instead of this the timeout is doubled on each failure until the segments get through the first time. This solution is called as Karn's algorithm. Most TCP implementations use it."

2.4.4.2 Karn's Algorithm

- Suppose that a segment is not acknowledged during the retransmission period and is therefore retransmitted.
- When the sending TCP receives an acknowledgement for this segment, it does not know if the acknowledgement is for the original segment or for the retransmitted one.
- The value of the new RTT is based on the departure of the segment.
- However, if the original segment was lost and acknowledgement is for retransmitted one, the value of the current RTT must be calculated from the time the segment was retransmitted.
- This problem has been solved by Karn.
- Karn's solution is very simple.
- Do not consider Round Trip Time of a retransmitted segment in the calculation of the new RTT. Do not update the value of RTT until you send a segment and receive acknowledgement without the need of retransmission.

2.4.4.3 Other Types of TCP Timers

1. Persistence Timer :

- To deal with a zero-window-size advertisement, TCP needs another timer.
- If the receiving TCP announces a window size of zero, the sending TCP stops transmitting the segments until the receiving TCP sends an acknowledgement segment announcing a non-zero window size.
- This acknowledgement segment can be lost.
- Remember that acknowledgement segments are not acknowledged in TCP.
- If this acknowledgement is lost, the receiving TCP thinks that it has done its job and waits for sending TCP to send more segments.
- There is no retransmission timer for the segment containing only acknowledgement.
- The sending TCP has not received an acknowledgement and waits for the other TCP to send an acknowledgement advertising the size of the window.
- Both TCPs can continue to wait for each other forever, which creates a deadlock.

- To correct this deadlock, TCP uses a persistence timer for each connection.
- When the sending TCP receives an acknowledgement with a window size of zero, it starts a persistence timer.
- When persistence timer goes off, the sending TCP sends a special segment called as probe.
- This segment (probe) contains only one byte of data.
- It has a sequence number; but this sequence number is never acknowledged.
- The probe alerts the receiving TCP that the acknowledgement was lost and must be resent.
- The value of persistence timer is set to the value of retransmission time.
- However, if response is not received from the receiver, another probe segment is sent and the value of the persistence timer is doubled and reset.
- The sender continues sending the probe segments and doubling and resetting the value of the persistent timer until the value reaches a threshold (usually 60 sec).
- After that the sender sends one probe segment every 60 sec until the window is reopened.

2. **Keepalive Timer :**
   - It is used in some implementations to prevent a long idle connection between two TCPs.
   - Suppose that a client opens a TCP connection to a server, transfers some data, and becomes silent. Perhaps the client has crashed. In this case, the connection remains open forever.
   - To remedy this situation, most implementations equip a server with a keepalive timer.
   - Each time the server hears from a client, it resets this timer.
   - The timeout is usually 2 hours.
   - If the server does not hear from the client after two hours, it send a probe segment.
   - If there is no response after 10 probes, each of which is 75 sec apart, it assumes that the client is down and terminates the connection

3. TIME-WAIT Timer :

It is used during connection termination. This timer is set to a time equal to twice the maximum packet lifetime to ensure that after closing a connection all the packets created by it die off.

2.5 CONGESTION CONTROL ALGORITHMS

Congestion control in the network can be controlled by employing traffic shaping mechanism. Traffic shaping is a mechanism to control the amount and the rate of the traffic sent to the network. Two techniques can shape traffic: leaky bucket and token bucket.

2.5.1 Leaky Bucket

- If a bucket has a small hole at the bottom, the water leaks from the bucket at a constant rate as long as there is water in the bucket.
- The rate at which the water leaks does not depend on the rate at which the water is in put to the bucketunlessthe bucketis empty.
- The input rate can vary, but the output rate remains constant. Similarly, in networking, a technique called leaky bucket can smooth out bursty traffic.
- Bursty chunks are stored in the bucket and sent out at an average rate. Fig. 2.17 shows aleaky bucket and its effects.

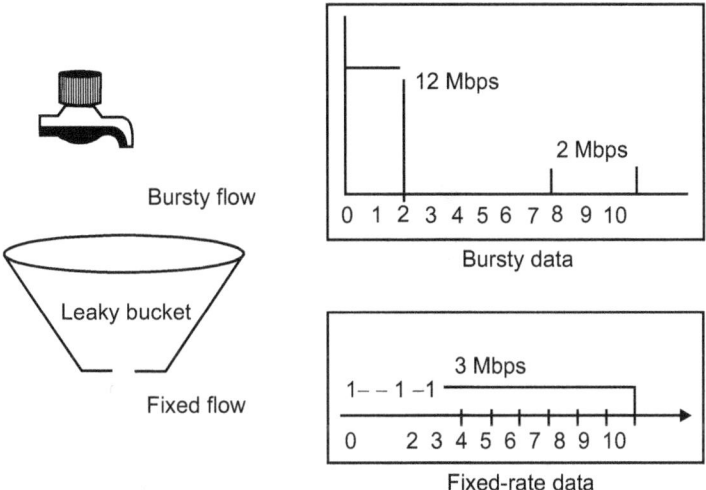

Fig. 2.17 : Leaky Bucket

- In the Fig. 2.17, we assum that the network has committed a bandwidth of 3Mbps for a host. The use of the leaky bucket shapes the input traffic to make it conform to this commitment. In Fig. 2.17 the host sends a burst of data at a rate of 12 Mbps for 2s, for a total of 24 Mbits of data.
- The host is silent for 5 s and then sends data at a rate of 2Mbps for 3s, for a total of 6Mbits of data. Inall, the host has sent 30 Mbits of data in lOs. The leaky bucket smooths the traffic by sending out data at a rate of 3 Mbps during the same 10s. Without the leaky bucket, the beginning burst may have hurt the network by consuming more bandwidth than is set aside for this host. We can also see that the leaky bucket may prevent congestion. As an analogy, consider the free way during rush hour (bursty traffic). If, instead, commuters could stagger their working hours, congestion o' nour freeways could be avoided.
- A simple leaky bucket implementatio is shown in Fig. 2.17. A FIFO queue holds the packets. If the traffic consists of fixed-size packets (e.g., cells in ATM networks),the process removes a fixed number of packets from the queue at each tick of the clock.

- If the traffic consists of variable length packets, the fixed output rate must be base do the number of by orbits.

The following is an algorithm for variable length packets:

1. Initialize a counter to n at the tick of the clock.
2. If n is greater than the size of the packet, send the packet and decrement the counter by the packet size. Repeat this step until n is smaller than the packet size.
3. Reset the counter and goto step1.

2.5.2 Token Bucket

- The leaky bucket is very restrictive. It does not credit an idle host. For example, if a host is not sending for a while, its bucket becomes empty. Now if the host has bursty data, the leaky bucket allows only an average rate. The time when the host was idle is not taken into account.

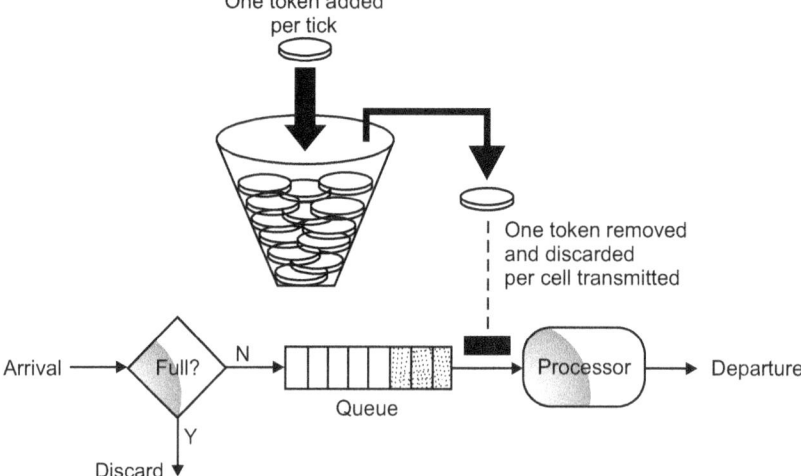

Fig. 2.18 : Token bucket

- On the other hand, the token bucket algorithm allow sidle hosts to accumulate credit for the future in the form of tokens.
- For each tick of the clock, the system sends n tokens to the bucket. The system removes one token for every cell (or byte) of data sent. For example, if n is 100 and the host is idle for 100 ticks, the bucket collects 10,000 tokens. Now the host can consume all these tokens in one tick with 10,000 cells, or the host takes 1000 ticks with 10 cells per tick.
- In other words, the host can send bursty data as long as the bucket is not empty Fig. 2.18 shows the idea.
- The token bucket can easily be implemented with a counter. The token is initialized to zero. Each time a token is added, the counter is incremented by 1. Each time a unit of data is sent, the counter is decremented by 1. When the counter is zero, the host can not send data.

2.6 CONGESTION AVOIDANCE

- As long as non-duplicate ACKs are received, the congestion window is additively increased by one MSS every round trip time. When a packet is lost, the likelihood of duplicate ACKs being received is very high (it's possible though unlikely that the stream just underwent extreme packet reordering, which would also prompt duplicate ACKs). The behavior of Tahoe and Reno differ in how they detect and react to packet loss:

2.6.1 RTT Estimation

- For each connection, TCP maintains a variable called RTT that is the best current estimate of the round-trip time (RTT) to the destination.
- When a segment is sent, a timer is started, to see how long the acknowledgement takes and to trigger a retransmission if it takes too long.
- If the acknowledgement gets back before the timer goes off, TCP measures how long the acknowledgement took (say M). It then updates *RTT* according to the formula;

$$RTT = \alpha RTT + (1 - \alpha) M$$

where α is a smoothing factor. Typically $\alpha = 7/8$.

- For a given good value of *RTT*, choosing a suitable retransmission timeout is not an easy task.
- By studying all these facts, Jacobson proposed a new smoothing factor that has been given below;

$$D = \alpha D + (1 - \alpha) | RTT - M |$$

- And the corresponding timeout is calculated by

$$\text{Time out} = 4D + RTT$$

- One problem that occurs with the dynamic estimation of *RTT* is what to do when a segment times out and is sent again ?
- The solution to this problem is "don't update *RTT* on any segments that have been retransmitted. Instead of this the timeout is doubled on each failure until the segments get through the first time. This solution is called as Karn's algorithm. Most TCP implementations use it."

2.6.2 Retransmission

- The heart of the error control mechanism is the retransmission of segments. When a segment is corrupted, lost, or delayed, it is retransmitted. In modern implementations, a segment is retransmitted on two occasions: when are transmission timer expires or when the send er receives three duplicate ACKs.
- In modern implementations, aretransmission occurs if there transmission timer expires or three duplicate ACK segments have arrived.

- Note that more transmission occurs for segments that do not consume sequence numbers. In particular, there is no transmission for an ACK segment.
- No retransmission timer is set for an ACK segment.

2.6.2.1 Retransmission After RTO
- A recent implementation of TCP maintains one retrans-mission time-out(RTO) timer for all outstanding (sent, but not acknowledged segments. When the timer matures, the earliest outstanding segment is retransmitted even though lack of a received ACK can be due to a delayed segment, a delayed ACK, or a lost acknowledgment. Note that no time-out timer is set for a segment that carries only an acknowledgment, which means that no such segment is resent.
- The value of RTO is dynamic in TCP and is updated based on the round-trip time (RTT) of segments. An RTI is the time needed for a segment to reach a destination and for an acknowledgment to be received.

2.6.2.2 Retransmission After Three Duplicate ACK Segments
- The previous rule about retransmission of a segment is sufficient if the value of RTO is not very large. Sometimes, however, one segment is lost and the receiver receives so many out-of-order segments that they can not be saved (limited buffer size).
- To alleviate this situation, most implementations today follow the three duplicate-ACKs rule and retransmit the missing segment immediately. This feature is referred to as fast retransmission, which we will see in an example shortly.

2.6.2.3 Fast Retransmission
- When the receiver receives the fourth, fifth, and sixth segments, it triggers an acknowledgment. The sender receives four acknowledgments with the same value (three duplicates).
- Although the timer for segment has not matured yet, the fast transmission requires that segment 3, the segment that is expected by all these acknowledgments, be resent immediately. Note that only one segment is retransmitted although four segments are not acknowledged. When the sender receives the retransmitted ACK, it knows that the four

Segments are safe and sound because acknowledgment is cumulative.

2.6.3 TCP Tahoe
Triple duplicate ACKS are treated the same as a timeout. Tahoe will perform "fast retransmit", set the slow start threshold to half the current congestion window, reduce congestion window to 1 MSS, and reset to slow-start state.

2.6.4 Fast Recovery
There is a variation to the slow-start algorithm known as Fast Recovery, which uses fast retransmit followed by Congestion Avoidance.

In the Fast Recovery algorithm, during Congestion Avoidance mode, when packets are not received (detected through three duplicate ACKs), the congestion window size is reduced to the slow-start threshold, rather than the smaller initial value.

2.7 SOCKET

- Sockets are commonly used for client/server communication.
- Typical system configuration places the server on one machine, with the clients on other machines.
- The clients connect to the server, exchange information, and then disconnect.
- The client and server processes only communicate with each other if and only if there is a socket at each end.
- There are three types of sockets
    1. The stream socket
    2. The packet/datagram socket
    3. The row socket

All these sockets can be used in TCP/IP environment. These are explained below :

1. The Stream Socket :

Features of stream socket are as follows :
- connection-oriented
- two way communication
- reliable (error free), in order delivery
- can use the Transmission Control Protocol (TCP)
- e.g. telnet, ssh, http

2. The Datagram Socket :

Features of datagram socket are as follows :
- connectionless, does not maintain an open connection, each packet is independent
- can use the User Datagram Protocol (UDP)
- e.g. IP telephony

3. Row Socket :
- Use protocols like ICMP or OSPF because these protocols do not use either stream packets or datagram packets.

Fig. 2.19 (a) shows all types of sockets.

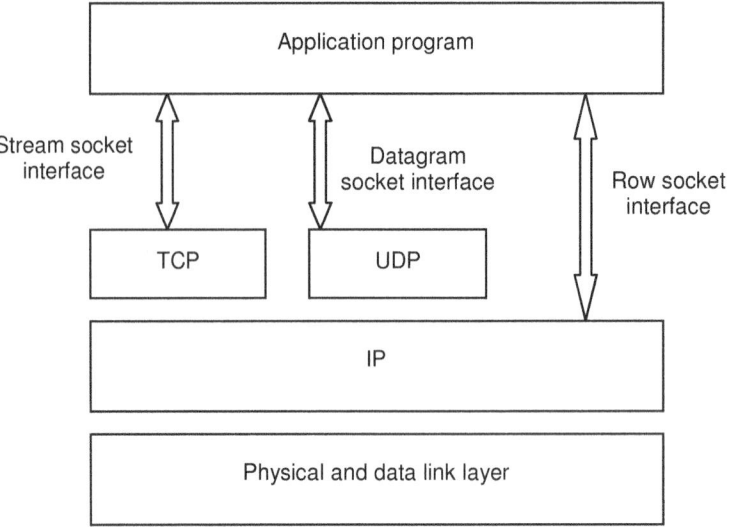

Fig. 2.19 : Types of Sockets

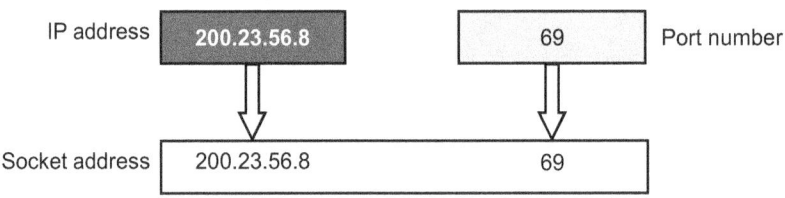

Fig. 2.20 : Socket Address

Socket Address :
- Process to process delivery needs two addresses.
    1. IP address and
    2. Port number at each end to make a connection
- Socket address is the combination of IP address and the port number.

Socket Characteristics :
- A socket is represented by an integer value. That integer is called a "socket descriptor".
- A socket exists as long as the process maintains an open link to the socket.
- You can name a socket and use it to communicate with other sockets in a communication domain.
- Sockets perform the communication when the server accepts connections from them, or when it exchanges messages with them.

2.8 BERKELEY SOCKET PREMITIVES

Let us now briefly inspect another set of transport primitives, the socket primitives used in Berkeley UNIX for TCP.

Primitive	Meaning
SOCKET	Used to create a new communication end point
BIND	It provides a local address to a socket
LISTEN	It shows willingness to accept connections
ACCEPT	Block the client as long as a connection attempt does not arrive
CONNECT	It tries to establish a connection
SEND	Send data
RECEIVE	Receive data
CLOSE	It releases the connection

Following four are Server Side Primitives :
- The SOCKET primitive creates a new end point and allocates table space for it within the transport entity.
- A successful SOCKET call returns an ordinary file descriptor (normally an integer value) for use in future.
- Newly-created sockets do not have network addresses. These are assigned using the BIND primitive.
- Once a server has bound an address to a socket, remote clients can connect to it.
- Next comes the LISTEN call, which allocates space to queue incoming calls for the case that several clients try to connect at the same time.
- To block waiting for an incoming connection, the server executes an ACCEPT primitive.
- ACCEPT returns a normal file descriptor, which can be used for reading and writing in the standard way, the same as for files.

Following are Client Side Primitives :
- Here, too, a socket must first be created using the SOCKET primitive, but BIND is not required since the address used does not matter to the server.
- The CONNECT primitive blocks the caller and actively starts the connection process. When it completes (i.e., when the appropriate TPDU is received from the server), the client process is unblocked and the connection is established.

- Both sides can now use SEND and RECV to transmit and receive data over the full-duplex connection.
- Connection release with sockets is symmetric. When both sides have executed a CLOSE primitive, the connection is released.

2.9 STEPS IN SOCKET PROGRAMMING

Fig. 2.21 specifies an outline of client server network interaction diagram.

By observing Fig. 2.21, we can state the steps followed for socket programming

Server Side :

1. Firstly server creates a socket. On successful creation of socket, socket primitive returns a file descriptor (also called as socket descriptor) that has been used in the future to refer the server socket.
2. Assigns local address and port number to the newly created socket using BIND. We need to associate an IP address and port number to our application. A client that wants to connect to our server needs both of these details in order to connect to our server. Notice the difference between bind function and the connect function of the client. The connect function specifies a remote address that the client wants to connect to, while here, the server is specifying to the bind function a local IP address of one of its Network Interfaces and a local port number.
3. LISTEN call allocates some space. Queue is implemented by using this space. When number of clients tries to connect the server, they send the connection requests. These connection requests are then stored in the queue and after that these requests are processed by the server one by one by using FIFO method.
4. ACCEPT is used for blocking the waiting incoming connections.

Client Side :

1. Creates a socket using SOCKET primitive
2. Uses CONNECT primitive for initiating the connection process with the server.
3. When server accepts the connection, the connection gets established.
4. After that data is send and receive from the server.
5. Connection release with sockets is symmetric. When both sides have executed a CLOSE primitive, the connection is released.

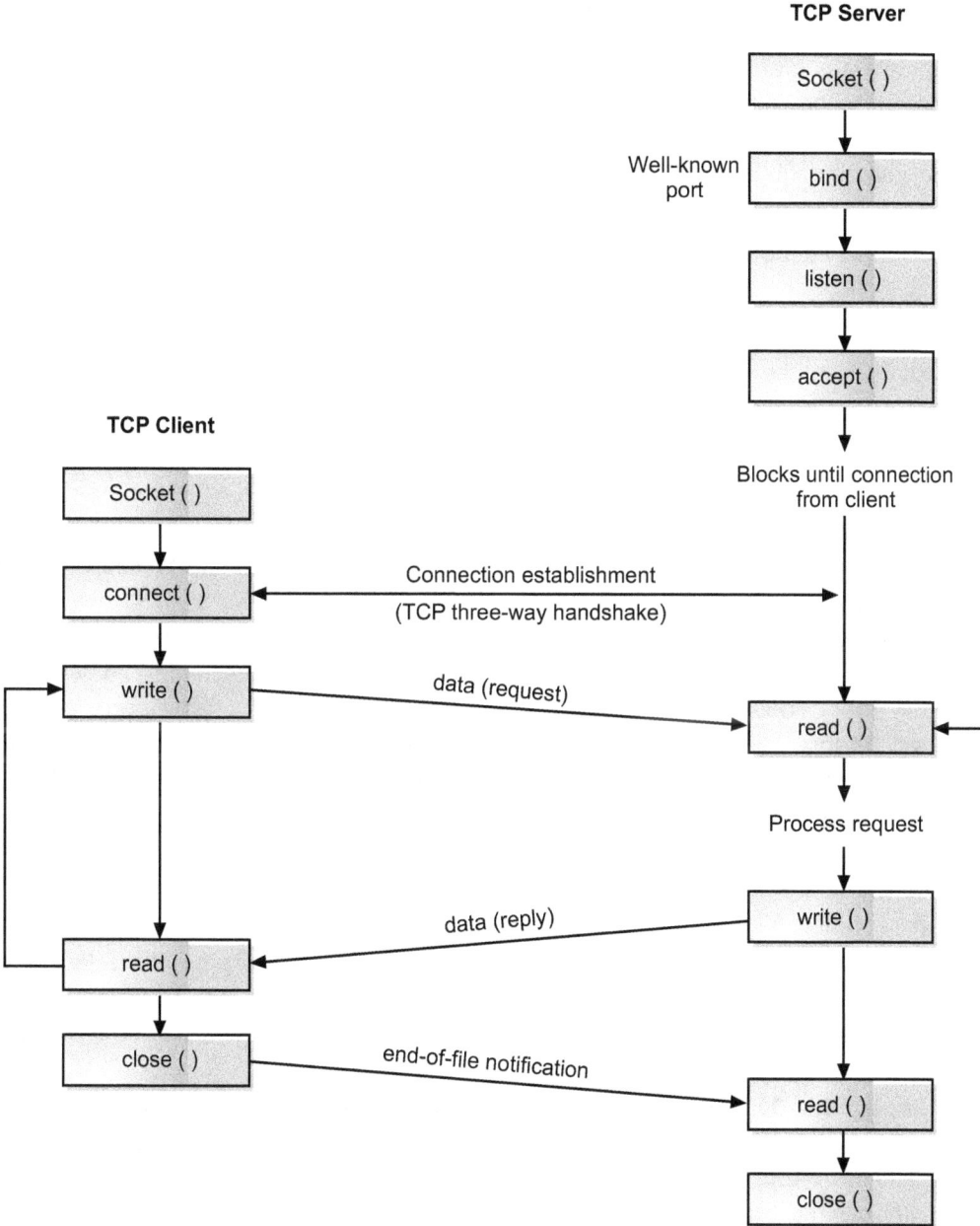

Fig. 2.21 : Client-servers network interaction

2.10 PERFORMANCE ISSUES

Performance issues are very important in computer networks. When hundreds or thousands of computers are interconnected, complex interactions, with unexpected consequences, are common. This complexity leads to poor performance. In the following sections, we will examine many issues related to network performance to see what kinds of problems exist and what can be done about them.

In this section, we will look at the following five aspects of network performance:

1. Performance problems.
2. Measuring network performance.
3. System design for better performance.
4. Fast TPDU processing.
5. Protocols for future high-performance networks.

The details are given below:

1. **Performance Problems :**
   - **Congestion :** Congestion can be caused by temporary resource overload. If more traffic suddenly arrives at a router than the router can handle, congestion will build up and performance will suffer.
   - **Resource Imbalance :** Performance also degrades when there is a structural resource imbalance. For example, if a gigabit communication line is attached to a low-end PC, the poor CPU will not be able to process the incoming packets fast enough and some will be lost. These packets will eventually be retransmitted, adding delay, wasting bandwidth, and generally reducing performance.
   - **Software Overhead :** Reduce/maintain the packet count to reduce the software overhead. If the number of packets increased tremendously on the network, the software overhead will get increased as it has to process those many number of packets, it results in the performance degradation.
   - **Timeouts :** When a TPDU is sent, a timer is typically set to protect the loss of the TPDU. If the timeout is set too short, unnecessary retransmissions will occur, blocking the wires. If the timeout is set too long, unnecessary delays will occur after a TPDU is lost.
   - **Bandwidth-Delay Product :** It is obtained by multiplying the bandwidth (in bits/sec) by the round-trip delay time (in sec). The product is the capacity of the pipe from the sender to the receiver and back (in bits). For good performance, the receiver's window must be at least as large as the bandwidth-delay product, preferably somewhat larger.
   - **Jitter :** Jitter is another performance problem that occurs with time-critical applications like audio and video.

2. How to Measure Network Performance :
- When a network performs poorly, its users often complaint about it, demanding improvements.
- To improve the performance, the operators must first determine exactly what is going on.
- To find out what is really happening, the operators must make measurements.
- The basic loop used to improve network performance contains the following steps :
  1. Measure the relevant network parameters and performance.
  2. Try to understand what is going on.
  3. Change one parameter.
- Measurements can be made in many ways and at many locations. The most basic kind of measurement is to start a timer when beginning some activity and see how long that activity takes. Consider the following parameters :
  - Make Sure That the Sample Size Is Large Enough
  - Make Sure That the Samples Are Representative
  - Be Careful When Using a Coarse-Grained Clock
  - Be Sure That Nothing Unexpected Is Going On during Your Tests
  - Caching can cause disaster.
  - Understand What You Are Measuring
  - Take accurate measurement and measure the correct timing of each reading.

3. System Design for Better Performance :
Design the system in such a way that it will give good performance. Consider the following parameters while designing the system :
- **Speed :** CPU speed is more important than the network speed. CPU speed automatically increases the network speed.
- **Software Overload :** Reduce the packet count to reduce the software overload.
- **Bandwidth :** Using Fiber Optic cable as a transmission media, one can increase the bandwidth of the network tremendously.
- **Network Congestion :** Avoid network congestion. When the network is congested, packets are lost, bandwidth is wasted and useless delays are introduced.
- **Timeouts :** Timeouts should be minimized.
- Minimize the context switches.
- Minimize copying.

4. Fast TPDU Processing :
- TPDU processing overhead has two components : overhead per TPDU and overhead per byte. Both must be attacked.

- The key to fast TPDU processing is to separate out the normal case (one-way data transfer) and handle it specially.
- Although a sequence of special TPDUs is needed to get into the *ESTABLISHED* state, once there, TPDU processing is straightforward until one side starts to close the connection.
- Let us begin by examining the sending side in the *ESTABLISHED* state when there are data to be transmitted. The first thing the transport entity does is test to see if this is the normal case: the state is *ESTABLISHED*, neither side is trying to close the connection, a regular (i.e., not an out-of-band) full TPDU is being sent, and enough window space is available at the receiver. If all conditions are met, no further tests are needed and the fast path through the sending transport entity can be taken. Typically, this path is taken most of the time.

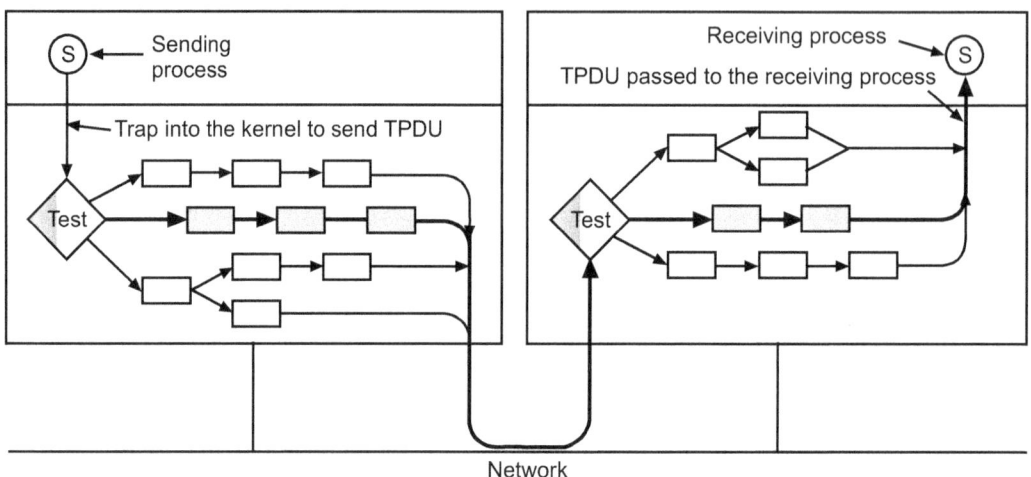

Fig. 2.22 : The fast path from sender to receiver is shown with a heavy line. The processing steps on this path are shaded

- In the usual case, the headers of consecutive data TPDUs are almost the same. To take advantage of this fact, a prototype header is stored within the transport entity. At the start of the fast path, it is copied as fast as possible to a scratch buffer, word by word. Those fields (such as the next sequence number) that change from TPDU to TPDU are then overwritten in the buffer.
- Now let us look at fast path processing on the receiving side of Fig. 2.22. Step 1 is locating the connection record for the incoming TPDU. For TCP, the connection record can be stored in a hash table for which some simple function of the two IP addresses and two ports is the key. Once the connection record has been located, both addresses and both ports must be compared to verify that the correct record has been found.
- The TPDU is then checked to see if it is a normal one: the state is *ESTABLISHED*, neither side is trying to close the connection, the TPDU is a full one, no special flags are set,

- and the sequence number is the one expected. These tests take just a handful of instructions. If all conditions are met, a special fast path TCP procedure is called.
- The fast path updates the connection record and copies the data to the user. While it is copying, it also computes the checksum, eliminating an extra pass over the data. If the checksum is correct, the connection record is updated and an acknowledgement is sent back. The general scheme of first making a quick check to see if the header is what is expected and then having a special procedure handle that case is called header prediction. Many TCP implementations use it.
- When this optimization and all the other ones are used together, it is possible to get TCP to run at 90 percent of the speed of a local memory-to-memory copy, assuming the network itself is fast enough.

2.10.1 Throughput

- The throughput is a measure of how fast we can actually send data through a network. Although, at first glance, bandwidth in bits per second and throughput seem the same, they are different .
- A link may have a bandwidth of B bps, but we can only send T bps through this link with T always less than B.In other words, the bandwidth is a potential measurement of a link; the throughput is an actual measurement of how fast we can send data. For example, we may have alink with abandwidthof1Mbps,but the devices connected to the end of the link may handle only 200kbps.
- This means that we can not send more than 200kbps through this link. Imagine a highway designed to transmit 1000 cars per minute from one point to another. However, if there is congestion on the road, this figure may be reduced to 100 cars per minute.The bandwidth is 1000 cars per minute; the throughput is 100cars per minute.

2.10.2 Delay

- The latency or delay define show long it takes for an entire message to completely arrive at the destination from the time the first bit is sent out from the source. We can say that latency is made off our components: propagation time, transmission time, Queuing time and processing delay.

Latency = propagation time + transmission time + queuing time + processing delay

Propagation time measures the time required for a bit to travel from the source to the destination. The propagation time is calculated by dividing the distance by the propagation speed

2.10.3 Network Reliability

In addition to accuracy of delivery, network reliability is measured by the frequency of failure, the time it takes alink to recover from a failure, and the network's robustness in a catastrophe.

COMPUTER NETWORK TECHNOLOGY (T.E. I.T.) TRANSPORT LAYER

QUESTIONS

1. Explain TCP with its header format.
2. What is a socket ? Explain various socket primitives used in client-server interaction.
3. Explain the multiplexing technique used in transport layer.
4. Explain how TCP provide flow control.
5. What is silly window syndrome ?
6. Explain the three-way handshake algorithm for TCP connection establishment.
7. How will you differentiate a stream socket from a raw socket ? How data transmissions happen in a datagram mode?
8. List and discuss the performance issues of the transport layer.
9. Why does UDP exist ? Would it not have been enough to just let user processes send raw IP packet ?
10. In a network assume that maximum TPDU size of 128 bytes, a maximum TPDU lifetime of 30 seconds, and an 8-bit sequence number. Calculate the maximum data rate per connection.
11. Describe any two flow control mechanisms. How timer plays the role in the flow control ?
12. What is a socket ? Explain various socket primitives used in client-server interaction.
13. Explain with a suitable diagram, the parameters involved in process to process communication. Give the different types of parts with their ranges.
14. Explain how TCP provide flow control mechanism.
15. What is silly window syndrome ? How to overcome it ?
16. How will you differentiate a stream socket from a datagram socket ? How data transmissions happen in a datagram mode without acknowledgement ?
17. List and discuss the performance issues of the transport layer.
18. What do you mean by flow control ? What are the different methods to achieve it ?
19. Give two functions of four different timers used in TCP.
20. Explain how TCP provide a flow control mechanism.
21. What is silly-window syndrome ? Explain at least two methods to overcome it.
22. What is a socket ? Where do we use it ? Explain important primitives used in socket programming.
23. List and discuss performance issues of transport layer.
24. Compare and contrast between RPC and UDP.
25. Explain what is Silly Window Syndrome Problem ? Explain at least 2 methods to overcome it.
26. List and discuss performance issues of the transport layer.

Unit - III

APPLICATION LAYER

3.1 CLIENT SERVER MODEL

- The purpose of a network is to provide services to the users. A user at one site wants to receive a service from another site.
- A user that seeks a service from another site runs an application program, called as client. The site which provides the service runs another application program called as server.

3.1.1 Server

- It is a program running on a remote machine which provides the service to the client.
- When a server starts it receives the requests from clients. When initiated it never provides the service until it is requested to do so.
- A server program is an infinite program. When it starts, it runs infinitely unless some problem occurs.
- It waits for request from clients and when it arrives it responds to the requests.

3.1.2 Client

- It is a program running on a local machine which requests the service from a server.
- Client program is a finite program. It is started by user or by some other application and it terminates when the request is completed.
- A client opens the communication channel using the IP address of and a well-known port number of a server machine. After a communication channel is established the client sends its request and receives response. This cycle of sending request and receiving response may be repeated several times but the whole process is finite and after some time come to end.

3.2 TELNET

3.2.1 Introduction

Where the TCP protocol makes it possible to connect the remote computers, the TELNET protocol makes it possible to use them. The TELNET protocol offers a user the possibility to connect and log on to any other hosts in the network from user's own computer by offering a remote log on capability. Historically, TELNET was the first TCP/IP application and still is widely used as a terminal emulator. Today, while the applications are more and more equipped with the graphical user interface, the terminal-based applications are becoming minority among the applications. The TELNET has found its future as a tool kit lying below several client/server software. For example : FTP, SMTP, SNMP, NNTP and HTTP are more or less dependent on the TELNET protocol.

3.2.2 Telnet Model

For the connections, TELNET uses the TCP protocol. The TELNET service is offered in the host machine's TCP port 23. The user at the terminal interacts with the local telnet client. The TELNET client acts as a terminal accepting any keystrokes from the keyboard, interpreting them and displaying the output on the screen. The client on the computer makes the TCP connection to the host machine's port 23 where the TELNET server answers. The TELNET server interacts with applications in the host machine and assists in the terminal emulation.

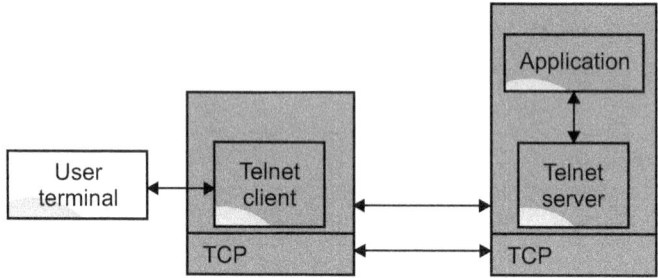

Fig. 3.1 : TELNET Protocol Model

As the connection is setup, the both ends of the TELNET connection are assumed to be originated and terminated at the Network Virtual Terminal (NVT). The NVT is a network wide terminal which is host independent so that both the server and the client in the connection may not need to keep any information about each other's terminal's characteristics as both sees each other as a NVT terminal. As there are several types of terminals, which may be able to provide additional services from those provided by the NVT, the TELNET protocol contains a negotiation method for the user and the server to negotiate changes to the terminal provided in the NVT. Typically, the client and the server stays in the NVT just as long as it takes to negotiate some terminal type to be emulated.

3.2.3 Options

The TELNET has a set of options and these options can be negotiated through a simple protocol inside the TELNET. The negotiation protocol contains commands DO, WILL, WON'T and DON'T. Following examples present the accepted command sequences:

- DO (sender wants receiver to enable the option)
- WILL (receiver acknowledges)
- DO (sender wants receiver to enable the option)
- WON'T (receiver will not acknowledge the request)
- WILL (sender wants to enable the option)
- DO (receiver gives permission)
- WILL (sender wants to enable the option)
- DON'T (receiver does not give permission to do so)

- WON'T (sender wants to disable option)
- DON'T (receiver has to answer OK)
- DON'T (sender wants receiver to disable option)
- WON'T (receiver must say OK)

Mostly, the options are used in the beginning of the connection to setup a desired set of options for the TELNET. In some cases, the options are changed during the session. The key option to be negotiated is the terminal type.

The symmetry in the negotiation protocol indicates that some loops are possible. Without any further restrictions, the following sequence could take place:

- DO TERMINAL TYPE VT100
- WILL TERMINAL TYPE VT100
- DO TERMINAL TYPE VT100

...

For this situation and similar situations the protocol introduces set of rules:

- Parties may only request a change in the option (this rule overcomes previous problem).
- If a party receives a request enter some mode that it is already in, the request should not be acknowledged.
- If the option affects the way, how the data is processed, the command must be inserted in the data stream exactly in the place where it is desired to take effect.
- The rejected request should not be repeated until something changes in the operating environment. For example, the process runs other program or other user commands is executed.

The options are set through TELNET commands. To indicate that the next byte is a command byte, the IAC (interpret as command) byte (0xFF) is sent. The data byte 0xFF is sent as two consecutive 0xFF bytes. The option negotiation requires three bytes: IAC, request (WILL, WON'T, DO, DON'T) and the option ID byte to be enabled or disabled. The negotiations are either symmetrical or non-symmetrical.

With a symmetrical option both sides may start the negotiation sequence. A non-symmetrical option is always requested by the other part. An example of a non-symmetrical option can be the line-mode option, which can only be requested by the client. The negotiation may require suboption negotiations. These negotiations take place when the option does not have only two modes: enable and disable. An example for such subnegotiation is a terminal type negotiation. The Terminal type option is first enabled with a normal 3 byte negotiation:

IAC, WILL, 24 (24 = terminal type)

The server responds hopefully:

IAC, DO, 24

The server then asks the terminal type of the client:

IAC, SB, 24, 1, IAC, SE

(SB = suboption, 24 = suboption terminal type, 1 = sent your terminal type, SE = suboption end)

Client responds:

IAC, SB, 24, 0, 'V', 'T', '1', '0', '0', IAC, SE

(0 = my terminal type, string VT100)

3.2.4 TELNET Commands

Typical for the terminals directly connected to a computer are that the keystrokes by the user are immediately interpreted by the computer's operating system. For the purpose certain keystroke combinations were invented. For example by pressing ctrl+'z', the processes were suspended or ctrl+'c' was used for killing current process. The TELNET cannot transmit such codes as they are since the codes are commands containing two keystrokes and do not map to the 7-bit ASCII chart used in the NVT. This requires that the client has to translate the terminal's control codes to the TELNET commands and transmit the commands to the server host's operating system.

As explained earlier, the TELNET commands are presented with IAC byte with a followed command and parameters. All the TELNET commands are presented in the Table 3.1. The TELNET command IP can be used for send what would be ctrl + 'c' in the keyboard and the command EC for what would be the backspace. The IP command is not always the right choice for interrupting the process because it acts similarly with the command sent from real terminal, which is interpreted right away while the IP signal may take some time to be transmitted over the connection and through the buffered data. For overcoming this problem the data mark (DM) command is introduced. With the DM command, the client gets server's attention faster and the client tells the server to throw away all the data but the commands.

The client uses the Synch Signal TCP segment for the purpose. The Synch signal is marked as an urgent data. The server will throw away everything except the commands until DM is reached. The DM marks the spot where the data is no longer discarded and the TELNET resumes the normal operating mode.

Table 3.1 : TELNET commands

Name	Code	Description
EOF	236	End of file
SUSP	237	Suspend process
ABORT	238	Abort process
EOR	239	End of record

Cont....

SE	240	Suboption end
NOP	241	No operation
DM	242	Data mark
BRK	243	Break
IP	244	Interrupt process
AO	245	Abort output
AYT	246	Are you there
EC	247	Escape character
EL	248	Erase line
GA	249	Go ahead
SB	250	Suboption
WILL	251	Option negotiation
WONT	252	Option negotiation
DO	253	Option negotiation
DONT	254	Option negotiation
IAC	255	Interpret as command

3.2.5 TELNET for Client/Server Applications

The TELNET can be used as a tool set to build the client/server applications. As a basis for the application, TELNET rarely requires the terminal extensions and the negotiations but the TELNET operates in the basic NVT mode. The NVT is bi-directional half-duplex device, which contains a terminal and a keyboard. Basically, the keyboard is the user keyboard. The keyboard produces client's outgoing data sent over the TELNET connection to the server. The printer is the user's display where the TELNET server sends the characters. The NVT is half duplex.

This means that in the TELNET protocol either the client or the server has the control. The control from the client to the server is changed by the CR/LF. The server uses the CR/LF for changing the line, not for returning the control to the client. The client receives the control after receiving the data from the server and accepting the GO AHEAD control code.

3.2.6 Telnet and Security

Since the eavesdropping and the snooping are easy to implement to any machine connected to a LAN and the fact that the password and the user IDs are sent through the TELNET connection which is unencrypted, if not otherwise required, the TELNET protocol is a security risk. Therefore, the TELNET protocol defines an option for the authentication. The actual authentication is exchanged in the authentication subnegoation. The TELNET's authentication options support such authentication standards like Kerberos, SPX, RSA, LOKI and SSA.

3.3 HYPER TEXT TRANSFER PROTOCOL (HTTP)

Now-a-days for us internet becomes very essential. If we want to access the information on any topic we just search the topic in World Wide Web. Now the public has become aware of the power of internet through WWW.

- HTTP protocol is used to access the data on World Wide Web.
- This protocol normally transfers the data in the form of plain text, hypertext, audio, video and so on.
- It is called as Hypertext Transfer Protocol because it is used in an environment where there are rapid jumps from one document to another.
- HTTP functions like a combination of FTP and SMTP.
- It is said to be similar to FTP because it transfers files.
- It is said to be similar to SMTP because the data transferred between the client and server are similar to the SMTP messages.
- However, HTTP differs from SMTP in the way the messages are sent from client to server and from server to client. In case of SMTP, messages are only transferred from server to client.

How HTTP Works ?

- The working of HTTP is very simple.
- A client sends a request and server sends a reply (response) to the client. See Fig. 3.2.
- HTTP uses the services of TCP on well known port 80.

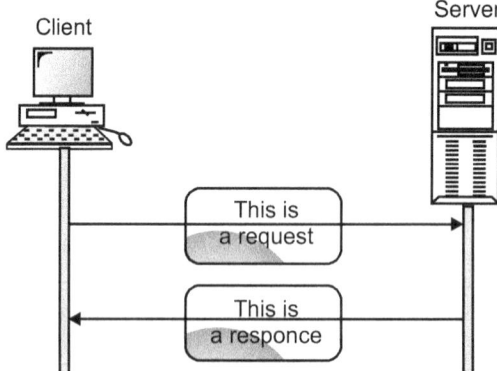

Fig. 3.2 : HTTP Transaction

- Although HTTP uses the services of TCP, HTTP itself is a **"stateless protocol"**. The client initializes the transaction by sending a request message. The server replies by sending a response.

3.3.1 Types of HTTP Messages

There are two types of HTTP messages :
(1) Request Message
(2) Response Message

(1) Request Message :

Request message consists of a request line, headers and sometimes a body. See the following figure.

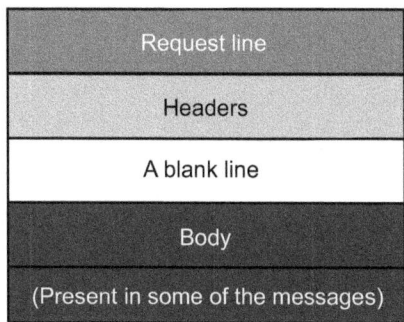

Fig. 3.3 : Request Message

Fields of request message are described as below :

Request Line :

The request line defines the request type, Uniform resource locator (URL) and HTTP version as shown in Fig. 3.4.

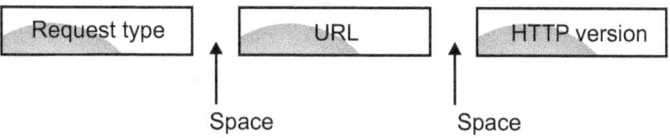

Fig. 3.4 : Request Line

- **Request Type :** It categorizes the request message into several methods, which will be discussed later.
- **Uniform Resource Locator (URL) :** A client that wants to access a web page needs an address. HTTP uses URL to facilitate the access of any document distributed over the world. The URL defines four things : method, host computer, port and path as shown in Fig. 3.5.

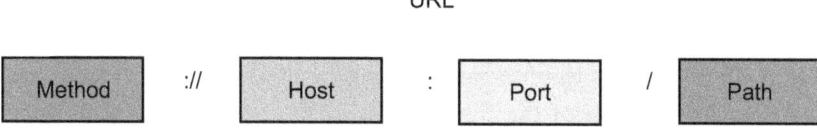

Fig. 3.5 : URL

- **Method :** It is a protocol such as FTP, HTTP that is used to retrieve the document from the web.
- **Host :** Host is a computer where the URL specific information is located. This information can be in terms of webpages or audio-video files or other types of files such as doc files or pdf files etc.

- **Port :** URL can originally contain the port number of the server. If the port number is included, it is inserted between the host and the path, and it should be separated from the host by a colon.
- **Path :** It is the pathname of the file where the information is located.
- **Version :** The latest version of HTTP is 1.1 but the versions 0.9 and 1 are also used.

Methods in the URL Field :

The request method is the actual request that a client issues to the server. Following are some of the important methods :

1. **GET :** The GET method is used when the client wants to retrieve a document from the server. The address of the document is defined in the URL; this is the main method for retrieving a document. The server usually responds with the contents of the document in the body of the response message unless there is an error.
2. **HEAD :** The HEAD method is used when the client wants some information about a document but not the document itself. It is similar to GET, but the response from the server does not contain a body.
3. **POST :** The POST method is used by the client to provide some information to the server. e.g. it can be used to send input to a server.
4. **PUT :** The PUT method is used by the client to provide a new or replacement document to be stored on the server. The document is included in the body of the request and stored in the location defined by the URL.
5. **PATCH :** PATCH is similar to PUT, except that the request contains a list of differences that should be implemented in the existing file.
6. **COPY :** The COPY method copies a file to another location. The location of the source file is given in the request line (URL). The location of the destination is given in the entity header.
7. **MOVE :** The MOVE method moves a file to another location. The location of the source file is given in the request line (URL); the location of the destination is given in the entity header.
8. **DELETE :** The DELETE method removes a document on the server.
9. **LINK :** The LINK method creates a link or links from a document to another location. The location of the file is given in the request line (URL); the location of the destination is given in the entity header.
10. **UNLINK :** The UNLINK method deletes links created by the LINK method.
11. **OPTION :** The OPTION method is used by the client to ask the server about the available options.

(2) Response Message :

A response message consists of a status line, a header and sometimes a body. Refer Fig. 3.6 (a).

Status Line:

The status line defines the status of the response message. It consists of the HTTP version, a status code and a status phrase as shown in Fig. 3.6 (b).

- **HTTP Version:** This field is the same as the corresponding field in the request line.
- **Status Code:** The status code field is similar to those in the FTP and the SMTP protocol. It consists of three digits.
- **Status Phrase:** This field explains the status code in text form.

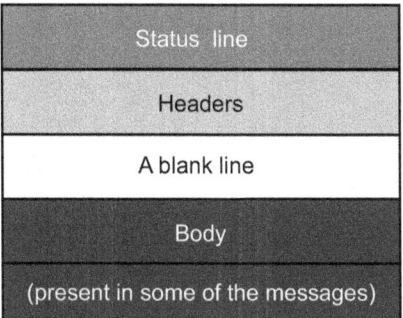

Fig. 3.6 (a) : Response Message

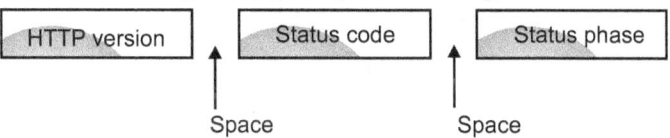

Fig. 3.6 (b) : Status Line

Headers:

- The headers exchange additional information between the client and the server.
- The header can be of one or more lines. Each header line is made of a header name, a colon, a space and a header value as shown in the following figure.

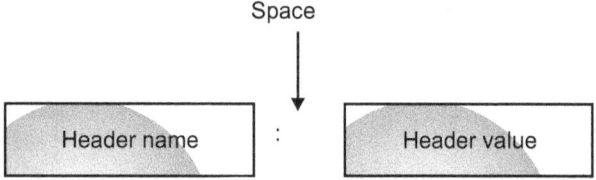

Fig. 3.7 : Header Format

- The header lines can be of four categories :
  (1) General Header, (2) Request Header, (3) Response Header, (4) Entity Header
- A request message can contain general request and entity headers while response message can contain general response and entity headers.

A comparison of request message and response message is shown in Fig. 3.8.

(1) General Header : It gives general information about the message. It is present in request as well as response message.

(2) Request Header : It can be present only in request message, which is used to specify client's configuration and client's preferred file format.

(3) Response Header : It can be present only in the response message. It is used for specifying the server's configuration.

(4) Entity Header : It is used for giving the information about the body of the document. It can be present in the request message as well as the response message.

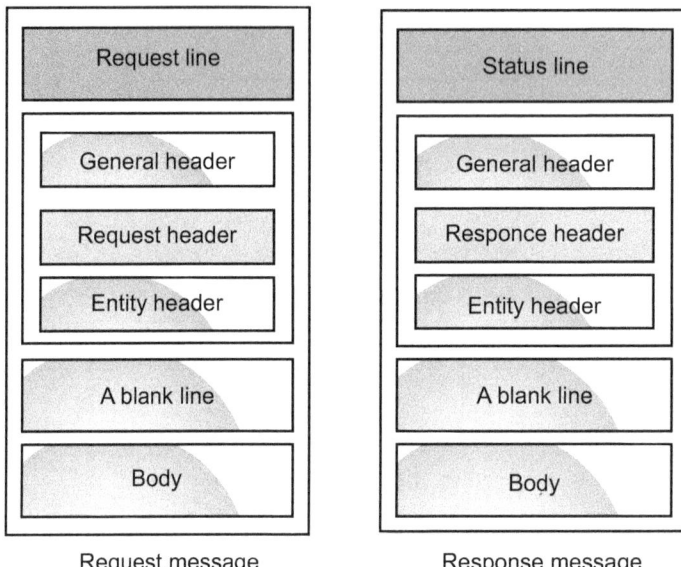

Fig. 3.8 : Request and Response Message Headers

3.3.2 HTTP is a Stateless Protocol

- In this protocol, the server does not store any information about the state of current transaction.
- So when the client does a request for some files, server sends these files to client without storing any state information about the client.
- If same client asks for the same information again and again to the server, so the server would not understand that it has already transferred this information to the same client, so server resends this information back to the client again and again as and when the client requests for those files.
- As HTTP server does not maintain any information about the state of client, it is called as **"stateless protocol"**.

3.3.3 HTTP Connections Types

HTTP connections are of two types :
1. Persistent Connections
2. Non-Persistent Connections.

These are explained in detail as follows :

(1) Persistent Connections :
- It is specified in HTTP version 1.1.
- In persistent connection the server leaves the connection open for more requests after sending a response.
- The server can close the connection at the request of a client or if timeout has been reached.
- The sender usually sends a length of the data with each response.
- However, there are certain situations where the sender does not know the length of the data. [In such situation the document is created dynamically.]
- In such cases, the server informs the client that the length of the data is not known and closes the connection after sending the data so the client knows that the end of the data has been reached.

HTTP version 1.1 by default specifies a persistent connection.

(2) Non-persistent Connection :
- In this type one TCP connection is made for each request/response by using the following steps :

    (i) The client opens a TCP connection and sends a request.

    (ii) The server sends a response and closes the connection.

    (iii) The client reads the data until it encounters an end-of-file marker; the client then closes the connection.

3.3.4 Cookies

- As we have seen repeatedly, the HTTP is basically stateless. There is no concept of a login session. The browser sends a request to a server and gets back a file. Then the server forgets that it has ever seen that particular client.
- At first, when the Web was just used for retrieving publicly available documents, this model was perfectly adequate.
- But as the Web started to acquire other functions, it caused problems. For example, some Web sites require clients to register (and possibly pay money) to use them. This raises the question of how servers can distinguish between requests from registered users and everyone else. A second example is from e-commerce. If a user wanders around an electronic store, tossing items into her shopping cart from time to time, how does the

server keep track of the contents of the cart? A third example is customized Web portals such as Yahoo. Users can set up a detailed initial page with only the information they want (e.g., their stocks and their favorite sports teams), but how can the server display the correct page if it does not know who the user is ?

- To solve this problem, Netscape devised a much-criticized technique called **cookies**. The name derives from ancient programmer slang in which a program calls a procedure and gets something back that it may need to present later to get some work done. In this sense, a UNIX file descriptor or a Windows object handle can be considered as a cookie.

- When a client requests a Web page, the server can supply additional information along with the requested page. This information may include a cookie, which is a small (at most 4 kB) file (or string). Browsers store offered cookies in a cookie directory on the client's hard disk unless the user has disabled cookies. Cookies are just files or strings, not executable programs. In principle, a cookie could contain a virus, but since cookies are treated as data, there is no official way for the virus to actually run and do damage. However, it is always possible for some hacker to exploit a browser bug to cause activation.

- A cookie may contain up to five fields, as shown in the following table. The *Domain* tells where the cookie came from. Browsers are supposed to check that servers are not lying about their domain. Each domain may store not more than 20 cookies per client. The *Path* is a path in the server's directory structure that identifies which parts of the server's file tree may use the cookie. It is often /, which means the whole tree.

Domain	Path	Content	Expires	Secure
toms-casino.com	/	CustomerID=497793521	15-10-02 17:00	Yes
joes-store.com	/	Cart=1.00501;1-07031;2-13721	11-10-02 14:22	No
aportal.com	/	Prefs=Stk:SUNW+ORCL;Spl:Jets	31-12-10 23:59	No
sneaky.com	/	UserID=3627239101	31-12-12 23:59	No

- The *Content* field takes the form *name = value*. Both *name* and *value* can be anything the server wants. This field is where the cookie's content is stored.

- The *Expires* field specifies when the cookie expires. If this field is absent, the browser discards the cookie when it exits. Such a cookie is called a **non-persistent cookie**. If a time and date are supplied, the cookie is said to be **persistent** and is kept until it expires. Expiration times are given in Greenwich Mean Time. To remove a cookie from a client's hard disk, a server just sends it again, but with an expiration time in the past.

- Finally, the *Secure* field can be set to indicate that the browser may only return the cookie to a secure server. This feature is used for e-commerce, banking, and other secure applications.
- We have now seen how cookies are acquired, but how are they used? Just before a browser sends a request for a page to some Web site, it checks its cookie directory to see if any cookies there were placed by the domain the request is going to. If so, all the cookies placed by that domain are included in the request message. When the server gets them, it can interpret them any way it wants to.
- To maintain some privacy, some users conFig. their browsers to reject all cookies. However, this can give problems with legitimate Web sites that use cookies. To solve this problem, users sometimes install cookie-eating software. These are special programs that inspect each incoming cookie upon arrival and accept or discard it depending on choices the user has given it (e.g., about which Web sites can be trusted). This gives the user fine-grained control over which cookies are accepted and which are rejected. Modern browsers, such as Mozilla (www.mozilla.org), have elaborate user-controls over cookies built in.

3.4 WORLD WIDE WEB (WWW)

- It is an information repository spread all over the world and linked together.
- The WWW is distributed client-server service, in which a client using a browser can access a service provided by the server.
- This service is distributed to many locations using the websites.

Hypertext and Hypermedia :

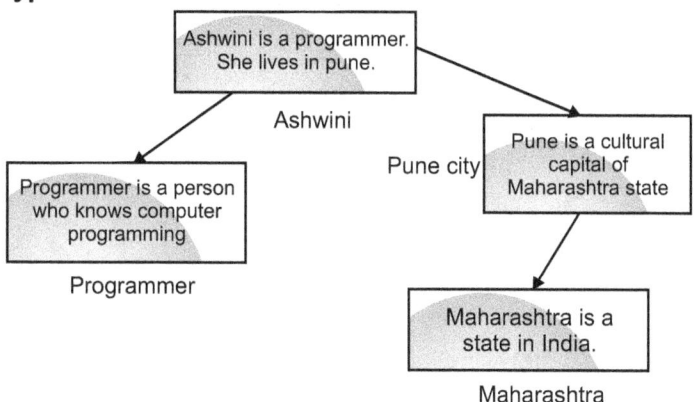

Fig. 3.9 : Hypertext

- In hypertext, set of documents containing information are linked using the concept of pointers.
- An item can be associated with another document by a pointer.

- The reader, who is browsing through the document, can move to other documents by clicking the items that are linked to other documents. (e.g. if user clicks on Pune city, then he/she will get more information on Pune city. If user clicks on Maharashtra then he/she will get some more information about Maharashtra state)
- Fig. 3.9 shows the concept of hypertext.
- Hypertext documents contain only text.
- Hypermedia documents can contain pictures, graphics and sounds.
- The hypertext and hypermedia available on the web in the form of webpages.
- The main page of the website is called as homepage.

3.4.1 Browser Architecture

- Refer the following Fig. 3.10.

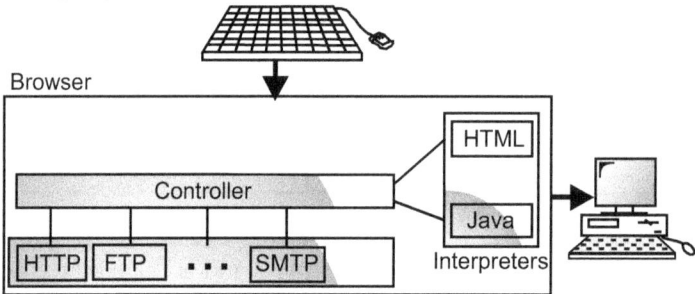

Fig. 3.10 : Browser Architecture

- Different vendors provide different browsers (such as internet explorer, Firefox mozilla, Netscape etc.).
- Although the browsers are different which have been developed by different vendors, they are having nearly same architecture.
- Each browser usually has three parts :
  (i) A controller
  (ii) A client program
  (iii) Interpreters
- A controller receives input from the keyboard or mouse and uses client program to access the document.
- After the document has been accessed, the controller uses one of the interpreter to display the document on the screen.
- The client programs can be one of the protocols, such as HTTP, FTP or SMTP.
- The interpreter can be HTML or JAVA depending on the type of the document.

3.4.2 Categories of Web Documents

- There are three types of web document as shown in Fig. 3.11.

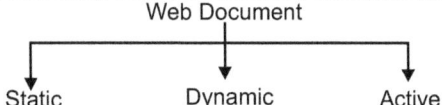

Fig. 3.11 : Categories of Web Documents

Static Documents :

- The contents of the static documents are fixed and that are created and stored in the server.
- The client can get a copy of a document when it does the request to the server.
- User cannot change the content of the document, but it is possible to change the content of the document at the server side. (See Fig. 3.12)

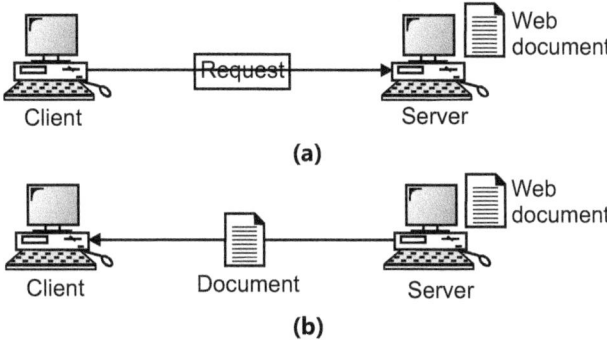

Fig. 3.12 : Static Document

3.5 HYPERTEXT MARKUP LANGUAGE

- By using this language the web pages are created.
- Book publishing agencies normally use the word markup language. (Before a book is typeset and printed, a copy editor reads the manuscript and puts a lot of marks on it. These marks tell the designer how to format the text.)
- For example : in case of HTML, if we want to give a heading in the page, then we must include the beginning and ending tags (marks) in the text as given below :

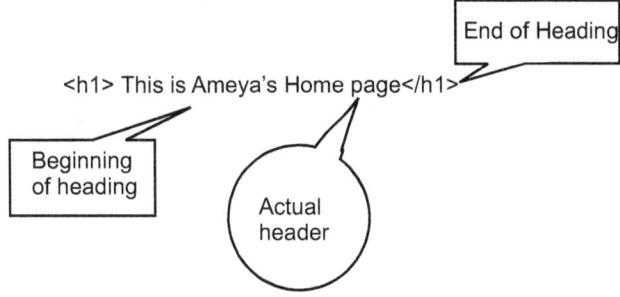

Fig. 3.13 : Heading Tags

- The two tags <h1> and </h1> are instructions for the browser. When the browser sees these two marks, it knows that the text is a heading in the document.
- As HTML allows embedding the formatting instructions inside the file itself, it is called as markup language.
- With the help of these embedded instructions, the browser at client side can read these instructions and format the text accordingly.
- HTML lets the user to use only ASCII characters for both the main text and formatting instructions.
- In this way, every computer can receive the whole document as an ASCII document. The main text is used as a data and formatting instructions can be used by the browser to format the data.

3.5.1 Web Page Structure

Web page is made up of two parts :

1. Head and
2. Body

(1) Head : The head is the first part of the webpage. The head contains the title of the page and other parameters that the browser will use.

(2) Body :

- The actual content of the page are in the body, which includes the text and the formatting tags.
- The text is the actual information contained in a page and tags define the appearance of the document.
- A tag can have a list of attributes, each of which is followed by an equal sign and a value associated with the attribute. Fig. 3.14 shows the format of the tags.

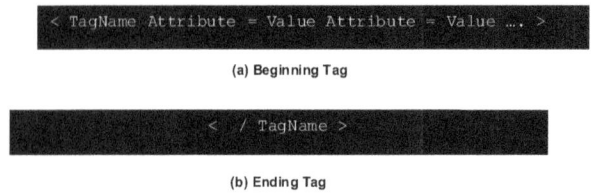

(a) Beginning Tag

(b) Ending Tag

Fig. 3.14 : Beginning and Ending Tags

3.5.2 Some Common HTML Tags

Beginning Tag	Ending Tag	Meaning
Skeletal Tags		
<HTML>	</HTML>	Defines a HTML document
<HEAD>	</HEAD>	Defines Head of the Document
<BODY>	</BODY>	Defines the body of the document
Title and Header Tags		
<TITLE>	</TITLE>	Defines the title of the document
Text Formatting Tags		
<B>	</B>	Boldface
<I>	</I>	Italic
<U>	</U>	Underlined
Data Flow Tags		
<CENTER>	</CENTER>	Centered
 		Line Break
Image Tags		
<IMG>		Defines an Image
Hyperlink Tags		
<A>	</A>	Defines an address

3.5.3 Dynamic Documents

- Dynamic documents are created by the server whenever it gets request from the client's browser.
- This document does not exist in predefined format.
- Whenever, the request comes from the client, the web server runs the application program which creates the dynamic document. The server returns the output of the program as a response to the browser that requested the document.

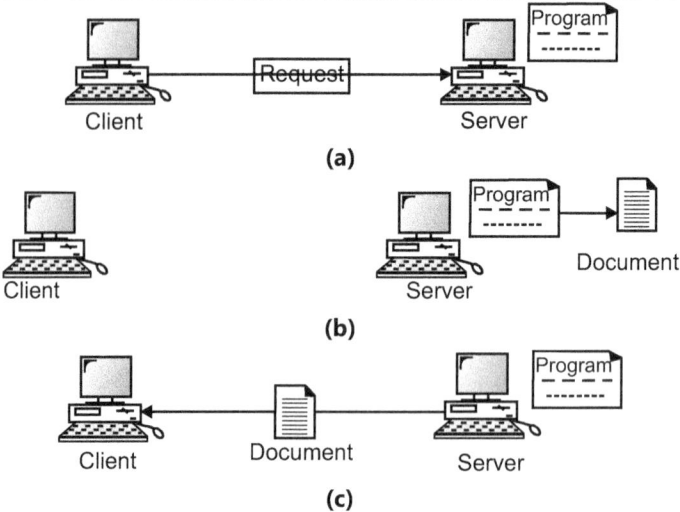

Fig. 3.15 : Dynamic Document

- Because the fresh document is created for each request, the contents of the dynamic document may vary from one request to another.
- A very simple example of dynamic document is getting the time and date from the server. (Time and date changes from moment to moment.)
- Observe Fig. 3.15.
- Server follows the following steps to handle the dynamic documents :
  (a) The server examines the URL to find if it defines a dynamic document.
  (b) If the URL defines a dynamic document, the server executes the program.
  (c) It sends the output of the program to the client.

3.5.4 Common Gateway Interface (CGI)

- CGI technology creates and handles dynamic documents.
- CGI is a set of standards that defines how a dynamic document should be written, how input data should be supplied to the program and how the output result should be used.
- Remember that, CGI is not a new language; instead it allows programmers to use any of several languages such as C, C++, Perl etc.
- The only thing is that CGI defines a set of rules and terms that the programmer should follow.
- The word 'common' in CGI shows that this standard defines some rules which are common to any language.
- The term 'Gateway' here means that a CGI program is a gateway that can be used to access the resources such as databases and graphics packages.
- The term 'interface' means that there is a set of predefined terms, calls, variables etc. which can be used in any CGI program.

3.5.5 Active Documents

- Active documents are the programs that run on the client side.
- For example, imagine we want to run a program that creates animated graphics on the screen or interacts with the user.
- When the browser requests an active document, the server sends a copy of the document in the form of **byte code**. The document is then run on the client browser.
- Active document does not create an overhead to the server because it is stored in the form of **binary code** in the server and server does not run it.
- When the client receives the document, it can also store the document in its own storage area; due to that client can run that document again and again without making another request to the server. (e.g. Applets in Java programming can be an example of active document.)
- Server sends an active document to the client in the binary form.
- While sending the document, it is compressed at server side and is decompressed at the client side, which saves both, bandwidth and transmission time.

Creation, Compilation and Execution of Active Document :

- Programmer writes a source code and deploys it on the server side.
- At server side, the program is compiled and binary code is created, which is stored in a file.
- The client requests a copy of binary code, which is transmitted in the compressed form from server to the client.
- The client converts the received program from binary code to executable code using its own browser software.
- The client runs the program and creates the result that can include animation or interaction with the user.

3.6 FILE TRANSFER PROTOCOL (FTP)

- The main purpose of computer networks is data and resource sharing.
- File transfer is a very common operation on the computer network.
- We require two types of protocols for transferring the files on the network : (1) FTP and (2) TFTP

- FTP is a standard mechanism provided by TCP/IP for copying a file from one host to another.
- There are some problems associated with file transfer mechanism from one machine to another, which can be as follows :
    - Two systems may have different ways to represent text and data.
    - These systems may have different directory structure.
- It is necessary for the FTP to solve all such sort of problems for transferring a file.
- For transferring a file, FTP establishes two connections between the hosts. One connection is used for data transfer, and other for control information (commands and responses).
- Separation of commands and data transfer makes FTP more efficient.
- Data connection uses very complex rules for transmission of data (due to variety of data types transferred); on the other hand control connection uses very simple rules of communication.

Points to be remembered :
- FTP uses the service of TCP.
- It needs two TCP connections.
- Port 21 is used for control connection &
- Port 20 is used for data connection.
- Following Fig. 3.16 explains the basic architecture of FTP. The server has two major components and the client has two major components as given in Fig. 4.17.

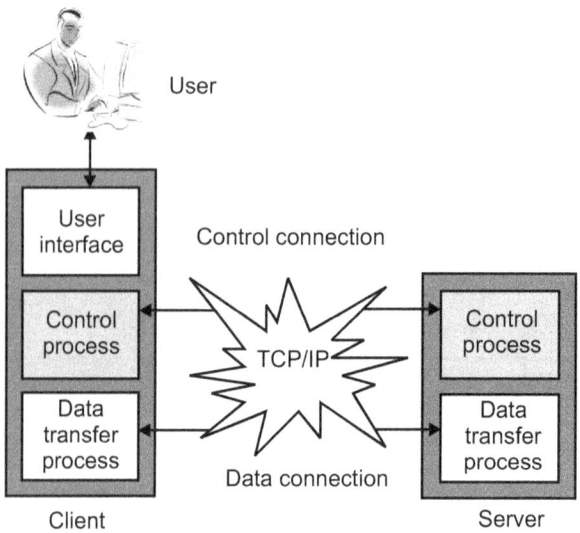

Fig. 3.16 : FTP

COMPUTER NETWORK TECHNOLOGY (T.E. I.T.) — APPLICATION LAYER

- The control connection is made between the control processes at server and client side while the data connection is made between the data transfer processes.
- One more thing that is very important about the control and data connection is that, the control connection remains open during the entire FTP interactive session, while the data connection is opened when the user wants to transmit a file and then it is closed after the file transfer. In short the data connection is opened and closed for each file transferred.

3.6.1 Control Connection

- The process of opening the control connection is shown in Fig. 3.17. There are two steps :
    1. The server issues a passive open on well-known port 21 and waits for a client.
    2. The client uses a temporary (ephemeral) port and issues an active open.

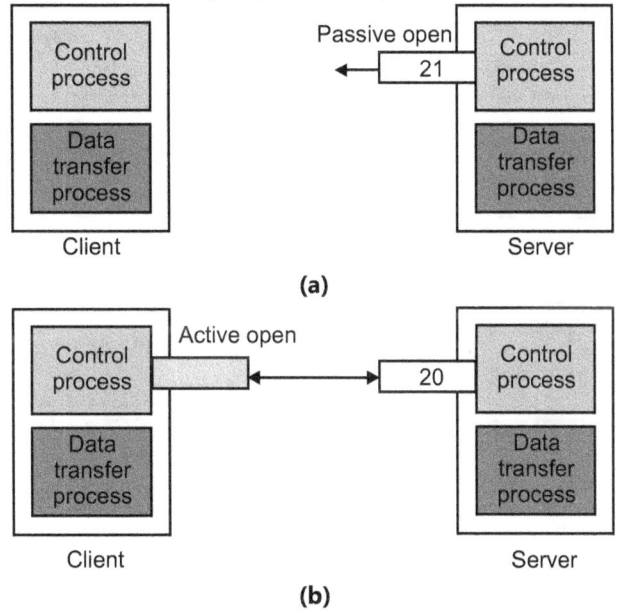

Fig. 3.17 : Opening the Control Connection

- The control connections remain alive during the entire process.
- The IP uses minimize delay type service because this is an interactive connection between a user and a server.

3.6.2 Data Connections

- Data connection uses port 20 at server side.
- Following steps are required for creating data connections :
    - The client issues a passive open using a temporary (ephemeral) port.
    - The client sends this port number to the server using PORT command.
    - The server receives the port number and issues an active open using port 20 and the received ephemeral port number.

These steps for creating the initial data connection are shown in Fig. 3.18.

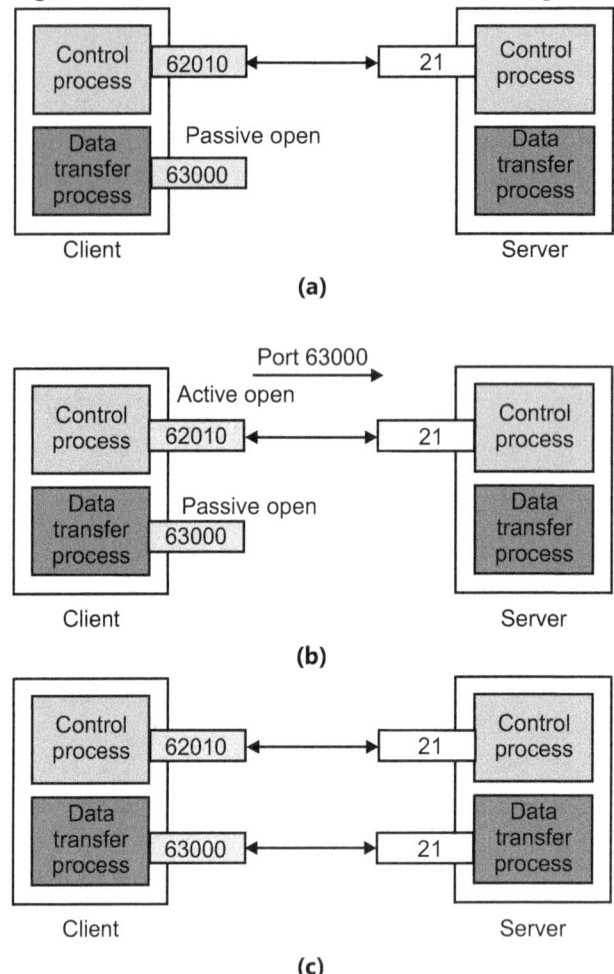

Fig. 3.18 : Creating Data Connections

3.6.3 Communication Over Control Connection

- Similar to the TELNET and SMTP, FTP communicate across the control connection.
- It uses NVT ASCII character set for communication as shown in the following Fig. 3.19.

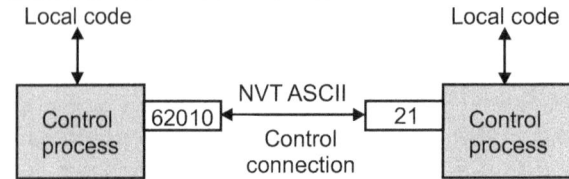

Fig. 3.19 : Using the Control Connection

- Communication is normally done using commands and responses.

- Only one command or response is sent at a time during the control connection.
- Each command or response is only one short line, so we need not worry about the file format or file structure.
- Every line is terminated with two characters i.e. carriage return and line feed.

3.6.4 Communication Over Data Connection

- Data connection is used to transfer files.
- Before transmission of the files, the client must specify :
- The type of the file to be transferred
- The structure of the data and
- Mode of data transmission.

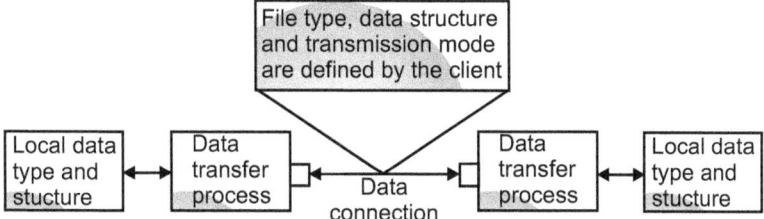

Fig. 3.20: Using the Data Connection

- Before sending the file using data connection, we have to send proper control signals through the control connection.
- The problem of heterogeneity is solved by defining the above three communication attributes i.e. File type, data structure and transmission mode. These attributes are explained below. Refer Fig. 3.20.
- **File Type :** FTP can transfer ASCII file, EBCDIC file or Image file.
  - **ASCII File :** Text files are by default transferred using ASCII format.
  - **EBCDIC File :** If one or both ends of the connection use EBCDIC encoding, the file can be transferred using EBCDIC encoding.
  - **Image File :** This is default format of transferring binary files.
- **Data Structure :** FTP can use the following data structures :
  - **File Structure :** The file has no structure; it is continuous stream of bytes.
  - **Record Structure :** In this case, the text files are divided into records.
  - **Page Structure :** The file is divided into pages, in which each page is having a page number and page header. The pages can be accessed randomly or sequentially.
- **Transmission modes :** FTP uses stream, block and compressed mode for file transfer.

- o **Stream Mode :** In this case, data is transferred in continuous stream of bytes.
- o **Block Mode :** In this case, data is transferred in the form of blocks.
- o **Compressed Mode :** In this method, by using run length encoding data is compressed.

3.6.5 File Transfer

File transfer takes place over the data connection in association with the control connection. File transfer in FTP means one of the following :

1. **Retrieving a file :** A file is copied from server to the client.
2. **Storing a file :** A file can be copied from client to the server.
3. A Server sends a list of directory or file names to the client. FTP treats such a list of directory as a file. The file transfer has been shown in the following Fig. 3.21.

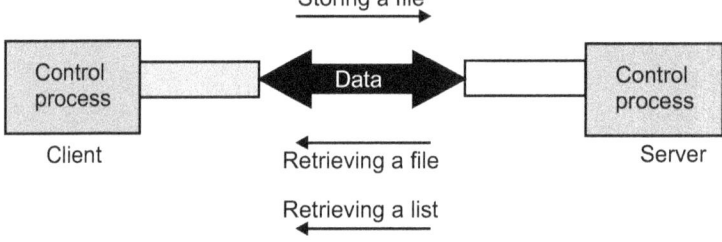

Fig. 3.21 : File Transfer

3.6.6 FTP Commands

- FTP creates a control connection between a client control process and server control process.
- During this communication, commands are sent from the client to the server and responses are sent from the server to the client.
- FTP commands are roughly divided into six groups : (1) access, (2) file management, (3) data formatting, (4) port defining, (5) file transferring and (6) miscellaneous commands.
- These commands are given in the following table :

Sr. No.	Command	Description
		Access Commands
1.	USER	User Information
2.	PASS	Password
3.	ACCT	Account Information
4.	REIN	Reinitialize
5.	QUIT	Log out of the system
6.	ABOR	Abort the previous command

Cont...

		Data Formatting Commands
1.	**TYPE**	Defines the file type and if necessary the print format
2.	**STRU**	Defines the organization of data
3.	**MODE**	Defines the transmission mode
		File Management Commands
1.	**CWD**	Change to another directory
2.	**CDUP**	Change to parent directory
3.	**DELE**	Delete a File
4.	**LIST**	List subdirectories or files
5.	**MKD**	Create (make) new directory
6.	**PWD**	Display name of current (present working) directory
7.	**RMD**	Delete (remove) directory
8.	**RNFR**	Identify a file to be renamed (rename from)
9.	**RNTO**	Rename the file (rename to)
		Port Defining Commands
1.	**PORT**	Client chooses a port
2.	**PASV**	Server chooses a port
		File Transfer Commands
1.	**RETR**	Retrieve files
2.	**STOR**	Store files: files are transferred from client to server
3.	**APPE**	Similar to STOR except if file exists, data must be appended to it
4.	**STOU**	Similar to STOR except that the file name will be unique in the directory
5.	**ALLO**	Allocate the storage space for the files at the server
6.	**REST**	Position a file marker at a specified data point
7.	**STAT**	Return the status of the files
		Miscellaneous Commands
1.	**HELP**	Ask information about the server
2.	**NOOP**	Check if server is alive
3.	**SITE**	Specify the site specific commands
4.	**SYST**	Ask about the operating system used by the server

3.7 TRIVIAL FILE TRANSFER PROTOCOL (TFTP)

- **Trivial File Transfer Protocol** (**TFTP**) is a file transfer protocol, with the functionality of a very basic form of File Transfer Protocol (FTP); it was first defined in 1980.
- Due to its simple design, TFTP could be implemented using a very small amount of memory.
- It is therefore useful for booting computers such as routers which did not have any data storage devices.
- It is still used to transfer small amounts of data between hosts on a network when a remote X Window System terminal or any other thin client boots from a network host or server.
- The initial stages of some network based installation systems (such as Solaris, Symantec Ghost and Windows NT's Remote Installation Services) use TFTP to load a basic kernel that performs the actual installation.
- Trivial File Transfer Protocol (TFTP) is a simple protocol to transfer files. It has been implemented on top of the User Datagram Protocol (UDP) using port number 69.
- TFTP is designed to be small and easy to implement, therefore, lacks most of the features of a regular FTP.
- TFTP only reads and writes files (or mail) from/to a remote server.
- It cannot list directories, and currently has no provisions for user authentication.

3.7.1 TFTP Operation

- In TFTP, any transfer begins with a request to read or write a file, which also serves to request a connection.
- If the server grants the request, the connection is opened and the file is sent in fixed length blocks of 512 bytes.
- Each data packet contains one block of data, and must be acknowledged by an acknowledgement packet before the next packet can be sent.
- A data packet of less than 512 bytes signals termination of a transfer.
- If a packet gets lost in the network, the intended recipient will timeout and may retransmit his last packet (which may be data or an acknowledgement), thus causing the sender of the lost packet to retransmit that lost packet.
- The sender has to keep just one packet on hand for retransmission, since the lock step acknowledgement guarantees that all older packets have been received.
- One sends data and receives acknowledgements; the other sends acknowledgements and receives data.

3.7.2 Modes of TFTP

Three modes of transfer are currently supported by TFTP :
- **Netascii :** That it is 8 bit ascii.
- **Octet :** This replaces the "binary" mode of previous versions of this document.
- **Mail :** netascii characters sent to a user rather than a file.

3.7.3 Uses

- TFTP is used to read files from, or write files to, a remote server.
- Due to the lack of security, it is dangerous over the open Internet. Thus, TFTP is generally only used on private, local networks.

3.7.4 Disadvantages of TFTP

- TFTP cannot list directory contents.
- TFTP has no authentication or encryption mechanisms.
- TFTP allows big data packets which may burst and cause delay in transmission.
- TFTP cannot download files larger than 1 Terabyte.

3.7.5 Comparison between FTP and TFTP [Dec. 2007]

Sr. No.	Parameter	FTP	TFTP
1.	Operation	Transferring Files	Transferring Files
2.	Authentication	Yes	No
3.	Control and Data	Separated	Not separated
4.	Protocol	TCP	UDP
5.	Ports	21-Control, 20-Data	Port 3214, 69, 4012
6.	Data Transfer	Reliable	Unreliable
7.	Number of connections	Two connections	One connection
8.	Commands	Provides many commands	Provides only 5 commands

3.8 SIMPLE MAIL TRANSFER PROTOCOL

E-mail system is implemented with the help of Message Transfer Agents (MTA).
- There are normally two MTAs in each mailing system : One for sending e-mails and another for receiving e-mails.
- The formal protocol that defines the MTA client and server in the internet is called Simple Mail Transfer Protocol (SMTP).

- Fig. 3.22 shows the range of SMTP protocol.

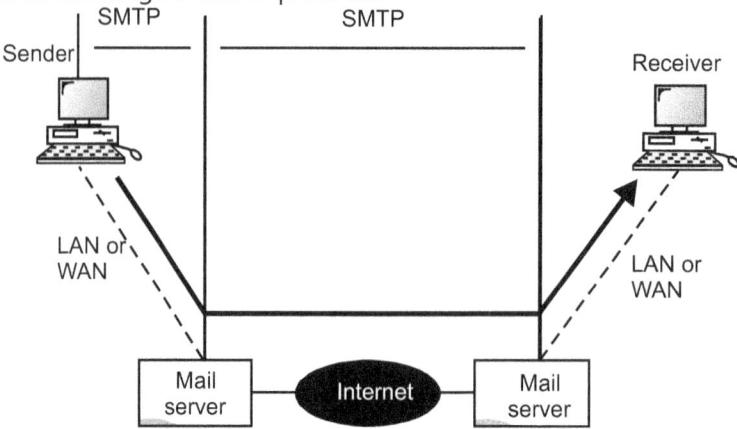

Fig. 3.22 : SMTP Range

- By referring the above diagram, we can say that SMTP is used two times. That is between the sender and sender's mail server and between the sender's mail server and receiver's mail server.
- Another protocol is used between the receiver's mail server and receiver.
- SMTP simply defines how commands and responses must be sent back and forth.
- SMTP is a simple ASCII protocol.
- It establishes a TCP connection between a sender and port number 25 of the receiver.
- No checksums are generally required because TCP provides a reliable byte stream.
- After exchanging all the e-mail, the connection is released.

3.8.1 Commands and Responses

- SMTP uses commands and responses to transfer messages between an MTA client and MTA server.
- Each command or reply is terminated by a two character (carriage return and line feed) end-of-line token.

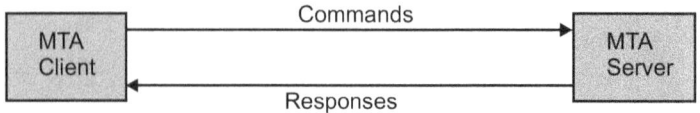

Fig. 3.23 : Commands and Responses

Commands :

- Client sends commands to the server. SMTP defines 14 commands.
- Out of that first 5 commands are mandatory; every implementation must support these commands.
- The next three commands are often used and are highly recommended.
- Last six commands are hardly used.
- Following table shows FTP commands.

Keyword	Description
HELO	Used by the client to identify itself. The argument is domain name of the client host. The format is : **HELO :** mail.viit.ac.in
MAIL FROM	Used by the client to identify the sender of the message. The argument is email address of the sender. Format is **MAIL FROM :** amol.dhumane@gmail.com
RCPT TO	Used by the client to identify the intended recipient of the message. The argument is the email address of the recipient. The format is: **RCPT TO :** ashwini.dhumane@yahoo.co.in
DATA	This command is used to send the actual message. The lines following DATA command are treated as mail message. Format is: **DATA** There is an important meeting on this Sunday. So please be present for it. Regards; Nitin Sakhare
QUIT	It terminates the message. The format is : **QUIT**
RSET	It aborts the current email transaction. The stored information of the sender and receiver is deleted after executing the command. The connection gets reset. The format is : **RSET**
VRFY	This command is used to verify the address of the recipient. In this sender asks the receiver to confirm that a name identifies a valid recipient. Its format is: **VRFY :** sai@puneatoz.net
NOOP	By using this command the client checks the status of the recipient. It requires an answer from recipient. Its format is : **NOOP**
TURN	It reverses the role of sender and receiver.
EXPN	It asks the receiving host to expand the mailing list.
HELP	It sends system specific documentation. The format is : **HELP :** mail
SEND FROM	This command specifies that the mail is to be delivered to the terminal of the recipient, and not the mailbox. If the recipient is not logged in, the mail is bounced back. The argument is the address of the sender. The format is : **SEND FROM :** amol.dhumane@gmail.com
SMOL FROM	This command specifies to send the mail to the terminal if possible, otherwise to the mailbox.
SMAL FROM	It sends mail to the terminal and mail box.

3.8.2 Working

SMTP works in the following three stages :
1. Connection Establishment
2. Message Transfer
3. Connection Termination

These are explained below :

1. Connection Establishment :
- Once the TCP connection is made on port no. 25, SMTP server starts the connection phase.
- This phase involves following three steps which are explained in the Fig. 3.24.
- The server tells the client that it is ready to receive mail by using the code 220. If the server is not ready, it sends code 421 which tells that service is not available.

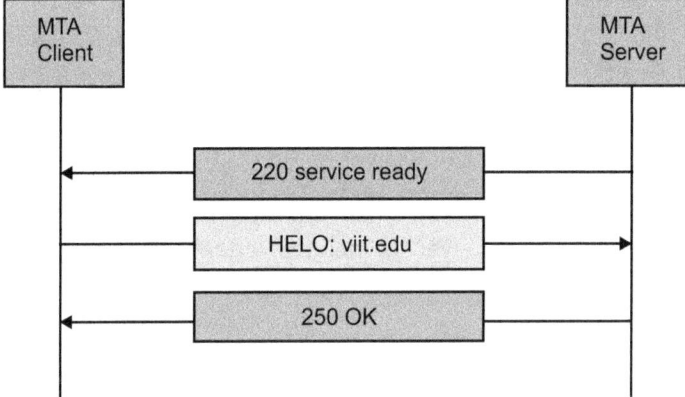

Fig. 3.24 : Connection Establishment

- Once the server becomes ready to receive the mails, client sends HELO message to identify itself using the domain name address. This is important step which informs the server of the domain name of the client. Remember that during TCP connection establishment, the sender and receiver know each other through their IP addresses.
- Server responds with code 250 which tells that the request command is completed.

2. Message Transfer :
- Once the connection has been established, SMTP server sends messages to SMTP receiver.
- The messages are transferred in three stages :
    1. A MAIL command identifies the message originator.
    2. RCPT command identifies the receiver of the message.
    3. DATA command transfers the message text.

3. Connection Closing :
- After the message is transferred successfully, the client terminates the connection.
- The connection is terminated in two steps :
  1. The client sends the quit command.
  2. The server responds with code 221 or some other appropriate code.

After the connection termination phase, the TCP connection must be closed.

3.9 POST OFFICE PROTOCOL (POP)

- In the first and second stage of mail delivery, SMTP protocol is used.
- As SMTP is a push protocol, it is not used into the third stage of mailing system.
- SMTP is called as push protocol because it pushes the messages from the client to the server.
- On the other hand, the third stage needs a pull protocol; the client must pull messages from the server.
- The direction of the bulk of data is from server to the client, where client pulls the messages from the server. Refer following figure.

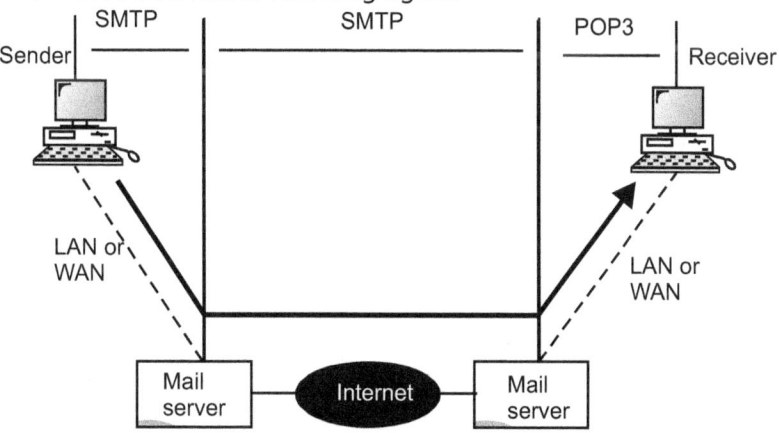

Fig. 3.25 : POP3

3.9.1 POP3

- This version of post office protocol is simple and is having limited functionality.
- The client's POP3 software is installed on the recipient computer and server's POP3 software is installed on mail server.
- When the user wants to read its mail, the user downloads its mails from the mailbox on the mail server.
- For downloading the mails from the mail server, the client opens a TCP connection with the mail server on port no. 110.

- By giving appropriate username and password, the user does its authentication.
- The user can then retrieve the mail messages one by one.
- Following Fig. 3.26 shows the working of POP3 protocol.

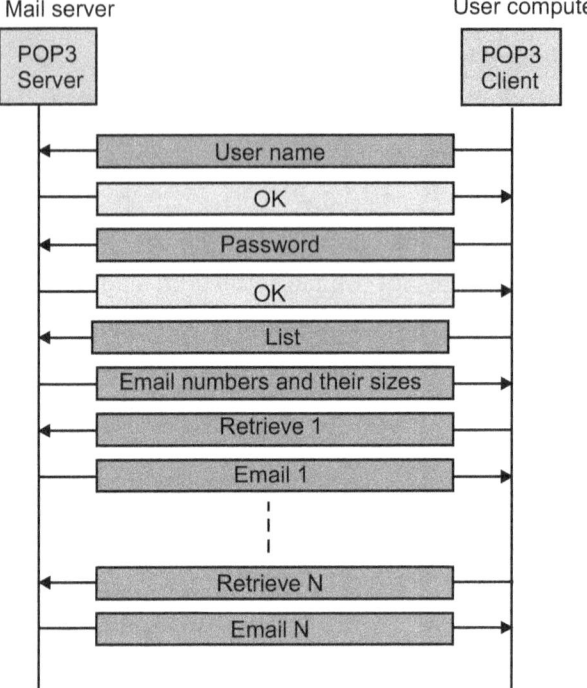

Fig. 3.26 : POP3

- POP3 works in two modes :
    1. Delete Mode
    2. Keep Mode
- **Delete Mode :** The mail is deleted from the mailbox after each retrieval. This mode is normally used when the user is working at her own computer, and can save and organize received mails after reading and replying.
- **Keep Mode :** The mail remains in the mailbox after retrieval. The keep mode is normally used when the user access her mail away from her primary computer. The mail is read but kept in the system for later retrieval and organizing.

3.9.2 Limitations of POP3 Protocol

1. POP3 does not allow organization of email on the server.
2. The user cannot have different folders on the server.
3. The user cannot partially check the content of email before downloading.

3.10 INTERNET MAIL ACCESS PROTOCOL (IMAP4)

Internet mail access protocol (IMAP4) is similar to POP3, but it has more features which are stated below:

- In IMAP4, before downloading the email, the user can check email header.
- It is possible for the user to search for the content of email before downloading it.
- By using IMAP4 protocol, user can partially download the email.
- In this case user can create, delete or rename mailboxes on the mail server.
- It is possible for the user to create hierarchy of mailboxes in a folder for email storage.

3.10.1 Comparison between IMAP and POP3

Sr. No	Parameter	POP3	IMAP
1.	Email is stored at	Users PC	Server
2.	Email is read	Off line	On line
3.	Multiple mail boxes	No	Yes
4.	Downloads partial message	No	Yes
5.	TCP port used	110	143
6.	Connection time	Small	large

3.11 MULTIPURPOSE INTERNET MAIL EXTENSIONS (MIME)

- Email can send message only in NVT 7-bit ASCII format.
- Email has some limitations, e.g. one cannot use it for writing the mail in the languages which are not supported by 7-bit ASCII characters. (French, German, Russian are some of the languages that can't be represented by 7-bit ASCII format).
- Also, it can not be used to send binary files or video or audio data.

Remember :

- MIME protocol allows non ASCII data to be sent through email.
- MIME transforms non-ASCII data at the sender site to NVT-ASCII data & delivers it to the client MTA to be sent through the internet.
- The message at the receiving side is transformed back to the original data (Non-ASCII).
- From the point of normal user, MIME is a set of software functions that transforms non-ASCII data to ASCII data and vice versa as shown in Fig. 3.27 given below :

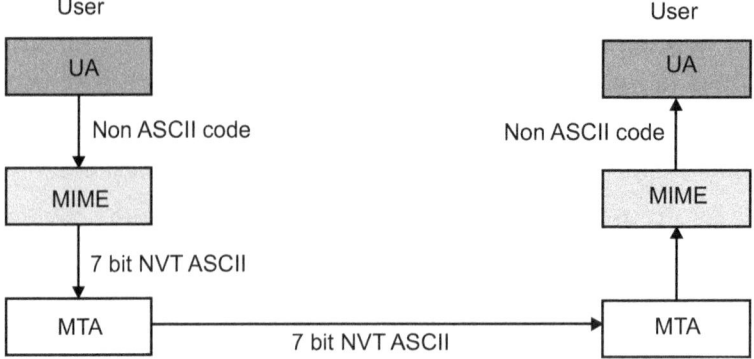

Fig. 3.27 : MIME

- MIME defines five headers that can be added to the original email header.
  1. MIME-Version
  2. Content-Type
  3. Content-Transfer-Encoding
  4. Content-ID
  5. Content-Description

  Fig. 4.29 shows the MIME header.

1. **MIME Version :** This field defines the version of MIME used. Current version of MIME is 1.1

2. **Content-Type :** This field defines the type of the data used in the message body. The data can be of different types such as text, image, audio, video multipart or application data. These data types are further divided into subtypes. E.g. text data type is further divided into plain text & HTML, Image data type is further divided into JPG images, GIF images etc.

3. **Content-Transfer-Encoding :** This field gives information about the encoding type of the message. Five types of encoding methods are listed below :

   (a) **7 Bit :** used for NVT ASCII characters and short lines

   (b) **8 Bit :** used for Non ASCII characters and short lines

   (c) **Binary :** used for Non ASCII characters with unlimited length lines

   (d) **Base 64 :** 6 bits block of data are encoded into 8 bit ASCII characters.

   (e) **Quoted Printable :** Non-ASCII characters are encoded as an equal sign followed by an ASCII code.

Email Header
MIME-Version: 1.1 **Content-Type:** type/subtype **Content-Transfer-Encoding:** encoding type **Content-Id:** message id **Content-Description:** Textual Explanation of nontextual contents
Email Body

Fig. 3.28 : MIME Header

4. **Content-Id :** This header uniquely identifies the whole message in a multiple message environment.
5. **Content-Description :** This header defines whether the body is image, audio or video (non textual).

3.12 DOMAIN NAME SYSTEM

- DNS provides a protocol that allows client and servers to communicate with each other.
- To identify a computer on the internet, IP address is used by the TCP/IP protocol suit.
- However, it is difficult to remember so many IP addresses, for that people used to prefer names (such as www.puneatoz.net) instead of the numeric IP addresses.
- Therefore we need a system that can map a name to an IP address or an IP address to a name.
- Domain Name System provides this facility.

3.12.1 Working of DNS

- To map a URL name with IP address, the application program calls a library procedure called as 'Resolver'.
- The URL name is passed to the Resolver as an argument.
- This Resolver sends a UDP packet to local DNS server which goes through its database, finds out the corresponding IP address associated with the URL name, and returns this IP address to the application program.
- After getting the actual IP address, the application program establish the connection with the destination.

3.12.2 Domain Name Space

- Domain name space is hierarchical, which is similar to unix file system.
- In this design, names are defined in an inverted tree structure with the root at the top.
- Domain names are case insensitive (i.e. com and COM are same thing).
- Every node has a label of maximum 63 characters long.

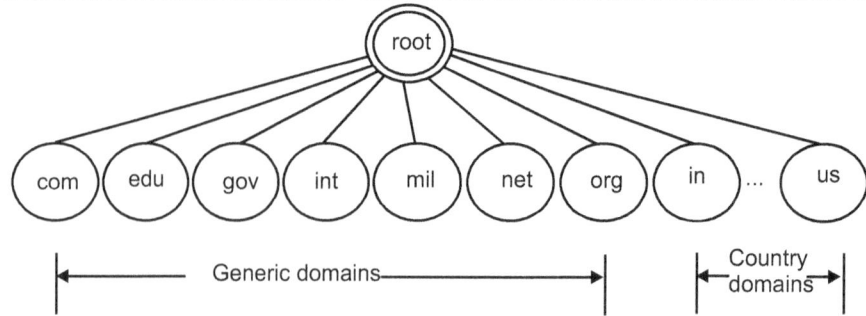

Fig. 3.29 : Hierarchical Organization of DNS

- The root label is null string.
- A domain name that ends with a period is called as absolute domain name or fully qualified domain name.
- Top level domains are divided into two areas; i.e. generic and countries as shown in Fig. 3.30.
- Three character domains are called as generic domains
- Two character domains are called as country domains (e.g. **in** for India, **us** for United States, **nz** for New Zealand).
- The generic domains .GOV and .MIL are restricted to the United States only.
- Each domain is named by the path upward from it to the root. The components are separated by periods. This is called as hierarchical routing.
- As we know that root label is null, this means that a full domain name always ends in null label; this means the last character is dot because the null string is nothing.
- Following Fig. shows some domain names :

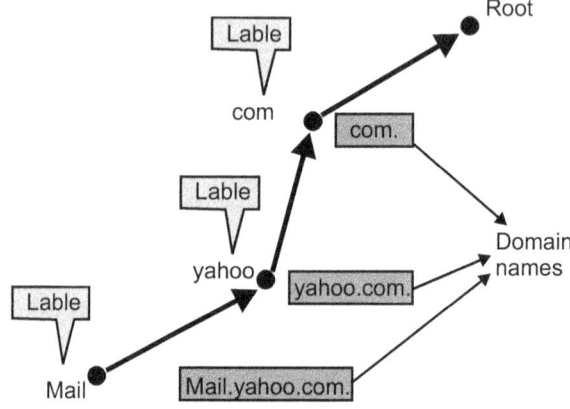

Fig. 3.30 : Domain Names and Labels

3.12.3 Fully Qualified Domain Names

- If a label is terminated by a null string, it is called as a Fully Qualified Domain Name (FQDN).
- A fully qualified domain name contains full name of the host. e.g. mail.yahoo.com.
- It is also called as absolute domain name. It always ends with a period (a dot).

3.12.4 Partially Qualified Domain Names

- If a label is not terminated by a null string, it is called as a partially qualified domain name (PQDN).
- PQDN starts from a node but never reach to the root node.
  e.g. mail.yahoo.com
- It is also called as relative domain name. It never ends with a period (a dot).

3.12.5 Domain

- A domain is a subtree of domain name space.
- The name of the domain is the domain name of the node at the top of the subtree.
- Following Fig. 3.31 shows .com and .edu domains.

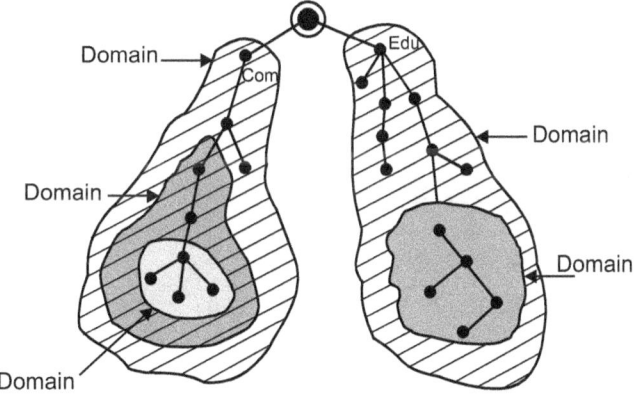

Fig. 3.31 : Domains

- Note that a domain may itself be divided into domains or subdomains as they are sometimes called.

3.12.6 Domain Name Servers

Need :
- The information contained in domain name space must be stored.
- As the information is tremendous (now a days the websites becomes countless), so it is not possible to store such a huge amount of information only on one computer.
- Even if we put the information on single computer, still it is very inefficient because for a single computer, responding to requests from all over the world will not be possible. (The load will be very heavy for a single computer to handle).

- Also, from the point of reliability, it can cause disaster because of machine failure. (The entire data on that machine will be inaccessible).
- So the solution to these problems is to distribute the information among many computers called DNS servers.
- Firstly, the whole space is divided into many first level domains. The root server stands alone and can create as many first level domains as required.
- The first level domains are further divided into smaller domains called as subdomains.
- Each server can be responsible for either a large or small domain.
- In short, we have hierarchy of servers similar to the hierarchy of names.
- The whole DNS namespace is divided into non overlapping zones. We can define a zone as a contiguous part of the entire tree.
- The zones are explained below.

3.12.7 Zone

- Since the complete domain name hierarchy can not be stored on a single server, it is divided among many servers.
- Server is responsible for a zone.
- We can define a zone as a **contiguous part of the entire tree**.
- If a server accepts responsibility of a domain and does not divide the domain into smaller domains, the domain and the zone refer to the same thing.
- A server makes a database called a "zone file" and keeps all the information for every node under that domain.
- However, if the server divides its domain into subdomains and pass on a part of its authority to other servers then domain and zone will be different from each other. This is shown in the following figure.
- The information about the nodes in the subdomains is stored in the servers at the lower levels, with the original server keeping some sort of reference to these lower-level servers.

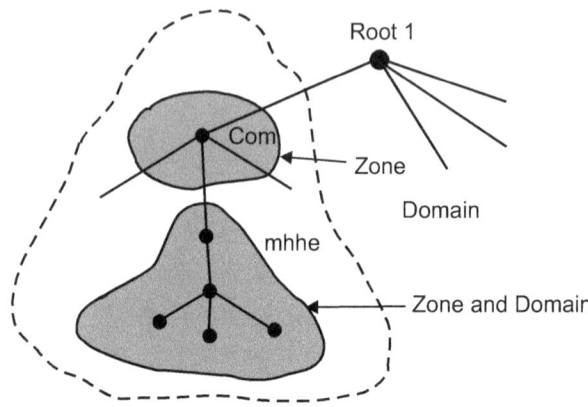

Fig. 3.32 : Zones and Domains

3.12.8 Root Server
- Root server is a server whose zone consists of the whole tree.
- Root server does not store any information about domains but pass on its authority to other servers.
- There are several root servers distributed all over the world.

3.12.9 Primary and Secondary Servers
- There are two types of DNS servers :
  - Primary Server
  - Secondary Server
- Primary server stores a file about the zone for which it is an authority.
- Primary server is responsible for creating, maintaining and updating a zone file. It stores the zone file on a local disk.
- A secondary server is a server that transfers the complete information about a zone from another server (primary and secondary) and stores the file on its local disk.
- The secondary server neither create nor update the zone files, updating is done only by the primary server, which further sends the updated zone file to the secondary.
- A primary server loads all information from the disk file; the secondary server loads all information from the primary server.
- **Zone Transfer :** When the secondary, downloads the information from the primary server, it is called as zone transfer.

3.12.10 Resolution
The mechanism of mapping a name to an address or an address to a name is called as name-address resolution.
Resolver :
- DNS is a client-server application.
- A resolver program is called by the client when a host wants to map an address to a name or a name to address.
- For this purpose the nearest DNS server is accessed by the resolver.
- If this server has information, it satisfies the resolver; otherwise, it refers the resolver to other servers or asks other servers to provide the information.
- After receiving the correct mapping, resolver delivers the result to the process that requested it.

Mapping Names to Addresses :
- Many times, the resolver gives a domain name to the DNS server and asks for the corresponding address.
- Here, server checks the generic or country domains to find mapping.
- If the domain name is from the generic domain area, the resolver receives the domain name such as "mail.viit.edu.".

- The query is sent by the resolver to the local DNS for resolution.
- If the local DNS server seems unable to solve the query, it either refers the resolver to other servers or it itself contact to other DNS servers.

Mapping Addresses to Names :
- In this case, client sends an IP address to a server to be mapped to a domain name. This type of query is called as PTR query.
- To solve such queries, DNS uses the inverse domain.
- For example, if the resolver receives an IP address 129.132.12.37, the resolver first inverts the address and then adds the two labels before sending.
- The domain name sent is "129.132.12.37.in-addr.arpa", which is received by the local DNS and resolved.

Recursive Resolution :
- The client can ask for a recursive answer from a name server.
- This means that the resolver expects the server to supply the final answer.
- If the server is the authority for the domain name, it checks its database and responds.
- If the server is not the authority, it sends the request to another server and waits for the response.
- If the parent is the authority, it responds; otherwise it sends the query to yet another server.
- When the query is finally resolved, the response travels back until it finally reaches the requesting client.
- Refer following figure.

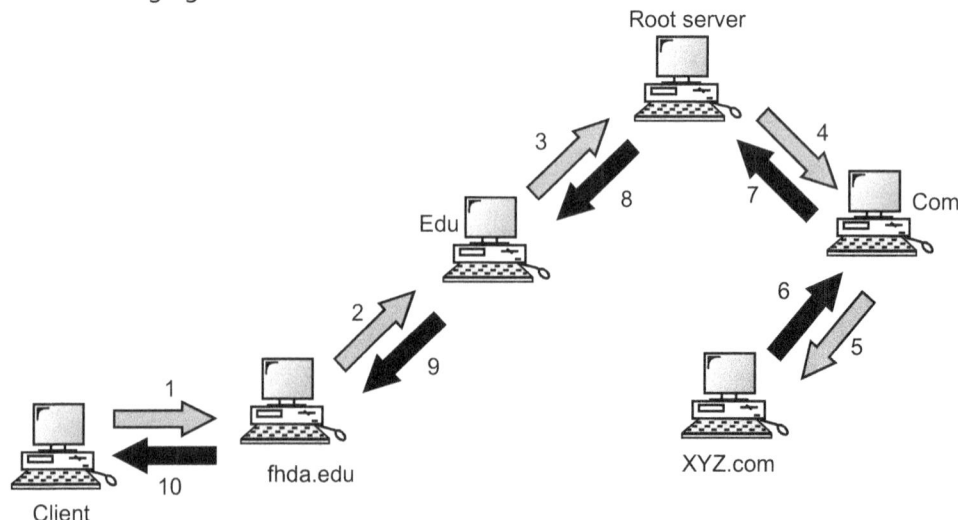

Fig. 3.33 : Recursive Resolution

Iterative Resolution :

- If the client does not ask for a recursive answer, the mapping can be done iteratively.
- If the server is an authority for the name, it sends the answer. If it is not, it returns the IP address of the server that it thinks can resolve the query.
- The client has to repeat the query to the second server. If the new server can resolve the problem, it answers the query with the IP address: otherwise it returns the IP address of the new server to the client.
- Now the client once again repeats the query to the third server. The process becomes iterative as the client is repeating the same query to multiple servers.
- Refer the following figure for the same.

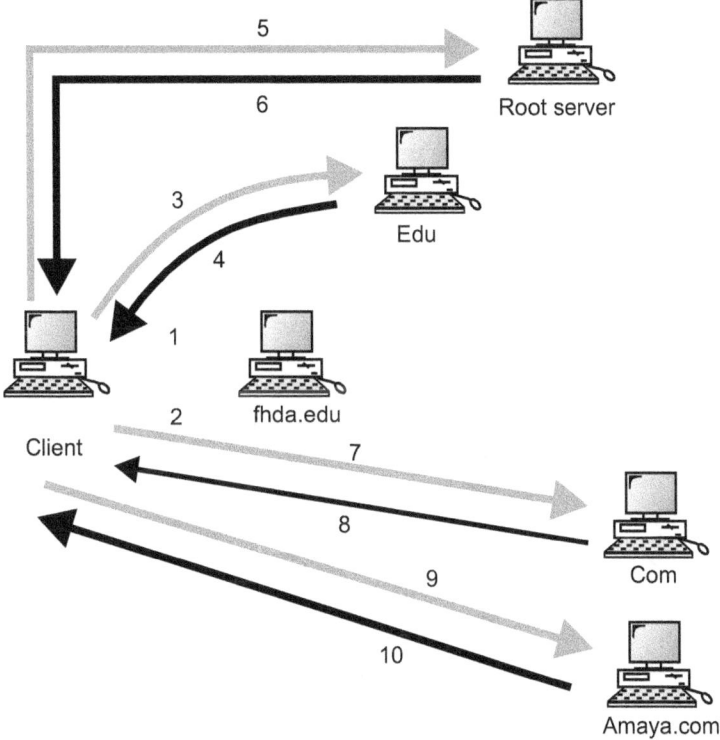

Fig. 3.34 : Iterative Resolution

Caching :

- After getting the query, server does searching in the database.
- Searching mechanism requires some time. Reduction of this search time can increase the server efficiency.
- For reducing the search time, DNS uses a mechanism known as caching.
- When a server asks for mapping from another server and receives the response, it stores this information in its cache memory before sending it to client.

- If the same or another client asks for the same mapping, it can check the cache memory and resolve the problem, so it reduces the time that is required for searching in the database.
- Caching speeds up the resolution, but it can also be problematic. If the server caches a mapping for a long time, it may send outdated mapping to the client.
- There are two solutions on this problem. First, the authority server always adds information to the mapping called time-to-live (TTL).
- It defines the time in seconds that the receiving server can cache the information. After that time, the mapping is invalid and any query must be sent again to the authority server.
- In the second solution, DNS server requires that each server keep a TTL counter for each mapping it caches. The cache memory must be searched periodically and those mapping with an expired TTL must be washed out.

3.12.11 DNS Messages

DNS has two types of messages : query and response. See the following figure.

Fig. 3.35 : DNS Messages

Both types have same format. The query message consists of a header and question record; the response message consists of a header, question records, authoritative records and additional records. Refer the following Fig. 3.36.

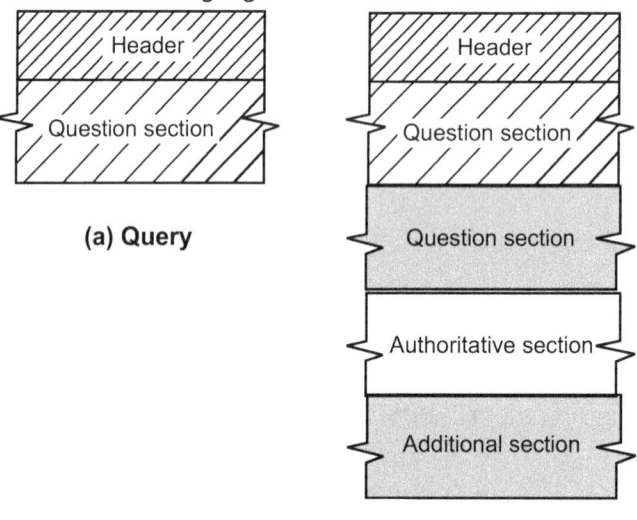

Fig. 3.36 : Query and Response Messages

Header :

Both the query and response messages have the same header format with some fields set to zero for the query message.

The header is of 12 bytes. The format of the header is shown in the following Fig. 3.37..

Identification	Flags
Number of question records	Number of answer records (all 0s in query message)
No. of authoritative records (all 0s in query message)	No. of additional records (all 0s in query message)

Fig. 3.37 : Header Format

The header fields are as follows :

- **Identification :** This is 16 bit field used by the client to match the response with the query.
- **Flags :** This is 16 bit field, which is a collection of subfields that defines the type of the message, type of the answers requested, type of the desired resolution and so on.
- **Number of question records :** It contains the number of queries in the question section of the message.
- **Number of answer records :** It contains the number of answer records in the answer section of the response message. Its value is zero in the query message.
- **Number of authoritative records :** It contains the number of authoritative records in the authoritative section of the response message. Its value is zero in the query message.
- **Number of additional records :** It contains the number of additional records in the additional section of the response message. Its value is zero in the query message.

Question section : This section consists of one or more question records. It is present on both query and response messages.

Answer Section : This is a section consisting of one or more resource records. It is present only in response message.

Authoritative Section : This section consists of one or more resource records. It is present only on response message. This section gives information about one or more authoritative servers for the query.

Additional Information Section : This is a section consisting of one or more resource records. It is present only on response message. This section provides additional information that may help the resolver.

3.13 RESOURCE RECORDS (RR)

- DNS distributed database stores resource records (RR) for the hostname to IP address mapping
- Each DNS reply message carries one or more resource records.
- Resource record is a four-tuple that contains the following fields :

{Name, Value, Type, TTL}

- TTL is the Time to live of the resource record; it determines the time at which the record should be removed from the cache memory. In the examples given below we will ignore the TTL field.
- The meaning of **Name** and **Value** tuples depends on **Type**.
- If Type=A, then Name is a Hostname and Value is the IP address of the Hostname. Thus, a Type A record provides the standard Hostname to IP address mapping.
  e.g. { relay1.bar.foo.com, 123.23.145.28, A} is a Type A record.
- If Type=NS, then Name is a domain (such as foo.com) and Value is the hostname of authoritative name server that knows how to obtain the IP addresses for hosts in the domain. This record is used to route DNS queries further along in the query chain. As an example, { foo.com, dns.foo.com, NS} is a Type NS record.
- If Type=CNAME, then Value is canonical hostname for the alias hostname. This record can provide querying hosts the canonical name for a hostname. As an example,
  { foo.com, relay1.bar.foo.com, CNAME } is a CNAME record.
- If Type=MX, then the value is canonical name of the mail server that has an alias hostname Name. As an example, { foo.com, mail.bar.foo.com, MX} is an MX record.
- If a name server is authoritative for a particular hostname, then the name server will contain a Type A record for the hostname.
- If a name server is not authoritative for a hostname, then the server will contain a Type NS record for the domain that includes the hostname; it will also contain a Type A record that provides a IP address of the name server in the value field of the NS record.

3.14 SIMPLE NETWORK MANAGEMENT PROTOCOL (SNMP)

- It is used for managing the networked devices on the internet.
- For managing these devices, it uses TCP/IP protocol suite.
- It provides a set of fundamental operations for monitoring and maintaining an internet.

3.14.1 Concept

- SNMP is an application level protocol.
- SNMP uses the concept of manager (host) and agent.
- Manager controls and monitors a set of agents. The agents are usually routers. See following figure.

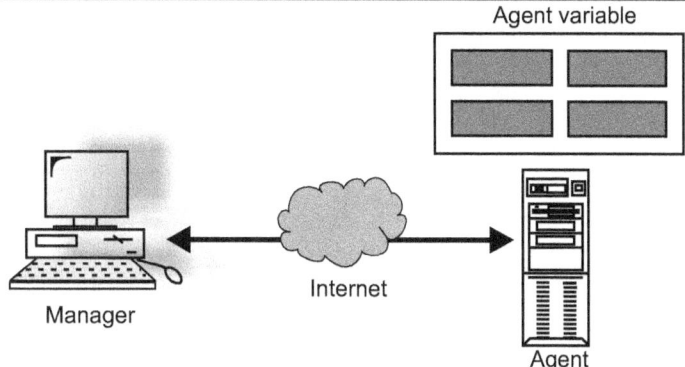

Fig. 3.38 : SNMP Concept

- The main aim of designing this protocol at the application layer is that, it can monitor devices manufactured by different vendors and installed on different physical networks.

Managers and Agents :
- Manager runs SNMP client program.
- A managed station, called agent is a router that runs SNMP server program.
- Management is achieved through simple interaction between a manager and an agent.
- The agent keeps performance information in a database.
- The manager has access to the values in the database.
- The manager can make the agent (router) to perform certain actions.
- Agent can also helps in the management process. The server program running on the agent can check the environment and if it notice something unusual, it can send a warning message (trap) to a manager.

In short...
1. The manager checks the behaviour of the agent time to time by accessing its performance information from its database
2. The manager forces an agent to perform certain tasks by modifying the values in the agent database.
3. If some unusual situation occurs, the agent informs the management about it by sending a warning message (trap) to the manager.

SNMP provides three ways to access management information.

1. **Manager to Agent :** Manager sends a request to an agent and agent responds to it. The request is usually to retrieve or modify the management information associated with the agents (such as routers).
2. **Manager to another Manager :** Manager sends a request to another manager and latter responds to the request. The request is usually to notify the other manager about the management information associated with the manager.
3. **Agent to Manager :** Agent sends a request to the manager. The request is usually to notify a manager of an unusual situation.

3.14.2 SNMPv3 Defines Eight Types of Packets

GetRequest, GetNextRequest, GetBulkRequest, SetRequest, Response, Trap, InformRequest and Report. Refer following Fig. 3.39.

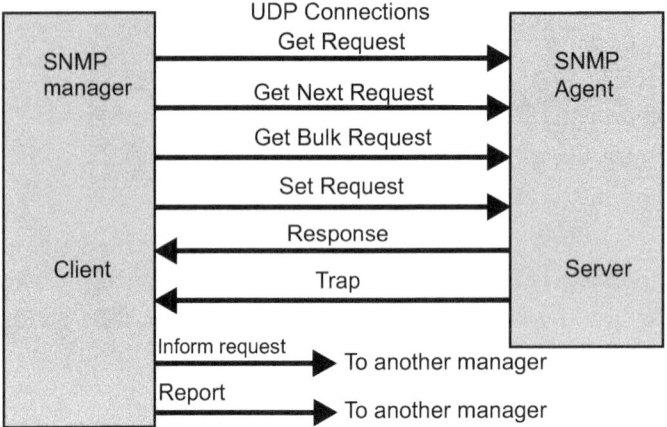

Fig. 3.39 : SNMP PDU

(i) **Get Request :** This PDU is sent from the manager to the agent to retrieve the value of a variable (or variables).

(ii) **Get Next Request :** If the agent variables are in the form of a table, the manager can not use GetRequest message, as it does not know where the current table pointer is pointing. This message is used in such cases.

(iii) **Get Bulk Request :** This is sent from the manager to the agent to retrieve a large amount (bulk) of data. Instead of using multiple GetRequest and GetNextRequest messages, GetBulkRequest is preferred.

(iv) **Set Request :** This is send from the manager to the agent to set a value of a variable.

(v) **Response :** It is sent from the agent to the manager in response to GetRequest or GetNextRequest. It contains the value(s) of variable(s) requested by the manager.

(vi) **Trap :** The agent can report an unusual event (it can be an error) to manager using this message.

(vii) **Inform Request :** It is sent from one manager to another remote manager to get the value of some variables from agents under the control of remote manager.

(viii) **Report :** It is not yet in use but it is designed to report some types of errors between the managers.

EXERCISE

1. Write a short note on session layer.
2. Explain session layer services.
3. Explain presentation layer. Why it is required ?
4. What is the use of HTTP ?
5. Write a short note on HTTP messages.
6. Explain methods in URL field.
7. Why HTTP is a stateless protocol ?
8. Explain HTTP connection types.
9. Write a short note on WWW.
10. Explain browser architecture in detail.
11. What are the types of web documents ? Explain each one of them.
12. Write a short note on HTML.
13. Explain the structure of web page.
14. Write down some of the HTML tags that you know.
15. What is common gateway interface ?
16. Write a short note on Active Documents.
17. Explain File Transfer Protocol in detail.
18. Write down the various FTP commands that you are aware of.
19. What is Trivial File Transfer Protocol ? How it is different from normal File Transfer Protocol ?
20. Compare FTP and TFTP.
21. What is Simple Mail Transfer Protocol ? Why to use it ?
22. Write a short note on Post Office Protocol (POP)
23. Explain IMAP4 in detail.
24. What is Multipurpose Internet Mail Extensions (MIME) ?
25. Write a short note on the working of Domain Name System.
26. What is domain name space ?
27. How domain name-address resolution take place ?

28. Explain following terms :
    (a) Recursive resolution
    (b) Iterative resolution.
29. Explain the types of DNS messages.
30. What is Resource Records (RRs) ?
31. Write a short note on Simple Network Management Protocol (SNMP) ?
32. Explain various packet types of SNMPv3.
33. What is caching ?

QUESTIONS

1. What do you mean by statelessness and cookies ? Explain.
2. What are dynamic and active pages ?
3. Explain how name resolution happens in DNS. Enlist all the resource records and its function.
4. Differentiate between FTP and TFTP.
5. Discuss various management categories used in network management.
6. Explain SNMP model with its major components.
7. In SMTP, if we send a one line message between two users, how many lines of commands and responses are exchanged ? Give the example.
8. Why Common Gateway Interface (CGI) is required in dynamic web pages ?
9. Discuss the role of SMI in SNMP. Give the data types supported by SMI.
10. Explain the MIB along with its structure
11. List and describe seven message types in SNMP.
12. How to receive the information about device interface and routing information of remote host by using SNMP protocol ?
13. Can a computer have two DNS names that fall in two different top level domains ? If so, give an example. If not, explain why not.
14. Compare between FTP and TFTP.
15. Why cookies are important ? What will happen if cookies are omitted?
16. POP3 allows users to fetch and download e-mail from a remote mailbox. Does this mean that the internal format of mailboxes has to be standardized so any POP3 program on the client side can read the mailbox on any mail server ? Discuss your answer.

17. What is the need of SMI ? Describe the structure of SMI.
18. How SNMP messages are used to monitor and to control the network elements ?
19. What is FTP ? Where and when it is used ? Why does not require 2 ports ? Explain at least 5 user commands used in FTP ?
20. Differentiate between persistent and non-persistent HTTP connection.
21. What is the difference between IMAP and POP 3 protocols ? Explain when and where they are used ?
22. What is the purpose of SMI and MIB in relation to SNMP ?
23. Explain the terms : managing entity, managed device, management agents, MIB in network management context.
24. List the five areas of network management and explain the necessity of each.
25. In SMTP, if we send a one line message between two users, how many lines of commands and responses are exchanged ? Give the example.
26. Explain how DNS service works.
27. Why Common Gateway Interface (CGI) is required in dynamic web pages ?
28. Compare between FTP and TFTP.
29. Explain the MIB along with its structure.
30. Discuss the role of SMI in SNMP. Give the data types supported by SMI.
31. Compare and contrast FTP and TFTP.
32. Explain at least 8 commands of FTP in brief.
33. Explain how DNS service works.
34. Where and why do we use MIME ?
35. List the similarities and differences between POP3 and IMAP. Which protocol is better and why ?
36. Explain RSVP. Why this protocol is needed ?
37. Explain what is MIB along with its structure.
38. What is the purpose of SMI and MIB in relation to SNMP ?
39. How SNMP messages are used to monitor and to control the network elements ?
40. List and explain the principle components of network management architecture.
41. List the 5 areas of network management and explain the necessity of each.
42. What is CGI ? Where and how it is used ?
43. Compare between FTP and TFTP.

44. Explain how DNS works.
45. What is cookie ? Where and how it is used ?
46. Differentiate between POP3 and IMAP.
47. Write a note on MIME.
48. What is MIB ? Explain its structure.
49. Discuss the role of SMI in SNMP. Give the data types supported by SMI.
50. How SNMP messages are used to monitor and control the network elements ?

Unit - IV
WIRELSS LANS, PANS AND MANS

4.1 INFRASTRUCTURE AND AD HOC NETWORKS

The IEEE standard defines the ad-hoc mode as Independent Basic Service Set (IBSS), and the infrastructure mode as Basic Service Set (BSS).

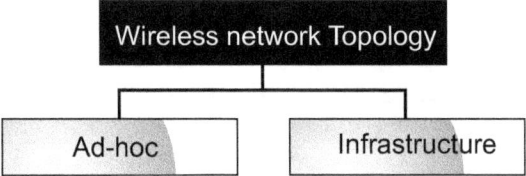

Fig. 4.1 : Wireless Network Topology

4.1.1 Ad-Hoc (Peer-to-Peer) Network

In the most basic form, stations communicate directly with each other on a peer-to-peer level sharing a given cell coverage area.

There is no base and no one gives permission to talk. Mostly these networks are spontaneous and can be setup rapidly.

This type of networks is spatially limited and is often formed on a temporary basis, and is commonly referred to as an ad-hoc network, or Independent Basic Service Set (IBSS). e.g. communication and data transfer between two Bluetooth enabled mobile phones.

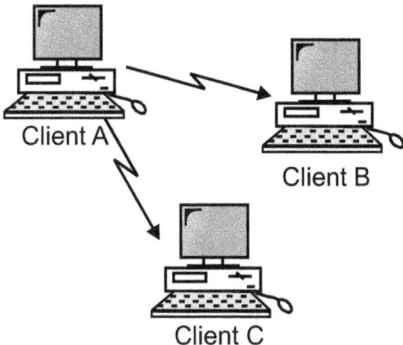

Fig. 4.2 : ad-hoc Network

In ad-hoc mode, each client communicates directly with the other clients within the network (without the help of access points).

Ad-hoc mode is designed such that only the clients within transmission range (within the same cell) of each other can communicate.

Infrastructure Network

In infrastructure mode, each client sends all of it's communications to a central station, or access point (AP). The access point acts as an Ethernet bridge and forwards the communications onto the appropriate network, either the wired network, or the wireless network.

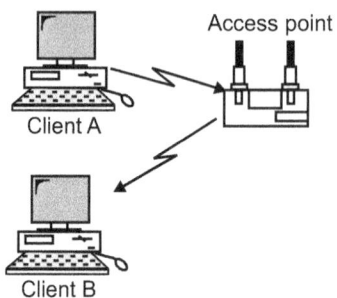

Fig. 4.3 : Infrastructure Network

In most instances, the BSS contains an Access Point (AP). The main function of an AP is to form a bridge between wireless and wired LANs. The AP is analogous to a base station used in cellular phone networks. When an AP is present, stations do not communicate on a peer-to-peer basis. All communications between stations or between a station and a wired network client go through the AP. APs are not mobile, and form part of the wired network infrastructure. A BSS in this configuration (Fig. 4.3) is said to be operating in the infrastructure mode.

4.1.2 HOW CLIENT JOIN BSS OR INFRASTRUCTURE WIRELESS NETWORK ?

All access points transmit a beacon management frame at fixed interval. To associate with an access point and join a BSS, a client listens for beacon messages to identify the access points within range. The client then selects the BSS to join in a vendor independent manner. For instance on the Apple Macintosh, all of the network names (or service set identifiers (SSID)) which are usually contained in the beacon frame are presented to the user so that they may select the network to join. A client may also send a **probe** request management frame to find an access point affiliated with a desired SSID. After identifying an access point, the client and the access point perform a mutual authentication by exchanging several management frames as part of the process.

After successful authentication, the client moves into the second state, authenticated and unassociated. Moving from the second state to the third and final state, authenticated and associated, involves the client sending an association request frame, and the access point responding with an association response frame. After this process, the client becomes a peer on the wireless network, and can transmit data frames on the network.

4.2 COMPARISON OF WIRELESS NETWORKS IN ISM BAND

Wireless means transmitting signals using radio waves as the medium instead of wires. Wireless technologies are used for tasks as simple as switching off the television or as complex as supplying the sales force with information from an automated enterprise application while in the field. Now cordless keyboards and mice, PDAs, pagers and digital and cellular phones have become part of our daily life.

Some of the inherent characteristics of wireless communications systems which make it attractive for users, are given below:

- **Mobility:** A wireless communications system allows users to access information beyond their desk and conduct business from anywhere without having a wire connectivity.
- **Reachability:** Wireless communications systems enable people to be better connected and reachable without any limitation of any location.
- **Simplicity:** Wireless communication system are easy and fast to deploy in comparison of cabled network. Initial setup cost could be a bit high but other advantages overcome that high cost.
- **Maintainability:** Being a wireless system, you do no need to spend too much to maintain a wireless network setup.
- **Roaming Services:** Using a wireless network system, you can provide service any where any time including train, buses, aeroplanes etc.
- **New Services:** Wireless communications systems provide new smart services like SMS and MMS

(1) Bluetooth over IEEE 802.15.1

Bluetooth, also known as the IEEE 802.15.1 standard is based on a wireless radio system designed for short-range and cheap devices to replace cables for computer peripherals, such as mice, keyboards, joysticks, and printers. This range of applications is known as wireless personal area network (WPAN). Two connectivity topologies are defined in Bluetooth: the piconet and scatternet. A piconet is a WPAN formed by a Bluetooth device serving as a master in the piconet and one or more Bluetooth devices serving as slaves. A frequency-hopping channel based on the address of the master defines each piconet. All devices participating in communications in a given piconet are synchronized using the clock of the master.

Slaves communicate only with their master in a point-to-point fashion under the control of the master. The master's transmissions may be either point-to-point or point-tomultipoint. Also, besides in an active mode, a slave device can be in the parked or standby modes so as to reduce power consumptions. A scatternet is a collection of operational Bluetooth piconets overlapping in time and space. Two piconets can be connected to form a scatternet. A Bluetooth device may participate in several piconets at the same time, thus allowing for the possibility that information could flow beyond the coverage area of the single piconet. A device in a scatternet could be a slave in several piconets, but master in

only one of them.

(2) UWB over IEEE 802.15.3

UWB has recently attracted much attention as an indoor short-range high-speed wireless communication. One of the most exciting characteristics of UWB is that its bandwidth is over 110 Mbps (up to 480 Mbps) which can satisfy most of the multimedia applications such as audio and video delivery in home networking and it can also act as a wireless cable replacement of high speed serial bus such as USB 2.0 and IEEE 1394. Following the United States and the Federal Communications Commission (FCC) frequency allocation for UWB in February 2002, the Electronic Communications Committee (ECC TG3) is progressing in the elaboration of a regulation for the UWB technology in Europe. From an implementation point of view, several solutions have been developed in order to use the UWB technology in compliance with the FCC's regulatory requirements.

Among the existing PHY solutions, in IEEE 802.15 Task Group 3a (TG3a), multiband orthogonal frequency-division multiplexing (MB-OFDM), a carrier-based system dividing UWB bandwidth to sub-bands, and direct-sequence UWB (DS-UWB), an impulse-based system that multiplies an input bit with the spreading code and transmits the data by modulating the element of the symbol with a short pulse have been proposed by the WiMedia Alliance and the UWB Forum, respectively. The TG3a was established in January 2003 to define an alternative PHY layer of 802.15.3. However, after three years of a jammed process in IEEE 802.15.3a, supporters of both proposals, MB-OFDM and DS-UWB, supported the shut down of the IEEE 802.15.3a task group without conclusion in January 2006. On the other hand, IEEE 802.15.3b, the amendment to the 802.15.3 MAC sublayer has been approved and released in March 2006.

(3) ZigBee over IEEE 802.15.4

ZigBee over IEEE 802.15.4, defines specifications for low rate WPAN (LR-WPAN) for supporting simple devices that consume minimal power and typically operate in the personal operating space (POS) of 10m. ZigBee provides self-organized, multi-hop, and reliable mesh networking with long battery Lifetime. Two different device types can participate in an LR-WPAN network: a full-function device (FFD) and a reduced-function device (RFD). The FFD can operate in three modes serving as a PAN coordinator, a coordinator, or a device. An FFD can talk to RFDs or other FFDs, while an RFD can talk only to an FFD.

An RFD is intended for applications that are extremely simple, such as a light switch or a passive infrared sensor. They do not have the need to send large amounts of data and may only associate with a single FFD at a time. Consequently, the RFD can be implemented using minimal resources and memory capacity. After an FFD is activated for the first time, it may establish its own network and become the PAN coordinator. All star networks operate independently from all other star networks currently in operation. This is achieved by choosing a PAN identifier, which is not currently used by any other network within the radio sphere of influence. Once the PAN identifier is chosen, the PAN coordinator can allow other devices to join its network. An RFD may connect to a cluster tree network as a leave node at the end of a branch, because it may only associate with one FFD at a time. Any of the FFDs may act as a coordinator and provide synchronization services to other devices or other coordinators. Only one of these coordinators can be the overall PAN coordinator, which may have greater computational resources than any other device in the PAN.

(4) Wi-Fi over IEEE 802.11a/b/g

Wireless fidelity (Wi-Fi) includes IEEE 802.11a/b/g standards for wireless local area networks (WLAN). It allows users to surf the Internet at broadband speeds when connected to an access point (AP) or in ad hoc mode. The IEEE 802.11 architecture consists of several components that interact to provide a wireless LAN that supports station mobility transparently to upper layers. The basic cell of an IEEE 802.11

LAN is called a basic service set (BSS), which is a set of mobile or fixed stations. If a station moves out of its BSS, it can no longer directly communicate with other members of the BSS. Based on the BSS, IEEE 802.11 employs the independent basic service set (IBSS) and extended service set (ESS) network configurations. As shown in Fig. , the IBSS operation is possible when IEEE 802.11 stations are able to communicate directly without any AP. Because this type of IEEE 802.11 LAN is often formed without pre-planning, for only as long as the LAN is needed, this type of operation is often referred to as an ad hoc network. Instead of existing independently, a BSS may also form a component of an extended form of network that is built with multiple BSSs. The architectural component used to interconnect BSSs is the distribution system (DS). The DS with APs allow IEEE 802.11 to create an ESS network of arbitrary size and complexity. This type of operation is often referred to as an infrastructure network.

(5) WiMAX over 802.16

- Acronym for Worldwide Interoperability for Microwave Access.
- Based on Wireless MAN technology.
- A wireless technology optimized for the delivery of IP centric services over a wide area.
- A scaleable wireless platform for constructing alternative and complementary broadband networks.

- A certification that denotes interoperability of equipment built to the IEEE 802.16 or compatible standard. The IEEE 802.16 Working Group develops standards that address two types of usage models:
  - A fixed usage model (IEEE 802.16-2004).
  - A portable usage model (IEEE 802.16e).

WiMAX is one of the hottest broadband wireless technologies around today. WiMAX systems are expected to deliver broadband access services to residential and enterprise customers in an economical way. Loosely, WiMax is a standardized wireless version of Ethernet intended primarily as an alternative to wire technologies (such as Cable Modems, DSL and T1/E1 links) to provide broadband access to customer premises. More strictly, WiMAX is an industry trade organization formed by leading communications, component and equipment companies to promote and certify compatibility and interoperability of broadband wireless access equipment that conforms to the IEEE 802.16 and ETSI HIPERMAN standards.

WiMAX would operate similar to WiFi but at higher speeds over greater distances and for a greater number of users. WiMAX has the ability to provide service even in areas that are difficult for wired infrastructure to reach and the ability to overcome the physical limitations of traditional wired infrastructure.

WiMAX was formed in April 2001, in anticipation of the publication of the original 10-66 GHz IEEE 802.16 specifications. WiMAX is to 802.16 as the WiFi Alliance is to 802.11

WiMAX is such an easy term that people tend to use it for the 802.16 standards and technology themselves, although strictly it applies only to systems that meet specific conformance criteria laid down by the WiMAX Forum.

The 802.16a standard for 2-11 GHz is a wireless metropolitan area network (MAN) technology that will provide broadband wireless connectivity to Fixed, Portable and Nomadic devices. It can be used to connect 802.11 hot spots to the Internet, provide campus connectivity, and provide a wireless alternative to cable and DSL for last mile broadband access.

WiMax Speed and Range:

WiMAX is expected to offer initially up to about 40 Mbps capacity per wireless channel for both fixed and portable applications, depending on the particular technical configuration chosen, enough to support hundreds of businesses with T-1 speed connectivity and thousands of residences with DSL speed connectivity. WiMAX can support voice and video as well as Internet data. WiMax will be to provide wireless broadband access to buildings, either in competition to existing wired networks or alone in currently unserved rural or thinly populated areas. It can also be used to connect WLAN hotspots to the Internet. WiMAX is also intended to provide broadband connectivity to mobile devices. It would not be as fast as in these fixed applications, but expectations are for about 15 Mbps capacity in a 3 km cell coverage area. With WiMAX users could really cut free from today's Internet access arrangements and be able to go online at broadband speeds, almost wherever they like from within a MetroZone.

WiMAX could potentially be deployed in a variety of spectrum bands: 2.3GHz, 2.5GHz, 3.5GHz, and 5.8GHz

- WiMAX can satisfy a variety of access needs. Potential applications include extending broadband capabilities to bring them closer to subscribers, filling gaps in cable, DSL and T1 services, WiFi and cellular backhaul, providing last-100 meter access from fibre to the curb and giving service providers another cost-effective option for supporting broadband services.
- WiMAX can support very high bandwidth solutions where large spectrum deployments (i.e. >10 MHz) are desired using existing infrastructure keeping costs down while delivering the bandwidth needed to support a full range of high-value multimedia services.
- WiMAX can help service providers meet many of the challenges they face due to increasing customer demands without discarding their existing infrastructure investments because it has the ability to seamlessly interoperate across various network types.
- WiMAX can provide wide area coverage and quality of service capabilities for applications ranging from real-time delay-sensitive voice-over-IP (VoIP) to real-time streaming video and non-real-time downloads, ensuring that subscribers obtain the performance they expect for all types of communications.
- WiMAX, which is an IP-based wireless broadband technology, can be integrated into both wide-area third-generation (3G) mobile and wireless and wireline networks allowing it to become part of a seamless anytime, anywhere broadband access solution.

Ultimately, WiMAX is intended to serve as the next step in the evolution of 3G mobile phones, via a potential combination of WiMAX and CDMA standards called 4G.

4.3 FUNDAMENTALS OF WIRELESS LAN

Need of Wireless LAN :

There are many reasons :

- An increasing number of LAN users are becoming mobile.
- These mobile users require that they should be connected to the network regardless of where they are because they want simultaneous access to the network.
- This makes the use of cables, or wired LANs, impractical if not impossible.
- Wireless LANs are very easy to install.
- There is no requirement for wiring every workstation and every room.
- This ease of installation makes wireless LANs inherently flexible.
- If a workstation must be moved, it can be done easily and without additional wiring, cable drops or reconfiguration of the network.

- Another advantage is its portability. If a company moves to a new location, the wireless system is much easier to move than ripping up all of the cables that a wired system would have snaked throughout the building.
- Most of these advantages also translate into monetary savings.
- Ad Hoc networks (discussed later) are easily set up in a wireless environment.

How Wireless LAN Work ?
- Wireless LAN (WLAN) uses electromagnetic airwaves (radio and infrared) to communicate information from one point to another without relying on any physical connection.
- Radio waves are often referred to as radio carriers because they simply perform the function of delivering energy to a remote receiver.
- The data being transmitted is superimposed on the radio carrier so that it can be accurately extracted at the receiving end.
- This is generally referred to as modulation of the carrier by the information being transmitted.
- Once data is superimposed (modulated) onto the radio carrier, the radio signal occupies more than a single frequency, since the frequency or bit rate of the modulating information adds to the carrier.
- Multiple radio carriers can exist in the same space at the same time without interfering with each other if the radio waves are transmitted on different radio frequencies.
- In a typical WLAN configuration, a transmitter/receiver (transceiver) device, called an access point (AP), connects to the wired network from a fixed location using standard Ethernet cable.
- At a minimum, the access point receives, buffers, and transmits data between the WLAN and the wired network infrastructure.
- A single access point can support a small group of users and can function within a range of less than one hundred to several hundred feet.
- The access point (or the antenna attached to the access point) is usually mounted high but may be mounted essentially anywhere that is practical as long as the desired radio coverage is obtained.
- End users access the WLAN through wireless LAN adapters, which are implemented as USB adapters, PC cards in notebook computers, ISA or PCI cards in desktop computers, or fully integrated devices within handheld computers. WLAN adapters provide an interface between the client network operating system (NOS) and the airwaves (via an antenna).

The nature of the wireless connection is transparent to the network operating system.

Advantages of Wireless LANs :

Wireless networks offer the following productivity, service, convenience, and cost advantages over traditional wired networks :

1. **Mobility improves productivity and service :** Wireless LAN systems can provide LAN users with access to real-time information anywhere in their organization. This mobility supports productivity and service opportunities not possible with wired networks.
2. **Installation Speed and Simplicity :** Installing a wireless LAN system can be fast and easy and can eliminate the need to pull cable through walls and ceilings.
3. **Installation Flexibility :** Wireless technology allows the network to go where wire cannot go.
4. **Reduced Cost-of-Ownership :** While the initial investment required for wireless LAN hardware can be higher than the cost of wired LAN hardware, overall installation expenses and life-cycle costs can be significantly lower. Long-term cost benefits are greatest in dynamic environments requiring frequent moves, adds, and changes.
5. **Scalability :** Wireless LAN systems can be configured in a variety of topologies to meet the needs of specific applications and installations. Configurations are easily changed and range from independent networks suitable for a small number of users to full infrastructure networks of thousands of users that allow roaming over a broad area.

Applications of Wireless LANs :

- LAN extensions
- Ad-hoc networks
- Nomadic access and so many...

4.4 ARCHITECTURE OF WIRELESS NETWORK

Each computer, mobile which is portable or fixed, is referred to as a station in 802.11 wireless networks. When two or more stations come together to communicate with each other, they form a Basic Service Set (BSS).The minimum BSS consists of two stations. 802.11 LANs use the BSS as the standard building block. The BSS can be either without AP (Access Point) or with AP (Access Point) which is as shown in Fig. 4.4. The BSS without AP can not send data to another BSS. So it is called as standalone or ad-hoc network.

Two or more BSSs are interconnected using a Distribution System or DS. This concept of DS increases network coverage, which can be either wired or wireless. Entry to the DS is accomplished with the use of access points. An access point is a station, thus addressable. So data moves between the BSS and the DS with the help of these access points. Creating large and complex networks using BSSs and DSs leads us to the next level of hierarchy, the Extended Service Set or ESS.

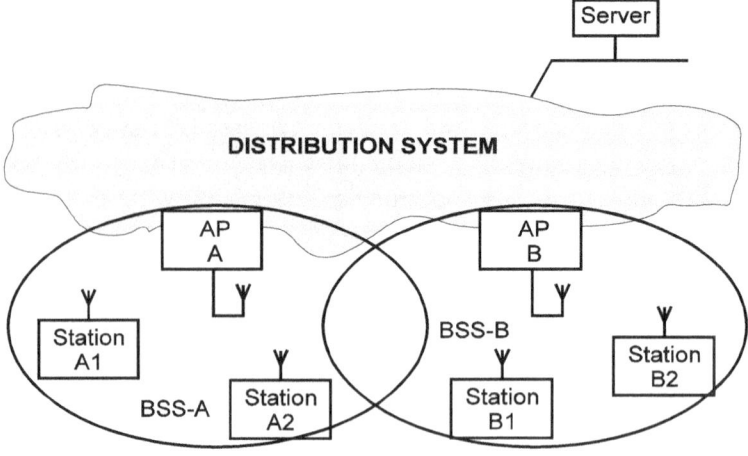

Fig. 4.4 : Components of Wireless Local Area Network

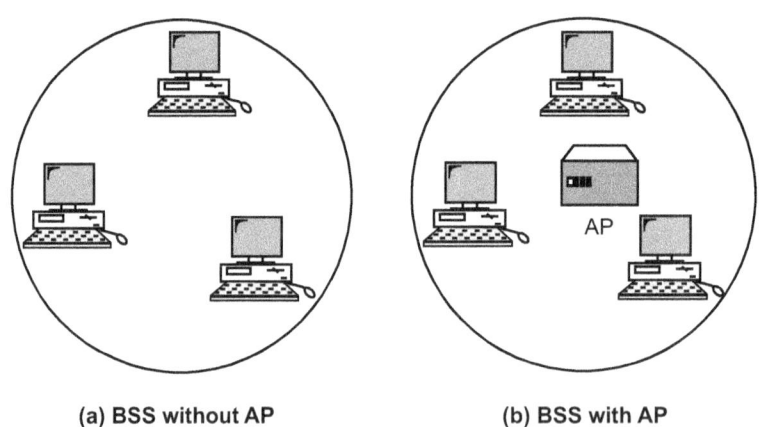

(a) BSS without AP (b) BSS with AP

Fig. 4.5 : Types of BSS

An Extended Service set contains two or more BSS with APs. The BSSs in the system are connected to each other via a distribution system which is generally a wired LAN as shown in Fig. 4.5. The beauty of the ESS is the entire network looks like an independent basic service set.

This means that stations within the ESS can communicate or even more between BSSs transparently. The implementation of the DS is not specified by 802.11. So a distribution system may be created from existing or new technologies. As the implementation for the DS is not specified, 802.11 does specify the services, which the DS must support. Services are divided into two sections, Station Services (SS) and Distribution System Services (DSS).

4.5 DSS SERVICES

There are five services provided by the DSS : Association, Re-association, Disassociation, Distribution, and Integration. The first three services deal with station mobility.

No-Transition : If a station is moving within its own BSS or is not moving, the stations mobility is termed as No-transition.

BSS Transition : If a station moves between BSSs within the same ESS, its mobility is termed as BSS transition.

ESS Transition : If the station moves between BSSs of differing ESSs, it is ESS transition.

The DSS services are explained below :

1. **Association :**
   - A station must affiliate itself with the BSS infrastructure if it wants to use the LAN.
   - This is done by associating itself with an access point.
   - Associations are dynamic in nature because stations move, turn on or turn off.
   - A station can only be associated with one AP. This ensures that the DS always knows where the station is.
   - Association supports no-transition mobility but is not enough to support BSS transition.

2. **Re-association :**
   - This service allows the station to switch its association from one AP to another.
   - Both association and re-association are initiated by the station.

3. **Disassociation :**
   - It is when the association between the station and the AP is terminated.
   - This can be initiated by either party.
   - A disassociated station cannot send or receive data.

4. **Distribution :**
   - This service determines how to route frames sent to the recipient.
   - The message is sent to the local AP (input AP), then distributed through the DS to the AP (output AP) that the recipient is associated with.
   - If the sender and receiver are in the same BSS, the input and output APs are the same. So the distribution service is logically invoked whether the data is going through the DS or not.

5. **Integration :**
   - This service handles situation when a frame needs to be sent through a non 802.11 network with a different addressing scheme or frame format, this service handles required translation. Thus 802.x LANs are integrated into the 802.11 DS.

Notice that I have not mentioned ESS-transition. That is because it is not supported. A station can move to a new ESS but will have to reinitiate connections.

4.6 SS SERVICES

Station services are **Authentication, De-authentication, Privacy, and MAC Service Data Unit (MSDU) Delivery**.

1. **Authentication :**
   - With a wireless system, the medium is not exactly bounded as with a wired system.
   - In order to control access to the network, stations must first establish their identity.
   - This is much like trying to enter a radio net in the military. Before you are acknowledged and allowed to converse, you must first pass a series of tests to ensure that you are who you say you are. That is really all authentication is.
   - There are two types of authentication services offered by 802.11.
     a. **Open System Authentication :** This means that anyone who attempts to authenticate will receive authentication.
     b. **Shared Key Authentication :** In order to become authenticated the users must be in possession of a shared secret. The shared secret is implemented with the use of the Wired Equivalent Privacy (WEP) algorithm. The shared secret is delivered to all stations ahead of time in some secure method (such as someone walking around and loading the secret onto each station).

2. **De-authentication :**
   - It is when either the station or AP wishes to terminate a stations authentication.
   - When this happens the station is automatically disassociated.

3. **Privacy :**
   - It is an encryption algorithm, which is used so that other 802.11 users cannot eavesdrop (maliciously get the data) on your LAN traffic.
   - IEEE 802.11 specifies Wired Equivalent Privacy (WEP) as an optional algorithm to satisfy privacy. If WEP is not used then stations are "in the clear" or "in the red", meaning that their traffic is not encrypted.
   - Data transmitted in the clear are called plaintext. Data transmissions, which are encrypted, are called ciphertext.
   - All stations start "in the red" until they are authenticated.

4. **MSDU Delivery :**
   - Data transmission over 802.11 is not guaranteed to be completely reliable.
   - MSDU delivery ensures that the information in the MAC service data unit is delivered between the medium access control service access points with detecting and correcting errors.

Authentication is basically a network wide password. Privacy is whether or not encryption is used.

4.7 THE 802.11 PROTOCOL STACK

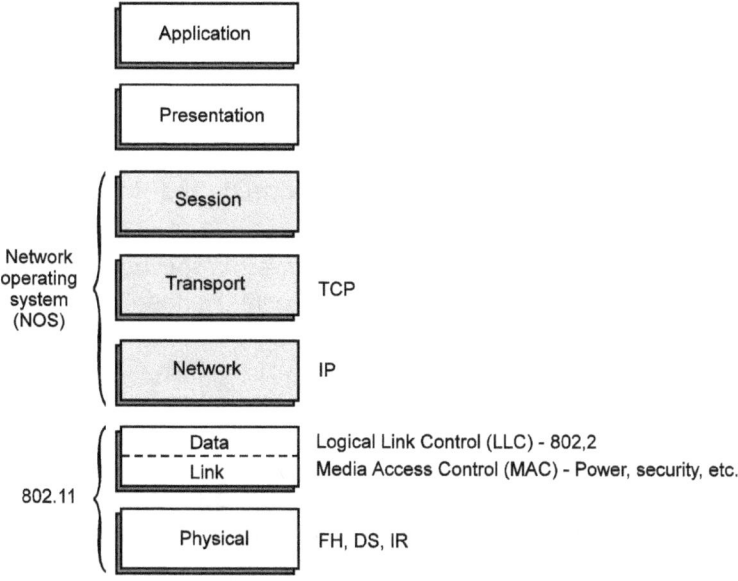

Fig. 4.6 : Protocol stack of 802.11

4.7.1 Physical Layer

There are three media that can be used for transmission over wireless LANs.
1. Infrared,
2. Radio frequency and
3. Microwave.

In 1985, the United States released the industrial, scientific, and medical (ISM) frequency bands.

These bands are 902-928MHz, 2.4 - 2.4853 GHz, and 5.725 - 5.85 GHz and do not require licensing by the Federal Communications Commission (FCC).

- This prompted most of the wireless LAN products to operate within ISM bands.

4.7.1.1 Infrared

- Infrared (IR) systems use very high frequencies to carry data.
- Like light, IR cannot penetrate opaque objects; it is either directed (line-of-sight) or diffuse technology.
- Inexpensive directed systems provide very limited range (3ft) and typically are used for personal area networks but occasionally are used in specific wireless LAN applications.
- Diffuse (or reflective) IR wireless LAN systems do not require line-of-sight, but cells (BSS) are limited to individual rooms.

- Infrared systems are simple in design and therefore inexpensive.
- They use the same signal frequencies used on fiber optic links.
- IR systems detect only the amplitude of the signal and so interference is greatly reduced.
- These systems are not bandwidth limited and thus can achieve transmission speeds greater than the other systems.
- Infrared transmission operates in the light spectrum and does not require a license from the FCC to operate.
- The drawbacks to IR systems are that the transmission spectrum is shared with the sun and other things such as fluorescent lights. If there is enough interference from other sources it can make the LAN useless.
- IR systems require a clear line of sight (LOS). IR signals cannot penetrate opaque objects.

4.7.1.2 Microwave

Microwave (MW) systems operate at less than 500 milliwatts of power in compliance with FCC regulations. They use narrow-band transmission with single frequency modulation and are set up mostly in the 5.8 GHz band. The big advantage to Microwave systems is higher throughput achieved.

4.7.1.3 Radio Frequency

Radio frequency technique can be implemented in two ways narrowband technology or spread spectrum technology. Radio frequency systems must use spread spectrum technology since it doesn't require license from FCC. This spread spectrum technology currently comes in two types : direct sequence spread spectrum (DSSS) and frequency hopping spread spectrum (FHSS).

1. Direct-Sequence Spread Spectrum (DSSS)

Direct-sequence spread spectrum (DSSS) generates a redundant bit pattern for each bit to be transmitted. This bit pattern is called a chip (or chipping code). The longer the chip, the greater the probability that the original data can be recovered and, of course, the more bandwidth required. Each bit is transmitted as 11 chips using a Barker Sequence. Even if one or more bits in the chip are damaged during transmission, statistical techniques embedded in the radio can recover the original data without the need for retransmission.

To an unintended receiver, DSSS appears as low-power wideband noise and is rejected (ignored) by most narrowband receivers. With direct sequence spread spectrum the transmission signal is spread over an allowed band.

A random binary string is used to modulate the transmitted signal. This random string is called the spreading code. The data bits are mapped to into a pattern of "chips" and mapped back into a bit at the destination. The number of chips that represent a bit is the spreading ratio.

The higher the spreading ratio, the more the signal is resistant to interference. The lower the spreading ratio, the more bandwidth is available to the user. The FCC dictates that the spreading ratio must be more than 10. IEEE 802.11 standard requires a spreading ratio of 11. The transmitter and the receiver must be synchronized with the same spreading code.

2. Frequency-Hopping Spread Spectrum (FHSS)

Frequency-hopping spread spectrum (FHSS) uses a narrowband carrier that changes frequency in a pattern known to both transmitter and receiver. To an unintended receiver, FHSS appears to be short-duration impulse noise. This technique splits the band into small 79 sub channels, each 1-MHz wide. The signal then hops from sub channel to sub channel transmitting short bursts of data on each channel for a set period of time, called dwell time. The hopping sequence must be synchronized at the sender and the receiver or information is lost. The FCC requires that the band is split into at least 75 subchannels and that the dwell time is no longer than 400 ms.

Frequency hopping is less susceptible to interference because the frequency is constantly shifting. This feature gives FH systems a high degree of security. In order to jam a frequency hopping system the whole band must be jammed. Most new products in wireless LAN technology are currently being developed with FHSS technology. Its only problem is its low bandwidth.

4.7.2 Medium Access Layer

With more and more companies and individuals requiring portable and mobile computing, the need for wireless local area networks continues to rise throughout the world. Because of this growth, IEEE formed a working group to develop a Medium Access Control (MAC) and Physical Layer (PHY) standard for wireless connectivity for stationary, portable, and mobile computers within a local area. This working group is IEEE 802.11.

4.7.2.1 Medium Access Control Protocol

Most wired LANs products use Carrier Sense Multiple Access with Collision Detection (CSMA/CD) as the MAC protocol. Carrier Sense means that the station will listen before it transmits. If there is already someone transmitting, then the station waits and tries again later. If no one is transmitting then the station goes ahead and sends what it has. But what if two stations send at the same time ? The transmissions will collide and the information will be lost. This is where Collision Detection comes into play. The station will listen to ensure that its transmission made it to the destination without collisions. If a collision occurred then the stations wait and try again later.

- The time the station waits is determined by the back off algorithm.

    This technique works great for wired LANs but wireless topologies can create a problem for CSMA/CD.

    The problem is the hidden node problem.

- **Hidden Node problem**

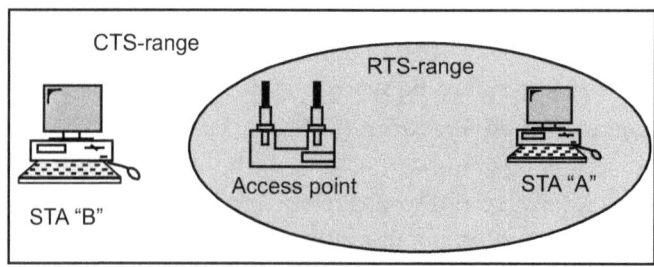

Fig. 4.7 : Hidden Node Problem

Since not all the stations are within radio range of each other, transmission going on in one part of a cell may not be received elsewhere in the same cell. In this Hidden Node problem, STA-B cannot hear request of STA-A since RTS-Range of STA-A is limited. So if node STA-A is transmitting, STA-B will not know and may transmit as well. This will result in collisions. To combat this problem, a second carrier sense mechanism is available. Virtual Carrier Sense enables a station to reserve the medium for a specified period of time through the use of RTS/CTS frames. In the case described above, STA-A sends a RTS frame to the AP. The RTS will not be heard by STA-B. The RTS frame contains a duration and ID field, which specifies the period of time for which the medium is reserved for a subsequent transmission.

The reservation information is stored in the Network Allocation Vector (NAV : internal reminders to keep quiet for a certain period of time) of all stations detecting the RTS frame. Upon receipt of the RTS, the AP responds with a CTS frame, which also contains a duration and ID field specifying the period of time for which the medium is reserved. While STA-B did not detect the RTS, it will detect the CTS and update its NAV accordingly. Thus, collision is avoided even though some nodes are hidden from other stations. This solution is called Carrier Sense Multiple Access with Collision Avoidance or CSMA/CA. Now consider Fig. 4.8 in which station-2 is transmitting to station-1. If station-3 senses the medium, then since station-2 comes in range with station-3. So station-3 will sense the transmission going on. So it will falsely decide that it should not transmit to station-4. Note that transmission from 3 to 4 is OK, even when station-2 is transmitting. This problem is called as exposed station problem.

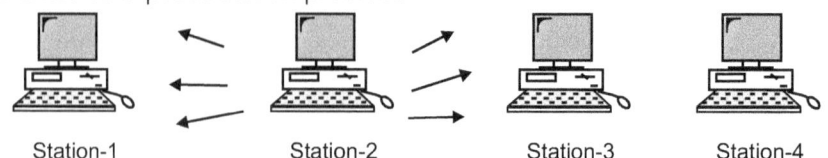

Fig. 4.8 : Exposed station problem

4.7.2.2 How CSMA/CA Work ?

1. The station listens before it sends. If someone is already transmitting, wait for a random period and try again. If no one is transmitting then it sends a short message. This

message is called the Ready To Send message (RTS). This message contains the destination address and the duration of the transmission.

2. Other stations now know that they must wait that long before they can transmit. The destination (AP) then sends a short message, which is the Clear To Send message (CTS). This message tells the source that it can send without fear of collisions.

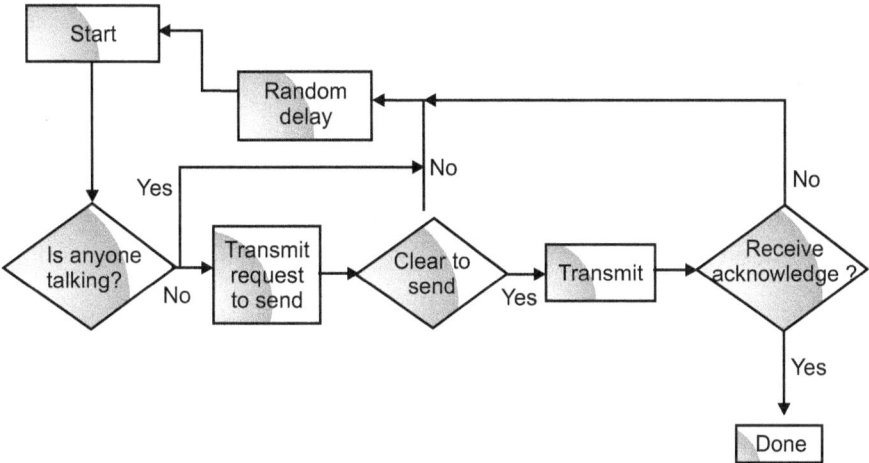

Fig. 4.9 : Working of CSMA/CA

3. Each packet is acknowledged. If an acknowledgement is not received, the MAC layer retransmits the data. This entire sequence is called the 4-way handshake (RTS->CTS->Data->ACK).

4.8 BLUETOOTH

Bluetooth is an emerging wireless communication technology that allows devices, within 10-100 meter proximity, to communicate with each other. The primary goal of this technology is to enable devices to communicate without physical cables. It is a worldwide specification for a small low-cost radio. It links mobile computers, mobile phones, other portable handheld devices, and provides Internet connectivity. It is developed, published and promoted by the Bluetooth Special Interest Group (SIG). Its key features are robustness, low complexity, low power and low cost. Bluetooth does not require direct line of sight and can also support multipoint communication in addition to point to point communication. The short range transceivers that are built into mobile gadgets to provide Bluetooth compatibility are designed to operate in the 2.45 GHz unlicensed radio band. It provides data rate up to 721 kbps as well as three 64 kbps voice channels. Through the use of frequency hopping, a Bluetooth transceiver can minimize the effect of interference from other signals by hopping to a new frequency after transmitting or receiving a packet.

(Bluetooth hop frequency is 1600 hops/second). Each Bluetooth gadget has a unique 12 bit address. In order for Bluetooth gadget A to connect with Bluetooth gadget B, gadget A must know the (12-bit) address of gadget B. Bluetooth supports gadget authentication and communications encryption. Bluetooth uses GFSK (Gaussian frequency shift keying) modulation technique.

4.8.1 Architecture

Bluetooth defines two type of networks :
1. Piconet &
2. Scatternet

We can assume piconet as a group of devices. A Bluetooth piconet consists of 1 master and 7 active slave device (all nodes must be within 10 meter range). All the slave devices are synchronized with the master device. There can be 255 parked nodes in the single piconet but at any time maximum 7 are communicating. A piconet is shown in Fig. 4.10.

Fig. 4.10 : A simple Piconet

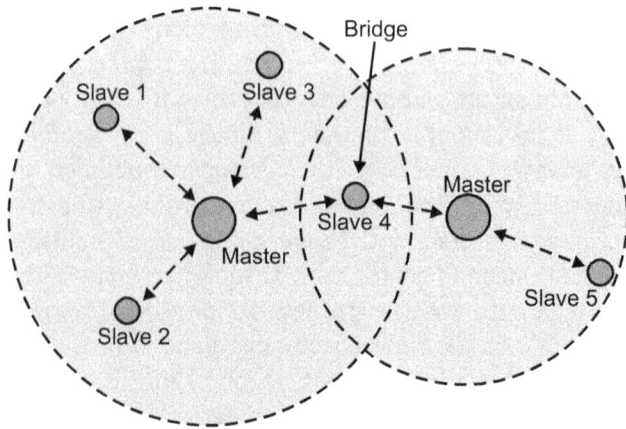

Fig. 4.11 : A simple scatternet

Two piconets can be connected through a common Bluetooth device (a gateway or bridge) to form a scatternet as shown in Fig. 4.11. These interconnected piconets within the scatternet can enable devices which are not directly communicating with each other, or which are out of range of another device, to exchange data through several hops in the scatternet. Current implementations of Bluetooth depend primarily on simple point-to-point data links between Bluetooth devices within direct range of each other.

4.8.2 The Bluetooth Protocol Stack

- The heart of the Bluetooth specification is the Bluetooth protocol stack. The protocol stack is shown in the figure given below :

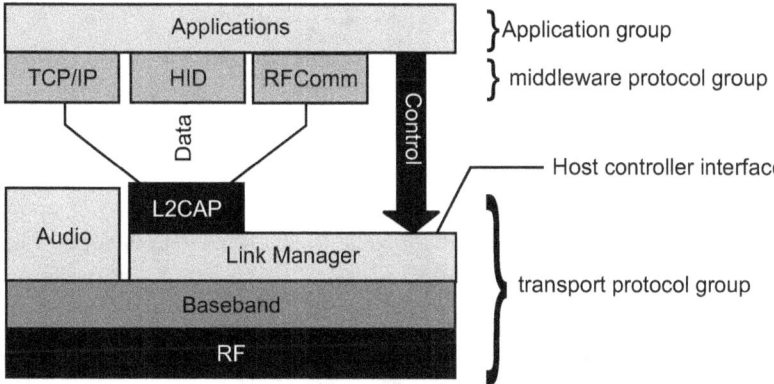

Bluetooth core protocol groups

Fig. 4.12 : Bluetooth protocol stack

The Bluetooth specification divides the Bluetooth protocol stack into three logical groups.

    (1) **Transport Protocol group,**

    (2) **Middleware Protocol group and**

    (3) **Application group**

The Transport group protocols allow Bluetooth devices to locate each other, and to manage physical and logical links with higher layer protocols and applications. The Radio, Baseband, Link Manager, Logical Link Control and Adaptation (L2CAP) layers and the Host Controller Interface (HCI) are included in the Transport Protocol group. These protocols support both asynchronous and synchronous transmission. All the protocols in the transport protocol group are required to support communications between Bluetooth devices.

The Middleware Protocol group includes third-party and industry-standard protocols, as well as Bluetooth SIG developed protocols. These protocols allow existing and new applications to operate over Bluetooth links.

Industry standard protocols include Point-to-Point Protocol (PPP), Internet Protocol (IP), Transmission Control Protocol (TCP), Wireless Application Protocols (WAP), and object exchange (OBEX) protocols.

Some of the layers in the transport protocol group are explained below :

- **(4) Radio layer :** The specification of the Radio layer is primarily concerned with the design of the Bluetooth transceivers.
- **(5) Baseband Layer :**
  - This layer defines how Bluetooth devices search for and connect to other devices.
  - The master and slave roles that a device may assume are defined here.
  - The master and slave communicate only in their pre-assigned time slots.
  - The devices use a time division duplexing (TDD), packet-based polling scheme for communication.
  - The Bluetooth specification doesn't establish a clear distinction between the responsibilities of the baseband and those of the link controller.
  - The best way to think about it is that the baseband portion of the layer is responsible for properly formatting data for transmission to and from the radio layer.
  - In addition, it handles the synchronization of links. The Baseband layer supports two types of links : Synchronous Connection- Oriented (SCO) and Asynchronous Connection-Less (ACL).
  - SCO links are characterized by a periodic, single-slot packet assignment, and are primarily used for voice transmissions that require fast, consistent data transfer. A device that has established a SCO link has, in essence, reserved certain time slots for its use. Its data packets are treated as priority packets, and will be serviced before any ACL packets.
  - A device with an ACL link can send variable length packets of 1, 3 or 5 time-slot lengths. But it has no time slots reserved for it.
- **(6) Link Manager Layer :** This layer implements the Link Manager Protocol (LMP). LMP manages bandwidth allocation for general data, bandwidth reservation for audio traffic, authentication using challenge response methods, and trust relationships between devices, encryption of data and control of power usage. Power usage control includes the negotiation of low power activity modes and the determination of transmission power levels.
- **(7) L2CAP layer :** The Logical Link Control and Adaptation Protocol (L2CAP) layer provides the interface between the higher- layer protocols and the lower-layer transport protocols. L2CAP supports multiplexing of several higher layer protocols, such as RFComm and SDP. This allows multiple protocols and applications to share the air-interface. L2CAP is also responsible for packet segmentation and reassembly, and for maintaining the negotiated service level between devices.

(8) HCI layer : The Host Controller Interface (HCI) layer defines a standard interface for upper level applications to access the lower layers of the stack. This layer is not a required part of the specification. Its purpose is to enable interoperability among devices and the use of existing higher level protocols and applications.

4.8.3 Bluetooth Frame Structure

There are several frame formats, the most important of which is shown in following Fig. 4.13. It begins with an **access code** that usually identifies the master so that slaves within radio range of two masters can tell which traffic is for them. Then comes a 54-bit header containing typical MAC sublayer fields. Then comes the data field, of up to 2744 bits (for a five-slot transmission).

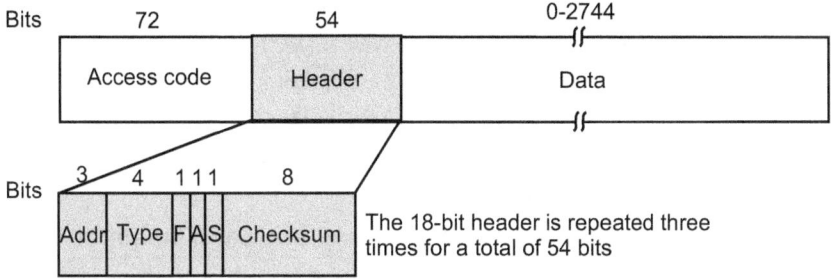

Fig. 4.13 : A Typical Bluetooth data frame

Header Field :

- **Address field :** The Address field identifies which of the eight active devices the frame is intended for.
- **Type :** The Type field identifies the frame type (ACL, SCO, poll, or null).
- **F :** The Flow bit is asserted by a slave when its buffer is full and cannot receive any more data.
- **A :** The Acknowledgement bit is used to piggyback an ACK onto a frame.
- **S :** The Sequence bit is used to number the frames to detect retransmissions. The protocol is stop-and-wait, so 1 bit is enough.
- **Checksum :** Then comes the 8-bit header Checksum. The entire 18-bit header is repeated three times to form the 54-bit header shown in figure.
- On the receiving side, a simple circuit examines all three copies of each bit. If all three are the same, the bit is accepted.
- If not, the majority opinion wins.

4.8.4 Advantages of Bluetooth

It is an open specification that is publicly available and royalty free; Its short-range wireless capability allows peripheral devices to communicate over a single air-interface, replacing cables that use connectors with a multitude of shapes, sizes and numbers of pins; Bluetooth supports both voice and data, making it an ideal technology to enable many types of devices to communicate; Bluetooth uses an unregulated frequency band available anywhere in the world.

4.9 BLUETOOTH SPECIFICATION

4.9.1 Radio specifications

This section describes the specifications of the Bluetooth link controller which carries out the baseband protocols and other low-level link routines. The Bluetooth radio specification is a short document that gives the details of radio transmission for Bluetooth devices. This specification defines three classes of transmitters based on output power.

Class 1: Outputs 100mW for maximum range and 1mW minimum. In this class, power control is mandatory, ranging from 4 to 20dBm. This class provides the greatest distance.

Class 2: Outputs 1.4mW at maximum and 0.25mW at minimum. Power control is optional.

Class 3: Lowest power. Nominal output is 1.

Table 4.1 Bluetooth radio and Baseband parameters

Topology	Up to 7 simultaneous links in a logical star
Modulation	GFSK
Peak data rate	1Mbps
RF bandwidth	220 kHz, 1Mhz
RF band	2.4 GHz, ISM band
RF carrier	3/79
Carrier spacing	1MHz
Transmit power	0.1 W
Piconet access	FH-TDD-TDMA
Frequency hop rate	1600 hops/s
Scatternet access	FH-CDMA

Bluetooth makes use of the 2.4-GHz band within the ISM (Industrial, Scientific, Medical) band. In most of the countries, the bandwidth is sufficient to define 79 1-MHz physical channels. Power control is used to control the devices so that they do not emit more RF power than necessary. The power control algorithm is implemented using link management protocol between a master and slaves in a piconet. Modulation for Bluetooth is Gaussian FSK, with a binary 1 is represented by a positive frequency deviation and a binary 0 is represented by a negative frequency deviation from the centre frequency.

Table 4.2: International Bluetooth Frequency Allocation

Area	Range	RF channels
US, Most of Europe	2.4 to 2.4835 GHz	f= 2.402+n MHz, n=0 to 78
Japan	2.471 to 2.497 GHz	f= 2.473+n MHz, n=0 to 22
Spain	2.445 to 2.475 GHz	f= 2.449+n MHz, n=0 to 22
France	2.4465 to 2.4835 GHz	f= 2.454+n MHz, n=0 to 22

4.9.2 Baseband Specification

This is one of the most complex specifications of Bluetooth.

Frequency Hopping (FH)

1. It provides resistance to interference and multipath effects
2. It provides a form of multiple access among co-located devices in different piconets

4.9.2.1 Channel Definition

The channel is represented by a pseudo-random hopping sequence hopping through the 79 or 23 RF channels. The hopping sequence is unique for the

piconet and is determined by the Bluetooth device address of the master; the phase in the hopping sequence is determined by the Bluetooth clock of the master. The channel is divided into time slots where each slot corresponds to an RF hop frequency. Consecutive hops correspond to different RF hop frequencies.

The nominal hop rate is 1600 hops/s. All Bluetooth units participating in the piconet are time- and hop-synchronized to the channel.

4.9.2.2 Time Slots

The channel is divided into time slots, each 625 μs in length. The time slots are numbered according to the Bluetooth clock of the piconet master. The slot numbering ranges from 0 to 227-1 and is cyclic with a cycle length of 227.

In the time slots, master and slave can transmit packets. A TDD scheme is used where master and slave alternatively transmit, see Fig. 4.14. The master shall start its transmission in even numbered time slots only, and the slave shall start its transmission in odd numbered time slots only. The packet start shall be aligned with the slot start. Packets transmitted by the master or the slave may extend over up to five time slots. The RF hop frequency shall remain fixed for the duration of the packet.

For a single packet, the RF hop frequency to be used is derived from the current Bluetooth clock value. For a multi-slot packet, the RF hop frequency to be used for the entire packet is derived from the Bluetooth clock value in the first slot of the packet. The RF hop frequency in the first slot after a multi-slot packet shall use the frequency as determined by the current Bluetooth clock value.

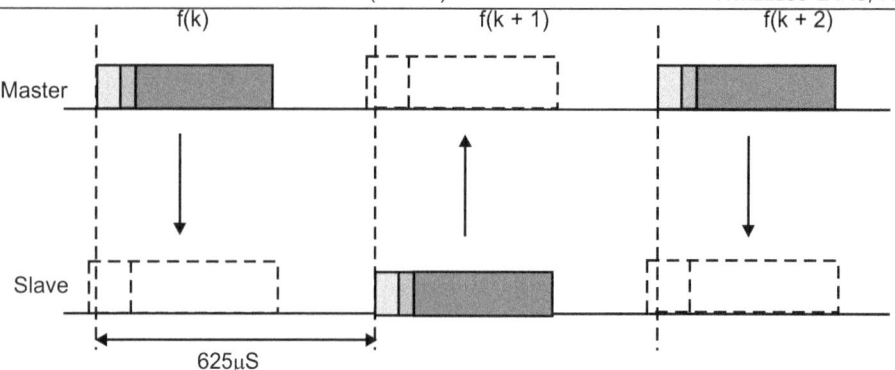

Fig. 4.14 TDD and Timing

Fig. 4.15 illustrates the hop definition on single and multi-slot packets. If a packet occupies more than one time slot, the hop frequency applied shall be the hop frequency as applied in the time slot where the packet transmission was started.

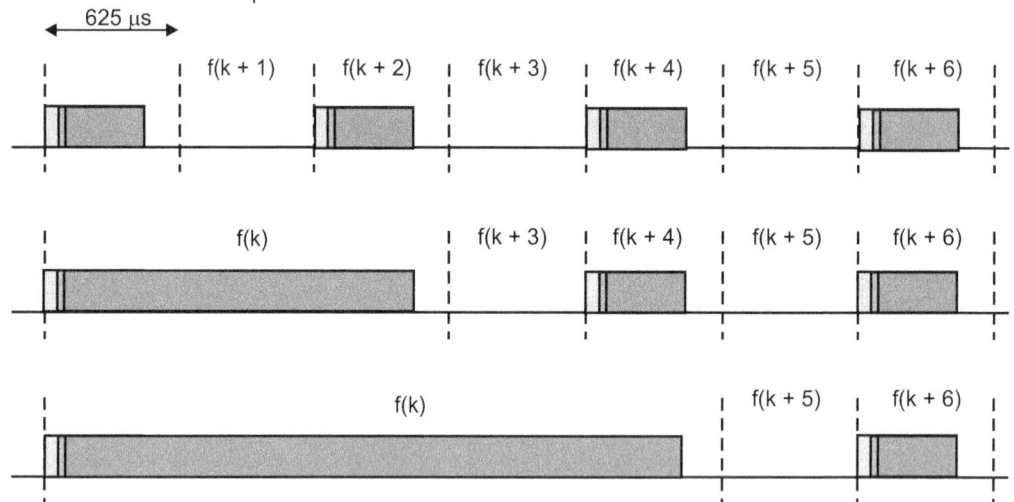

Fig. 4.15 Multislot packets

4.9.2.5 Physical Links

Between master and slave(s), different types of links can be established. Two link types have been defined:

- Synchronous Connection-Oriented (SCO) link
- Asynchronous Connection-Less (ACL) link

The SCO link is a point-to-point link between a master and a single slave in the

piconet. The master maintains the SCO link by using reserved slots at regular intervals. The ACL link is a point-to-multipoint link between the master and all the slaves participating on the piconet. In the slots not reserved for the SCO link(s), the master can establish an ACL link on a per-slot basis to any slave, including the slave(s) already engaged in an SCO link.

SCO LINK

The SCO link is a symmetric, point-to-point link between the master and a specific slave. The SCO link reserves slots and can therefore be considered as a circuit-switched connection between the master and the slave. The SCO link typically supports time-bounded information like voice. The master can support up to three SCO links to the same slave or to different slaves. A slave can support up to three SCO links from the same master, or two SCO links if the links originate from different masters. SCO packets are never retransmitted.

The master will send SCO packets at regular intervals, the so-called SCO interval T_{SCO} (counted in slots) to the slave in the reserved master-to-slave slots.

The SCO slave is always allowed to respond with an SCO packet in the following slave-to-master slot unless a different slave was addressed in the previous master-to-slave slot. If the SCO slave fails to decode the slave address in the packet header, it is still allowed to return an SCO packet in the reserved SCO slot.

The SCO link is established by the master sending an SCO setup message via the LM protocol. This message will contain timing parameters such as the SCO interval T_{SCO} and the offset D_{SCO} to specify the reserved slots.

In order to prevent clock wrap-around problems, an initialization flag in the LMP setup message indicates whether initialization procedure 1 or 2 is being used.

The slave shall apply the initialization method as indicated by the initialization flag. The master uses initialization 1 when the MSB of the current master clock

(CLK27) is 0; it uses initialization 2 when the MSB of the current master clock

(CLK27) is 1. The master-to-slave SCO slots reserved by the master and the slave shall be initialized on the slots for which the clock satisfies the following

equation:

CLK27-1 mod T_{SCO} = D_{SCO} for initialization 1

(CLK27,CLK26-1) mod T_{SCO} = D_{SCO} for initialization 2

The slave-to-master SCO slots shall directly follow the reserved master-toslave SCO slots. After initialization, the clock value CLK(k+1) for the next master- to-slave SCO slot is found by adding the fixed interval TSCO to the clock value of the current master-to-slave SCO slot: CLK(k+1) = CLK(k) + T_{SCO}

ACL LINK

In the slots not reserved for SCO links, the master can exchange packets with any slave on a per-slot basis. The ACL link provides a packet-switched connection between the master and all active slaves participating in the piconet.

Both asynchronous and isochronous services are supported. Between a master and a slave only a single ACL link can exist. For most ACL packets, packet retransmission is applied to assure data integrity.

A slave is permitted to return an ACL packet in the slave-to-master slot if and only if it has been addressed in the preceding master-to-slave slot. If the slave fails to decode the slave address in the packet header, it is not allowed to transmit. ACL packets not addressed to a specific slave are considered as broadcast packets and are read by every slave. If there is no data to be sent on the ACL link and no polling is required, no transmission shall take place.

4.9.2.6 Packets

GENERAL FORMAT

The bit ordering when defining packets and messages in the *Baseband*

Specification, follows the *Little Endian format*, i.e., the following rules apply:

- The *least significant bit* (LSB) corresponds to ;
- The LSB is the first bit sent over the air;
- In illustrations, the LSB is shown on the left side;

The linkcontroller interprets the first bit arriving from a higher software layer as

; i.e. this is the first bit to be sent over the air. Furthermore, data fields generated internally at baseband level, such as the packet header fields and payload header length, are transmitted with the LSB first. For instance, a 3-bit parameter X=3 is sent as over the air where 1 is sent first and 0 is sent last.

The data on the piconet channel is conveyed in packets. The general packet format is shown in Fig. 4.16. Each packet consists of 3 entities: the access code, the header, and the payload. In the figure, the number of bits per entity is indicated.

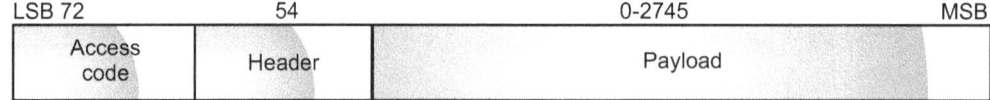

Fig. 4.16 Standard packet Format

The access code and header are of fixed size : 72 bits and 54 bits respectively.

The payload can range from zero to a maximum of 2745 bits. Different packet types have been defined. Packets may consist of the (shortened) access code only, of the access code + header, or of the access code + header + payload.

4.9.2.5 Access Code

Each packet starts with an access code. If a packet header follows, the access code is 72 bits long, otherwise the access code is 68 bits long. This access code is used for synchronization, DC offset compensation and identification. The access code identifies all packets exchanged on the channel of the piconet: all packets sent in the same piconet are preceded by the same channel access code. In the receiver of the Bluetooth unit, a sliding correlator correlates against the access code and triggers when a threshold is exceeded.

This trigger signal is used to determine the receive timing. The access code is also used in paging and inquiry procedures. In this case, the access code itself is used as a signalling message and neither a header nor a payload is present. The access code consists of a preamble, a sync word, and possibly a trailer, see fig 4.17.

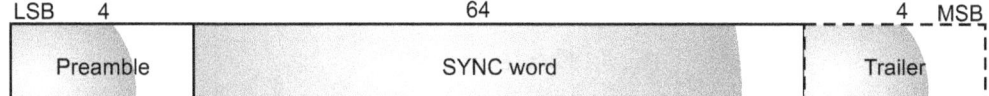

Fig. 4.17 : Access code format

Access code types

There are three different types of access codes defined:
- Channel Access Code (CAC)
- Device Access Code (DAC)
- Inquiry Access Code (IAC)

The CAC consists of a preamble, sync word, and trailer and its total length is 72 bits. When used as self-contained messages without a header, the DAC and IAC do not include the trailer bits and are of length 68 bits.

The preamble is a fixed zero-one pattern of 4 symbols used to facilitate DC compensation. The sequence is either 1010 or 0101, depending whether the

LSB of the following sync word is 1 or 0, respectively.

Sync Word

The sync word is a 64-bit code word derived from a 24 bit address (LAP); for the CAC the master's LAP is used; for the GIAC and the DIAC, reserved, dedicated

LAPs are used; for the DAC, the slave unit LAP is used. The construction guarantees large Hamming distance between sync words based on different LAPs. In addition, the good auto correlation properties of the sync word improve on the timing synchronization process.

Trailer

The trailer is appended to the sync word as soon as the packet header follows the access code. This is typically the case with the CAC, but the trailer is also used in the DAC and IAC when these codes are used in FHS packets exchanged during page response and inquiry response procedures.

The trailer is a fixed zero-one pattern of four symbols. The trailer together with the three MSBs of the syncword form a 7-bit pattern of alternating ones and zeroes which may be used for extended DC compensation. The trailer sequence is either 1010 or 0101 depending on whether the MSB of the sync word is 0 or 1, respectively. The choice of trailer is illustrated in Fig. 4.18.

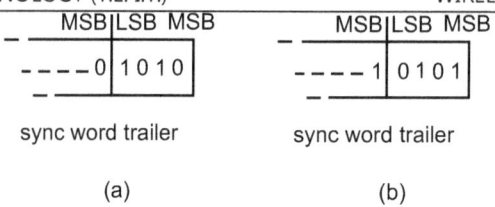

sync word trailer   sync word trailer

(a)   (b)

Fig. 4.18 Trailer in CAC

4.9.2.6 Packet Header

The header contains link control (LC) information and consists of 6 fields:
- AM_ADDR: 3- bit active member address
- TYPE: 4-bit type code
- FLOW: 1-bit flow control
- ARQN: 1-bit acknowledge indication
- SEQN: 1-bit sequence number
- HEC: 8-bit header error check

The total header, including the HEC, consists of 18 bits, see fig 4.19

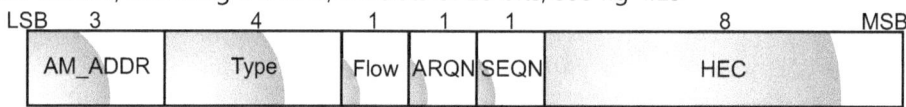

Fig. 4.19 Header format

and is encoded with a rate 1/3 FEC resulting in a 54-bit header. Note that the AM_ADDR and TYPE fields are sent with their LSB first. The function of the different fields will be explained next.

AM_ADDR

The AM_ADDR represents a member address and is used to distinguish between the active members participating on the piconet. In a piconet, one or more slaves are connected to a single master. To identify each slave separately, each slave is assigned a temporary 3-bit address to be used when it is active. Packets exchanged between the master and the slave all carry the AM_ADDR of this slave; that is, the AM_ADDR of the slave is used in both master-to-slave packets and in the slave-to-master packets. The all-zero address is reserved for broadcasting packets from the master to the slaves.

An exception is the FHS packet which may use the all-zero member address but is *not* a broadcast message. Slaves that are disconnected or parked give up their AM_ADDR. A new AM_ADDR has to be assigned when they re-enter the piconet.

Type

Sixteen different types of packets can be distinguished. The 4-bit TYPE code specifies which packet type is used. Important to note is that the interpretation of the TYPE code depends on the physical link type associated with the packet. First, it shall be determined whether the packet is sent on an SCO link or an ACL link. Then it can be determined which type of SCO packet or ACL packet has been received. The TYPE code also reveals how many slots the current packet will occupy. This allows the non-addressed receivers to refrain from listening to the channel for the duration of the remaining slots.

Flow

This bit is used for flow control of packets over the ACL link. When the RX buffer for the ACL link in the recipient is full and is not emptied, a STOP indication (FLOW=0) is returned to stop the transmission of data temporarily. Note, that the STOP signal only concerns ACL packets. Packets including only link control information (ID, POLL and NULL packets) or SCO packets can still be received. When the RX buffer is empty, a GO indication (FLOW=1) is returned.

When no packet is received, or the received header is in error, a GO is assumed implicitly. In this case, the slave can receive a new packet with CRC although its RX buffer is still not emptied. The slave shall then return a NAK in response to this packet even if the packet passed the CRC check.

ARQN

The 1-bit acknowledgment indication ARQN is used to inform the source of a successful transfer of payload data with CRC, and can be positive acknowledge

ACK or negative acknowledge NAK. If the reception was successful, an

ACK (ARQN=1) is returned, otherwise a NAK (ARQN=0) is returned. When no return message regarding acknowledge is received, a NAK is assumed implicitly.

NAK is also the default return information. The ARQN is piggy-backed in the header of the return packet. The success of the reception is checked by means of a cyclic redundancy check (CRC) code. An unnumbered ARQ scheme which means that the ARQN relates to the latest received packet from the same source, is used.

SEQN

The SEQN bit provides a sequential numbering scheme to order the data packet stream. For each new transmitted packet that contains data with CRC, the SEQN bit is inverted. This is required to filter out retransmissions at the destination; if a retransmission occurs due to a failing ACK, the destination receives the same packet twice. By comparing the SEQN of consecutive packets, correctly received retransmissions can be discarded.

HEC

Each header has a header-error-check to check the header integrity. The HEC consists of an 8-bit word generated by the polynomial 647 (octal representation).

Before generating the HEC, the HEC generator is initialized with an 8-bit value. For FHS packets sent in master page response state, the slave upper address part (UAP) is used. For FHS packets sent in inquiry response, the default check initialization is used. In all other cases, the UAP of the master device is used. After the initialization, a HEC is calculated for the 10 header bits. Before checking the HEC, the receiver must initialize the HEC check circuitry with the proper 8-bit UAP (or DCI). If the HEC does not check, the entire packet is disregarded.

Table 4.3 Bluetooth Packet Types

Type Code	Physical Link	Name	No. of slots	Description
0000	Common	NULL	1	Has no payload. Used to return link information to the source regarding the success of the previous transmission or the success of RX buffer. Not acknowledged
0001	Common	POLL	1	Has no payload. Used by master to poll a slave. Acknowledged.
0010	Common	FHS	1	Special control packet for revealing device address and the clock of the sender. Used in page master response inquiry response, and frequency hop synchronization. 2/3 FEC encoded.
0011	Common	DM1	1	Supports control messages and can also carry user data. 16 bit CRC. 2/3 FEC encoded
0101	SCO	HV1	1	Carries 10 information bytes; typically used for 64-kbps voice. 1/3 FEC encoded
0110	SCO	HV2	1	Carries 20 information bytes; typically used for 64-kbps voice. 2/3 FEC encoded
0111	SCO	HV3	1	Carries 30 information bytes; typically used for 64-kbps voice. No FEC encoded
1000	SCO	DV	1	Combined data (150 bits) and voice (50 bits) packet. Data field 2/3 FEC encoded.
0100	ACL	DH1	1	Carries 28 information bytes plus 16 bit CRC; typically used for high speed data. Not FEC encoded
1001	ACL	AUX1	1	Carries 30 information bytes plus 16 bit CRC; typically used for high speed data. Not FEC encoded
1010	ACL	DM3	3	Carries 123 information bytes plus 16 bit CRC; 2/3 FEC encoded
1011	ACL	DH3	3	Carries 185 information bytes plus 16 bit CRC; Not FEC encoded
1110	ACL	DM5	5	Carries 226 information bytes plus 16 bit CRC; Not FEC encoded
1111	ACL	DH5	5	Carries 341 information bytes plus 16 bit CRC; Not FEC encoded

Payload Format

For some packet types, the baseband specification defines a format for the payload field. For voice payloads, no header is defined. For all of the ACL packets and for data portion of the SCO DV packet, a header is defined. For data payload, the payload format consists of three fields.

- Payload header: An 8 bit header is defined for single slot packets and a 16 bit header is defined for multislot packets.
- Payload body: Contains user information
- CRC: A 16 bit CRC code is used on all data payloads except AUX1 packet.

4.9.2.7 Error Correction

There are three error correction schemes defined for Bluetooth:
- 1/3 rate FEC
- 2/3 rate FEC
- ARQ scheme for the data

The purpose of the FEC scheme on the data payload is to reduce the number of retransmissions. However, in a reasonable error-free environment, FEC gives unnecessary overhead that reduces the throughput. Therefore, the packet definitions have been kept flexible to use FEC in the payload or not, resulting in the **DM** and **DH** packets for the ACL link and the **HV** packets for the SCO link. The packet header is always protected by a 1/3 rate FEC; it contains valuable link information and should be able to sustain more bit errors. Correction measures to mask errors in the voice decoder are not included in this section.

FEC CODE: RATE 1/3

A simple 3-times repetition FEC code is used for the header. The repetition code is implemented by repeating the bit three times, see the illustration in fig 4.20 The 3-bit repetition code is used for the entire header, and also for the voice field in the **HV1** packet.

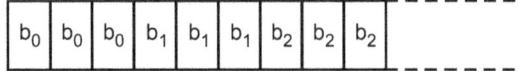

Fig. 4.20 : Bit repetition encoding scheme

FEC CODE: RATE 2/3

The other FEC scheme is a (15,10) shortened Hamming code. The generator polynomial is . This corresponds to 65 in octal notation. The LFSR generating this code is depicted in 4.21. Initially all register elements are set to zero. The 10 information bits are sequentially fed into the LFSR with the switches S1 and S2 set in position 1. Then, after the final input bit, the switches S1 and S2 are set in position 2, and the five parity bits are shifted out. The parity bits are appended to the information bits. Consequently, each block of 10 information bits is encoded into a 15 bit codeword. This code can correct all single errors and detect all double errors in each codeword. This 2/3 rate FEC is used in the **DM** packets, in the data field of the **DV** packet, in the **FHS** packet, and in the **HV2** packet.

Since the encoder operates with information segments of length 10, tail bits with value zero may have to be appended after the CRC bits. The total number of bits to encode, i.e., payload header, user data, CRC, and tail bits, must be a multiple of 10. Thus, the number of tail bits to append is the least possible that achieves this (i.e., in the interval 0...9). These tail bits are not included in the payload length indicator. The ARQ scheme is used with DM and DH packets and the data field of DV packets

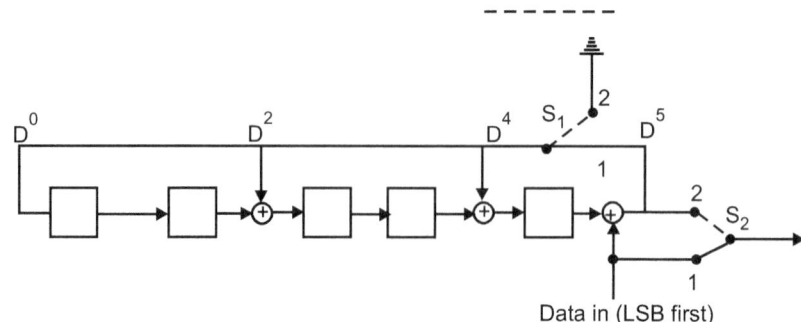

Fig. 4.21 : LFSR generating (15,10) shortened Hamming code

Error Detection :

The destination detects errors and discards packets that are in error. Error detection is achieved with a CRC error detecting code supplemented with the FEC code.

Positive Acknowledgement :

The destination returns a positive acknowledgement to successfully received, error free packets. Retransmission after timeout: The source retransmits a packet that has not been acknowledged after a predetermined amount of time. Negative acknowledgement and retransmission: The destination returns a negative acknowledgement to packets in which an error is detected. The source retransmits such packets.

4.9.2.8 Logical Channels

Bluetooth defines five types of logical channels to carry out different type of payload traffic.

Link Control (LC):

It is used to manage the flow of packets over the link interface. The LC channel is mapped to the packet header. This channel carries low level link control information like ARQ, flow control and payload characterization. The LC channel I carried in every packet except in the ID packet, which has no packet header.

Link manager (LM): Transports link management information between participating stations. This logical channel supports LMP traffic and can be carried over either an SCO or ACL link. User asynchronous (UA): Carries asynchronous user data. This channel is normally carried over the ACL link but may be carried in a DV packet on the SCO link. User isochronous (UI): Carries user isochronous user data.

This channel is normally carried over the ACL link but may be carried in a DV packet on he SCO link. At the baseband level UI channels are treated in the same way as a UA channel. User synchronous (US): Carries synchronous user data. This channel is carried over the SCO link.

Channel Control

The operation of a piconet can b understood in terms of the states of operation during link establishment and maintenance.

Two main states are

1. Standy : The default state. This is a low power state in which only the native clock is running

2. Connection : The device is connected to a piconet as a master or a slave.

In addition to these two states there are seven substates that can be used to add slaves to a piconet. The substates are as follows:

1. Page : Device has issued a page. Used by the master to activate and connect to slave. Master sends page message by transmitting slave's device access code (DAC) in different hop channels.

2. Page Scan : Device is listening for a page with its on DAC.

3. Master Response : A device acting as a master receives a page response from a slave. The device can now enter the connection state or return to the page state to page for other slaves.

4. Slave Response : A device acting as a slave responds to a page from master. If connection setup succeeds, the device enters the connection state or it returns to the page scan state.

5. Inquiry : Device has issued an inquiry, to find the identity of the devices within range.

6. Inquiry Scan : Device is listening for an inquiry

7. Inquiry Response : A device that has issued an inquiry receives an inquiry response.

Inquiry Procedure

The first step in establishing a piconet is for a potential master to identify devices in range that wish to participate in the piconet. A device begins an inquiry procedure for this purpose. Inquiry procedure begins when the potential master transmits an ID packet with an inquiry access code (IAC), which is code common to all Bluetooth devices. Out of 79 radio carrier, 32 are considered as wake up carriers. The master broadcasts the IAC over each of the 32 wake up carriers. This is done in Inquiry state. Meanwhile, devices in the Standby state periodically enter the Inquiry Scan state to search for IAC messages on the wake up carriers. When a device receives the inquiry, it enters the Inquiry response state and returns an FHS packet which contains its device address and timing information required by the master to initiate a connection. The master dos not respond to the FHS packet and may remain in the Inquiry state.

Once a device has responded to an Inquiry, it moves to the page scan state to await a page from the master in order to establish a connection. If collision occurs in the Inquiry Response phase, no page will be received and device may return to the Inquiry scan state to attempt another inquiry and response.

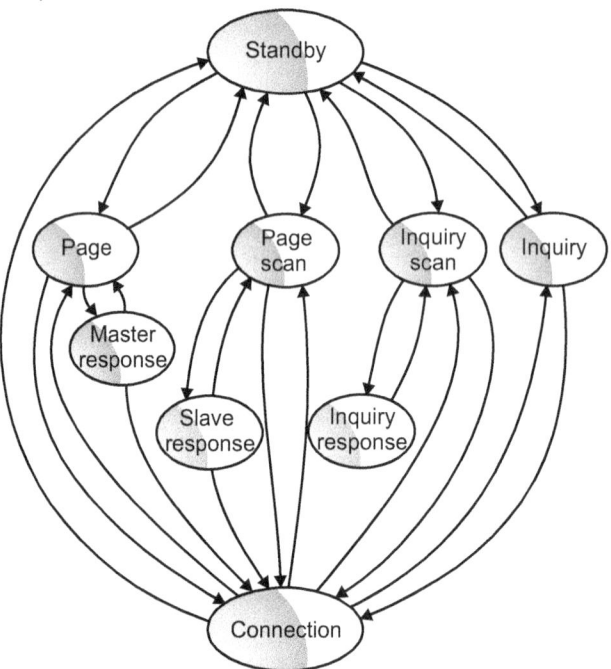

Fig. 4.22 : Bluetooth state transition diagram

Page Procedure

Once the master has found devices within its range, it is able to establish connections to each device, setting up a piconet. Master uses the device's address (BD_ADDR) in order to page that device. The master pages by using an ID packet with a device access code (DAC) of the specific slave. The slave responds by returning the same DAC ID packet to the master. The master responds to this with its own FHS packet, containing its own device address and its real time Bluetooth clock value. Once again, the slave sends a response DAC ID packet to the master to confirm the receipt of master's FHS packet. At this point slave transits from Response state to the connection state. Master may continue to page until it has connected to all the desired slaves, then master enters the connection state.

Connection State

In the CONNECTION state, the connection has been established and packets can be sent back and forth. In both units, the channel (master) access code and the master Bluetooth clock are used. The hopping scheme uses the *channel hopping sequence*. The master starts its transmission in even slots (CLK 1-0=00), the slave starts its transmission in odd slots (CLK 1-0=10)

The CONNECTION state starts with a POLL packet sent by the master to verify the switch to the master's timing and channel frequency hopping. The slave can respond with any type of packet. If the slave does not receive the POLL packet or the master does not receive the response packet for *newconnectionTO* number of slots, both devices will return to page/page scan substates. The first information packets in the CONNECTION state contain control messages that characterize the link and give more details regarding the Bluetooth units. These messages are exchanged between the link managers of the units.

For example, it defines the SCO links and the sniff parameters. Then the transfer of user information can start by alternately transmitting and receiving packets. The CONNECTION state is left through a detach or reset command. The detach command is used if the link has been disconnected in the normal way. All configuration data in the Bluetooth link controller is still valid. The reset command is a hard reset of all controller processes. After a reset, the controller has to be reconfigured. The Bluetooth units can be in several modes of operation during the CONNECTION state: active mode, sniff mode, hold mode, and park mode.

Active : The slave actively participates in the piconet by listening, transmitting and receiving packets. The master periodically transmits to he slaves to maintain synchronization.

Sniff : The slave does not listen on every receive slot but only on slots specified for its messages. The slave can operate in reduced power state for the rest of the time. In sniff mode the master designs specific number of slots for transmission to a specific slave.

Hold : The device in this mode does not support ACL packets and goes to reduced power status. The slave may still participate in SCO exchanges. During the period of inactivity slave is free to idle in reduced power state or participate in other piconet.

Park : When a slave does not need to participate on the piconet but still want to be the part of piconet, it can enter in park mode. This is a low power mode with very little activity.

4.10 BLUETOOTH PROFILES

- Bluetooth profiles Describe configuration of the Bluetooth stack for different types of applications.
- Specify minimum requirements from Bluetooth layers for each profile.
- Generic access profile give recommendations and common requirements for access procedures.

Bluetooth SIG (Special Interest Group) has defined three separate application profiles using OBEX. These profiles are briefly introduced in this section.

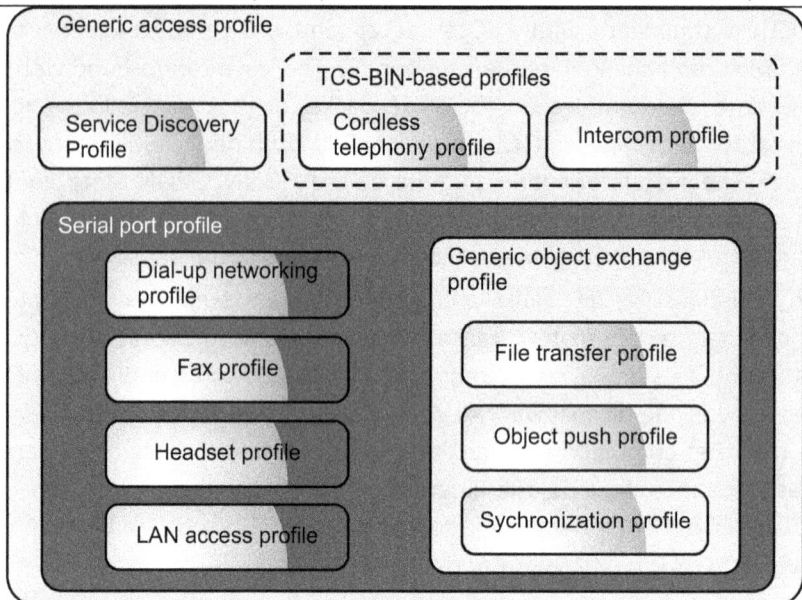

Fig. 4.23 Bluetooth Profile

4.10.1 Synchronization

Basically, the synchronization means comparing two object stores, determining their inequalities, and then unifying these two object stores. The Bluetooth devices supporting the synchronization may be desktop PCs, notebooks, PDAs, cellular phones, or smart phones.

The Bluetooth Synchronization profile uses the servers and clients compliant to the IrMC synchronization specified by IrDA. The Bluetooth Synchronization servers and clients must support the level 4 synchronization functionality specified in the IrMC specification.

The actual logic of the synchronization engines which process the synchronization algorithm at the client device is implementation-specific. It is therefore left to the participating software vendors, and is not considered in the Bluetooth specifications.

The synchronization is not limited to one type of application. The Bluetooth synchronization (i.e. the IrMC synchronization) enables four different application classes:

1. Phone Book – provides a means for a user to manage contact records

2. Calendar – enables a user to manage calendar items, and can also be used
for 'to-do' or task lists

3. Messaging – lets a user manage messages (e.g. e-mails)

4. Notes – provides a means for a user to manage small notes

The interoperability requirements for the Bluetooth Synchronization profile are
defined in the Synchronization Profile and Generic Object Exchange Profile
specifications.

4.10.2 File Transfer

At the minimum, the File Transfer profile is intended for sending and retrieving generic files to and from the Bluetooth device. The File Transfer service also facilitates the browsing of the remote Bluetooth device's folder. The interoperability requirements for the Bluetooth File Transfer profile are defined in the File Transfer Profile and Generic Object Exchange Profile specifications.

4.10.3 Object Push

The Object Push profile is the special case of the File Transfer Profile for beaming objects and optionally pulling the default objects. At a minimum, it offers the capability to exchange business cards, but is not limited to this service.

The interoperability requirements for the Object Push profile are defined in the

Object Push Profile and Generic Object Exchange Profile specifications.

4.11 DIFFERENCE BETWEEN 802.11 AND 802.16

IEEE 802.11 WLAN ARCHITECTURE

The IEEE 802.11 was the first international standard for WLANs.

The basic service set (BSS) is the fundamental building block of the IEEE 802.11 architecture. A BSS is defined as a group of stations that are under the direct control of a single coordination function (e.g. Direct Coordination Function (DCF) or Point Coordination Function (PCF)), which is defined below.

The geographical area covered by the BSS is known as the Basic Service Area (BSA), which is analogous to a cell in a cellular communication network. Conceptually, all stations in a BSS can communicate directly with all other stations in a BSS.

An ad-hoc network is a defined group of stations that are organized into a single BSS for the purposes of inter-networked communications, without the aid of any additional network infrastructure. Fig. 4.24 provides an illustration of a wireless infrastructure and independent BSS. The IEEE 802.11 Standard defines an ad-hoc network as an independent BSS.

Any station can establish a direct communication session with any other station in the BSS in an ad-hoc network, without having to channel all traffic through a centralized access point (AP).

Physical Layer

The IEEE specification calls for three different physical-layer implementations: Frequency Hopping Spread Spectrum (FHSS), Direct Sequence Spread Spectrum (DSSS), and Infrared.

The FHSS utilizes the 2.4 GHz Industrial, Scientific, and Medical (ISM) band (e.g. 2.4- 2.4835 GHz). In the United States, a maximum of 79 channels are specified in the hopping set. The first channel has a central frequency of 2.402 GHz, and all subsequent channels are spaced at 1 MHz intervals.

The 1 MHz separation is mandated by the FCC for the 2.4 GHz ISM band. The channel separation corresponds to 1 Mb/s of instantaneous bandwidth. Three different hopping sequence sets are established with 26 hopping sequences per set. Different hopping sequences enable multiple BSSs to coexist in the same geographical area, which may become necessary to alleviate congestion and maximize the total throughput of a single BSS. The minimum hop rate permitted is 2.5 hops/seconds. The basic access rate of 1 Mb/s uses two-level Gaussian frequency shift keying (GFSK).

The enhanced access rate of 2 Mb/s uses four-level GFSK. The DSSS also uses the 2.4 GHz ISM frequency band, where the 1 Mb/s basic rate is encoded using differential binary phase shift keying (DBPSK), and a 2 Mb/s enhanced rate uses differential quadrature phase shift keying (DQPSK). The spreading is done by dividing the available bandwidth into 11 sub-channels, each 11 MHz wide, and using an 11-chip Barker sequence to spread each data symbol. The maximum channel capacity is therefore (11 chips/symbol)/ (11 MHz) = 1 Mb/s if DBPSK is used.

In October 1997, the IEEE 802 Executive Committee approved two extensions for higher data rate transmissions. The first extension, IEEE 802.11a, defines requirements for a PHY layer operating in the 5.0 GHz frequency and data rate transmission ranging from 6 Mbps to 54 Mbps.

The second extension, IEEE 802.11b, defines a set of PHY layer specifications operating in the 2.4 GHz frequency band up to 11 Mbps. Both PHY layers are designed to operate with the existing MAC layer. The IEEE 802.11a PHY is one of the physical layer extensions of IEEE 802.11 and is referred to as orthogonal frequency division multiplexing (OFDM) and the IEEE 802.11b is referred to as high rate direct sequence spread spectrum (HR/DSSS). The HR/DSSS PHY provides two functions.

First, the HR/DSSS extends the PSDU data rates to 5.5 and 11 Mbps using an enhanced modulation technique, called Complementary Code Keying (CCK). Secondly, the HR/DSSS PHY provides a rate shift mechanism, which allows 11 Mbps networks to fall back to 1 and 2 Mbps and interoperates with the legacy IEEE 802.11 standard. The most recent Wired LAN commercial standard is IEEE 802.11g, approved in June 2003.

The IEEE 802.11g standard provides optional data rates transmission of up to 54 Mbps, and requires compatibility with 802.11b devices to protect the substantial investments in today's WLAN installations. The 802.11g standard includes mandatory and optional components. It specifies OFDM and CCK as the mandatory modulation schemes with 24 Mbps as the maximum mandatory data rates, but it also provides for optional higher data rates of 36, 48 and 54 Mbps.

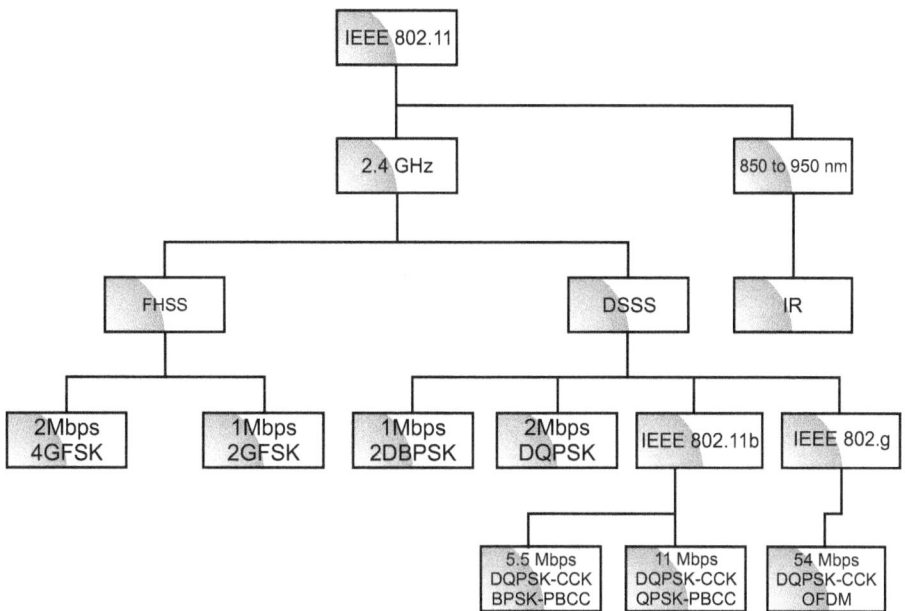

Fig. 4.24 : 802.11 Architecture

Medium Access Control Sub-layer

The MAC sub-layer is responsible for channel allocation procedures, protocol data unit (PDU) addressing, frame formatting, error checking, and data fragmentation and reassembly.

The transmission medium can operate in the contention mode exclusively, requiring all stations to contend for access to the channel for each packet transmitted. The medium can also alternate between the contention mode, known as the contention period (CP) under the Distribute Coordination Function (DCF), and a contention-free period (CFP) under the Point Coordination Function (PCF). During the CFP, medium usage is controlled (or mediated) by the AP, thereby eliminating the need for stations to contend for channel access.

The DCF is the fundamental access method used to support asynchronous data transfer on a best effort basis. The DCF operates exclusively in ad-hoc networks and is based on carrier sense multiple access with collision avoidance (CSMA/CA). In IEEE 802.11, carrier sensing is performed at both the air interface, referred to as physical carrier sensing and at the MAC sublayer, also called virtual carrier sensing. Physical carrier sensing detects the presence of other IEEE 802.11 WLAN users by analyzing all detected packets and also detecting activity in the channel via relative signal strength from other sources. A source station performs virtual carrier sensing by sending MPDU duration information in the header of request to send (RTS), clear to send (CTS), and data frames. The duration field indicates the amount of time (in microseconds) after the end of the present frame. The channel will then be utilized to complete the successful transmission of the data or management frame.

Stations in the BSS use the information in the duration field to adjust their network allocation vector (NAV), which indicates the amount of time that must elapse to complete a transmission session before the channel can be sampled again for idle status. The channel is marked busy if either the physical or virtual carrier sensing mechanisms indicates the channel is busy.

On the other hand, the PCF is an optional capability, which is connection-oriented, and provides contention-free (CF) frame transfer. The PCF relies on the point coordinator (PC) to perform polling, enabling polled stations to transmit without contending for the channel. The function of the PC is performed by the AP within each BSS.

4.11.1 Physical Layer of 802.11 G

The 802.11g physical (PHY) layer supports 4 modulation schemes. Two of these schemes, ERP-OFDM and ERP-CCK/DSSS, are mandatory and two, ERP-PBCC and DSSS-OFDM, are optional. Of the four schemes, only ERP-OFDM and DSSS-OFDM provide data rates of up to 54Mb/s using OFDM modulation schemes, while also providing explicit support for interoperating with 802.11b nodes. Such support is necessary as 802.11b nodes cannot detect or interpret OFDM modulated signals.

The ERP-OFDM scheme is a variant of the 802.11a PHY scheme modified for use in the 2.4 GHz band (Szczypiorski, and Lubacz, 2008). In this mode, all the data is sent by OFDM and can only be received by 802.11g stations. It is therefore known as 802.11g-only mode. The data rates are also 6, 9, 12, 18, 24, 36, 48, and 54 Mbps.

The ERP-CCK mode is used for compatibility with 802.11b stations. CCK stands for Complementary Code Keying; the data rates supported are 5.5 and 11Mbit/s. In the ERP-DSSS mode, data is transmitted using a technique called Direct Sequence Spread Spectrum (DSSS). ERP-DSSS provides backward compatibility with 802.11 stations supporting data rates of 1 and 2Mbit/s. The ERP-PBCC mode is optional and rarely used. PBCC, or Packet Binary Convolutional Coding, is used in conjunction with DSSS. The data rates achieved by ERP-PBCC are 5.5, 11, 22, and 33Mbit/s.

The DSSS-OFDM scheme is a hybrid modulation scheme that combines a DSSS and OFDM.

DSSS is employed to transmit the header of a PHY frame. Doing so allows 802.11b devices to receive information and update their NAVs dynamically. Therefore, 802.11b stations and 802.11g stations can be operated in the same network. The actual data is OFDM modulated and cannot be received by 802.11b stations. The data rates are 6, 9, 12, 18, 24, 36, 48, and 54Mbit/s.

4.11.2 PHY Frames

In order to transmit packets over the wireless link, the MAC frames are encapsulated into PHY frames. The format of the transmitted PHY Protocol Data Unit (PPDU) consists of a PLCP (Physical Layer Convergence Procedure) preamble, a PLCP header and a Physical Service Data

Unit (PSDU). Each PSDU consists of the MAC header, the frame body (MSDU), and extra bits (Tail/Pad bits) (IEEE Std 802.11b, 1999).

Figure 4.25 shows the format of an ERP-OFDM PPDU, which is common to the 802.11g PHY standard. ERP-OFDM is the most often implemented PPDU in the 802.11g standard, and supports data rates of 6, 9, 12, 18, 24, 36, 48, and 54 Mbps. The ERP-OFDM PPDU has three parts: Preamble, Header, and Data Field. The PLCP preamble is carefully designed to enable synchronization.

IEEE 802.11g typically uses the ERP-OFDM mode for the PLCP format. With the ERP-OFDM preamble, it takes just 16µs to train the receiver after first detecting a signal on the RF medium with respect to the 144µs for IEEE 802.11b. Failure in frame detection and/or synchronization results in a physical layer (PHY) error. The ERP-OFDM header carries the essential information needed by the receiver to properly decode the rest of the frame. The Data field consists of the Service subfield, PSDU, Tail subfield, and Pad Bits subfield. The Service subfield consists of 16 bits, with the first 7 bits as zeros to synchronize the receiver descrambler. The remaining 9 bits are reserved for future use and set to all 0s. As part of the Data field, the Service subfield is transmitted at the rate specified in the Signal field's Rate subfield.

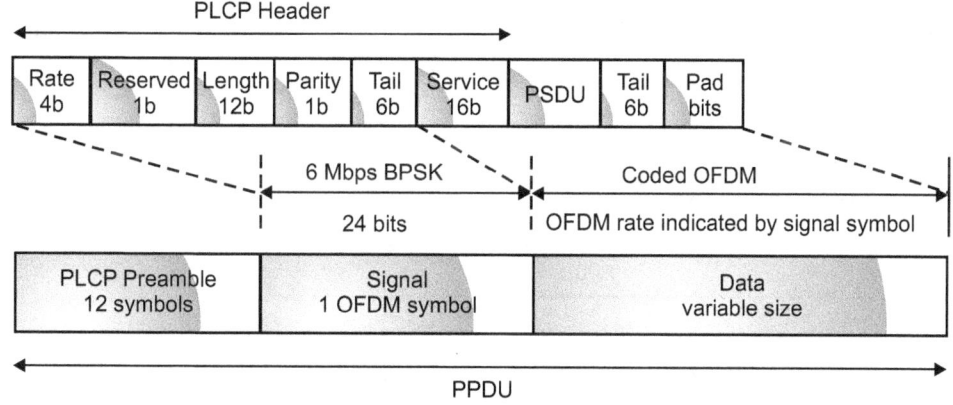

Fig. 4.25 : ERP OFDM PPDU Framing

In the 802.11g standard extends the use of the DSSS PHY by specifying an optional PPDU type consisting of the same DSSS preamble and header, but at the cost of accepting an ERP-OFDM PPDU as its PSDU.

The IEEE calls this new PPDU type DSSS-OFDM. Both long and short preambles are supported with DSSS-OFDM, and no protection mechanisms are required by DSSS-OFDM stations when operating with DSSS stations present in the BSA.

Figure 4.26 illustrates the construction of both long and short preamble formats for DSSS-OFDM PPDUs.

The preamble and header transmission rates apply to DSSS-OFDM as with DSSS.

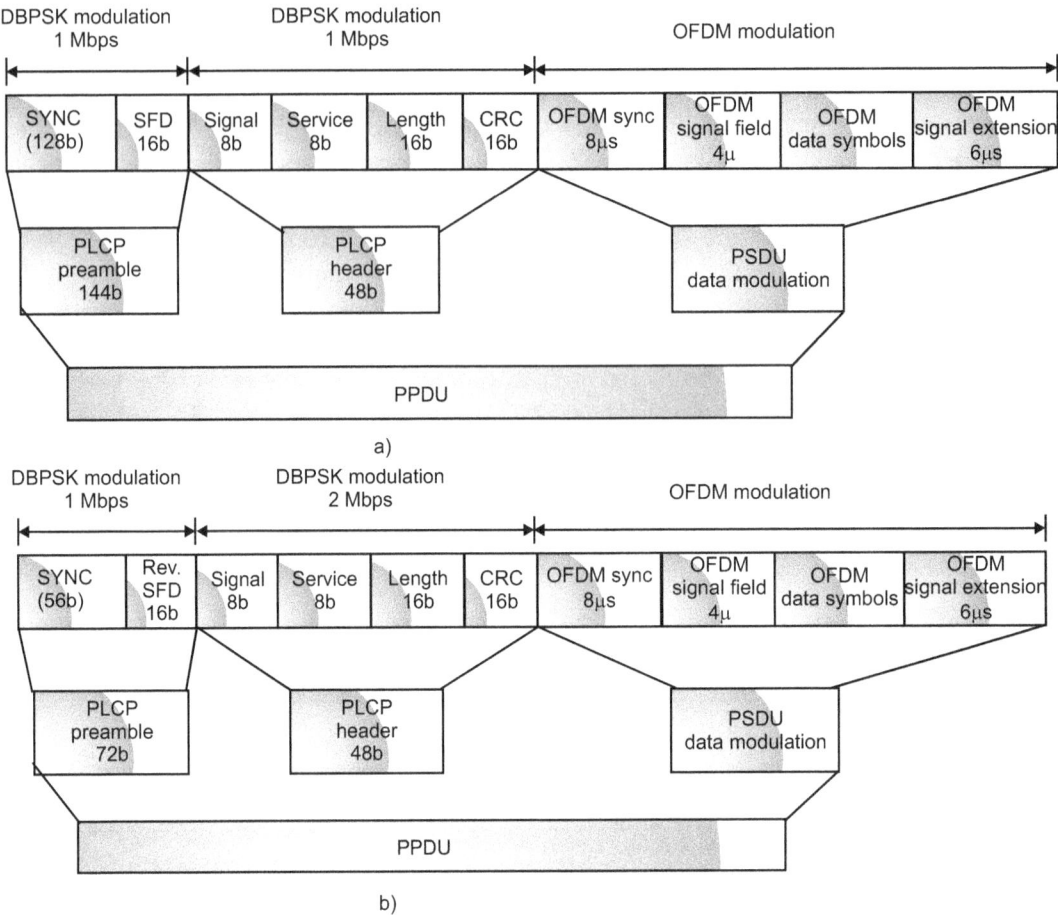

Fig. 4.26 DSSS OFDM PPDU framing a) long preamble b) short preamble

4.11.3 Medium Access Control of 802.11G

The IEEE 802.11g standard builds on the MAC protocol specifications defined for legacy 802.11 networks (IEEE Std 802.11, 1999; IEEE Std 802.11a, 1999; IEEE Std 802.11b,1999). In the 802.11 standard there are two different schemes that can be used in the medium control access. When the Point Coordination Function (PCF) is employed, the access point controls access to the medium by assigning time slots to each station. The Distributed Coordination Function (DCF) on the other hand, needs no central coordinator.

Because the PCF scheme is an optional access method of the 802.11 standard, only the functionality of the DCF will be described in this section. In addition, DCF defines a randomized access mechanism, which is based on the CSMA/CA (Carrier Sense Multiple Access/Collision Avoidance).

DCF constitutes the fundamental access mechanism of the original IEEE 802.11 standard.

According to DCF, a WLAN station must sense the medium before initiating the transmission of a packet. If the medium is sensed idle for a time interval greater than a Distributed InterFrame Space (DIFS), the station transmits the packet. Otherwise, the transmission is deferred and a backoff process begins. Specifically, the station initializes and begins decreasing a timer called a backoff counter.

As soon as the backoff counter expires, the station is authorized to access the medium. The initial value of the backoff counter is defined as the backoff window, which is a random time interval uniformly distributed in the range of [0,CWmin – 1]. The parameter CWmin constitutes the minimum contention window and is doubled after each unsuccessful retransmission attempt up to a maximum value CWmax called the maximum contention window.

Note that in the special case where the time elapsed between the last packet transmission and the current packet transmission is less than a DIFS, the station is obliged to execute the backoff process for the first transmission attempt. Given that collision detection is not possible in a WLAN environment, an Acknowledgement (ACK) is used to notify the sending station that the transmitted frame has been successfully received. The transmission of the acknowledgement is initiated at a time interval equal to the Short InterFrame Space (SIFS) after the end of the reception of the transmitted frame. The above described DCF mechanism is depicted in Fig. 4.27.

In addition to the basic access mechanism, the IEEE 802.11 standard includes a protection mechanism for dealing with the hidden terminal problem. This mechanism is based on the exchange of two short control frames: a Request To Send (RTS) frame that is sent by a potential transmitter to the receiver and a Clear To Send (CTS) frame that is sent from the receiver in response to the RTS frame. The RTS and CTS frames include a duration field that specifies the time interval necessary to completely transmit the data frame and the related acknowledgement. Other stations can hear either the sender (RTS frame), or the receiver (CTS frame), in order to refrain from transmitting until the data frame transmission is completed. The effectiveness of the RTS/CTS mechanism depends upon the length of the packet being protected.

Usually, a hybrid approach is used, where only packets with a size greater than a threshold called RTS Threshold are transmitted with the RTS/CTS mechanism. The operation of the

RTS/CTS protection mechanism is depicted in Figure 4.27. Moreover, this protection mechanism is used to improve the performance in 802.11b/g, and it communicates to 802.11g stations utilizing the CCK scheme. Other protection mechanism used in 802.11g is the CTS-toself. In this protection mechanism, a station sends a CTS message when it desires to send data, even though there is no RTS message received. Both of these mechanisms are designed to help reduce collisions.

IEEE 802.16 WMAN ARCHITECTURE

WiMAX (Worldwide Interoperability for Microwave Access) is an emerging wireless communication system that is expected to provide high data rate communications in metropolitan area networks (MANs). In the past few years, the IEEE 802.16 working group has developed a number of standards for WiMAX. The first standard was published in 2001, which supports communications in the 10-66 GHz frequency band. In 2003, IEEE 802.16a was introduced to provide additional physical layer specifications for the 2-11 GHz frequency band. These two standards were further revised in 2004 (IEEE 802.16-2004). Recently, IEEE 802.16e has also been approved as the official standard for mobile applications.

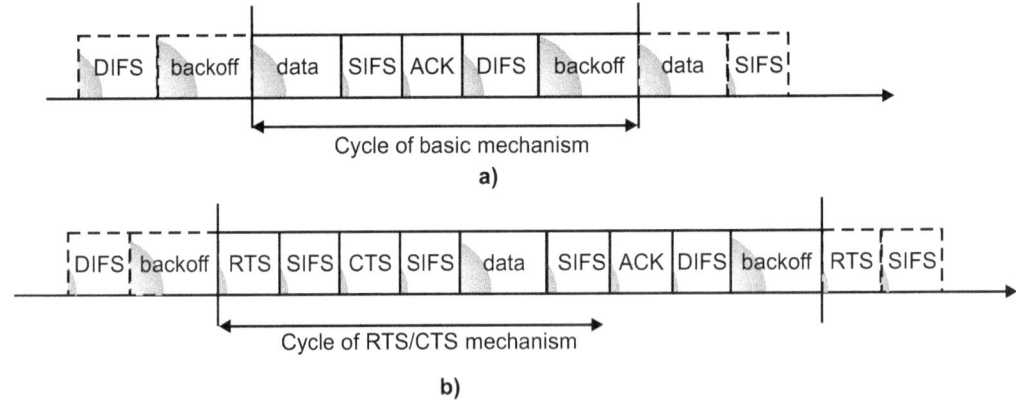

Fig 4.27: Access mechanisms a) Basic b) RTS/CTS

Physical Layer

In the physical (PHY) layer, IEEE 802.16 supports four PHY specifications for the licensed bands. These four specifications are Wireless-MAN-SC (single carrier), -SCa, -OFDM, (orthogonal frequency division multiplexing), and –OFDMA (orthogonal frequency –division multiple access).

In addition, the standard also supports different PHY specifications (-SCa, -OFDM, and –OFDMA) for the unlicensed bands: wireless high-speed unlicensed MAN (WirelessHUMAN). Most PHYs are designed for non-line-of-sight (NLOS) operation in frequency bands below 11

GHz, except –SC, which is for operation in the 10-66 GHz frequency band. To support multiple subscribers, IEEE 802.16 supports both time-division duplex (TDD) and frequency-division duplex (FDD) operations.

The mobile version of IEEE 80.16 also supports the following features to enhance the performance of the wireless system: 1) multiple input, multiple output (MIMO) technique such as transmit/receive diversity multiplexing, 2) multiple antennas schemes can also be used to increase the performance by increasing the transmitted data rates through spatial multiplexing, and 3) adaptive modulation and coding (AMC) is used to better match instantaneous channel and interference conditions.

Medium Access Control Sub-layer

In the medium access control (MAC) layer, IEEE 802.16 supports two modes: point-tomultipoint (PMP) and mesh.

The former organizes nodes into a cellular-like structure consisting of a base station (BS) and subscriber stations (SSs). The channels are divided into uplink (from SS to BS) and downlink (from BS to SS), and both uplink and downlink channels are shared among the SSs. PMP mode requires all SSs to be within the transmission range and clear line of sight (LOS) of the BS. On the other hand, in mesh mode, an ad hoc network can be formed with all nodes acting as relay routers in addition to their sender and receiver roles, although there may still be nodes that serve as BSs and provide backhaul connectivity.

In PMP, requests for resource allocations and data transmissions from SSs to the BS are carried in an uplink (UL) frame. Transmissions from the BS to SSs are carried by a downlink (DL) frame. A typical signaling frame for TDD includes a UL-frame (see Fig. 4.28 a) and a DL-frame (see Fig. 4.28) using a single channel frequency as illustrated in Fig. 4.28 (c). In FDD, these frames are transmitted at the same time using different channel frequencies as illustrated in Fig. 4.28.

The IEEE 802.16 MAC protocol regulates uplink (UL) channel access using Time Division Multiple Access (TDMA). Upon entering the BWA network, each Subscriber Station (SS) has to go throughout the initialization process setup, described as follows:

Subscriber stations need to synchronize with a downlink channel (DL-Ch) and an uplink channel (UL-ch). When a SS has tuned to a DL-ch, it gets the frame structure of the UL-ch, called a UL-MAP frame.

Then the ranging procedure is performed, where the round-trip delay and power calibration are determined for each SS, so that SS transmissions are aligned to the correct mini-slot boundary. Following this, the SS negotiates basic capabilities with the BS.

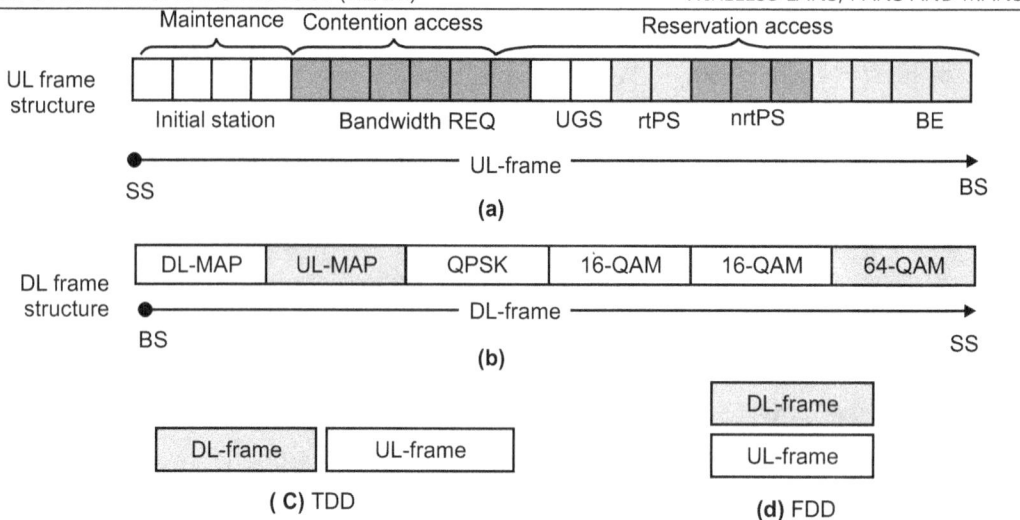

Fig. 4.28 : Frame Structure for TDD and FDD access

This is the phase where the SS and the BS exchange their supported parameters. Next, the SS should use the Privacy Key Management (PKM) protocol to receive authentication from the BS. Then the SS performs the registration process by establishing a security association that allows the SS to enter the network. The next step is to establish IP connectivity. The BS uses the DHCP mechanisms to obtain an IP address for the SS and any other parameters needed to establish IP connectivity.

Then, the SS establishes the time of the day, which is required for time-stamping logged events and key management. In the next step, the SS transfers control parameters via TFTP, such as boot information, QoS parameters, fragmentation, and packing, among others. The last step is to set up connections for pre-provisioned service flows belonging to the SS.

After the initialization process is completed, a SS can create one or more connections over which its data is transmitted to and from the BS. SSs contend for transmission opportunities using the contention access period (or contention block) of the current UL-frame. The BS collects these requests and determines the number of slots (grant size) that each SS will be allowed to transmit in the next UL-frame, using a UL_MAP sub-frame, as shown in Figure 4.28.

The UL-MAP frame contains Information Elements (IE), which describe the maintenance, contention or reservation access of the UL-frame. The UL-MAP is broadcasted in the DL channel by the BS in each DL-Frame. After receiving the UL-MAP, an SS can transmit data in the predefined reserved slots indicated in the IE. These reserved slots are transmission opportunities assigned by a scheduling algorithm using the following QoS service agreements.

Unsolicited Grant Service (UGS):

This service supports real-time service flows that generate fixed-size data packets on a periodic basis (CBR-like services), such as T1/E1, VoIP or videoconferencing. At the beginning of the connection setup, an SS provides the BS its service requirements, such as grant size, grant inter-arrival time, tolerated grant jitter and Poll bit. The UGS service also includes Activity Detection (AD) to examine the flow state. If the state is inactive, then the UGS-AD Service sets the Poll bit to 1 and periodically provides a unicast transmission opportunity, in which an SS can request the BS reestablish its UGS service, thus saving bandwidth.

Real-Time Polling Service (rtPS):

This service supports real-time service flows that generate variable size data packets on a periodic basis (VBR-like services), such as MPEG video streams. The rtPS service offers periodic transmission opportunity, which meets the flow's realtime needs and allow the SS to specify the size of the desired channel reservation. A SS should indicate its requirements to the BS at the beginning of the session, such as polling interval and tolerated poll jitter.

Non Real-Time Polling Service (nrtPS):

This type of service is similar to rtPS, however polling will typically occur at a much lower rate and may not necessarily be periodic. This applies to applications that have no requirement for a real time service but may need an assured high level of bandwidth. An example of this may be bulk data transfer (via FTP) or an Internet gaming application. The parameters required for this service are the polling interval, minimum and maximum sustained data rate.

Best Effort (BE):

This kind of service is for standard Internet traffic, where no throughput or delay guarantees are provided. The IEEE 802.16 MAC protocol can identify the type of service flow required by an SS using the following fields of the IEEE 802.16 protocol stack: source or destination MAC address, EtherType, source and destination IP address or network, IP protocol type, source or destination port number, IP type of service bits and any combination thereof. A simple example of how a classification might be used would be to match VoIP traffic from a particular source IP address and UDP port and to direct that traffic into a dynamically created service flow that has a QoS parameter set that provides a UGS mode of data transmission.

Once the service flows have been identified, the BS uses two modes of operation to allocate grants: 1) Grants per Connection (GPC) and Grants per Subscriber Station (GPSS).

In the first case, the BS grants bandwidth explicitly to each connection, whereas in the second case the bandwidth is granted to all the connections belonging to the SS. The latter case (GPSS) allows smaller uplink maps and allows more intelligent SSs to make last moment decisions and perhaps utilize the bandwidth differently than it was originally granted by the

BS. This may be useful for real-time applications that require a faster response time from the system.

QUESTIONS

1. Explain the difference between Infrastructure and Ad-hoc Networks.
2. Explain different wireless networks in ISM Band.
3. Explain network architecture of IEEE 802.11 with physical and MAC layer.
4. Explain CSMA/CA mechanism.
5. Explain following points in the context of bluettoth :
   (a) Specification.
   (b) Profiles.
6. Explain difference between IEEE 802.11 and 802.16.

Unit - V
AD HOC NETWORKS AND SENSOR NETWORKS

5.1 INTRODUCTION TO MANET

The field of wireless and mobile communication has grown extremely fast in the last decade. Current second generation (2G) cellular systems have enabled the worldwide mobile connectivity. Mobile users can access the Internet, check their mails from the cellular phone.

A trend of wireless LAN hot spots is also emerging rapidly which allows travellers with portable computers to access the Internet from any location. Meanwhile 2G cellular networks are shifting to 3G, offering higher data rates and location based or personalised services.

However, all these Networks are conventional wireless networks as they require fixed network infrastructure with centralised administration for their operation. This consumes a lot of time and money for setup and maintenance. On the other hand an increasing number of devices such as laptops, pocket PCs, smart phones are provided with short range wireless interfaces. Also these devices are getting smaller, cheaper, more user friendly and cheaper. This evolution is the driving force for new kind of mobile communication in which mobile devices form a self creating, self organising and self administrating wireless network called a Mobile Ad hoc Network (MANET).

A MANET is a self configuring network of mobile routers connected by wireless links. The union of this forms a random topology. These mobile routers are free to move randomly and organize themselves at random. This may change the network's topology rapidly and unpredictably. Such networks usually operate in standalone fashion. Minimal configuration and quick deployment make MANET suitable for monitoring emergency situations like natural or manmade disasters, military conflicts, emergency situations etc.

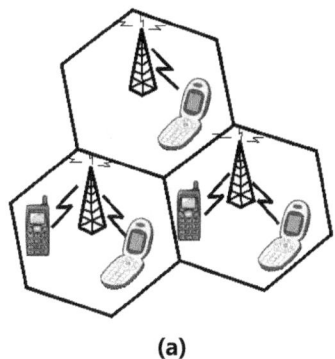

(a)

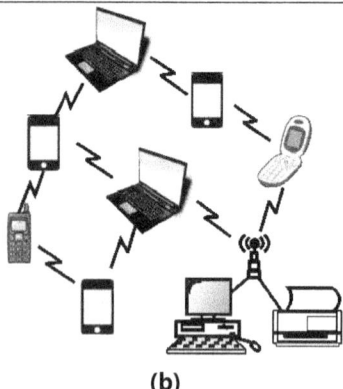

(b)

Fig. 5.1 : Cellular network versus MANET

Characteristics and Complexities of MANET :

- Autonomous and infrastructureless
- Multihop routing
- Dynamic network topology
- Device heterogeneity
- Network scalability
- Self creation, self organization, self administration
- Energy constrained operation
- Bandwidth constrained variable capacity links
- Limited physical security

Applications of MANET :

Application	Possible Scenarios/Services
Tactical networks	Military communication and operations Automated battlefields
Emergency services	Search and rescue operations Disaster recovery Policing and fire fighting Supporting doctors and nurses in hospitals
Commercial and civilian	E-commerce: electronic payments anytime and anywhere Business: dynamic database access, mobile offices Vehicular services: road or accident guidance, taxi cab network, inter-vehicle networks Sports stadiums, trade fairs, shopping malls

	Networks of visitors at airports
Home and enterprise	Home/office wireless networking
	Personal area networks (PAN), Personal networks (PN)
	Networks at construction sites
Education	Universities and campus settings
	Virtual classrooms
	Ad hoc communications during meetings or lectures
Entertainment	Multi-user games
	Outdoor Internet access
	Robotic pets
Sensor networks	Home applications: smart sensors and actuators embedded in consumer electronics
	Data tracking of environmental conditions, animal movements, chemical/biological detection
Context aware services	Follow-on services: call-forwarding, mobile workspace
	Information services: location specific services, time dependent services
Coverage extension	Extending cellular network access
	Linking up with the Internet, intranets, etc.

5.2 INTRODUCTION TO WIRELESS SENSOR NETWORK (WSN)

Efficient design and implementation of wireless sensor networks has become an important area of research in recent years, due to the vast potential of sensor networks to enable applications that connect the physical world to the virtual world. By networking large numbers of tiny sensor nodes, it is possible to obtain data about physical phenomena that was difficult or impossible to obtain in more conventional ways. In the coming years, as advances in micro-fabrication technology allow the cost of manufacturing sensor nodes to continue to drop, increasing deployments of wireless sensor networks are expected, with the networks eventually growing to large numbers of nodes (e.g., thousands). Potential applications for such large-scale wireless sensor networks exist in a variety of fields, including medical monitoring, environmental monitoring, surveillance, home security, military operations, and industrial machine monitoring. To understand the variety of applications that can be supported by wireless sensor networks. Consider the following two examples.

Surveillance : Suppose multiple networked sensors (e.g., acoustic, seismic, video) are distributed throughout an area such as a battlefield. A surveillance application can be designed on top of this sensor network to provide information to an end-user about the environment. In such a sensor network, traffic patterns are many-to-one, where the traffic can range from raw sensor data to a high level description of what is occurring in the environment, if data processing is done locally.

The application will have some Quality of Service (QoS) requirements from the sensor network, such as requiring minimum percentage sensor coverage in an area where a phenomenon is expected to occur, or requiring a maximum probability of missed detection of an event.

At the same time, the network is expected to provide this quality of service for a long time (months or even years) using the limited resources of the network (e.g., sensor energy and channel bandwidth) while requiring little to no outside intervention. Meeting these goals requires careful design of both the sensor hardware and the network protocols.

Medical Monitoring : A different application domain that can make use of wireless sensor network technology can be found in the area of medical monitoring. This field ranges from monitoring patients in the hospital using wireless sensors to remove the constraints of tethering patients to big, bulky, wired monitoring devices, to monitoring patients in mass casualty situations, to monitoring people in their everyday lives to provide early detection and intervention for various types of disease.

In these scenarios, the sensors vary from miniature, body-worn sensors to external sensors such as video cameras or positioning devices. This is a challenging environment in which dependable, flexible, applications must be designed using sensor data as input. Consider a personal health monitor application running on a PDA that receives and analyzes data from a number of sensors (e.g., ECG, EMG, blood pressure, blood flow, pulse oxymeter). The monitor reacts to potential health risks and records health information in a local database. Considering that most sensors used by the personal health monitor will be battery-operated and use wireless communication, it is clear that this application requires networking protocols that are efficient, reliable, scalable and secure.

To better understand why traditional network protocols are not suitable for these types of sensor network applications, in the remainder of this section, we will categorize the unique features of sensor networks and the performance metrics with which protocols for sensor networks should be evaluated.

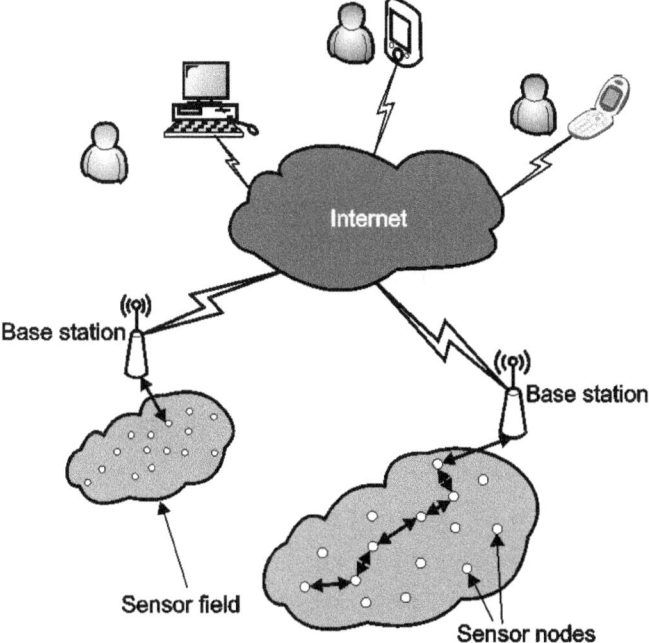

Fig. 5.2 : Accessing the WSNs through Internet

5.2.1 Context of Sensor Networks

As research in sensor networks has grown, so too has the range of applications proposed to make use of this rich source of data. Such diversity of sensor network applications translates to differing requirements from the underlying sensor network. To address these varying needs, many different network models have been proposed, around which protocols for different layers of the network stack have been designed. While there are many ways to classify different sensor network architectures, the following list highlights some fundamental differences in sensor networks that affect protocol design.

- **Data Sink(s) :** One of the most important aspects of a sensor network is the nature of the data sink(s). In some situations, the end user(s) may be embedded within the sensor network

    (e.g., actuator(s) that correct abnormalities in environmental conditions, access points that network with the outside world) or may be less accessible mobile access points that collect data once in a while. This distinction may be important, as efficient distributed data storage techniques may be effective depending on applications.

- **Sensor Mobility :** Another classification of sensor networks may be made based on the nature of the sensors being deployed. Typically, it can be assumed that sensors are immobile. In military operations, additional sensors may be mounted on soldiers or UAVs to interact with a deployed sensor network. The mobility of sensors can influence protocols at the networking layer as well as those for localization services.

- **Sensor Resources :** Sensor nodes may vary greatly in the computing resources available. It is obvious that memory and processing constraints should influence protocol design at nearly every level.
- **Traffic Patterns :** Another important aspect to consider is the traffic generated on the network. In many event-driven applications, sensors may operate in a sentry state for the majority of time, only generating data traffic when an event of interest is detected. In other applications such as environmental monitoring, data should be continuously generated.

As can be seen by the above discussion, there are many features of the sensors, the network and the application that should influence protocol design. Accordingly, much research has gone into designing protocols for these different scenarios.

5.2.2 Unique Features of Sensor Networks

It should be noted that sensor networks do share some commonalities with general ad hoc networks. Thus, protocol design for sensor networks must account for the properties of ad hoc networks.

- Lifetime constraints imposed by the limited energy supplies of the nodes in the network.
- Unreliable communication due to the wireless medium.
- Need for self-configuration, requiring little or no human intervention.

However, several unique features exist in wireless sensor networks that do not exist in general ad hoc networks. These features present new challenges and require modification of designs for traditional ad hoc networks.

- While traditional ad hoc networks consist of network sizes on the order of 10s, sensor networks are expected to scale to sizes of 1000s.
- Sensor nodes are typically immobile, meaning that the mechanisms used in traditional ad hoc network protocols to deal with mobility may be unnecessary and overweight.
- Since nodes may be deployed in harsh environmental conditions, unexpected node failure may be common.
- Sensor nodes may be much smaller than nodes in traditional ad hoc networks (e.g., PDAs, laptop computers), with smaller batteries leading to shorter lifetimes, less computational power, and less memory.
- Additional services, such as location information, may be required in wireless sensor networks.

- While nodes in traditional ad hoc networks compete for resources such as bandwidth, nodes in a sensor network can be expected to behave more co-operatively, since they are trying to accomplish a similar universal goal, typically related to maintaining an application-level quality of service (QoS), or fidelity.
- Communication is typically data-centric rather than address-centric, meaning that routed data may be aggregated/compressed/prioritized/dropped depending on the description of the data.
- Communication in sensor networks typically takes place in the form of very short packets, meaning that the relative overhead imposed at the different network layers becomes much more important.
- Sensor networks often have a many-to-one traffic pattern, which leads to a "hot spot" problem.

Incorporating these unique features of sensor networks into protocol design is important in order to efficiently utilize the limited resources of the network. At the same time, to keep the protocols as light-weight as possible, many designs focus on particular subsets of these criteria for different types of applications. This has led to quite a number of different protocols from the data-link layer up to the transport layer, each with the goal of allowing the network to operate autonomously for as long as possible while maintaining data channels and network processing to provide the application's required quality of service.

5.3 OPERATING ENVIRONMENT CONSTRAINTS

5.3.1 Need of Operating Environment Constraints

The traditional tasks of an operating system are controlling and protecting the access to resources (including support for input/output) and managing their allocation to different users as well as the support for concurrent execution of several processes and communication between these processes. These tasks are, however, only partially required in an embedded system as the executing code is much more restricted. Rather, an operating system or an execution environment for WSNs should support the specific needs of these systems. In particular, the need for energy-efficient execution requires support for energy management, for example, in the form of controlled shutdown of individual components or Dynamic Voltage Scaling (DVS) techniques. Also, external components – sensors, the radio modem, or timers – should be handled easily and efficiently, in particular, information that becomes available asynchronously (at any arbitrary point in time) must be handled.

All this requires an appropriate programming model, a clear way to structure a protocol stack, and explicit support for energy management – without imposing too heavy a burden on system resources like memory or execution time.

These three topics are treated in the following sections :

5.3.2 Programming Paradigms and Application Programming Interfaces

Concurrent Programming

One of the first questions for a programming paradigm is how to support concurrency. Such support for concurrent execution is crucial for WSN nodes, as they have to handle data communing from arbitrary sources, for example, multiple sensors or the radio transceiver – at arbitrary points in time. For example, a system could poll a sensor to decide whether data is available and process the data right away, then poll the transceiver to check whether a packet is available, and then immediately process the packet, and so on Fig. 5.3. Such a simple sequential model would run the risk of missing data while a packet is processed or missing a packet when sensor information is Single-node architecture processed. This risk is particularly large if the processing of sensor data or incoming packets takes substantial amounts of time, which can easily be the case. Hence, a simple, sequential programming model is clearly insufficient.

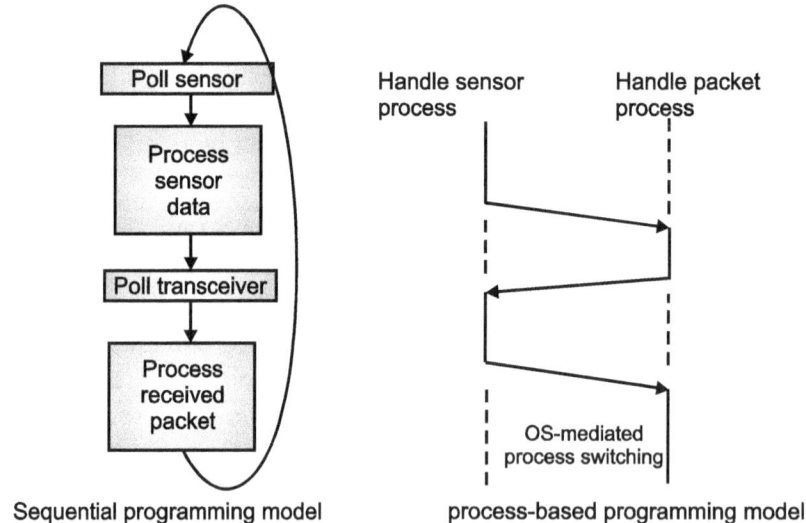

Fig. 5.3 : Programming models for WSN operating systems:

Process-based Concurrency

Most modern, general-purpose operating systems support concurrent (seemingly parallel) execution of multiple processes on a single CPU. Hence, such a process-based approach would be a first candidate to support concurrency in a sensor node as well; it is illustrated in (b) of Figure 3. But mapping such an execution model of concurrent processes to a sensor node shows has some problems. Equating individual protocol functions or layers with individual processes would entail a high overhead in switching from one process to another. This problem is particularly severe if often tasks have to be executed that are small with respect to the overhead incurred for switching between tasks – which is typically the case in sensor networks. Also, each process requires its own stack space in memory, which fits ill with the stringent memory constraints of sensor nodes.

Event-based Programming

For these reasons, a somewhat different programming model seems preferable. The idea is to embrace the reactive nature of a WSN node and integrate it into the design of the operating system. The system essentially waits for any event to happen, where an event typically can be the availability of data from a sensor, the arrival of a packet, or the expiration of a timer. Such an event is then handled by a short sequence of instructions that only stores the fact that this event has occurred and stores the necessary information for example, a byte arriving for a packet or the sensor's value – somewhere. The actual processing of this information is not done in these event handler routines, but separately, decoupled from the actual appearance of events.

This **event-based programming** model is shown in Fig. 5.4.

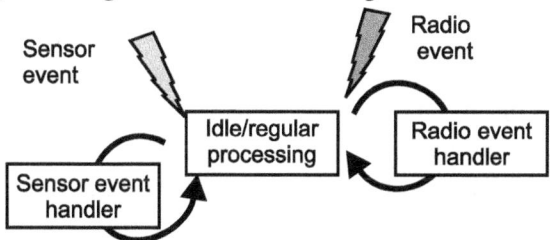

Fig. 5.4 : Event-based programming model

Such an event handler can interrupt the processing of any normal code, but as it is very simple and short, it can be required to run to completion in all circumstances without noticeably disturbing other code. Event handlers cannot interrupt each other but are simply executed one after each other. As a consequence, this event-based programming model distinguishes between two different "contexts": one for the time-critical event handlers, where execution cannot be interrupted and a second context for the processing of normal code, which is only triggered by the event handlers. It is actually comparable, on some levels, to communicating, extended finite state machines, which are used in protocol design formalisms as well as in some parallel programming paradigms.

5.3.3 Interfaces to the Operating System

In addition to the programming model that is stipulated, if not actually imposed, by the operating system, it is also necessary to specify some interfaces to how internal state of the system can be inquired and set. As the clear distinction between protocol stack and application programs vanishes somewhat in WSNs, such an interface should be accessible from protocol implementations and it should allow these implementations to access each other. This interface is also closely tied with the structure of protocol stacks.

Such an Application Programming Interface (API) comprises, in general, a "functional interface". Abstractions are wireless links, nodes, and so on; possible functions include state inquiry and manipulation, sending and transmitting of data, access to hardware (sensors, actuators, transceivers), and setting of policies, for example, with respect to energy/quality trade-offs.

While such a general API would be extremely useful, there is currently no clear standards are available. Until this change, de facto standards will continue to be used and are likely to serve reasonably well.

5.3.4 Structure of Operating Environment and Protocol Stack

The traditional approach to communication protocol structuring is to use layering: individual protocols are stacked on top of each other, each layer only using functions of the layer directly below. This layered approach has great benefits in keeping the entire protocol stack manageable, in containing complexity, and in promoting modularity and reuse. However, it is not clear whether such a strictly layered approach will work for WSNs.

As an example, consider the use of information about the strength of the signal received from a communication partner. This physical layer information can be used to assist in networking protocols to decide about routing changes (a signal becomes weaker if a node moves away and should perhaps no longer be used as a next hop), to compute location information by estimating distance from the signal strength, or to assist link layer protocols in channel-adaptive or hybrid FEC/ARQ schemes. Hence, one single source of information can be used to the advantage of many other protocols not directly associated with the source of this information. Such cross-layer information exchange is but one way to loosen the strict confinements of the layered approach. Also, WSNs are not the only reason why such exchanges are brought. Even in traditional network scenarios, efficiency considerations the there is need support handover mechanisms by physical layer information in cellular networks which have created a considerable pressure for a flexible, manageable, and efficient way of structuring and implementing communication protocols.

When departing from the layered architecture, the prevalent trend is to use a component model. Relatively large, monolithic layers are broken up into small, self-contained "components". These components only fulfil one well-defined function each, for example, computation of a Cyclic Redundancy Check (CRC) and interact with each other over clear interfaces. The main difference compared to the layered architecture is that these interactions are not confined to immediate neighbours in an up/down relationship, but can be with any other component. This component model not only solves some of the structuring problems for protocol stacks, it also fits naturally with an event-based approach to programming wireless sensor nodes. Wrapping of hardware, communication primitives, in-network processing functionalities all can be conveniently designed and implemented as components.

5.3.5 Dynamic Energy and Power Management

Switching individual components into various sleep states or reducing their performance by scaling down frequency and supply voltage and selecting particular modulation and codings are not the prominent for improving energy efficiency. To control these possibilities, decisions have to be made by the operating system, by the protocol stack, or potentially by an application when to switch into one of these states. Dynamic Power Management (DPM) on a system level is the problem at hand.

One of the complicating factors to DPM is the energy and time required for the transition of a component between any two states. If these factors were negligible, clearly it would be optimal to always & immediately go into the mode with the lowest power consumption possible. As this is not the case, more advanced algorithms are required, taking into account these costs, the rate of updating power management decisions, the probability distribution of time until future events, and properties of the used algorithms.

5.4 PROTOCOLS SUPPORTED BY WIRELESS NETWORKS

This section introduces the Bluetooth, UWB, ZigBee, and Wi-Fi protocols, which corresponds to the IEEE 802.15.1, 802.15.3, 802.15.4, and 802.11a/b/g standards, respectively.

(1) Bluetooth over IEEE 802.15.1 :

Bluetooth, also known as the IEEE 802.15.1 standard is based on a wireless radio system designed for short-range and cheap devices to replace cables for computer peripherals, such as mice, keyboards, joysticks, and printers. This range of applications is known as wireless personal area network (WPAN). Two connectivity topologies are defined in Bluetooth: the piconet and scatternet. A piconet is a WPAN formed by a Bluetooth device serving as a master in the piconet and one or more Bluetooth devices serving as slaves. A frequency-hopping channel based on the address of the master defines each piconet. All devices participating in communications in a given piconet are synchronized using the clock of the master. Slaves communicate only with their master in a point-to-point fashion under the control of the master. The master's transmissions may be either point-to-point or point-tomultipoint.

Also, besides in an active mode, a slave device can be in the parked or standby modes so as to reduce power consumptions. A scatternet is a collection of operational Bluetooth piconets overlapping in time and space.

Two piconets can be connected to form a scatternet. A Bluetooth device may participate in several piconets at the same time, thus allowing for the possibility that information could flow beyond the coverage area of the single piconet. A device in a scatternet could be a slave in several piconets, but master in only one of them.

(2) UWB over IEEE 802.15.3 :

UWB has recently attracted much attention as an indoor short-range high-speed wireless communication. One of the most exciting characteristics of UWB is that its bandwidth is over 110 Mbps (up to 480 Mbps) which can satisfy most of the multimedia applications such as audio and video delivery in home networking and it can also act as a wireless cable replacement of high speed serial bus such as USB 2.0 and IEEE 1394. Following the United States and the Federal Communications Commission (FCC) frequency allocation for UWB in February 2002, the Electronic Communications Committee (ECC TG3) is progressing in the elaboration of a regulation for the UWB technology in Europe. From an implementation point of view, several solutions have been developed in order to use the UWB technology in compliance with the FCC's regulatory requirements. Among the existing PHY solutions, in IEEE 802.15 Task Group 3a (TG3a), multiband orthogonal frequency-division multiplexing (MB-OFDM), a carrier-based system dividing UWB bandwidth to sub-bands, and direct-sequence UWB (DS-UWB), an impulse-based system that multiplies an input bit with the spreading code and transmits the data by modulating the element of the symbol with a short pulse have been proposed by the WiMedia Alliance and the UWB Forum, respectively. The TG3a was established in January 2003 to define an alternative PHY layer of 802.15.3. However, after three years of a jammed process in IEEE 802.15.3a, supporters of both proposals, MB-OFDM and DS-UWB, supported the shut down of the IEEE 802.15.3a task group without conclusion in January 2006. On the other hand, IEEE 802.15.3b, the amendment to the 802.15.3 MAC sublayer has been approved and released in March 2006.

(3) ZigBee over IEEE 802.15.4 :

ZigBee over IEEE 802.15.4, defines specifications for low rate WPAN (LR-WPAN) for supporting simple devices that consume minimal power and typically operate in the personal operating space (POS) of 10m. ZigBee provides self-organized, multi-hop, and reliable mesh networking with long battery.

Lifetime. Two different device types can participate in an LR-WPAN network: a full function device (FFD) and a reduced-function device (RFD). The FFD can operate in three modes serving as a PAN coordinator, a coordinator, or a device. An FFD can talk to RFDs or other FFDs, while an RFD can talk only to an FFD. An RFD is intended for applications that are extremely simple, such as a light switch or a passive infrared sensor. They do not have the need to send large amounts of data and may only associate with a single FFD at a time. Consequently, the RFD can be implemented using minimal resources and memory capacity. After an FFD is activated for the first time, it may establish its own network and become the PAN coordinator. All star networks operate independently from all other star networks currently in operation. This is achieved by choosing a PAN identifier, which is not currently used by any other network within the radio sphere of influence. Once the PAN identifier is chosen, the PAN coordinator can allow other devices to join its network. An RFD may connect to a cluster tree network as a leave node at the end of a branch, because it may only associate with one FFD at a time. Any of the FFDs may act as a coordinator and provide synchronization services to other devices or other coordinators. Only one of these coordinators can be the overall PAN coordinator, which may have greater computational resources than any other device in the PAN.

(4) Wi-Fi over IEEE 802.11a/b/g

Wireless fidelity (Wi-Fi) includes IEEE 802.11a/b/g standards for wireless local area networks (WLAN). It allows users to surf the Internet at broadband speeds when connected to an access point (AP) or in ad hoc mode. The IEEE 802.11 architecture consists of several components that interact to provide a wireless LAN that supports station mobility transparently to upper layers. The basic cell of an IEEE 802.11 LAN is called a basic service set (BSS), which is a set of mobile or fixed stations. If a station moves out of its BSS, it can no longer directly communicate with other members of the BSS. Based on the BSS, IEEE 802.11 employs the independent basic service set (IBSS) and extended service set (ESS) network configurations. As shown in Fig. , the IBSS operation is possible when IEEE 802.11 stations are able to communicate directly without any AP. Because this type of IEEE 802.11 LAN is often formed without pre-planning, for only as long as the LAN is needed, this type of operation is often referred to as an ad hoc network. Instead of existing independently, a BSS may also form a component of an extended form of network that is built with multiple BSSs. The architectural component used to interconnect BSSs is the distribution system (DS). The DS with APs allow IEEE 802.11 to create an ESS network of arbitrary size and complexity. This type of operation is often referred to as an infrastructure network.

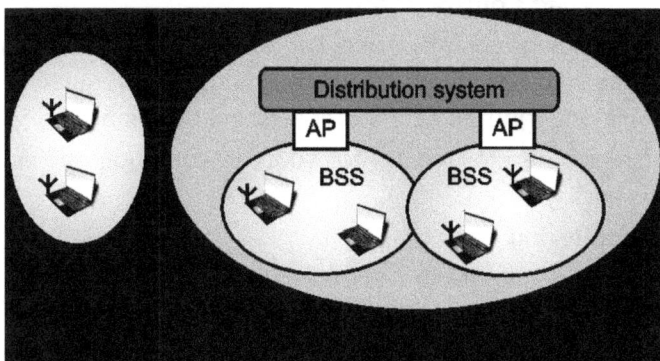

Fig. 5.5 : IBSS and ESS configurations in Wi-Fi networks

5.5 APPLICATIONS OF SENSOR NETWORKS

Unlike the Internet where TCP\IP is the standard transport protocol on which all the Internet applications can be built, sensor networks have no such common platform on which most applications can be built. Unique characteristics of each application are also an important reason behind it.

Following are some typical applications of sensor networks

(1) Asset and Warehouse Management

Sensor may be used to monitor and track assets such as trucks and other equipments especially in the area where no fixed network infrastructure is available. Sensor may also be used to manage assets for oil and gas industries, utility industries and aerospace. These tracking sensors can vary from GPS equipped locators to passive RFID tags.

The automated logging system can reduce errors in manual data entry. Businesses such as transport, construction and utility can significantly improve the asset utilization using real time information about equipment location and condition.

With the use of RFIDs warehouses and department stores are able to collect real time inventory and retail information and use the information to optimize for supply, delivery and storage.

(2) Automation

With emerging standards such as dedicated short range communications (DSRC) designed for vehicle to vehicle communication, cars will soon be able to talk to each other and to roadside infrastructures. A new application called sensors on wheels is very useful in emergency alerts and driver safety assistance. During an emergency brake, an alert message from the breaking can be broadcast to nearby cars so that preventive measures can be taken by them. Information about cars mechanical conditions can be linked to databases of maintenance shops so that timely repairs can be scheduled.

(3) Building Monitoring and Control

Sensors embedded in buildings can effectively cut down the energy costs by monitoring the temperature and lightening conditions in the buildings and regulating the heating and cooling systems, ventilators, lights and computer servers accordingly.

For example, cold air may be directed to hot spots in computer server rooms to prevent overheating and save energy.

(4) Environmental Monitoring

Environmental monitoring is one of the earliest applications of the sensor networks. Sensors can be used to monitor conditions and movements of wild animals or plants in wild life habitats. Sensors can be also used for monitoring air quality and track environmental pollutants, wildfires or other natural or manmade disasters. Sensors can also monitor biological or chemical hazards to provide early warnings.

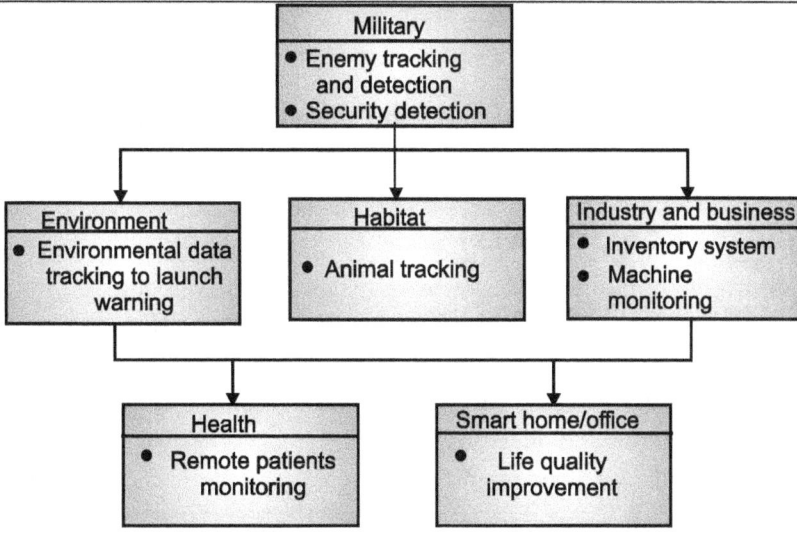

Fig. 5.6 : Application areas of sensor networks

(5) Health Care

Sensors can monitor vital signs of patient and are remotely connected to doctors' offices. Sensors deployed in homes can also alert doctors when patient falls or need immediate medical attention

For example, Intel consortium is developing a system to follow activities of elder people with Alzheimer's disease. This system when fully developed will deploy a network of sensors throughout patient's home tracking down his activities.

(6) Military Battlefield Awareness

Wireless sensors can be rapidly deployed, either by themselves, without an established infrastructure or embedding with other resources such as radar arrays and long haul communication links.

They are well suited to collect information about enemy presence and to track down their movement in a battlefield. These sensors can also be deployed over the hill to gather enemy troop movement data.

(7) Security and Surveillance

Security monitoring and surveillance for buildings, airports, subways and other critical infrastructures such as power and telecom grids and nuclear power plants is one of the most important applications of sensor networks. Sensors may also be used to improve the safety of roads by providing warnings of approaching cars at intersections. Image or video sensors can be very useful in identifying and tracking moving. However they require high bandwidth communication links.

5.6 SENSOR NODE ARCHITECTURE

nodes. These nodes must meet the requirements that emerge as a part of particular application. These nodes can be small, cheap and energy efficient. They have to be equipped with right sensors having suitable memory and computation resources. Also they require adequate communication facilities.

5.6.1 Hardware Components

Selection of hardware components for a wireless sensor node depends on the application's requirement. These requirements are governed by the factors such as size, cost and energy consumption of the nodes, quality of communication and computation facilities, cost etc.

There is no single standard available for the hardware components of wireless sensor node, nor will such single standard be able to support number of application types.

Basic sensor node has following five main components.

(1) Controller

Controller is the most important part of the sensor node. It collects the data from sensors, processes this data, decides when and where to send it and also receives data from other sensor nodes. Also it has to execute various programs such as time critical signal processing, communication protocols and application programs.

Controller is the central processing unit of the sensor node. Such variety of data processing tasks can be performed by controller with setting trade-offs between flexibility, performance, energy efficiency and cost. These data processing tasks can be performed by simpler processors that are more widely used in embedded systems. These processors are commonly referred as microcontrollers. The main advantage of using these microcontrollers are their flexibility in connecting with other devices like sensors, instruction set useful for time critical signal processing, low power consumption, built in memory and also they are also easily programmable.

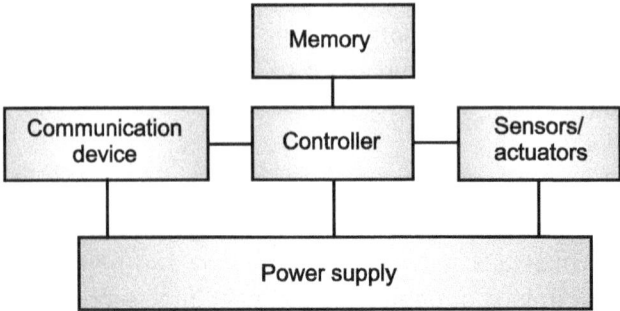

Fig. 5.7 : Block diagram of main components of a sensor node

These microcontrollers are also suitable for wireless sensor networks as they reduce the power consumption by going into sleep states and only required parts of controller are active.

Examples of microcontrollers

Texas Instruments MSP 430

It runs a 16 bit RISC core at lower clock frequencies and supports a wide range of interconnection possibilities and instruction set for handling different kinds of peripherals. It has on chip RAM with size ranging from 2 to 10 KB, 12 bit analog/digital converter and a real time clock. It is powerful enough to handle the computational tasks of wireless sensor node.

Atmel AT mega

It is a 8 bit microcontroller and provides external interfaces for common peripherals.

(2) Memory

Memory is required to store programs and intermediate data. Memory requirements are very much application dependant. Random Access Memory (RAM) can be used to store intermediate sensor readings, packets from other nodes, etc. It can be crucial with respect to manufacturing cost and power consumption. However its disadvantage is that it loses its content if power supply is interrupted. Flash memory can be also used as an intermediate storage of data when RAM is insufficient or RAM is to be switched off for some time.

(3) Sensors and Actuators

The possible range of sensors in the context of wireless sensor network is quite large. Hence it is possible to give only rough idea about them. Sensors and actuators are the devices that can monitor and control physical parameters of the environment. They serve as actual interface to the real world.

Sensors are classified into three categories:

(1) Passive, Unidirectional Sensors

These sensors are called as passive because they can measure a physical quantity at the point of sensor node without actually monitoring the environment. Some of these sensors are self powered as they obtain the energy they need from the environment. Typical examples of these sensors are thermometer, light sensors, microphones, smoke detectors and air pressures, etc.

(2) Passive, Narrow Beam Sensors

These sensors though passive, but have a well defined direction measurement. A typical example is camera, which can take measurement in a given direction.

(3) Active Sensors

These sensors are called as active because they actively monitor the environment, for example a sonar or a radar sensor which generates shock waves by small explosion. These explosions are not lightly taken actions, they require quite special attention.

Each sensor node has a certain area of coverage for which it can reliably and accurately report the particular quality that it is monitoring.

(4) Communication and Communicating Devices

Turning nodes on into network require a device for sending and receiving information over a wireless medium. In case of wireless communication first of all transmission medium is very important. Usually radio frequencies, optical communication or ultra sound can be used. However Radio Frequency (RF) based communication is best fitted for the requirements of most WSN applications. It provides long range, high data rates, and acceptable error rates with efficient energy expenditure. Also it does not require any line of sight between sender and receiver.

(5) Power Supply

Power supply is needed for the operation of sensor nodes. For sensor nodes, as there is no tethered power source is available, some form of batteries can be sued to provide them energy. Other advantage of using these batteries as power source is that they are self rechargeable. For this they obtain energy from environment. (Example: solar cells).

Conventional Energy Stores :

Traditional Batteries

Power source for sensor nodes is either primary batteries or secondary batteries. Primary batteries are non rechargeable. Secondary batteries have energy scavenging device that present on the node and they are rechargeable.

Example of primary battery is lithium batteries with energy 2880 J/cm^3 and secondary battery is NiMHd batteries with energy 860 J/ cm^3

Requirements of Batteries

Capacity : They should have high capacity at a small weight, small volume and low cost.

Capacity under load : They should be capable of withstanding variety of usage patterns as a sensor node can consume quite different levels of power over time.

Self discharge : Their self discharge should be large. They should last for long time.

Efficient recharging : Recharging should be efficient even at low and intermittently available recharge power.

Unconventional Energy Stores

Batteries alone are not sufficient as a single and main power source for a sensor node. One major problem is the reduction of a battery's voltage as its capacity drops. Less power is delivered to the sensor node's circuitry and battery becomes weak. A node on weak battery will have a smaller transmission range than with the full battery.

DC-DC Conversion

A DC-DC conversion can be used to overcome the problem of battery's voltage reduction. DC-DC conversion regulates the voltage delivered to the sensor node's circuitry. It ensures a constant voltage even though battery's supply voltage drops by drawing higher current from the battery when the battery is already becoming weak.

Energy Scavenging

Some of the unconventional energy stores such as fuel cells, convert energy from some stored, secondary form into an electricity in easy to use way than normal batteries do. For long lasting nodes and wireless sensor networks, such a limited energy store is not acceptable. Energy scavenging is an important effect that taps the energy from node's environment and make sure that it is available to the node.

Energy scavenging can be achieved by following approaches

(1) Photovoltaic

Solar cells can be used to power sensor nodes. The available power depends on whether nodes are used outdoors or indoors, time of the day, etc.

The resulting power is somewhere between $10\mu W/cm^2$ for indoors to $15mW/cm^2$ for outdoors. Single cell achieves a fairly stable output voltage of about 0.6 V as long as the current the drawn current does not exceeds as critical threshold.

(2) Temperature Gradient

Different temperature can be directly converted to electrical energy. Theoretically even a small difference of temperature (about 5 K) can produce considerable power. But practically fall very short of theoretical upper limits.

5.7 SENSOR NETWORK ARCHITECTURE

Wireless sensor network (WSN) is a network made of a numerous number of sensor nodes with sensing, wireless communications and computation capabilities. These sensor nodes are scattered in an unattended environment (i.e., sensor field) situated far from the user as shown in Fig. 5.8. The upper side of the architecture above in Fig. 5.8 represents the communication architecture for (WSNs).

The main entities that build up the architecture are

- The Sensor nodes that form the sensor network. Their main objectives are making discrete, local measurement about phenomenon surrounding these sensors, forming a wireless network by communicating over a wireless medium, and collect date and rout data back to the user via sink (Base Station).
- The sink (Base Station) communicates with the user via internet or satellite communication. It is located near the sensor field or well-equipped nodes of the sensor network. Collected data from the sensor field routed back to the sink by a multi-hop infrastructure less architecture through the sink.
- Phenomenon which is an entity of interest to the user to collect measurements about. This phenomenon sensed and analyzed by the sensor nodes.

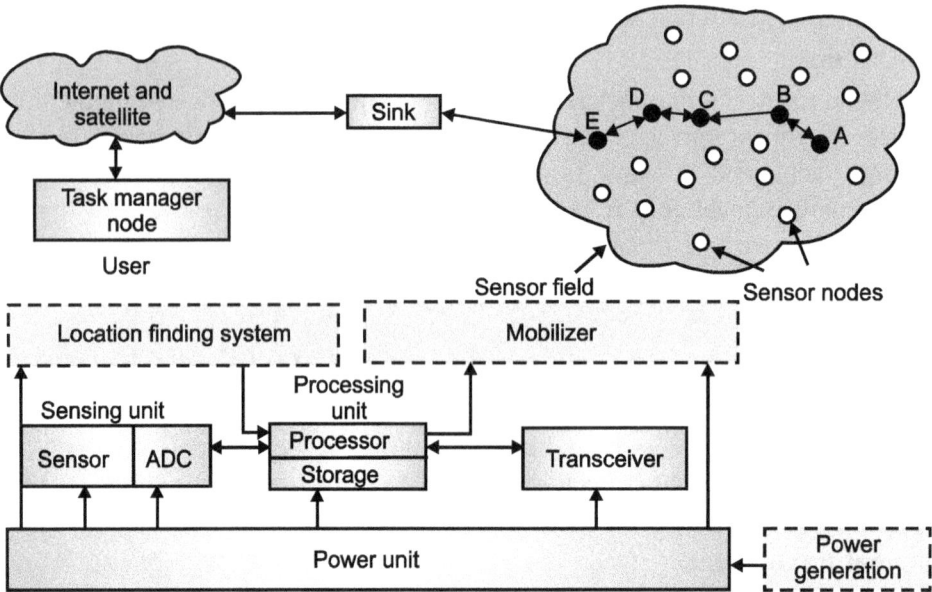

Fig. 5.8 : Sensor node's scattering

- The user who is interested in obtaining information about specific phenomenon to measure/monitor its behavior.

5.7.1 Design Factors and Requirements

The designed factors mentioned below serve as guidelines to design a protocol or algorithm for WSNs.

Reliability :

Reliability or fault tolerance or of a sensor node is the ability to maintain the sensor network functionalities without any interruption due to sensor node failure. Sensor node may fail due to lack of energy, physical damage, communications problem, inactivity (a node becomes suspended), or environmental interference. Reliability

is modelled using the Poisson distribution to capture the probability of not having a failure within the time interval (0,t):

$Rk(t) = e^{-\lambda} k^z$

Where λ_z is the failure rate of sensor node k and t is the time period.

Density and Network Size/Scalability :

hundreds, thousands or millions of sensor nodes may be deployed to study a phenomenon of interest to users. The density of these nodes affects the degree of coverage area of interest. The networks size affects reliability, accuracy, and data processing algorithms. The density can range from a fewer sensor nodes to a hundred in a region that can be less than 10m in diameter.

Sensor Network Topology :

The topology of a network affects many of its characteristics like; latency, capacity, and robustness. Also, the complexity of data routing and processing depends on the network topology. Densely deploying thousands of sensor nodes in sensor field requires careful handling of network topology maintenance. There three phases related to topology maintenance. (1) Predeployment and deployment phase, (2) Postdeployment

phase, and (3)Redeployment of additional nodes phase.

Energy Consumption :

One of the components of sensor nodes is the power source which is limited enough. A sensor node is battery operated. Hence; life time of a sensor node depends strongly on the battery life time, especially where no power source replenishment is possible in some applications scenarios.

Since the main objectives of sensor nodes are sensing/collecting events, data processing, and data transmission through routing; then the power resource can be divided among these three operations (sensing, computation, and communications). On the other hand; life time of a sensor node plays a key role on energy efficiency and robustness of sensor node.

Data Aggregation/Data Fusion :

It is the task of reducing data size by summarizing the data into a set of meaningful information via computation while data are propagating through the wireless sensor network. As sensor networks made of large number of sensor nodes; this can easily congest the network and flooding it with information. Hence; a solution to data congestion in sensor networks is to use computation to aggregate or fuse data within WSN, then transmit only the aggregated data to the controller.

Many approaches within the context of WSNs are proposed to facilitate data aggregation, also known as data fusion, such as;

(1) diffusion algorithms which assume that homogeneous data propagate to destination throughout the network by transmitting data from one node to another, then these data may be aggregated using diffusion algorithms, (2) Streaming queries are based on SQL extension for continuous querying, And (3) Event Algebra which assists in composing simple events into composite ones with the help of event graph.

Transmission Media :

In a multi-hop sensor network, a wireless medium is used to link nodes for communications goal. These links can be formed by radio (e.g., Bluetooth compatible 2.4 GHz transceiver), Infrared which is license free and robust to interference from electrical devices, and Optical media.

Security :

Security aspects in WSNs have been focused on the centralized communications approaches. Some of the threats to a WSN are categorized as follows: Passive Information Gathering, False Node, Node Outage, Supervision of a Node, Node Malfunction, Message Corruption, Denial of Service, and Traffic Analysis. There is a need to develop distributed security approaches for wireless sensor network.

Self-Configuration :

It is essential for wireless sensor network. to be self-organize; since the densely deployed sensor nodes in a sensor field may fail due to many reasons (e.g., lack of energy, physical destruction, environment interference, communications problem, inactivity, etc) and new nodes may join the network. On the other hand; sensor nodes work unattended in a dynamic environment; so they need to be self-configuration to establish a topology that supports communications under severe energy constraints. It is worthy mention that self-configuration in WSN is an essential factor to maintain a WSN functions properly and serve its purpose.

Network Dynamics :

In many applications, the movement of sensor nodes or the base station (sink) is essential. This means that sensor nodes are moving nodes (i.e., not stationary as assumed by many of network architectures). This has arisen the routing stability issues as well as energy, bandwidth, etc. Moreover, the specific sensed phenomenon may be either dynamic (e.g., target detection/ tracking applications) or stationary (e.g., forest monitoring) depending on the applications.

Quality of Service :

For some applications, data delivery within a bounded latency (i.e., time constrained applications) is of great importance; otherwise, the sensed data that delivered after certain latency will be useless. In other applications (e.g., not time-constrained applications), the conservation of power is more important than the quality of the sent data. Hence; there is a trade off between the quality of service/the quality of data sent and the energy conservations or consumption depending on the applications.

Coverage :

The sensor node's view of the environment that it is situated in is limited both in range and in accuracy. This means the ability of sensor nodes to cover physical area of the environment is limited.

Connectivity :

A permanent connection between any two individual sensor nodes that are densely deployed in a sensor network defines the network connectivity. The connectivity is of great importance, since it influences communications protocols' design and data dissemination techniques. Also, it is worth mentioning that connectivity of sensor network may not prevent the network topology from being variable and the network size from reduction as a result of the death or failure of some sensor nodes.

5.8 RADIO PROPAGATION AND PROPAGATION IMPAIRMENTS

Propagation Modes

Radio wave propagation is the study of the transfer of energy at radio frequencies from one point, a transmitter, to another, a receiver. Radio waves are part of the broad electromagnetic spectrum that extends from the very low frequencies which are produced by electric power facilities up to the extremely high frequencies of cosmic rays. Between these two extremes are bands of frequencies that are found in every day uses: audio frequencies used in systems for the reproduction of audible sounds, radio frequencies, infrared light and ultraviolet light and x-rays. All electromagnetic waves propagate at the same velocity, regardless of the frequency. Light is an electromagnetic wave, and thus the propagation velocity is often referred to as "the speed of light" (c), which for a vacuum is approximately 3 2 108 m/sec. The velocity of any wave is dependent upon the medium in which it is travelling, but for simplicity is usually considered with respect to a vacuum. The frequency of a wave is defined in terms of the number of cycles per second or hertz (Hz) and is related to the wavelength by the expression $f = c/\lambda$. Radio frequencies are generally considered to be the portion of the electromagnetic spectrum below the infrared frequencies. At present, the practical upper limit of radio frequencies is roughly 100 GHz.1 Within the radio frequency spectrum are bands of frequencies that have been allocated to the broadcast service.

Components of radio waves :

The basic shape of the wave generated by a transmitter is that of a sine wave. The wave radiated out into space, however, may or may not retain the characteristics of the sine wave.

A sine wave can be one cycle or many cycles. The number of cycles of a sine wave that are completed in 1 second is known as the *frequency* of the sine wave.

The frequencies falling between 3000 hertz (3 kHz) and 300,000,000,000 hertz (300 GHz) are called RADIO FREQUENCIES (abbreviated rf) since they are commonly used in radio communications. This part of the radio frequency spectrum is divided into bands, each band being 10 times higher in frequency than the one immediately below it. This arrangement serves as a convenient way to remember the range of each band. The rf bands are shown in table 1. The usable radio-frequency range is roughly 10 kilohertz to 100 gigahertz.

Any frequency that is a whole number multiple of a smaller basic frequency is known as a HARMONIC of that basic frequency. The basic frequency itself is called the first harmonic or, more commonly, the FUNDAMENTAL FREQUENCY. A frequency that is twice as great as the fundamental frequency is called the second harmonic; a frequency three times as great is the third harmonic; and so on.

For example:

First harmonic (Fundamental frequency)	3000 kHz
Second harmonic	6000 kHz
Third harmonic	9000 kHz

The PERIOD of a radio wave is simply the amount of time required for the completion of one full cycle. If a sine wave has a frequency of 2 hertz, each cycle has a duration, or period, of one-half second.

If the frequency is 10 hertz, the period of each cycle is one-tenth of a second. Since the frequency of a radio wave is the number of cycles that are completed in one second, you should be able to see that as the frequency of a radio wave increases, its period decreases.

A wavelength is the space occupied by one full cycle of a radio wave at any given instant.

Wavelengths are expressed in meters. The velocity (or speed) of a radio wave radiated into free space by a transmitting antenna is equal to the speed of light—186,000 miles per second or 300,000,000 meters per second. Because of various factors, such as barometric pressure, humidity, molecular content, etc., radio waves travel inside the Earth's atmosphere at a speed slightly less than the speed of light. Normally, in discussions of the velocity of radio waves, the velocity referred to is the speed at which radio waves travel in free space.

The frequency of a radio wave has nothing to do with its velocity. A 5-megahertz wave travels through space at the same velocity as a 10-megahertz wave. However, the velocity of radio waves is an important factor in making wavelength-to-frequency conversions.

Table 1: Radio Frequency Bands

Description	Abbreviation	Frequency
Very Low	VLF	3 to 30 KHz
Low	LF	30 to 300 KHz
Medium	MF	300 to 3000 KHz
High	HF	3 to 30 MHz
Very High	VHF	30 to 300 MHz
Ultrahigh	UHF	300 to 3000 MHz
Super High	SHF	3 to 30 GHz
Extremely High	EHF	30 to 300 GHz

The AM band frequency allotments are contained in what is referred to as medium frequencies (MF), 300 kHz to 3 MHz. The FM band frequencies and a portion of the TV band are contained in the VHF band which extends from 30 MHz to 300 MHz. The remaining TV allocations are contained in the UHF band of 300 MHz to 3 GHz. Allocations for broadcast auxiliary services such as remote pickup, studio/transmitter links, intercity relays, MDS, and ITFS are included within the MF, VHF, UHF and SHF (super high frequency) bands.

Propagation modes and impairments

There are two principal ways in which electromagnetic (radio) energy travels from a transmitting antenna to a receiving antenna. One way is by GROUND WAVES and the other is by SKY WAVES. Ground waves are radio waves that travel near the surface of the Earth (surface and space waves). Sky waves are radio waves that are reflected back to Earth from the ionosphere.

Ground Waves

The ground wave is actually composed of two separate component waves. These are known as the SURFACE WAVE and the SPACE WAVE. The determining factor in whether a ground wave component is classified as a space wave or a surface wave is simple. A surface wave travels along the surface of the Earth. A space wave travels over the surface.

Surface Wave :

The surface wave reaches the receiving site by travelling along the surface of the ground as shown in Fig. 5.9. A surface wave can follow the contours of the Earth because of the process of diffraction. When a surface wave meets an object and the dimensions of the object do not exceed its wavelength, the wave tends to curve or bend around the object.

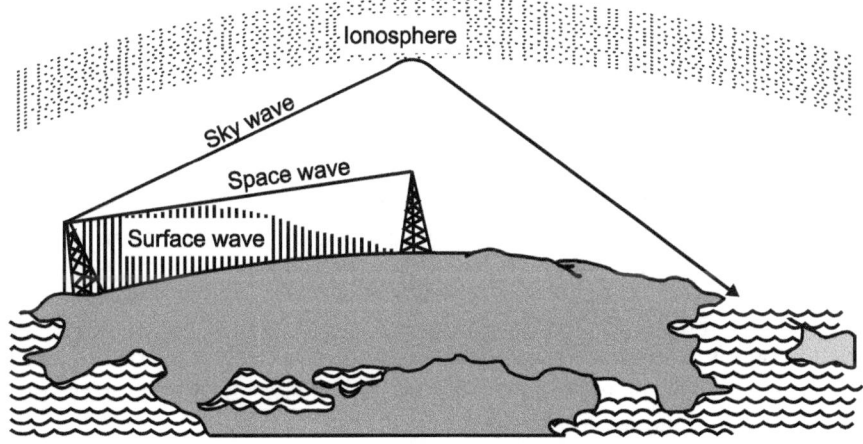

Fig. 5.9 : Ground waves and sky waves

Space Wave

The space wave follows two distinct paths from the transmitting antenna to the receiving antenna—one through the air directly to the receiving antenna, the other reflected from the ground to the receiving antenna. This is illustrated in Fig. 5.10.

The primary path of the space wave is directly from the transmitting antenna to the receiving antenna. So, the receiving antenna must be located within the radio horizon of the transmitting antenna. Because space waves are refracted slightly, even when propagated through the troposphere, the radio horizon is actually about one-third farther than the line-of-sight or natural horizon.

Sky wave

The sky wave, often called the ionospheric wave, is radiated in an upward direction and returned to Earth at some distant location because of refraction from the ionosphere. This form of propagation is relatively unaffected by the Earth's surface and can propagate signals over great distances. Usually the high frequency (hf) band is used for sky wave propagation.

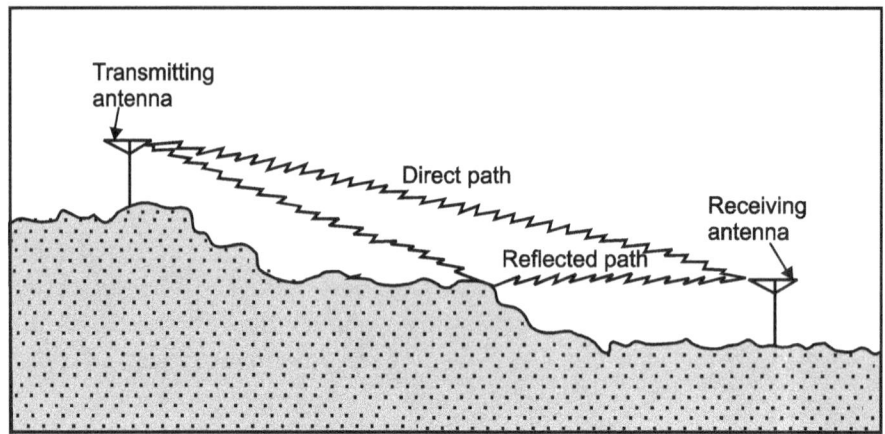

Fig. 5.10 : Space wave propagation

Radio Wave Transmission Impairments

(1) Fresnel zone

Radio waves diffracted by objects can affect the strength of the received signal. This happens even though the obstacle does not directly obscure the direct visual path. This area, known as the "Fresnel Zone", and must be kept clear of all obstructions.

$$d1 \text{ and } d2 = km, f = GHz, h = meters$$

The 1st Fresnel zone is a spheroid space formed within the trajectory of the path when the path difference when radio wave energy reaches the receiver by the shortest distance, and when it gets there by another route, is within $\lambda/2$.

Odd-numbered Fresnel zones have relatively intense field strengths, whereas even numbered Fresnel zones are nulls.

When the radio signal pass from site A to site B, the lack of adequate Fresnel Zone clearance caused signal diffraction, and degradation of the radio signal.

If the 1st Fresnel zone is not clear, then free-space loss does *not* apply and an adjustment term must be included. To avoid this have to:

1. Use an antenna with higher gain.
2. Raise the antenna mounting point on Site A and/or Site B.

(2) Free Space Loss

Radio waves travel from a source into the surrounding space at the "speed of light" (approximately 3.0×10^8 meters per second) when in "free space". Literally, "free space" should mean a vacuum, but clear air is a good approximation to this.

Free Space Path Loss(dB) = 27.6(dB) − 20*LOG[Frequency(MHz)] − 20*LOG[Distance(m)]

The equations for free-space loss and link-loss can be used between two antennas only for distances greater than the near-field distance of each antenna.

(3) Atmospheric Absorption

The atmosphere, due to the many different gases, water and particles contained there in, absorbs and transmits many different wavelengths of electromagnetic radiation. The wavelengths that pass through the atmosphere unabsorbed constitute the "atmospheric windows."

A significant atmospheric effect is that of attenuation due to rain. Below about 10 GHz, rain fading is not very significant, but, at higher microwave frequencies, it becomes the major factor limiting path length, particularly in areas that experience high levels of rainfall. In addition to the attenuation of electromagnetic waves, rain and other precipitation tend to cause depolarization of the wave.

(4) Ducting

A duct is something that will confine whatever is travelling along it into a narrow 'pipe'.

The atmosphere can assume a structure that will produce a similar effect on radio waves. When a radio wave enters a duct it can travel with low loss over great distances. The atmosphere will then act in the manner of a giant optical fibre, trapping the radio wave within the layer of high refractive index.

A wave trapped in a duct can travel beyond the radio horizon with very little loss, producing signal levels within a few dB of the free-space level.

(5) Scattering

When an electromagnetic wave is incident on a rough surface, the wave is not so much reflected as "scattered".

Scattering is the process by which small particles suspended in a medium of a different index of refraction diffuse a portion of the incident radiation in all directions. Scattering occurs when incoming signal hits an object whose size in the order of the wavelength of the signal or less.

(6) Reflection

Reflection occurs when signal encounters a surface that is large relative to the wavelength of the signal. Radio waves may be reflected from various substances or objects they meet during travel between the transmitting and receiving sites.

The amount of reflection depends on the reflecting material.
- Smooth metal surfaces of good electrical conductivity are efficient reflectors of radio waves.
- The surface of the Earth itself is a fairly good reflector.

The radio wave is not reflected from a single point on the reflector but rather from an area on its surface. The size of the area required for reflection to take place depends on the wavelength of the radio wave and the angle at which the wave strikes the reflecting substance. When radio waves are reflected from flat surfaces, a phase shift in the alternations of the wave occurs. The shifting in the phase relationships of reflected radio waves is one of the major reasons for fading.

(7) Refraction

Refraction it is the bending of the waves as they move from one medium into another in which the velocity of propagation is different. This bending, or change of direction, is always toward the medium that has the lower velocity of propagation.

(8) Diffraction

Diffraction is the name given to the mechanism by which waves enter into the shadow of an obstacle. Diffraction occurs at the edge of an impenetrable body that is large compared to wavelength of radio wave. A radio wave that meets an obstacle has a natural tendency to bend around the obstacle. The bending, called diffraction, results in a change of direction of part of the wave energy from the normal line-of-sight path. This change makes it possible to receive energy around the edges of an obstacle.

The ratio of the signal strengths without and with the obstacle is referred to as the diffraction loss. The diffraction loss is affected by the path geometry and the frequency of operation. The signal strength will fall by 6 dB as the receiver approaches the shadow boundary, but before it enters into the shadow region.

Deep in the shadow of an obstacle, the diffraction loss increases with 10*log(frequency). So, if double the frequency, deep in the shadow of an obstacle the loss will increase by 3 dB. This establishes a general truth, namely that radio waves of longer wavelength will penetrate more deeply into the shadow of an obstacle.

(9) Multipath

Multipath is a term used to describe the multiple paths a radio wave may follow between transmitter and receiver. Such propagation paths include the ground wave, ionospheric refraction, re-radiation by the ionospheric layers, reflection from the Earth's surface or from more than one ionospheric layer, etc.

If the two signals reach the receiver in-phase (both signals are at the same point in the wave cycle when they reach the receiver), then the signal is amplified. This is known as an "upfade." If the two waves reach the receiver out-of-phase (the two signals are at opposite points in the wave cycle when they reach the receiver), they weaken the overall received signal. If the two waves are 180° apart when they reach the receiver, they can completely cancel each other out so that a radio does not receive a signal at all. A location where a signal is cancelled out by multipath is called a "null" or "downfade."

If the reflecting surfaces that cause the multipath situation do not move, the locations of the maxima and minima will not move, hence the name 'standing wave'.

The depth of the null in a standing wave pattern is dependent upon the magnitude of the reflection coefficient of any reflecting surface.

The Effects of Multipath Propagation
- Multiple copies of a signal may arrive at different phases
- If phases add destructively, the signal level relative to noise declines, making detection more difficult.
- Delay Spread resulting in Intersymbol interference (ISI) - one or more delayed copies of a pulse may arrive at the same time as the primary pulse for a subsequent bit

(10) Fading

There is a large dependence of fading on distance.
- The probability of a fade of a particular depth increases with the cube of distance. Thus, as the distance is doubled, the probability of a particular fade depth increases by a factor of eight. Or, alternatively, the fade for a given probability increases by 9 dB. So, doubling the distance will increase the free space loss by 6 dB, and increase the probability of fading by 9 dB, thus increasing the overall link-budget loss by 15 dB.

There is a slight dependence of fading on frequency. Increasing the frequency by 1GHz will decrease the probability of a fade by a factor of 1.08. There is a fairly strong dependence of fading on the height of the path above sea level.
- There is simply less atmosphere at higher altitudes and therefore the effect of atmospheric fading is smaller.
- For every 1000 meter increase in altitude the required fade margin reduces by 10 dB.

Types of Fading
- Fast fading - occurs when the coherence time of the channel is small relative to the delay constraint of the channel. Fast fading causes rapid fluctuations in phase and amplitude of a signal if a transmitter or receiver is moving or there are changes in the radio environment (e.g. car passing by). If a transmitter or receiver is moving, the fluctuations occur within a few wave lengths. Because of its short distance fast fading is considered as small-scale fading.
- Slow fading - arises when the coherence time of the channel is large relative to the delay constraint of the channel. Slow fading occurs due to the geometry of the path profile. This leads to the situation in which the signal gradually gets weaker or stronger.
- Flat fading – occurs when the coherence bandwidth of the channel is larger than the bandwidth of the signal.

- Selective fading – occurs when the coherence bandwidth of the channel is smaller than the bandwidth of the signal.
- Rayleigh fading - assume that the magnitude of a signal that has passed through a communications channel will vary randomly.
- Ricean fading - occurs when one of the paths, typically a line of sight signal, is much stronger than the others.
- Nakagami fading - occurs for multipath scattering with relatively larger time delay spreads, with different clusters of reflected waves.
- Weibull fading - considers a signal composed of clusters of one multipath wave, each propagating in a non-homogeneous environment.

5.9 MEDIUM ACCESS CONTROL (MAC) PROTOCOL

5.9.1 Fundamentals of MAC protocol

MAC protocol is the first protocol layer above the physical layer. Its fundamental task is to regulate the access of number of nodes to a shared medium so as to satisfy certain performance requirements. These requirements include delay, throughput and fairness.

Within the OSI reference model, the MAC protocol is considered as a part of data link layer, however there clear separation between the functionalities handled by MAC and remaining part of the data link layer. The MAC protocol determines the time for a node when it accesses the medium, controls and transmits a data to another node (unicast) or to a set of nodes (multicast, broadcast).

5.9.2 Requirements and Design Constraints for Wireless MAC Protocol

Throughput, efficiency, stability, fairness, low access delay, low transmission delay as well as low overhead are the requirements of MAC protocol. Per packet overhead, collision may cause overhead in MAC protocol. Collision can happen if the MAC protocol allows two or more nodes to send packets at the same time. Collision results in the inability of the receiver to read a packet correctly causing above layers to perform a retransmission. For time-critical applications, it is important to provide deterministic or stochastic guarantees on delivery time or minimal available data rate. Sometimes, preferred treatment of important packets over unimportant ones is required, leading to the concept of **priorities**.

The operation and performance of MAC protocols is heavily influenced by the properties of the underlying physical layer. Since WSNs use a wireless medium, they inherit all the well-known problems of wireless transmission. One problem is time-variable, and sometimes quite high, error rates, which is caused by physical phenomena like slow and fast fading, path loss, attenuation, and man-made or thermal noise. Depending on modulation schemes, frequencies, distance between transmitter and receiver, and the propagation environment, instantaneous bit error rates in the range of 10−3 ... 10−2 can easily be observed.

The received power decreases with the distance between transmitting and receiving node. This path loss combined with the fact that any transceiver needs a minimum signal strength to demodulate signals successfully leads to a maximum range that a sensor node can reach with a given transmit power. If two nodes are out of reach, they cannot hear each other. This gives rise to the well-known hidden-terminal/exposed-terminal problems

The **hidden-terminal problem** occurs specifically for the class of Carrier Sense Multiple Access (CSMA) protocols, where a node senses the medium before starting to transmit a packet. If the medium is found to be busy, the node defers its packet to avoid a collision and a subsequent retransmission. Consider the example in Fig. 5.11. Here, we have three nodes A, B, and C that are arranged such that A and B are in mutual range, B and C are in mutual range, but A and C cannot hear each other. Assume that A starts to transmit a packet to B and sometime later node C also decides to start a packet transmission. A carrier-sensing operation by C shows an idle medium since C cannot hear A's signals. When C starts its packet, the signals collide at B and both packets are useless. Using simple CSMA in a hidden-terminal scenario thus leads to needless collisions.

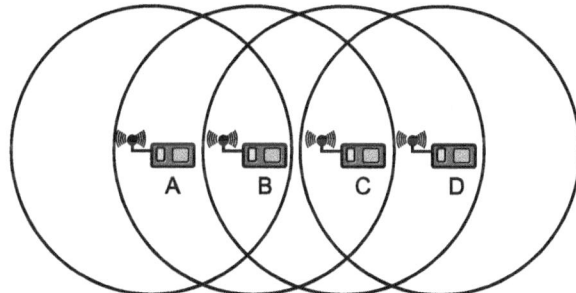

Fig. 5.11 : Hidden Terminal scenario (circle indicates the transmission range)

In the **exposed-terminal scenario**, B transmits a packet to A, and some moment later, C wants to transmit a packet to D. Although this would be theoretically possible since both A and D would receive their packets without distortions, the carrier-sense operation performed by C suppresses C's transmission and bandwidth is wasted. Using simple CSMA in an exposed terminal scenario thus leads to needless waiting.

5.9.3 Important Classes of MAC Protocols

MAC protocols can be categorised into following classes.

(a) Fixed assignment

(b) Demand assignment

(c) Random access

Fixed Assignment Protocols

In this class of MAC protocol, the available resources are allocated between the nodes in such a way that the resource assignment is long term and each node can use resources allocated to it exclusively without any collision. Typical protocols of this class are Time Division Multiple Access (TDMA), Frequency Division Multiple Access (FDMA), Code Division Multiple Access (CDMA) and Space Division Multiple Access (SDMA).

TDMA scheme divides the time axis into fixed length superframes and each superframe is subdivided into a fixed number of time slots. Further these time slots are allotted to nodes exclusively and node can transmit in this time slot periodically in every superframe.

FDMA scheme divides the available frequency band into number of sub channels. These sub channels are assigned to nodes and nodes can exclusively transmit on their channel.

In CDMA scheme nodes spread their signals over much larger bandwidth than needed, using different codes to separate their transmissions. The receiver must know the code used by the transmitter. In SDMA spatial separation of nodes is used to separate their transmission.

Demand Assignment

In demand assignment protocols resources are allocated to nodes exclusively for short amount time. These protocols are sub divided as centralised and distributed protocols. In centralised protocols the nodes send requests for bandwidth allocation to a central node which either accepts or rejects the request. If resource is successfully allocated to a requesting node then confirmation is transmitted back to it along with the description of a allocated resource.

An example of distributed demand assignment protocol is token passing protocol. In this protocol a token frame is rotated among nodes arranged in a logical ring in a broadcast medium. Special ring management techniques are needed to include and exclude nodes from the ring or to handle failures like token loss. As token circulation times are available, a node must always be able to receive the token. For this node's transceiver must be switched on most of the time.

Random Access Protocols

Sensor nodes have no coordination among them and protocols operate in fully distributed manner. These packets may have random packet arrival times. ALOHA, slotted ALOHA and CSMA are important protocols of this class.

ALOHA

In pure ALOHA protocol, a node which wants transmit a new packet, transmits it immediately. There is no coordination with other nodes and protocol has to accept the risk of collision at the receiver. For detecting the collision, receiver is required to send an immediate acknowledgement for a received packet. When transmitter does not receive an acknowledgement frame, it interprets is as a collision. It then backs-off for a random time and then starts again. ALOHA provides the short access and transmission delays under light loads. For heavier loads the number of collisions increases which in turn decreases the throughput efficiency and increases the transmission delays.

Slotted ALOHA

In slotted ALOHA the time is divided number of time slots and node x is allowed to transmit the pocket only at the beginning of a slot. A slot is large enough to accommodate a packet of maximum length. Only other nodes starting their packet transmission in the same slot can destroy node x's packet. If any other node wants to start later, it has to wait for the beginning of the next time slot and has no chance to destroy the node x's packet. This synchronization reduces the probability of collisions and slotted ALOHA has higher throughput than pure ALOHA.

CSMA protocol

In CSMA protocols, a node which wants to transmit the packet respects the ongoing transmission. Node is required to listen to the medium. This is called as carrier sensing. If medium is idle then the node starts transmission. It the medium is found to be busy, node does not transmit for an amount of time determined by one of the several possible algorithms. In non persistent CSMA, the node has a random waiting time, after which it senses the medium again. Before this time, node does not care about the state of the medium. In persistent CSMA, after sensing that the medium is busy, the node waits for the ongoing transmission.

5.10 SPARSE TOPOLOGY AND ENERGY MANAGEMENT (STEM)

STEM protocol provides a solution for the idle listening problem. STEM focuses on the networks that are deployed to wait for and report the behaviour of a certain event. The network has a monitor state in which nodes are idle and do nothing. It also has transfer state in which nodes exhibit significant sensing and communication functions. STEM tries to eliminate idle listening in a monitor state and provides a fast transition into the transfer state.

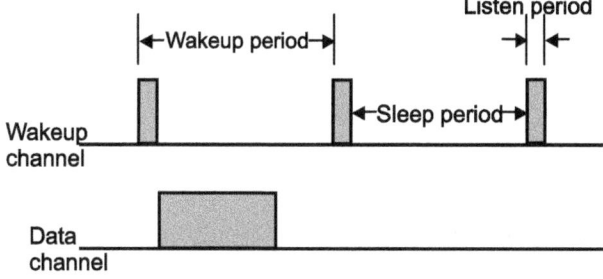

Fig. 5.12 : STEM Duty Cycle Diagram

In STEM two different channels are used: the wake up channel and the data channel and two transceivers are required in each node. The data channel is always in a sleep mode except when transmitting or receiving data packets. On the wake up channel, time is divided into fixed length wake periods of length T. A wake up period is further divided into a listen period of length $T_{RX} \ll T$ and a sleep period in which wake up channel's transceiver enters in sleep mode. When node enters the listen period, it switches on its receiver for the wake up channel and waits for the incoming signal. If nothing is received during time T_{RX}, the node returns to the sleep mode. Otherwise the transmitter and receiver start a packet transfer on the data channel. There are two different variants for the transmitter to acquire the receiver's attention:

In STEM-B, the transmitter issues so-called **beacons** on the wakeup channel periodically and without prior carrier sensing. Such a beacon indicates the MAC addresses of transmitter and receiver. As soon as the receiver picks up the beacon, it sends an acknowledgment frame back on the wakeup channel (causing the transmitter to stop beacon transmission), switches on the transceiver for the data channel, and both nodes can proceed to execute the regular MAC protocol on the data channel, like for example an RTS/CTS handshake. Any other node receiving the beacon on the wakeup channel recognizes that the packet is not destined for it and goes back to sleep mode. The transmitter sends these beacons at least for one full wakeup period to be sure to hit the receivers listen period.

In STEM-T, the transmitter sends out a simple busy tone on the control channel (the T in STEM-T comes from "tone") for a time long enough to hit the receiver's listen period. Since the busy tone carries no address information, all the transmitter's neighbors (the receiver as well as other nodes) will sense the busy tone and switch on their data channel, without sending an acknowledgment packet. The other nodes can go back to sleep when they can deduce from the packet exchange on the data channel that they are not involved in the data transfer. A transceiver capable of generating and sensing busy tones can be significantly cheaper and less energy-consuming than a transceiver usable for data transmission but requires proper frequency synchronization.

5.11 S-MAC

The S-MAC (Sensor-MAC) protocol provides mechanisms to circumvent idle listening, collisions, and overhearing. It does not require two different channels.

S-MAC employs a periodic wakeup scheme as each node alternates between a fixed-length listen period and a fixed-length sleep period according to its **schedule**. The listen period of S-MAC can be used to receive *and transmit* packets.

S-MAC attempts to coordinate the schedules of neighbouring nodes such that their listen periods start at the same time.

A node x's listen period is subdivided into three different phases:

In the first phase (**SYNCH phase**), node *x* accepts SYNCH packets from its neighbours. In these packets, the neighbors describe their own schedule and *x* stores their schedule in a table (the **schedule table**). Node *x*'s SYNCH phase is subdivided into time slots and *x*'s neighbors contend according to a CSMA scheme. Each neighbour y wishing to transmit a SYNCH packet picks one of the time slots randomly and starts to transmit if no signal was received in any of the previous slots. In the other case, y goes back into sleep mode and waits for x's next wakeup. In the other direction, since x knows a neighbour y's schedule, x can wake at appropriate times and send its own SYNCH packet to y (in broadcast mode). It is not required that x broadcasts its schedule in every of y's wakeup periods. However, for reasons

of time synchronization and to allow new nodes to learn their local network topology, x should send SYNCH packets periodically. The according period is called **synchronization period**.

In the second phase (**RTS phase**), x listens for RTS packets from neighbouring nodes. In order to reduce the collision of data packets due to hidden terminal problem RTS/CTS handshake is used and interested neighbors contend in this phase according to

a CSMA scheme with additional back-off.

In the third phase (**CTS phase**), node x transmits a CTS packet if an RTS packet was received in the previous phase. After this, the packet exchange continues, extending into x's nominal sleep time. In general, when competing for the medium, the nodes use the RTS/CTS handshake, including the virtual carrier-sense mechanism, whereby a node maintains a NAV variable. The NAV mechanism can be readily used to switch off the node during ongoing transmissions to avoid overhearing.

When transmitting in a broadcast mode (for example SYNCH packets), the RTS and CTS packets are dropped and the nodes use CSMA with back-off.

If we can arrange the schedules of node x and its neighbors are synchronized, node x and all its neighbors wake up at the same time and x can reach all of them with a single SYNCH packet. The S-MAC protocol allows neighbouring nodes to agree on the same schedule and to create **virtual clusters**. The clustering structure refers solely to the exchange of schedules; the transfer of data packets is not influenced by virtual clustering.

The S-MAC protocol proceeds as follows to form the virtual clusters: A node x, newly switched on, listens for a time of at least the (globally known) synchronization period. If x receives any SYNCH packet from its neighbours, it adopts the announced schedule and broadcasts it in one of the neighbour's next listen periods. In the other case, node x picks a schedule and broadcasts it.

If x receives another node's schedule during the broadcast packet's contention period, it drops its own schedule and follows the other one. It might also happen that a node x receives a different schedule after it already has chosen one, for example, because bit errors destroyed previous SYNCH packets. If node x already knows about the existence of neighbors who adopted its own schedule, it keeps its schedule and in the future has to transmit its SYNCH and data packets according to both schedules. On the other hand, if x has no neighbour sharing its schedule, it drops its own and adopts the other one. Since there is always a chance to receive SYNCH packets in error, node x periodically listens for a whole synchronization period to relearn its neighbourhood.

The periodic wakeup scheme adopted by S-MAC allows nodes to spend much time in the sleep mode, but there is also a price to pay in terms of latency. Without further modifications, the per-hop latency of S-MAC will be approximately equal to the sleep period on average when all nodes follow the same schedule.

5.12 LOW ENERGY ADAPTIVE CLUSTERING HIERARCHY (LEACH) PROTOCOL

LEACH protocol considers a dense sensor network of homogeneous, energy constrained nodes which shall report their data to a sink node. In LEACH, a TDMA based MAC protocol is integrated with clustering and simple routing protocol.

LEACH forms the cluster of nodes and each cluster a dedicated node called as cluster head is responsible for creating and maintaining a TDMA schedule. All other nodes of a cluster are called as member nodes. For all member nodes, TDMA slots are assigned which can be used for exchanging data between member node and the cluster head. When not in this time slots, member nodes spend their time in sleep state. Cluster head aggregates the data from member nodes and transmits it to the sink node or to other nodes for further relaying. Cluster head has to spend significant energy for this transmission as sink is often far away. For member nodes it is much cheaper to reach the cluster head than to transmit directly to the sink.

Cluster head's role is time consuming since it is always switched on and is responsible for long range communication. If fixed node is assigned for the role of cluster head it will lose its energy quickly and get died. Without cluster head other member nodes are useless. Therefore this responsibility is rotated among the nodes.

Selection of Cluster Head :

A node that has not been a cluster head for a long time is more likely to elect itself than a node serving just recently. In this protocol all nodes make decision whether to become a cluster head at the same time. Non cluster head nodes choose their cluster head based on received signal strength. After the clusters have been formed, each cluster head picks a random CDMA code for its cluster, and broadcasts this code. Member nodes subsequently use this code. This avoids a situation where a border node belonging to cluster head A distorts transmission directed to cluster head B.

LEACH protocol is organized in rounds and each round is sub divided into a set up phase and steady state phase. The set up phase starts with self election of nodes to become a cluster head.

In advertisement phase, the cluster heads inform their neighbourhood with an advertisement packet. Non cluster head nodes pick the advertisement packet with the strongest received signal strength. Non cluster head nodes pick the advertisement with the strongest received signal strength. Cluster head knows the number of members and their identities after set up phases.

Fig. 5.13 : Intercluster Interference

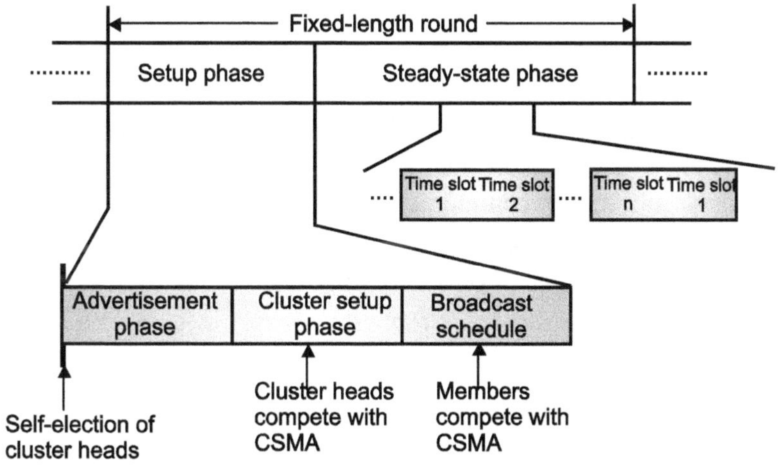

Fig. 5.14 : Organization of LEACH rounds

Because of collisions of advertisement or join packets, the protocol cannot guarantee if each non cluster head node is part of cluster. But it can guarantee that nodes belong to at most one cluster. Disadvantage of LEACH protocol is that as the distance between cluster head and sink is few miles it does not have enough energy to reach the sink at all. Hence LEACH protocol would not be able to cover large geographical area.

5.13 IEEE 802.15.4

The institute of Electrical and Electronics Engineers (IEEE) finalized the IEEE 802.15.4 standard. This standard covers the physical layer and MAC layer of a low rate wireless personal area network (WPAN). Sometimes people confuse between IEEE 802.15.4 with Zigbee. Zigbee uses the services offered by 802.15.4. The targeted applications for IEEE 802.15.4 are in the area of WSN, home automation, home networking, home security, and so on. Most of these applications require low to medium bit rates and up to few hundreds of kbps.

5.13.1 Network Architecture and Types on Nodes

IEEE 802.15.4 distinguishes nodes in two types.

(a) Full Function Device (FFD)

(b) Reduced Function Device (RFD)

FFD can operate in three different roles. It can be a Personal Area Network (PAN) coordinator, a simple coordinator or a device.

RFD can operate only as a device.

A device must be associated with a coordinator node (FFD) and communication with this only forms a star network. Coordinator can operate in peer to peer fashion. Multiple coordinators can form a Personal Area Network (PAN). One of these coordinators is designated as a PAN coordinator which performs following tasks.

- It manages a list of associated devices. Devices can associate with a coordinator using certain signalling packets.
- It allocates short addresses to its devices. IEEE 802.15.4 nodes have a 64 bit device address. When a device associates with a coordinator, it may request 16 bit short address for all subsequent communication between device and coordinator.
- In the beaconed mode, it regularly transmits frame beacon packets and announces the PAN identifier and a list of outstanding frames.

Coordinators can also accept and process requests to reserve fixed time slots to nodes and these allocations are indicated in the beacon.

5.13.2 Superframe Structure

The coordinator of a star network operating in beacon mode organizes channel access and data transmission with the help of superframe structure.

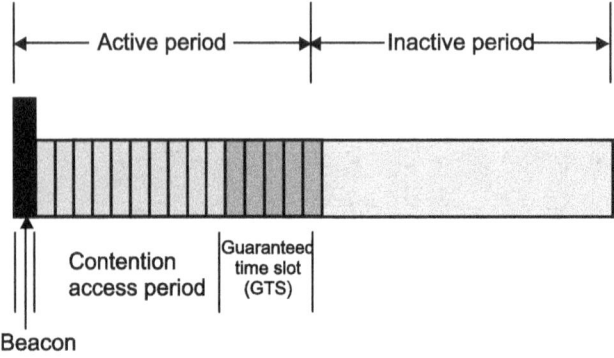

Fig. 5.15 : Superframe Structure

All superframes have the same length. The coordinator starts each superframe by sending frame beacon packet. This frame beacon packet includes a superframe specification which describes the length of the various components of superframe.

Superframe is sub divided into two parts: an active period and an inactive period.

In the inactive period, all nodes including the coordinator can switch off their transceivers and go to sleep state. Nodes have to wake up immediately before the inactive period ends to receive the next beacon.

The active period is sub divided into 16 time slots. First slot is occupied by the beacon frame and remaining time slots are partitioned into Contention access period (CAP) followed by a number of contiguous guaranteed time slots (GTS).

The length of the active and inactive period, length of a single time slot and usage of GTS slots are configurable. During entire active period the coordinator is active. The devices associated with it are active in the GTS phase only in the time slots allocated to them. In all other GTS slots they can enter sleep mode. In the CAP, a device can shut down transceiver if it does not want to transmit or receive.

5.13.3 GTS Management

Device is allocated a GTS by the coordinator only when is send appropriate request packets during the CAP. Request packet has a flag which indicates whether requested time slot is a transmit slot or a receive slot. In the transmit slot, device sends packets to the coordinator and in receive slot it receives packet from the coordinator. Coordinator sends the immediate acknowledgement packet indicating device that it has received the request packet properly. After receiving the acknowledgement packet, device tracks the coordinator's beacon for some specified time called as GTSDescPersistanceTime. When the coordinator has sufficient resources, it inserts corresponding GTS descriptor into one of the next beacon frames. This descriptor specifies the short address of the requesting node and the number and the position of the time slots within the GTS phase of the superframe. When the coordinator announces the devices in the GTS descriptor, they can use their allotted slots.

A GTS is allocated to a device on a regular basis until it is explicitly deallocated. Such explicit deallocation can be requested by the device by means of special control frame. After sending this frame, the device shall not use the allocated resources further.

5.13.4 Data Transfer procedures

Assume that a device wants to send a data packet to the coordinator. If the device has an allocated transmit GTS, it wakes up before the starting of the time slot and sends its packet immediately without performing any carrier sense and collision avoidance operation. However device can do this only when the data packet and immediate acknowledgement sent by the coordinator fit into the allocated time slots. In case of data transfer from the coordinator to a device, if the device has allocated a receive GTS and when acknowledgement fits in that GTS coordinator simply transmits the packet. Receiving device has to acknowledge the data packet.

5.13.5 Non beaconed Mode

The IEEE 802.15.4 protocol offers a **nonbeaconed mode** besides the beaconed mode. Some important differences between these modes are the following:

- In the nonbeaconed mode, the coordinator does *not* send beacon frames nor is there any GTS mechanism. The lack of beacon packets takes away a good opportunity for devices to acquire time synchronization with the coordinator.
- All packets from devices are transmitted using an unslotted (because of the lack of time synchronization) CSMA-CA protocol. As opposed to the slotted CSMA-CA protocol, there is no synchronization to back-off period boundaries and, in addition, the device performs only a single CCA operation. If this indicates an idle channel, the device infers success.
- Coordinators must be switched on constantly but devices can follow their own sleep schedule.

Devices wake up for two reasons: (i) to send a data/control packet to the coordinators, or (ii) to fetch a packet destined to itself from the coordinator by using the data request/acknowledgment/data/acknowledgment handshake (fetch cycle) discussed above. When the coordinator has a data packet for the device, it transmits it using the unslotted CSMA-CA access method and the device sends an immediate acknowledgment for the data. Therefore, the device must stay awake for a certain time after sending the data request packet. The rate by which the device initiates the fetch cycle is application dependent.

QUESTIONS

1. Explain in short MANET and Sensor Networks.
2. Write short note on operating environment constraints for MANET and WSNS.
3. Explain the application sof sensor networks.
4. Explain (a) Sensor node architecture, (b) Sensor network architecture.
5. Write short not eon radio propagation and propagation impairments.
6. Explain the following MAC protocols :
   (a) STEM, (b) S-MAC, (c) LEACH.
7. Explain IEEE 802.15.4.

Unit - VI
ROUTING IN SENSOR NETWORKS AND RECENT TRENDS

6.1 ROUTING PROTOCOLS IN MANET

In order to facilitate communication within the network, a routing protocol is used to discover routes between nodes. The primary goal of such an ad-hoc network routing protocol is correct and efficient route establishment between a pair of nodes so that messages may be delivered in a timely manner. Route construction should be done with a minimum of overhead and bandwidth consumption. An Ad-hoc routing protocol is a convention or standard that controls how nodes come to agree which way to route packets between computing devices in a

MANET. In ad-hoc networks, nodes do not have a priori knowledge of topology of network around them, they have to discover it. The basic idea is that a new node announces its presence and listens to broadcast announcements from its neighbours. The node learns about new near nodes and ways to reach them, and announces that it can also reach those nodes. As time goes on, each node knows about all other nodes and one or more ways how to reach them.

Routing Algorithms have to :
- Keep routing table reasonably small;
- Choose best route for given destination (this can be the fastest, most reliable, highest throughput, or cheapest route);
- Keep table up-to-date when nodes die, move or join;
- Require small amount of messages/time to converge;

As shown in Figure 1 below, these routing protocols may generally be categorized as:

(a) table-driven

(b) source-initiated on-demand driven.

Solid lines in this figure represent direct descendants while dotted lines depict logical descendants. Despite being designed for the same type of underlying network, the characteristics of each of these protocols are quite distinct. Such protocols must deal with the typical limitations of these networks, which include high power consumption, low bandwidth, and high error rates.

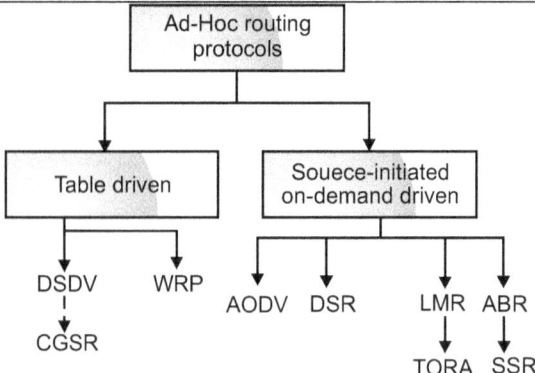

Fig. 6.1 : Classification of Ad Hoc Routing Protocols

(1) Table-Driven Routing Protocols

The table-driven routing protocols attempt to maintain consistent, up-to-date routing information from each node to every other node in the network. These protocols require each node to maintain one or more tables to store routing information, and they respond to changes in network topology by propagating updates throughout the network in order to maintain a consistent network view. The areas where they differ are the number of necessary routing-related tables and the methods by which changes in network structure are broadcast.

(i) Destination-Sequenced Distance-Vector Routing (DSDV)

The Destination-Sequenced Distance-Vector Routing protocol (DSDV) is a table-driven algorithm based on the classical Bellman-Ford routing mechanism. The improvements made to the Bellman-Ford algorithm include freedom from loops in routing tables.

Every mobile node in the network maintains a routing table in which all of the possible destinations within the network and the number of hops to each destination are recorded. Each entry is marked with a sequence number assigned by the destination node. The sequence numbers enable the 2 mobile nodes to distinguish stale routes from new ones, thereby avoiding the formation of routing loops. Routing table updates are periodically transmitted throughout the network in order to maintain table consistency. To help ease the potentially large amount of network traffic that such updates can generate, route updates can employ two possible types of packets. The first is known as a "full dump." This type of packet carries all available routing information and can require multiple network protocol data units (NPDUs). During periods of occasional movement, these packets are transmitted infrequently. Smaller "incremental" packets are used to relay only that information which has changed since the last full dump. Each of these broadcasts should fit into a standard size NPDU, thereby decreasing the amount of traffic generated. The mobile nodes maintain an additional table where they store the data sent in the incremental routing information packets.

New route broadcasts contain the address of the destination, the number of hops to reach the destination, the sequence number of the information received regarding the destination, as well as a new sequence number unique to the broadcast. The route labelled with the most recent sequence number is always used. In the event that two updates have the same sequence number, the route with the smaller metric is used in order to optimize (shorten) the path. Mobiles also keep track of the settling time of routes, or the weighted average time that routes to a destination will fluctuate before the route with the best metric is received. By delaying the broadcast of a routing update by the length of the settling time, mobiles can reduce network traffic and optimize routes by eliminating those broadcasts that would occur if a better route was discovered in the very near future.

(ii) Clusterhead Gateway Switch Routing (CGSR)

The Clusterhead Gateway Switch Routing (CGSR) protocol differs from the previous protocol in the type of addressing and network organization scheme employed. Instead of a "fat" network, CGSR is a clustered multihop mobile wireless network with several heuristic routing schemes. By having a cluster head controlling a group of ad-hoc nodes, a framework for code separation (among clusters), and channel access, routing and bandwidth allocation can be achieved. A cluster head selection algorithm is utilized to elect a node as the cluster head using a distributed algorithm within the cluster. The disadvantage of having a cluster head scheme is that frequent cluster head changes can adversely affect routing protocol performance since nodes are busy in cluster head selection rather than packet relaying. Hence, instead of invoking cluster head reselection every time the cluster membership changes, a Least Cluster Change (LCC) clustering algorithm is introduced. Using LCC, cluster heads only change when two cluster heads come into contact, or when a node moves out of contact of all other cluster heads. CGSR uses DSDV as the underlying routing scheme, and hence has much of the same overhead as DSDV. However, it modifies DSDV by using a hierarchical cluster head-to-gateway routing approach to route traffic from source to destination. Gateway nodes are nodes that are within communication range of two or more cluster heads.

A packet sent by a node is first routed to its cluster head, and then the packet is routed from the cluster head to a gateway to another cluster head, and so on until the cluster head of the destination node is reached. The packet is then transmitted to the destination. Using this method, each node must keep a "cluster member table" where it stores the destination cluster head for each mobile node in the network. These cluster member tables are broadcast by each node periodically using the DSDV algorithm. Nodes update their cluster member tables on the reception of such a table from a neighbour. In addition to the cluster member table, each node must also maintain a routing table, which is used to determine the next hop in order to reach the destination.

On receiving a packet, a node will consult its cluster member table and routing table to determine the nearest cluster head along the route to the destination. Next the node will check its routing table to determine the node in order to reach the selected cluster head. It then transmits the packet to this node.

(iii) The Wireless Routing Protocol (WRP)

The Wireless Routing Protocol (WRP) is a table-based protocol with the goal of maintaining routing information among all nodes in the network. Each node in the network is responsible for maintaining four tables: (a) distance table, (b) routing table, (c) link-cost table, and (d) message retransmission list (MRL) table. Each entry of the MRL contains the sequence number of the update message, a retransmission counter, an acknowledgment-required flag vector with one entry per neighbour, and a list of updates sent in the update message. The MRL records which updates in an update message need to be retransmitted and which neighbours should acknowledge the retransmission.

Mobiles inform each other of link changes through the use of update messages. An update message is sent only between neighbouring nodes and contains a list of updates (the destination, the distance to the destination, and the predecessor of the destination), as well as a list of responses indicating which mobiles should acknowledge (ACK) the update. Mobiles send update messages after processing updates from neighbours or detecting a change in a link to a neighbour. In the event of the loss of a link between two nodes, the nodes send update messages to their neighbours. The neighbours then update their distance table entries and check for new possible paths through other nodes. Any new paths are relayed back to the original nodes so that they can update their tables accordingly.

Nodes learn of the existence of their neighbours from the receipt of acknowledgments and other messages. If a node is not sending messages, it must send a hello message within a specified time period to ensure connectivity. Otherwise, the lack of messages from the node indicates the failure of that link; this may cause a false alarm. When a mobile receives a hello message from a new node, that new node is added to the mobile's routing table, and the mobile sends the new node a copy of its routing table information. In WRP, routing nodes communicate the distance and second-to-last hop information for each destination in the wireless networks. WRP belongs to the class of path finding algorithms with an important exception. It avoids the "count-to-infinity" problem by forcing each node to perform consistency checks of predecessor information reported by all its neighbours. This ultimately (though not instantaneously) eliminates looping situations and provides faster route convergence when a link failure event occurs.

(2) Source-Initiated On-Demand Routing

A different approach from table-driven routing is source-initiated on-demand routing. This type of routing creates routes only when desired by the source node. When a node requires a route to a destination, it initiates a route discovery process within the network. This process is completed once a route is found or all possible route permutations have been examined.

Once a route has been established, it is maintained by some form of route maintenance procedure until either the destination becomes inaccessible along every path from the source or until the route is no longer desired.

(i) Ad-hoc On-Demand Distance Vector Routing (AODV)

The Ad-hoc On-Demand Distance Vector (AODV) routing protocol builds on the DSDV algorithm previously described. AODV is an improvement on DSDV because it typically minimizes the number of required broadcasts by creating routes on an on-demand basis, as opposed to maintaining a complete list of routes as in the DSDV algorithm. The authors of AODV classify it as a pure on-demand route acquisition system, as nodes that are not on a selected path do not maintain routing information or participate in routing table exchanges.

When a source node desires to send a message to some destination node and does not already have a valid route to that destination, it initiates a Path Discovery process to locate the other node. It broadcasts a route request (RREQ) packet to its neighbours, which then forward the request to their neighbours, and so on, until either the destination or an intermediate node with a "fresh enough" route to the destination is located. AODV utilizes destination sequence numbers to ensure all routes are loop-free and contain the most recent route information. Each node maintains its own sequence number, as well as a broadcast ID. The broadcast ID is incremented for every RREQ the node initiates, and together with the node's IP address, uniquely identifies a RREQ. Along with its own sequence number and the broadcast ID, the source node includes in the RREQ the most recent sequence number it has for the destination. Intermediate nodes can reply to the RREQ only if they have a route to the destination whose corresponding destination sequence number is greater than or equal to that contained in the RREQ.

During the process of forwarding the RREQ, intermediate nodes record in their route tables the address of the neighbour from which the first copy of the broadcast packet is received, thereby establishing a reverse path. If additional copies of the same RREQ are later received, these packets are discarded. Once the RREQ reaches the destination or an intermediate node with a fresh enough route, the destination/intermediate node responds by unicasting a route reply (RREP) packet back to the neighbour from which it first received the RREQ. As the RREP is routed back along the reverse path, nodes along this path set up forward route entries in their route tables which point to the node from which the RREP came. These forward route entries indicate the active forward route. Associated with each route entry is a route timer which will cause the deletion of the entry if it is not used within the specified lifetime. Because the RREP is forwarded along the path established by the RREQ, AODV only supports the use of symmetric links.

Routes are maintained as follows. If a source node moves, it is able to reinitiate the route discovery protocol to find a new route to the destination. If a node along the route moves, its upstream neighbour notices the move and propagates a link failure notification message (a RREP with infinite metric) to each of its active upstream neighbours to inform them of the erasure of that part of the route. These nodes in turn propagate the link failure notification to their upstream neighbours, and so on until the source node is reached. The source node may then choose to reinitiate route discovery for that destination if a route is still desired.

(ii) Dynamic Source Routing (DSR)

The Dynamic Source Routing (DSR) protocol is an on-demand routing protocol that is based on the concept of source routing. Mobile nodes are required to maintain route caches that contain the source routes of which the mobile is aware. Entries in the route cache are continually updated as new routes are learned.

The protocol consists of two major phases: route discovery and route maintenance. When a mobile node has a packet to send to some destination, it first consults its route cache to determine whether it already has a route to the destination. If it has an unexpired route to the destination, it will use this route to send the packet. On the other hand, if the node does not have such a route, it initiates route discovery by broadcasting a route request packet. This route request contains the address of the destination, along with the source node's address and a unique identification number. Each node receiving the packet checks whether it knows of a route to the destination. If it does not, it adds its own address to the route record of the packet and then forwards the packet along its outgoing links. To limit the number of route requests propagated on the outgoing links of a node, a mobile only forwards the route request if the request has not yet been seen by the mobile and if the mobile's address does not already appear in the route record.

A route reply is generated when either the route request reaches the destination itself, or when it reaches an intermediate node which contains in its route caches an unexpired route to the destination. By the time the packet reaches either the destination or such an intermediate node, it contains a route record yielding the sequence of hops taken. If the node generating the route reply is the destination, it places the route record contained in the route request into the route reply. If the responding node is an intermediate node, it will append its cached route to the route record and then generate the route reply. To return the route reply, the responding node must have a route to the initiator. If it has a route to the initiator in its route cache, it may use that route. Otherwise, if symmetric links are supported, the node may reverse the route in the route record. If symmetric links are not supported, the node may initiate its own route discovery and piggyback the route reply on the new route request.

Route maintenance is accomplished through the use of route error packets and acknowledgments. Route error packets are generated at a node when the data link layer encounters a fatal transmission problem. When a route error packet is received, the hop in error is removed from the node's route cache and all routes containing the hop are truncated at that point. In addition to route error messages, acknowledgments are used to verify the correct operation of the route links. Such acknowledgments include passive acknowledgments, where a mobile is able to hear the next hop forwarding the packet along the route.

(iii) Temporally-Ordered Routing Algorithm (TORA)

TORA (Temporally-Ordered Routing Algorithm) is a highly adaptive, loop-free, and distributed routing algorithm based on the concept of link reversal. TORA is proposed to operate in a highly dynamic mobile networking environment. It is source-initiated and provides multiple routes for any desired source/destination pair. The key design concept of TORA is the localization of control messages to a very small set of nodes near the occurrence of a topological change. To accomplish this, nodes need to maintain routing information about adjacent (1-hop) nodes. The protocol performs three basic functions: (a) route creation, (b) route maintenance, and (c) route erasure.

During the route creation and maintenance phases, nodes use a "height" metric to establish a directed acyclic graph (DAG) rooted at the destination. Thereafter, links are assigned a direction (upstream or downstream) based on the relative height metric of neighbouring nodes. This process of establishing a DAG is similar to the query/reply process proposed in LMR (Lightweight Mobile Routing). In times of node mobility, the DAG route is broken and route maintenance is necessary to re-establish a DAG rooted at the same destination. Upon failure of the last downstream link, a node generates a new reference level which results in the propagation of that reference level by neighbouring nodes, effectively coordinating a structured reaction to the failure. Links are reversed to reflect the change in adapting to the new reference level. This has the same effect as reversing the direction of one or more links when a node has no downstream links.

Timing is an important factor for TORA because the "height" metric is dependent on the logical time of a link failure; TORA assumes all nodes have synchronized clocks (accomplished via an external time source such as Global Positioning System). TORA's metric is a quintuple comprised of five elements, namely: (a) logical time of a link failure, (b) the unique ID of the node that defined the new reference level, (c) a reflection indicator bit, (d) a propagation ordering parameter, and (e) the unique ID of the node. The first three elements collectively represent the reference level. A new reference level is defined each time a node loses its last downstream link due to a link failure. TORA's route erasure phase essentially involves flooding a broadcast "clear packet" (CLR) throughout the network to erase invalid routes.

(iv) Associativity-Based Routing (ABR)

The Associativity-Based Routing (ABR) protocol is free from loops, deadlock, and packet duplicates, and defines a new routing metric for ad-hoc mobile networks. This metric is known as the degree of association stability. In ABR, a route is selected based on the degree of association stability of mobile nodes. Each node periodically generates a beacon to signify its existence. When received by neighbouring nodes, this beaconing cause their associativity tables to be updated. For each beacon received, the associativity tick of the current node with respect to the beaconing node is incremented. Association stability is defined by connection stability of one node with respect to another node over time and space. A high degree of association stability may indicate a low state of node mobility, while a low degree may indicate a high state of node mobility. Associativity ticks are reset when the neighbours of a node or the node itself moves out of proximity. A fundamental objective of ABR is to derive longer-lived routes for ad-hoc mobile networks.

The three phases of ABR are: (a) route discovery, (b) route re-construction (RRC), and (c) route deletion. The route discovery phase is accomplished by a broadcast query and awaits reply (BQ-REPLY) cycle. A node desiring a route broadcasts a BQ message in search of mobiles that have a route to the destination. All nodes receiving the query (that are not the destination) append their addresses and their associativity ticks with their neighbours along with QoS information to the query packet. A successor node erases its upstream node neighbours' associativity tick entries and retains only the entry concerned with itself and its upstream node. In this way, each resultant packet arriving at the destination will contain the associativity ticks of the nodes along the route to the destination. The destination is then able to select the best route by examining the associativity ticks along each of the paths. In the case where multiple paths have the same overall degree of association stability, the route with the minimum number of hops is selected. The destination then sends a REPLY packet back to the source along this path. Nodes propagating the REPLY mark their routes as valid. All other routes remain inactive and the possibility of duplicate packets arriving at the destination is avoided.

(v) Signal Stability Routing (SSR)

Unlike the algorithms described so far, SSR selects routes based on the signal strength between nodes and on a node's location stability. This route selection criterion has the effect of choosing routes that have "stronger" connectivity. SSR can be divided into two cooperative protocols: the Dynamic Routing Protocol (DRP) and the Static Routing Protocol (SRP).

The DRP is responsible for the maintenance of the Signal Stability Table (SST) and the Routing Table (RT). The SST records the signal strength of neighbouring nodes, which is obtained by periodic beacons from the link layer of each neighbouring node. The signal strength may be recorded as either a strong or weak channel. All transmissions are received by, and processed in, the DRP. After updating all appropriate table entries, the DRP passes a received packet to the SRP.

The SRP processes packets by passing the packet up the stack if it is the intended receiver or looking up the destination in the RT and then forwarding the packet if it is not. If no entry is found in the RT for the destination, a route-search process is initiated to find a route. Route requests are propagated throughout the network but are only forwarded to the next hop if they are received over strong channels and have not been previously processed (to prevent looping). The destination chooses the first arriving route-search packet to send back because it is most probable that the packet arrived over the shortest and/or least congested path. The DRP then reverses the selected route and sends a route-reply message back to the initiator. The DRP of the nodes along the path update their RTs accordingly.

Route-search packets arriving at the destination have necessarily chosen the path of strongest signal stability, as the packets are dropped at a node if they have arrived over a weak channel. If there is no route-reply message received at the source within a specific timeout period, the source changes the PREF field in the header to indicate that weak channels are acceptable, as these may be the only links over which the packet can be propagated.

When a failed link is detected within the network, the intermediate nodes send an error message to the source indicating which channel has failed. The source then initiates another route-search process to find a new path to the destination. The source also sends an erase message to notify all nodes of the broken link.

6.2 NAMING AND ADDRESSING IN WSN

Naming and addressing schemes are used to denote and to find things. In networking, names and addresses often refer to individual nodes as well as to data items stored in them. Addresses/names have a particular format, which has a certain length when considered as a string of bits. As opposed to other types of networks, representation size is a critical issue in wireless sensor networks, since addresses are present in almost any packet. However, coordination among nodes is needed to assign reasonably short addresses.

A second key aspect is content-based addressing, where not nodes or network interfaces but data is addressed. Content-based addressing can be integrated with data-centric routing and is also a key enabler of in-network processing.

6.2.1 Use of Addresses and Names in (Sensor) Networks

In most computer and sensor networks, the following types of names, addresses, and identifiers can be found

A Unique Node Identifier (UID) : is a persistent data item unique for every node. An example of a UID might be a combination of a vendor name, a product name, and a serial number, assigned at manufacturing time. Such a UID may or may not have any function in the protocol stack.

MAC Address :

A MAC address is used to distinguish between one-hop neighbors of a node. This is particularly important in wireless sensor networks using contention-based MAC protocols, since by including a MAC addresses into unicast MAC packets a node can determine which packets are *not* destined to it and go into sleep mode while such a packet is in transit. This overhearing avoidance is an important method of conserving energy at the MAC layer.

Network Address :

A network address is used to find and denote a node over multiple hops and therefore network addresses are often connected to routing.

Network Identifiers :

In geographically overlapping wireless (sensor) networks of the same type and working in the same frequency band, it is also important to distinguish the networks by means of network identifiers.

Resource Identifiers :

A name or resource identifier is represented in user-understandable terms or in a way that is understandable to the user. For example, upon reading the name

www.xyz.org, an experienced user knows that (i) the thing the name refers to is likely

a web server and (ii) the user can find information about the thing.

In contrast, upon looking at the IP address 195.182.163.136, hardly any user draws either conclusion. Names can refer to nodes, groups of nodes, data items, or similar abstractions.

A single node can have many names and addresses. For example, the WWW server www.xyz.org has the name www.xyz.org, it has the IP address 195.182.163.136 and, assuming that the server is attached to an Ethernet, it has a 48-bit IEEE MAC address. The mapping between user-friendly names like www.xemacs.org and the addresses relevant for network operation is done by binding service. This mapping is also often referred to as name resolution. The domain name service (DNS) provides the mapping from the name to the IP address while the address resolution protocol (ARP) maps the IP address to a MAC address

6.2.2 Uniqueness of Addresses

Globally Unique :

A globally unique address or identifier is supposed to occur at most once all over the world. An example is the 48-bit IEEE MAC addresses used in Ethernet and Token Ring networks. The binary representation of such addresses must be sufficiently large to accommodate all devices worldwide.

Networkwide Unique :

A networkwide unique address is supposed to be unique within a given network, but the same address can be used in different networks

Locally Unique :

A locally unique address might occur several times in the same network, but it should be unique within a suitably defined **neighbourhood**.

6.2.3 Address Management Tasks

Following are the fundamental tasks of address management, which are independent of the type of addresses:

Address Allocation

This task is the assignment of an address to an entity from an address pool.

Address Deallocation

In on-demand addressing schemes, the address space often has a small-to-moderate size. The node population in sensor networks is intrinsically dynamic, with nodes dying or moving away and new nodes being added to the network. If the addresses of the leaving nodes were not put back into the address pool for reuse, the address pool would be exhausted eventually and no addresses could be allocated to new nodes. Address deallocation can be either graceful or abrupt. In graceful deallocation, a node explicitly sends out control packets to give up its address. In abrupt deallocation, the node disappears or crashes and consequently does not send appropriate control packets, leaving the responsibility to detect and deallocate the node's address to the network. When very large address spaces are used, like for example the IEEE 802.3 MAC addresses of 48-bits length, address deallocation is not an issue.

Address Representation

A format for representing addresses needs to be negotiated and implemented.

Conflict Detection/Resolution

Address conflicts can occur in networks with distributed assignment of on-demand addresses or in case of mergers of so-far distinct networks. If conflicts cannot be tolerated, they must be resolved.

Binding

If several addressing layers are used, a mapping between the different layers has to be provided. For example, in IP networks, an IP address has to be mapped to a MAC address using the ARP protocol.

6.2.4 Assignment of MAC Addresses

Assignment of globally unique MAC addresses is undesirable in sensor networks with mostly small packets. This section contains the assignment methods for MAC address.

A prior assignment of networkwide unique addresses is feasible only if it can be done with reasonable effort. But there can be the overhead to represent addresses as address space is not as large as in globally unique addresses. For example, up to 16,384 nodes can be addressed with 14 bits and this number is much friendlier than 48 bits used for globally unique IEEE addresses. Therefore, we concentrate on dynamic and distributed assignment of networkwide and local addresses.

6.2.5 Distributed Assignment of Locally Unique Addresses

A protocol is discussed in this section that assigns locally unique MAC addresses to nodes by utilizing a localized protocol in which a node communicates only with immediate neighbors. By restricting the uniqueness requirement to a small local neighbourhood, fewer bits are needed for address representation than for networkwide or globally unique addresses. The energy reduction due to the saved address bits can be significant if the size of the data payload has the same order of magnitude as the address size. By using locally unique addresses, we can reuse the same address several times in the overall network.

Address Assignment Algorithm

The assignment algorithm must take the existence of asymmetric links into account. Asymmetric links are the links which are links where a node A may hear some other node B but not vice versa. It is assumed that each node has already discovered its bidirectional and inbound neighbours from a previous run of a neighbourhood discovery protocol. An inbound neighbour of a node A is a neighbour whose transmissions A can hear but not vice versa. Similarly, an outbound neighbour of A is a node that receives A's transmissions but not vice versa.

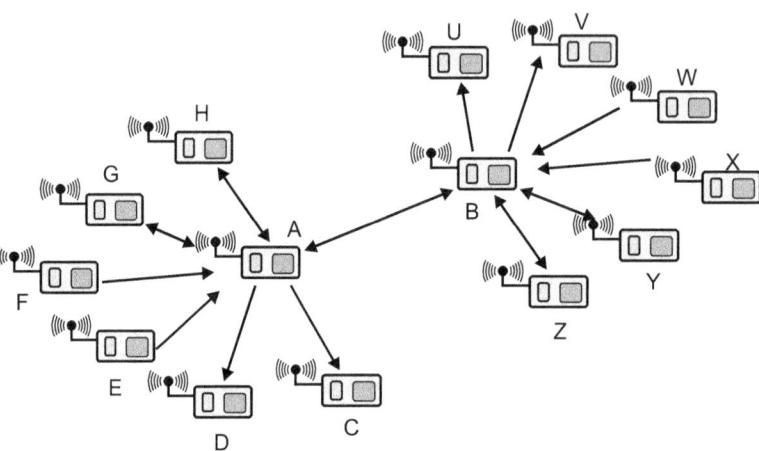

Fig. 6.2 : Address assignment with bidirectional, inbound, outbound neighbours

Consider the situation shown in Fig. 6.2. We want to assign addresses to nodes A and B. The requirements are:

- Node A and B are assigned different addresses.
- The address of node A is different from those of nodes W, X, Y, and Z since all these nodes can direct packets to B.
- By symmetry, B's address must be different from the addresses of E, F, G, and H.
- Do B's and C's (or D's) addresses have to be different?

If they are the same, all packets from node A destined to node B would also be received by C. If, however, the link between A and C is perfectly unidirectional and if the additional constraint is introduced that any node accepts packets only from bidirectional neighbors, there is no need to let C choose another address than B (how shall C tell A about the conflict anyway?). By the same argument, both A and B can also have the same address as W and X, since B would not accept packets from any of these. It is not even required that W and X have different addresses as far as node B is concerned.

Under the assumption that nodes communicate only with bidirectional neighbors, then for any node A all its bidirectional neighbors must have distinct addresses. Furthermore, the address of any inbound neighbour must be different from the address of all bidirectional neighbors.

After a node A has performed neighbourhood discovery, it starts by broadcasting a HELLO message. The bidirectional and outbound neighbors of A reply to this message by sending INFO messages.4 With reference to 2, let us assume that node B replies with an INFO packet. This packet contains the following information:

- The unique node identifier of B, which can also be a networkwide or globally unique and routable address;
- B's MAC address;
- The MAC addresses of all bidirectional neighbors of B.

Only neighbors that already have a MAC address send INFO messages. By assumption, node A will only hear the INFO messages of its bidirectional neighbors and therefore knows their identity. To see why it is useful that B includes its neighbors as well, remember that A must choose its MAC address distinct from nodes Y and Z.

The time that node A listens for INFO messages is bounded. After this time has elapsed, node A knows the entire one-hop and two-hop neighbourhood. Now, two important cases can occur:

- If all of A's one-hop neighbors have different addresses, there is no conflict and A can choose an address such that this address is unique within A's two-hop neighbourhood.
- If there is a conflict between A's one-hop neighbors, node A issues a CONFLICT message, indicating the conflicting address. Reception of this message by the conflicting nodes triggers a new address selection round.

6.2.6 Content-Based and Geographic Addressing

Traditional fixed and ad hoc networks offer services and protocols that allow a number of independent users to exchange data among each other and with the remaining world. On the other hand, in wireless sensor networks, the nodes interact with the physical environment, and they *collaborate*, that is they are not independent of each other. A user of a wireless sensor network ultimately wants to know something about the physical environment the network interacts with, but he typically does not care about the individual sensor nodes. It is preferable to allow users to *name the data they are interested in and not the (set of) nodes producing the data*. In traditional IP-based networks, this requirement corresponds to introducing a naming system *on top of* IP addresses and to introducing appropriate binding services like DNS or other directory services, providing a mapping from names (meaningful to the user) to IP addresses (meaningful for the routing protocol). In sensor networks, however, these levels of indirection can be eliminated and the user-specified attributes can be directly used to find (groups of) nodes. This idea is often referred to as data-centric addressing. Such an approach to make the application data meaningful to the operation of network (especially routing) protocols is also a key enabler for in-network processing techniques.

Geographic addressing can be regarded as a special case of content-based addressing. Here, some of the user-specifiable attributes refer to spatial coordinates. Geographic addressing assumes that each node knows its own location with respect to some agreed-upon coordinate system. Thus, location techniques are essential for working with geographic addresses. Both content-based and geographic addressing are no replacements for MAC protocols but can be used, for example, on the network layer to help with routing decisions.

Content-Based addressing
A Low-Level-Naming Mechanism

In this approach, content-based addressing is integrated with directed diffusion routing. In directed diffusion a sink node issues an interest message, specifying a set of attributes to describe the desired data. This message is disseminated into the network. The nodes that can produce sensor data matching the interest are called source nodes. A data packet generated by a source node travels through intermediate nodes to the sink. An intermediate node stores the interest along with (set of) possible upstream neighbors in the interest cache. Upon receiving a data packet, the intermediate node searches its cache for an interest matching the data and forwards the data packet to the associated upstream neighbour.

Both the interests and the data packets are represented as sets of Attribute Value Operation (AVO) tuple. The set of attributes is predefined and each attribute possesses a unique, well known key as well as an understanding of the data type for the corresponding value.

The different operators and their meaning are shown in Table 6.1. The IS operator specifies that the corresponding attribute actually has the indicated value and is typically generated by the data source; IS is also called an **actual operator**.

Table 6.1 : Set of Operators

Operator Name	Meaning
EQ	Matches if actual value is equal to value
NE	Matches if actual value is not equal to value
LT	Matches if actual value is smaller than value
GT	Matches if actual value is greater than value
LE	Matches if actual value is smaller or equal to value
GE	Matches if actual value is larger or equal to value
EQ	ANY matches anything, value is meaningless
IS	Specifies a literal attribute

All the other operators are called formal operators, and they are used to specify the interests against which the actual values generated by the source are matched.

The intermediate nodes use an operation called one-way match to decide which interest a received data packet matches. Basically, for a given interest, the intermediate node goes through all its formal attributes and checks whether (i) the data packet possesses a corresponding attribute at all and (ii) whether the actual value carried in the data packet's attribute matches the formal operator in the interest.

Geographic Addressing

It is often convenient for users to express their queries to a sensor network in terms of not only the *type* and modality of data they want to receive but also the *region* or *location* from where the data should originate. By the same token, as for content-based addresses, users do not want to separately specify each node belonging to the region of interest but they prefer to specify a region and let the network figure out which sensors are appropriate. Furthermore, if the location of a sensor node is known, geographic routing schemes can be applied, which are discussed in later section. There are many different ways to specify a region, for example

- Specify a single point.
- Specify a circle or a sphere by giving centre point and radius.
- Specify a rectangle or a parallelepiped by giving two or three corner points.
- Specify a polygon (two-dimensional) or a polytope (three-dimensional) by giving a list of points.

Geographic addressing requires that a sensor can check whether its position lies within a given area. This test can be complex if general polygons/polytopes are used to specify the region of interest. Such a point-in-polygon test is a standard task in computational geometry. The use of more complex shapes also has the disadvantage that more points and thus more data bits are needed to specify them.

6.3 ROUTING IN SENSOR NETWORKS CHALLENGES AND DESIGN ISSUES

Wireless sensor network (WSN) is widely considered as one of the most important technologies for the twenty-first century. In the past decades, it has received tremendous attention from both academia and industry all over the world. A WSN typically consists of a large number of low-cost, low-power, and multifunctional wireless sensor nodes, with sensing, wireless communications and computation capabilities. These sensor nodes communicate over short distance via a wireless medium and collaborate to accomplish a common task, for example, environment monitoring, military surveillance, and industrial process control.

The basic philosophy behind WSNs is that, while the capability of each individual sensor node is limited, the aggregate power of the entire network is sufficient for the required mission. In many WSN applications, the deployment of sensor nodes is performed in an ad hoc fashion without careful planning and engineering. Once deployed, the sensor nodes must be able to autonomously organize themselves into a wireless communication network. Sensor nodes are battery-powered and are expected to operate without attendance for a relatively long period of time. In most cases it is very difficult and even impossible to change or recharge batteries for the sensor nodes. WSNs are characterized with denser levels of sensor node deployment, higher unreliability of sensor nodes, and sever power, computation, and memory constraints. Thus, the unique characteristics and constraints present many new challenges for the development and application of WSNs.

Due to the severe energy constraints of large number of densely deployed sensor nodes, it requires a suite of network protocols to implement various network control and management functions such as synchronization, node localization, and network security. The traditional routing protocols have several shortcomings when applied to WSNs, which are mainly due to the energy-constrained nature of such networks.

A large number of research activities have been carried out to explore and overcome the constraints of WSNs and solve design and application issues.

6.3.1 Network Characteristics and Design Objectives

The characteristics of sensor networks and application requirements have a significant impact on the network design objectives in term of network capabilities and network performance.

(1) Network Characteristics :

As compared to the traditional wireless communication networks such as mobile ad hoc network (MANET) and cellular systems, wireless sensor networks have the following unique characteristics and constraints:

(2) Dense Sensor Node Deployment :

Sensor nodes are usually densely deployed and can be several orders of magnitude higher than that in a MANET.

(3) Battery-Powered Sensor Nodes :

Sensor nodes are usually powered by battery and are deployed in a harsh environment where it is very difficult to change or recharge the batteries.

(4) Severe Energy, Computation, and Storage Constraints :

Sensors nodes are having highly limited energy, computation, and storage capabilities.

(5) Self-Configurable :

Sensor nodes are usually randomly deployed and autonomously configure themselves into a communication network.

(6) Unreliable Sensor Nodes :
Since sensor nodes are prone to physical damages or failures due to its deployment in harsh or hostile environment.

(7) Data Redundancy :
In most sensor network application, sensor nodes are densely deployed in a region of interest and collaborate to accomplish a common sensing task. Thus, the data sensed by multiple sensor nodes typically have a certain level of correlation or redundancy.

(8) Application Specific :
A sensor network is usually designed and deployed for a specific application. The design requirements of a sensor network change with its application.

(9) Many-to-one Traffic Pattern :
In most sensor network applications, the data sensed by sensor nodes flow from multiple source sensor nodes to a particular sink, exhibiting a many-to-one traffic pattern.

(10) Frequent Topology Change :
Network topology changes frequently due to the node failures, damage, addition, energy depletion, or channel fading.

(11) Network Design Objectives :
Most sensor networks are application specific and have different application requirements. Thus, all or part of the following main design objectives is considered in the design of sensor networks:

(12) Small Node Size :
Since sensor nodes are usually deployed in a harsh or hostile environment in large numbers, reducing node size can facilitate node deployment. It will also reduce the power consumption and cost of sensor nodes.

(13) Low Node Cost :
Since sensor nodes are usually deployed in a harsh or hostile environment in large numbers and cannot be reused, reducing cost of sensor nodes is important and will result into the cost reduction of whole network.

(14) Low Power Consumption :
Since sensor nodes are powered by battery and it is often very difficult or even impossible to charge or recharge their batteries, it is crucial to reduce the power consumption of sensor nodes so that the lifetime of the sensor nodes, as well as the whole network is persists for a long time.

(15) Scalability :
Since the number sensor nodes in sensor networks are in the order of tens, hundreds, or thousands, network protocols designed for sensor networks should be scalable to different network sizes.

(16) Reliability :

Network protocols designed for sensor networks must provide error control and correction mechanisms to ensure reliable data delivery over noisy, error-prone, and time-varying wireless channels.

(17) Self-Configurability :

In sensor networks, once deployed, sensor nodes should be able to autonomously organize themselves into a communication network and reconfigure their connectivity in the event of topology changes and node failures.

(18) Adaptability :

In sensor networks, a node may fail, join, or move, which would result in changes in node density and network topology. Thus, network protocols designed for sensor networks should be adaptive to such density and topology changes.

(19) Channel Utilization :

Since sensor networks have limited bandwidth resources, communication protocols designed for sensor networks should efficiently make use of the bandwidth to improve channel utilization.

(20) Fault Tolerance :

Sensor nodes are prone to failures due to harsh deployment environments and unattended operations. Thus, sensor nodes should be fault tolerant and have the abilities of self-testing, self-calibrating, self-repairing, and self-recovering.

(21) Security :

A sensor network should introduce effective security mechanisms to prevent the data information in the network or a sensor node from unauthorized access or malicious attacks.

(22) QoS Support :

In sensor networks, different applications may have different quality-of-service (QoS) requirements in terms of delivery latency and packet loss. Thus, network protocol design should consider the QoS requirements of specific applications.

(23) Network Design Challenges and Routing Issues :

The design of routing protocols for WSNs is challenging because of several network constraints.

WSNs suffer from the limitations of several network resources, for example, energy, bandwidth, central processing unit, and storage. The design challenges in sensor networks involve the following main aspects:

(i) Limited Energy Capacity :

Since sensor nodes are battery powered, they have limited energy capacity. Energy poses a big challenge for network designers in hostile environments, for example, a battlefield, where it is impossible to access the sensors and recharge their batteries.

Furthermore, when the energy of a sensor reaches a certain threshold, the sensor will become faulty and will not be able to function properly, which will have a major impact on the network performance. Thus, routing protocols designed for sensors should be as energy efficient as possible to extend their lifetime, and hence prolong the network lifetime while guaranteeing good performance overall.

(ii) Sensor Locations :

Another challenge that faces the design of routing protocols is to manage the locations of the sensors. Most of the proposed protocols assume that the sensors either are equipped with global positioning system (GPS) receivers or use some localization technique to learn about their locations.

(iii) Limited Hardware Resources :

In addition to limited energy capacity, sensor nodes have also limited processing and storage capacities, and thus can only perform limited computational functionalities. These hardware constraints present many challenges in software development and network protocol design for sensor networks, which must consider not only the energy constraint in sensor nodes, but also the processing and storage capacities of sensor nodes.

(iv) Massive and Random Node Deployment :

Sensor node deployment in WSNs is application dependent and can be either manual or random which finally affects the performance of the routing protocol. In most applications, sensor nodes can be scattered randomly in an intended area or dropped massively over an inaccessible or hostile region. If the resultant distribution of nodes is not uniform, optimal clustering becomes necessary to allow connectivity and enable energy efficient network operation.

(24) Network Characteristics and Unreliable Environment :

A sensor network usually operates in a dynamic and unreliable environment. The topology of a network, which is defined by the sensors and the communication links between the sensors, changes frequently due to sensor addition, deletion, node failures, damages, or energy depletion.

Also, the sensor nodes are linked by a wireless medium, which is noisy, error prone, and time varying. Therefore, routing paths should consider network topology dynamics due to limited energy and sensor mobility as well as increasing the size of the network to maintain specific application requirements in terms of coverage and connectivity.

(i) Data Aggregation :

Since sensor nodes may generate significant redundant data, similar packets from multiple nodes can be aggregated so that the number of transmissions is reduced. Data aggregation technique has been used to achieve energy efficiency and data transfer optimization in a number of routing protocols.

(ii) Diverse Sensing Application Requirements :

Sensor networks have a wide range of diverse applications. No network protocol can meet the requirements of all applications. Therefore, the routing protocols should guarantee data delivery and its accuracy so that the sink can gather the required knowledge about the physical phenomenon on time.

(iii) Scalability :

Routing protocols should be able to scale with the network size. Also, sensors may not necessarily have the same capabilities in terms of energy, processing, sensing, and particularly communication. Hence, communication links between sensors may not be symmetric, that is, a pair of sensors may not be able to have communication in both directions. This should be taken care of in the routing protocols.

6.4 ROUTING PROTOCOLS

Routing in wireless sensor networks differs from conventional routing in fixed networks in various ways. There is no infrastructure, wireless links are unreliable, sensor nodes may fail, and routing protocols have to meet strict energy saving requirements. This section covers the details of some important routing protocols such as flooding, SPIN, PEAGASIS, Geographic routing

6.4.1 Flooding

Flooding (or network-wide broadcasting) is the simplest way to deliver data from a node to any other node in the network. In flooding, the source simply broadcasts the data packet to its neighbouring nodes via a MAC layer broadcast mechanism. Each node hearing the broadcast *for the first time* re-broadcasts it. Thus, the broadcast propagates in "layers" outwards from the source, eventually terminating when every node has heard the packet and transmitted it once. The rule "every node transmits only once" guarantees termination of the procedure and also avoids looping. This can be achieved using unique identifiers on all packets being flooded. The flooding technique delivers the data to every node in the connected component of the network. With flooding, no topological information needs to be maintained or known in advance. In network scenarios where node mobility is so high that a given unicast routing protocol may fail to keep up with the rate of topology changes, flooding may become the only alternative for routing data reasonably. However, in other scenarios where node mobility is traceable by a routing protocol, flooding can be a very inefficient option. This is because the total number of transmissions to deliver a single message to a destination with flooding is in the order of network size, as opposed to the network diameter with a unicast routing protocol (assuming that a route is already found).

Although flooding is not usually attractive for efficiently delivering data, it is still very useful in carrying out certain routing tasks such as route discovery and topology dissemination, and as a bootstrapping mechanism when nothing is known in prior about the network topology.

In the simple flooding protocol as described above (also called *pure flooding*), each node transmits (broadcasts) the data once. As a result, a node may receive the same packet from several neighbors. Thus, depending on the network density, simple flooding may take far more transmissions than necessary for the flood to reach every node. Such redundancy can be eliminated to achieve less contention and collisions at the radio link layer, thus increasing network utilization. Several efficient alternatives have been proposed that use only a small subset of nodes to transmit the data packet during a flood, however ensure that all nodes in the network receive the packet.

6.4.2 Sensor Protocols for Information via Negotiation (SPIN)

SPIN protocol was designed to improve classic flooding protocols and overcome the problems they may cause, for example, implosion and overlap. The SPIN protocols are resource aware and resource adaptive. The sensors running the SPIN protocols are able to compute the energy consumption required to compute, send, and receive data over the network. Thus, they can make informed decisions for efficient use of their own resources. The SPIN protocols are based on two key mechanisms namely *negotiation* and *resource adaptation*. SPIN enables the sensors to negotiate with each other before any data dissemination can occur in order to avoid injecting non-useful and redundant information in the network. SPIN uses *meta-data* as the descriptors of the data that the sensors want to disseminate. The notion of meta-data avoids the occurrence of overlap given sensors can name the interesting portion of the data they want to get. It may be noted here that the size of the meta-data should definitely be less than that of the corresponding sensor data. Contrary to the flooding technique, each sensor is aware of its resource consumption with the help of its own *resource manager* that is probed by the application before any data processing or transmission. This helps the sensors to monitor and adapt to any change in their own resources.

There are two protocols in the SPIN family: SPIN-I (or SPIN-PP) and SPIN-2 (or SPIN-EC).

While SPIN-I uses a negotiation mechanism to reduce the consumption of the sensors, SPIN-2 uses a resource-aware mechanism for energy savings. Both protocols allow the sensors to exchange information about their sensed data, thus helping them to obtain the data they are interested in. SPIN-I is a three-stage handshake protocol by which the sensors can disseminate their data. This protocol applies for those networks using point-to-point transmission media (or point-to-point networks), in which two sensors can communicate exclusively with each other without interfering with other sensors. SPIN-BC improves SPIN-PP by using one-to-many communication instead of many one-to-one communications.

It is a three-stage handshake protocol for broadcast transmission media, where the sensors in a network communicate with each other using a single shared channel. SPIN-2 differs from SPIN-I in that it takes into account the residual energy of sensors. If the sensors have plenty of energy, SPIN-2 is identical to SPIN-I, and hence has the same three stages. However, when a sensor has low residual energy, it controls its participation in a data dissemination process. While the family of SPIN protocols applies to lossless networks, it can be slightly updated to apply to lossy or mobile networks.

6.4.3 Power-Efficient Gathering in Sensor Information Systems (PEGASIS)

Clustering is an energy-efficient communication protocol that can be used by the sensors to report their sensed data to the sink. PEGASIS is a layered protocols in which a network is composed of several *clumps* (or *clusters*) of sensors. Each clump is managed by a special node, called *cluster head*, which is responsible for coordinating the data transmission activities of all sensors in its clump.

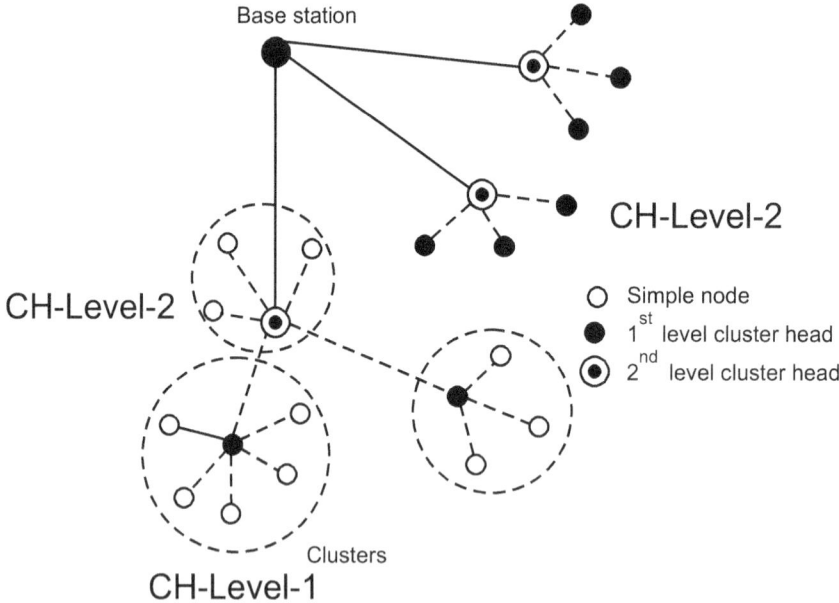

Fig. 6.3 : Cluster-based Hierarchical Model

As shown in Fig. 6.3, a hierarchical approach breaks the network into clustered layers.

Nodes are grouped into clusters with a cluster head that has the responsibility of routing from the cluster to the other cluster heads or base stations. Data travel from a lower clustered layer to a higher one. Although, it hops from one node to another, but as it hops from one layer to another it covers larger distances. This moves the data faster to the base station. Clustering provides inherent optimization capabilities at the cluster heads.

PEGASIS is an extension of the LEACH protocol, which forms chains from sensor nodes so that each node transmits and receives from a neighbour and only one node is selected from that chain to transmit to the base station (sink). The data is gathered and moves from node to node, aggregated and eventually sent to the base station. The chain construction is performed in a greedy way. Unlike

LEACH, PEGASIS avoids cluster formation and uses only one node in a chain to transmit to the base station (sink) instead of using multiple nodes. A sensor transmits to its local neighbors in the data fusion phase instead of sending directly to its CH as in the case of LEACH. In PEGASIS routing protocol, the construction phase assumes that all the sensors have global knowledge about the network, particularly, the positions of the sensors, and use a greedy approach. When a sensor fails or dies due to low battery power, the chain is constructed using the same greedy approach by bypassing the failed sensor. In each round, a randomly chosen sensor node from the chain will transmit the aggregated data to the BS, thus reducing the per round energy expenditure compared to LEACH.

Simulation results showed that PEGASIS is able to increase the lifetime of the network twice as much the lifetime of the network under the LEACH protocol. Such performance gain is achieved through the elimination of the overhead caused by dynamic cluster formation in LEACH and through decreasing the number of transmissions and reception by using data aggregation. Although the clustering overhead is avoided, PEGASIS still requires dynamic topology adjustment since a sensor node needs to know about energy status of its neighbors in order to know where to route its data. Such topology adjustment can introduce significant overhead especially for highly utilized networks.

6.4.4 Directed Diffusion

Directed diffusion is a data-centric routing protocol for sensor query dissemination and processing. It meets the main requirements of WSNs such as energy efficiency, scalability, and robustness. Directed diffusion has several key elements namely *data naming, interests and gradients, data propagation,* and *reinforcement*. A sensing task can be described by a list of attribute-value pairs. At the beginning of the directed diffusion process, the sink specifies a low data rate for incoming events. After that, the sink can *reinforce* one particular sensor to send events with a higher data rate by resending the original interest message with a smaller interval. Likewise, if a neighbouring sensor receives this interest message and finds that the sender's interest has a higher data rate than before, and this data rate is higher than that of any existing gradient, it will *reinforce* one or more of its neighbors.

6.4.5 Geographic Routing

Sometimes wireless sensor networks require a query packet to be forwarded to a particular region of interest in the network. A natural approach to perform this forwarding is to utilize geographic forwarding.

Geographic forwarding reduces the amount of routing overhead, which is largely due to route discovery, and requires little memory utilization for route caching compared to typical address-centric ad hoc routing protocols. Furthermore, geographic routing protocols can enable geographically distributed data storage techniques such as Geographic Hash Tables (GHT).

(1) Greedy Perimeter Stateless Routing (GPSR)

GPSR is a geographic routing protocol in which nodes make local packet forwarding decisions according to a greedy algorithm. Under normal circumstances, a packet that is destined for some node D is forwarded to the node's neighbour that enables the maximum progress toward D.

However, obstacles or a lack of adequate sensor density can cause voids in the network topology so that packets reach a hole, from which the packet cannot be progressed any further without first being sent backward. GPSR accounts for this by incorporating a perimeter routing mechanism. These voids can be detected by the nodes surrounding them and when a packet reaches these voids, alternate routes can be used. This approach has been shown in figure 3.

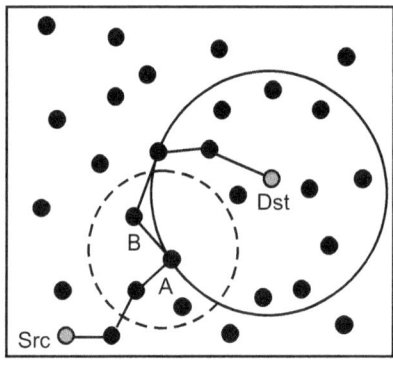 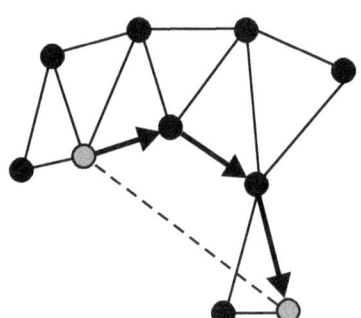

(a) Greedy forwarding Policy   (b) Perimeter routing algorithm

Fig. 6.4

(2) Trajectory Based Forwarding (TBF)

Trajectory Based Forwarding is a useful paradigm for geographic routing in wireless sensor networks. Rather than sending a packet along a straight path toward its destination (as methods such as GPSR would do under ideal scenarios with dense deployment and no obstructions), TBF allows packets to follow a source-specified trajectory, increasing the flexibility of an overall forwarding strategy. For example, multipath routing can be achieved by sending multiple copies of a single packet along separate geographic trajectories, increasing resilience to localized failures or congestion in certain parts of the network. Also, TBF can increase the efficiency of many different forwarding techniques, including multipath forwarding (Fig. 6.5 (a)), spoke broadcasting (Fig. 6.4 (b)), and broadcast to a remote sub region (Fig. 6.4 (c)).

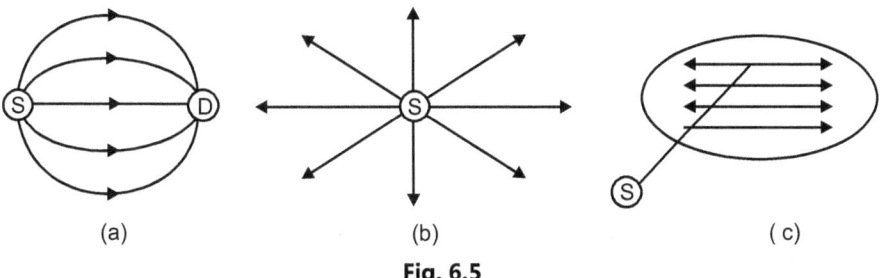

(a)   (b)   (c)

Fig. 6.5

6.5 RECENT TRENDS IN WSN

The recent developments in sensor nodes must produce very powerful and cost effective devices, so that they may be used in applications like underwater acoustic sensor systems, sensing based cyber-physical systems, time critical applications, cognitive sensing and spectrum management, and security and privacy management.

6.5.1 Software Defined Networks (SDN)

Managing a network requires support for multiple concurrent tasks, from routing and traffic monitoring, to access control and server load balancing. Software-Defined Networking (SDN) allows applications to realize these tasks directly, by installing packet-processing rules on switches.

Software-Defined Networking (SDN) can greatly simplify network management by offering programmers network-wide visibility and direct control over the underlying switches from a logically-centralized controller. The architecture of the physical network infrastructure significantly affects latency, resilience, and overall performance. SDNs will be far more flexible than traditional device-centric networking, but the new options they will provide and the new operational paradigm will bring about complexity with them. Improving architectural simplicity, automation, and resilience in the underlying physical network will, in fact, improve the performance and operational feasibility of SDNs. An application that performs multiple tasks (e.g., routing, monitoring, access control, and server load balancing) must ensure that packet-processing rules installed to perform one task do not override the functionality of another. This section introduces new abstractions for building applications out of multiple, independent modules that jointly manage network traffic. First, composition operators and a library of policies for forwarding and querying traffic are defined. Parallel composition operator allows multiple policies to operate on the same set of packets, while a novel sequential composition operator allows one policy to process packets after another.

```
Monitor                          Route                              Load-balance
srcip=5.6.7.8 → count            dstip=10.0.0.1 → fwd(1)            srcip=0*,dstip=1.2.3.4 → dstip=10.0.0.1
                                 dstip=10.0.0.2 → fwd(2)            srcip=1*,dstip=1.2.3.4 → dstip=10.0.0.2

Compiled Prioritized Rule Set for "Monitor | Route"        Compiled Prioritized Rule Set for "Load-balance >> Route"
srcip=5.6.7.8,dstip=10.0.0.1 → count.fwd(1)                srcip=0*,dstip=1.2.3.4 → dstip=10.0.0.1.fwd(1)
srcip=5.6.7.8,dstip=10.0.0.2 → count.fwd(2)                srcip=1*,dstip=1.2.3.4 → dstip=10.0.0.2.fwd(2)
srcip=5.6.7.8 → count
dstip=10.0.0.1 → fwd(1)
dstip=10.0.0.2 → fwd(2)
```

Fig. 6.6 : Parallel and sequential composition

Composition Operators

Many applications require the same traffic to be processed in multiple ways. For instance, an application may route traffic based on the destination IP address, while monitoring the traffic by source address. Or, the application may apply an access control policy to drop unwanted traffic, before routing the remaining traffic by destination address. Ideally, programmer would construct a sophisticated application out of multiple modules that each partially specifies the handling of the traffic. Conceptually, modules that need to process the same traffic could run in parallel or in series. Parallel composition gives each module

(e.g., routing and monitoring) the illusion of operating on its own copy of each packet. Whereas sequential composition allows one module to act on the packets already processed by another module (e.g., routing after access control).

Parallel and Sequential Composition Operators

Parallel and sequential compositions are two central mechanisms for specifying the relationship between packet-processing policies. These policies are specified via prioritized lists of OpenFlow-like rules. This is shown in Fig. 6.6. Each rule includes a pattern (field=value) that matches on bits in the packet header (e.g., source and destination MAC addresses, IP addresses, and TCP/UDP port numbers), and simple actions the switch should perform (e.g., drop, flood, forward out a port, rewrite a header field, or count1 matching packets). When a packet arrives, the switch identifies the first matching rule and performs the associated actions. Note that one may easily think of such a list of rules as a function: The function input is a packet at a particular inport on s and the function output is a multiset of zero or more packets on various outports of s (zero output packets if the matching rule drops the input packet; one output if it forwards the input; and one or more if it floods).

Parallel Composition

Parallel composition gives the illusion of multiple policies operating concurrently on separate copies of the same packets. Given two policy functions f and g operating on a located packet p, parallel composition computes the multiset union of f (p) and g(p) that is, every located packet produced by either policy. For example, suppose a programmer writes one module to monitor traffic by source IP address, and another to route traffic by destination IP address.

The monitoring module (Figure 5, top-left) comprises a simple policy that consists of a single rule applying the count action to packets matching source IP address 5.6.7.8. The routing module (Fig. 6.6, top-middle) consists of two rules, each matching on a destination IP address and forwarding packets out the specified port. Each module generates its policy independently, with the programmer using the "|" operator to specify that both the route and monitor functions should be performed simultaneously. These can be mechanically compiled into a single joint rule set (Fig. 6.6, bottom-left)

Sequential Composition (>>): Sequential composition gives the illusion of one module operating on the packets produced by another. Given two policy functions f and g operating on a located packet p, sequential composition applies g to each of the located packets produced by f (p), to produce a new set of located packets. For example, a programmer can write one module to load balance traffic destined to a public IP address 1.2.3.4, over multiple server replicas at private addresses 10.0.0.1 and 10.0.0.2, respectively, and another to route traffic based on the chosen destination server. The load-balancing module splits traffic destined to the public IP between the replicas based on the client IP address. Traffic sent by clients with an IP address whose highest-order bit is 0 go to the first server, while remaining traffic goes to the second server. As shown in Figure 5 (top-right), the load balancer performs a rewriting action to modify the destination address to correspond to the chosen server replica, without actually changing the packet's location. This load balancer can be composed sequentially with the routing policy introduced earlier. Here the programmer uses the ">>" operator to specify that load balancing should be performed first, followed by routing. Again, these may be mechanically compiled into a single joint rule set (Fig. 6.6, bottom-right).

6.5.2 Wi-Fi Offloads

Mobile network traffic is growing exponentially, and service providers must manage their networks efficiently to meet consumer demand. The only solution for increasing overall mobile network capacity is to increase the carrier-to-interference ratio while decreasing cell size and deploying small cell technologies.

The most efficient way to use small cells is to position them in locations where significant amounts of data are generated (shopping malls, stadiums, university campuses, public transportation hubs, etc.) and where subscribers spend most of their time and therefore consume significant amounts of data (homes, offices, etc.).

Wi-Fi, one of the small cell technologies, appeals to many operators as a cost-effective mean of offloading large amounts of mobile data traffic while delivering a variety of new services. It offers these features:

- Wide spread existing deployments.
- Availability of user devices that support the technology.
- Cost efficiency.

- Capability to address new users and devices without mobile subscription (without a subscriber identity module [SIM]).
- Globally available spectrum capacity.
- Standards availability for integration into mobile core networks.

Increased mobile data traffic will put a substantial strain on mobile operators' networks. Offloading a portion of data traffic to an alternate network is part of the mitigation strategy of most operators. Offloading of data provides better indoor coverage and decongestion of the 3G/4G network.

Overview of Wi-Fi Offload Architecture

The Third-Generation Partnership Project (3GPP) standard differentiates two types of Wi-Fi access (also referred to as non-3GPP IP access):

Untrusted :

Introduced in the early stages of the Wi-Fi specification in 3GPP Release 6 (2005), untrusted access includes any type of Wi-Fi access that either is not under control of the operator (public open hotspot, subscriber's home WLAN, etc.) or that does not provide sufficient security (authentication, encryption, etc.).

Trusted :

Trusted access generally refers to operator-built Wi-Fi access with over-the-air encryption and a secure authentication method. Trusted non-3GPP IP access was introduced only with the LTE standard in 3GPP Release 8 (2008). Although most of today's offload designs are build on the trusted model, 3GPP does not currently offer guidance for integration with the 3G or 2G packet core.

In the 3GPP specification, the Wi-Fi network is referred to as the Wi-Fi access network only. No details about the Wi-Fi network structures are specified. This document, however, separates the network into the access and gateway components. The Wi-Fi network infrastructure for mobile data offload consists of three parts :

- Wi-Fi radio access network (Wi-Fi RAN).
- Wi-Fi access gateway (WAG) and Wi-Fi back-end systems (this document expands the definition from 3GPP TS 23.234 to refer also to non-3GPP WAG).
- Packet core integration elements (multiple options).

If the Wi-Fi network is used for mobile data offload, it needs to take care of following tasks:

- Authentication : To help ensure that only authorized subscribers can access the network
- IP persistence : For service mobility between different access networks (3G to Wi-Fi, Wi-Fi to 3G, or across the Wi-Fi network).

Authentication

To control subscriber access to Wi-Fi networks, multiple authentication methods can be used. The choice of method is crucial to the usability of the network. The more transparent the authentication method is for the subscriber, the greater the likelihood that the subscriber will connect to the network. The authentication method also determines the subscriber and device types that can be addressed in a particular network (subscribers with or without SIM cards, the operator's subscribers, visiting subscribers, etc.).

In a typical modern Wi-Fi network, two types of authentication are available to address all possible subscribers and at the same time provide convenient access to the network for frequent Wi-Fi users. The first method, portal based authentication, targets customers without a permanent contract with the operator (vouchers, time-limited access, SMS payments, etc.). Alternatively, EAP authentication provides transparent and easy access for the operator's own subscribers with SIM cards or certificates.

Inter-Radio Handover

In mobile data networks, one of the most important procedures is handover - when a subscriber moves from one radio station to another. The handover procedure describes the behavior of the network when the subscriber switches from one radio type to another (for example, from 3G to Wi-Fi). Today, few handover types can be used. The one required in the operator's network needs to balance the expectations of subscribers and the complexity of the architecture.

Handover without IP address persistency (connectivity handover): When a subscriber connects to the Wi-Fi access network, the subscriber is authenticated transparently and is assigned a new IP address by the Wi-Fi network. All new communications can use the new IP address as the source. All established TCP and UDP connections can, however, still continue over the 3G network. If the user equipment logic disables the 3G interface, then these established sockets will need to be (automatically) re-established over Wi-Fi, using the new IP address.

Handover with IP Persistency (IP Handover) : When a subscriber connects to the Wi-Fi network, the subscriber will be assigned the same IP address as he used on the 3G or LTE network. If the established TCP and UDP connections are bound to a physical interface (because of the TCP/IP stack implementation of the UE), they will need to be (automatically) re-established using the new Wi-Fi interface, even though they will use the same IP address.

Session Handover (Transparent Handover) : This type of handover is similar to IP handover, but the handover must occur in a time range that allows real-time media applications (voice over IP, streaming video, etc.) - for example, using established UDP sockets for media and TCP sockets for the control-plane protocol - to continue without interruption or user-experience degradation as the device switches between Wi-Fi and 3G cellular connectivity.

6.5.3 100 G Ethernet and its Variants

Many organizations are encouraging telecommuting and business localization is being widely adopted. In such a scenario, be it for business discussions with remote customers or for communication between remote users or inter-branch connectivity, Internet based voice and video will be the solution. Most enterprises who use voice and video solutions have added real time, high definition, high quality, etc. in their immediate wish list. All these require a huge bandwidth capacity.

There are also factors like increase in number of business applications, more users due to business localization, need for efficient data centre connectivity and being future ready, skipping the 40G network and thus a possible dual migration.

Another interesting point is the efficiency of 100G Ethernet compared to link aggregation that is used today. As of now, a 10 x 10G Ethernet link aggregation can only give a throughput of up to 30Gbps. This limitation can be overcome with a true 100G connection which can give a 100Gbps bandwidth, thus allowing high capacity links to scale even further. Considering all these, if not this year or the next, 100G will be widely adopted soon.

The Need for Network Performance Monitoring

Before switching to 100G networks, there is one thing that every network admin should be ready with – a comprehensive plan for network performance monitoring which involves bandwidth monitoring, traffic analytics and anomaly detection.

The higher speed that comes with the 100G network does not mean that bandwidth monitoring or traffic analytics is no longer a requirement. E-Commerce is growing and therefore the importance and dependency enterprises have on Internet connectivity too has increased. Network performance monitoring is a necessity in any network, be it a small enterprise, who wants their bandwidth to be used only for business applications or a large enterprise, with high speed bandwidth and high traffic volume.

Constant network monitoring can help create high performance networks. By knowing traffic patterns and finding peak usage patterns, you can ensure optimal bandwidth usage and decide when to schedule the backup jobs. You also get to know when a threshold value is being reached or when it is violated. With this information, you get to know about the issues before someone else reports it and maybe even would have found the root cause.

You also need monitoring to know when an application usage is hitting a peak, when there is unwanted traffic to the application server or to find if an application has incorrect QoS priority. Visibility into application details helps keep out spam applications, measure and increase performance of business applications and thus ensure application delivery.

Something else that monitoring can help with is validating the performance of QoS policies. This way, you will know if VoIP really has higher priority over web traffic or if the QoS policy implemented to prioritize the CRM application traffic is actually causing a drop in web traffic.

Monitoring can also detect network behavior anomalies that surpass the intrusion detection system or firewalls. Most enterprises allow web traffic, but a number of threats and malwares too can reach your network disguised as web traffic. In certain cases, malwares may physically be carried in by an employee whose laptop was compromised. Internal and external traffic monitoring will detect all types of anomalies, be it those that spread from your network to the outside or those which enter your network over the WAN and thereby help mitigate the effect of a major malware. Monitoring also helps in planning network changes, find VoIP and video traffic usage and measure its performance, get data for SLA reports, capacity planning, etc.

All this leads to one advantage – Increased cost savings by reduced network downtime and better performance from business applications.

Transmission of 100 Gigabit Ethernet (GigE)

For now, 100 GigE is transmitted via several optical channels using the multilane concept. Three different physical interfaces are standardized as shown in table 6.2.

Table 6.2 : Standardization of physical interfaces

Physical Medium	100 GigE
Multimode optical fibre < 100m with OM-3 fibre	100GBase-SR10 • Ribbon Fibre • 850nm • 10*10Gbps
Single mode optical fibre > 10km	100GBase-LR4 • LAN-WDM 4.5 nm • 1310nm • 4 wavelengths * 25 Gbps
Single mode optical fibre > 40km	100GBase-ER4 • LAN-WDM 4.5 nm • 1310nm • 4 wavelengths * 25 Gbps

Two ranges are defined for transmission via a single mode fibre.

100GBase-LR4 (long range) describes the optical interface for four wavelengths within the range of 1310 nm with a channel spacing of 4.5 nm with an attainable transmission range of 10 km and 100GBase-ER4 (extended range) for a range of 40km. Another optical interface with 10 wavelengths in the range of 1550 nm is available. Although this interface was not standardized, it is technically the simpler solution as the multiplexers can be omitted in these transponders. For short connections within a computer centre, another interface for multimode fibre is defined in the wavelength range of 850 nm. 10 transmission channels run in parallel in a cable by means of ribbon fibres. The transmission channels are plugged together in an optical plug. By using OM-3 fibres, transmission lengths of at least 100m can be achieved. In addition to the optical interfaces, an electrical interface was also defined for both data transmission rates. Thus a maximum transmission range of 10m should be obtainable by 4 or 10 parallel signals.

6.5.4 Internet of Things and Web of Things

Ubiquitous sensing enabled by Wireless Sensor Network (WSN) technologies cuts across many areas of modern day living. This offers the ability to measure, infer and understand environmental indicators, from delicate ecologies and natural resources to urban environments. The proliferation of these devices in a communicating–actuating network creates the Internet of Things (IoT), wherein sensors and actuators blend seamlessly with the environment around us, and the information is shared across platforms in order to develop a common operating picture (COP).

The Internet of Things (IoT), sometimes referred to as the Internet of Objects, will change everything including ourselves. IoT represents the next evolution of the Internet, taking a huge leap in its ability to gather, analyze, and distribute data that we can turn into information, knowledge, and, ultimately, wisdom.

Already, IoT projects are under way that promise to close the gap between poor and rich, improve distribution of the world's resources to those who need them most, and help us understand our planet so we can be more proactive and less reactive. Even so, several barriers exist that threaten to slow IoT development, including the transition to IPv6, having a common set of standards, and developing energy sources for millions even billions of minute sensors. However, as businesses, governments, standards bodies, and academia work together to solve these challenges, IoT will continue to progress.

IoT as a Network of Networks

Currently, IoT is made up of a loose collection of disparate, purpose-built networks. Today's cars, for example, have multiple networks to control engine function, safety features, communications systems, and so on. Commercial and residential buildings also have various control systems for heating, venting, and air conditioning (HVAC); telephone service; security; and lighting. As IoT evolves, these networks, and many others, will be connected with added security, analytics, and management capabilities (see Fig. 6.7). This will allow IoT to become even more powerful in what it can help people achieve. Before we can begin to see the importance of IoT, it is first necessary to understand the differences between the Internet and the World Wide Web (or web) terms that are often used interchangeably.

The Internet is the physical layer or network made up of switches, routers, and other equipment. Its primary function is to transport information from one point to another quickly, reliably, and securely. The web, on the other hand, is an application layer that operates on top of the Internet. Its primary role is to provide an interface that makes the information flowing across the Internet usable.

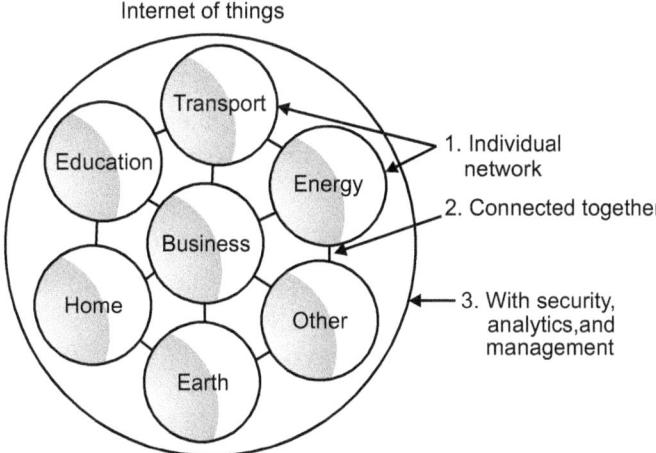

Fig. 6.7 : Internet of Things

The web has gone through several distinct evolutionary stages :

Stage 1 : First was the research phase, when the web was called the Advanced Research Projects Agency Network (ARPANET). During this time, the web was primarily used by academic for research purposes.

Stage 2 : The second phase of the web can be coined "brochureware." Characterized by the domain name "gold rush," this stage focused on the need for almost every company to share information on the Internet so that people could learn about products and services.

Stage 3 : The third evolution moved the web from static data to transactional information, where products and services could be bought and sold, and services could be delivered.

During this phase, companies like eBay and Amazon.com exploded on the scene. This phase also will be infamously remembered as the "dot-com" boom and bust.

Stage 4 : The fourth stage, where we are now, is the "social" or "experience" web, where companies like Facebook, Twitter, and Groupon have become immensely popular and profitable (a notable distinction from the third stage of the web) by allowing people to communicate, connect, and share information (text, photos, and video) about themselves with friends, family, and colleagues.

IoT: First Evolution of the Internet

By comparison, the Internet has been on a steady path of development and improvement, but arguably hasn't changed much. It essentially does the same thing that it was designed to do during the ARPANET era.

For example, in the early days, there was several communication protocols, including AppleTalk, Token Ring, and IP. Today, the Internet is largely standardized on IP. In this context, IoT becomes immensely important because it is the first real evolution of the Internet a leap that will lead to revolutionary applications that have the potential to dramatically improve the way people live, learn, work, and entertain themselves. Already, IoT has made the Internet sensory (temperature, pressure, vibration, light, moisture, stress), allowing us to become more proactive and less reactive.

In addition, the Internet is expanding into places that until now have been unreachable.

Patients are ingesting Internet devices into their own bodies to help doctors diagnose and determine the causes of certain diseases. Extremely small sensors can be placed on plants, animals, and geologic features, and connected to the Internet.

Humans evolve because they communicate.

This principle of sharing information and building on discoveries can best be understood by examining how humans process data (see Fig. 6.8). From bottom to top, the pyramid layers include data, information, knowledge, and wisdom. Data is the raw material that is processed into information. Individual data by itself is not very useful, but volumes of it can identify trends and patterns.

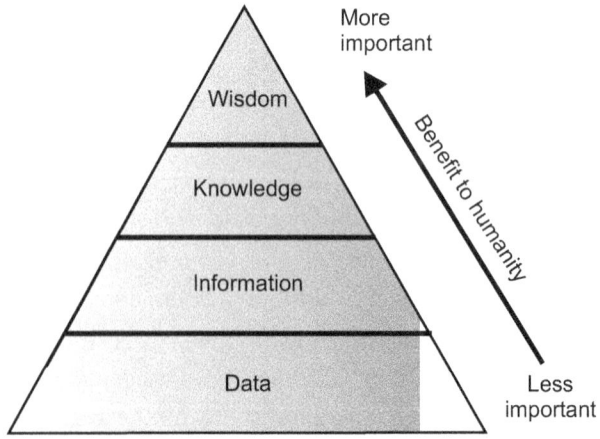

Fig. 6.8 : Pyramid of data processing

This and other sources of information come together to form knowledge. In the simplest sense, knowledge is information of which someone is aware. Wisdom is then born from knowledge plus experience. While knowledge changes over time, wisdom is timeless, and it all begins with the acquisition of data. It is also important to note there is a direct correlation between the input (data) and output (wisdom). The more data that is created, the more knowledge and wisdom people can obtain. IoT dramatically increases the amount of data available for us to process. This, coupled with the Internet's ability to communicate this data, will enable people to advance even further.

Challenges for IoT

Several challenges, however, have the potential to slow the development of IoT. The three Major challenges are the deployment of IPv6, power for sensors, and agreement on standards.

Deployment of IPv6 :

The world ran out of IPv4 addresses in February 2010. While no real impact has been seen by the general public, this situation has the potential to slow IoT's progress since the potentially billions of new sensors will require unique IP addresses. In addition, IPv6 makes the management of networks easier due to auto configuration capabilities and offers improved security features.

Sensor Energy :

For IoT to reach its full potential, sensors will need to be self-sustaining.

Imagine changing batteries in billions of devices deployed across the planet and even into space. Obviously, this isn't possible. What's needed is a way for sensors to generate electricity from environmental elements such as vibrations, light, and airflow. In a significant breakthrough, scientists announced a commercially viable nanogenerator—a flexible chip that uses body movements such as the pinch of a finger to generate electricity.

Standards :

While much progress has been made in the area of standards, more is needed, especially in the areas of security, privacy, architecture, and communications. IEEE is just one of the organizations working to solve these challenges by ensuring that IPv6 packets can be routed across different network types. Given the benefits of IoT, these issues will get worked out. It is only a matter of time.

6.5.5 Web of Things

From the 70s until the mid 90s, the Internet was just another network. In fact, in the early 90s there wasn't any strong indication that the "Information Superhighway" was going to be the

Internet. In 1990 there were only 300,000 Internet hosts, but by 2000 there were over 72 million, and today almost 700 million:

But along the way over the last two decades, the Web has turned many technologies which sit above TCP/IP into de facto standards also: HTTP, URIs, HTML, MIME encoded data, and JavaScript. IP is a critical enabling technology for the Web, but the Web itself is best described by its application layer protocols and formats:

- URI: are used to name and identify information
- MIME: is used to encode information
- HTTP: is used to retrieve transport information
- HTML: is used to display information

These Web technologies are now the de facto global standard for sharing information.

Web of Things

The Internet was a key enabler for the Web, but it was the Web itself which really transformed information technology and society as a whole. Likewise, the Internet of Things is just an enabler for what we really want: the Web of Things. The Internet of Things gives everyday devices an IP address and lets them plug into the Internet. But the Web of Things lets those devices integrate into the fabric of the Web itself and our lives.

It is the Web of Things which can truly unlock the potential of device networking. IP enables inter-networking, but Web technologies enable information sharing. The goal for the Web of Things is to provide URIs to all the information trapped inside smart devices, encode that information using standard MIME types, and transport that information via HTTP.

Applications and Services

Today smart device applications tend to follow the model of vertically oriented stove-piped silos. Increasingly the opportunities to create new value lie in horizontal solutions which cross-cut verticals. For example, building out the smart grid requires device networking across many siloed markets: residential, commercial, industrial, metering, and electricity distribution. Even today, many of these opportunities are not cost effective because it is too complex and too expensive to implement connectivity to the devices. But the Web of Things can change this by making it as easy to query information from a device as it is from a web-site.

Just as IP became the focal point for gluing networking technology to application protocols, the Web of Things can become the focal point for gluing devices across vertical domains to emerging applications and services. Making device information available as normal Web services will have a transformative effect upon the entire value chain by drastically simplifying how applications and services utilize networked devices.

Challenges for Web of Things

Although the Web of Things is starting to take shape, there are still a couple of missing pieces. Existing networking using Ethernet, Wifi, or cellular can already leverage Web technologies, although many verticals still cling to running fieldbus protocols over IP. But the ability to utilize Web technology over 15.4 and serial media remains immature, lacking many key standards. The key missing pieces:

IP over Serial

One of the biggest holes today is a standard for running IP over media such as twisted pair. The most obvious solution would be to extend 6LoWPAN to utilize another MAC layer. No matter how successful 802.15.4 may be, serial communications will never go away.

ROLL

Work is progressing within the IETF on the routing standards for setting up mesh 802.15.4 networks. However it will likely still take a couple years before things are really mature. Most likely ROLL will also be required to deal with how serial links are integrated into the PAN.

HTTP over 6LoWPAN

Although HTTP is the desired application protocol for the Web of Things, it will never successfully run directly over 802.15.4 or serial links. The memory and packet size requirements for TCP and text headers are an ill fit for the constraints of sensor networks and sleeping devices. This is really no different than why full IPv6 is unsuited for direct use over 15.4. But it doesn't mean we throw out what already exists, rather we figure out how to optimize it for the problem space and still maintain HTTP semantics, URIs, and MIME encoded data for seamless integration with the Web.

Security

Security concerns have the potential to limit the growth of the Web of Things. One of the biggest problems of sensor networks is the lack of TCP. Most smart devices don't have the resources to run TCP, so while they might be IP enabled, they are limited to UDP. But virtually all security techniques and protocols in wide use today are based on TCP. Many techniques for encryption and preventing replay attacks are based on packet ordering. So there is much work left to do.

The Web of Things has the potential to transform the planet in the same way that the Human Web has done over the last fifteen years (and continues to do). Most of the enabling infrastructure for the Web of Things is snapping into place, but there is still work left to do.

6.5.6 Bring Your Own Device

There is an unstoppable trend of easy-to-use mobile devices such as smart phones, laptops and tablet computers

Almost all of the companies surveyed reported that some workers are already using non-company-issued computing devices for work-related tasks. The survey also indicated that around 28 percent of the workforce is already using non-company-issued computing devices for work-related tasks.

So organizations must now consider policies that support their use. Indeed, 'bring your own' (BYO) policies that empower workers to choose their own computing equipment are rapidly being adopted.

Smart phones, laptops, tablets, netbooks and even personal desktops enable mobility and new ways of working. The predominant driver for companies in adopting a BYO policy is to increase productivity; better staff recruitment and worker retention run a very close second. With BYO, organizations are also able to reduce IT management of the vast numbers of diverse computing devices being requested and brought in by the workforce.

For some organizations, BYO creates concerns about security, application management and IT costs. Because all applications and data are accessed from the datacenter, this technology enables organizations to control IT costs while maximizing security. Further, workers have a great deal of flexibility because they get the same end user experience regardless of device or location. Indeed, desktop virtualization is central to enabling organizations to best benefit from BYO by enabling organizations to deliver the right desktop, to any device, in any location.

The Many Benefits of Bring Your Own

Organizations that have adopted a bring-your-own strategy often cite employee satisfaction and business productivity as key advantages. Other benefits include enhanced collaboration and mobility, expanded mobile access to resources, reduced spending on sourcing and support of devices, lessened responsibility for device lifecycle management, as well as consolidation of infrastructure and tools across many IT disciplines.

An infrastructure that allows access from a large set of device types must be secure. An advantage of a device-agnostic infrastructure is that security is integrated into the design; it is not, as with traditional infrastructure, an overlay. A BYOD strategy requires that organizations apply the controls typically found on endpoint devices to the network layer. As a result, a comprehensive device-agnostic approach can simplify and strengthen security of networks, data and applications.

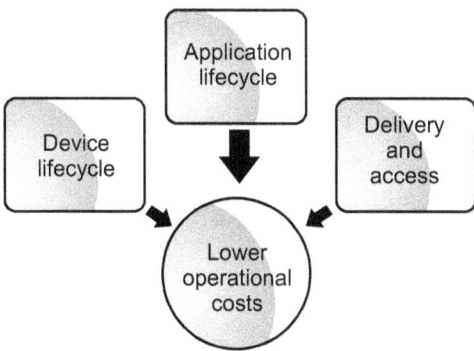

Fig. 6.9 : Benefits of BYOD

Allowing employee-owned devices to connect to corporate resources can also save costs when coupled with the right infrastructure and policies. In a BYOD world, IT is no longer responsible for sourcing and procuring hardware such as smart phones, laptops, tablets and even desktops. Instead, employees are offered a stipend to purchase the computing device of their choice, assuming it meets the company's baseline requirements.

Stipends also can be offered to cover all or part of an employee's smart phone data plan, a perk for the knowledge worker who does not use a company-issued handset as a primary device. At the same time, this approach frees the IT organization from procuring, maintaining and refreshing smart phones, and relieves IT of the responsibility of managing service plans.

BYOD also makes telecommuting more feasible and available to a broader set of employees, who often regard working from home as a coveted privilege. For the business, telecommuting enables operations to take advantage of cost-saving options such as the hoteling of office floor space, and can help centralize the IT support organization.

A BYOD strategy that frees application lifecycles from devices and consolidates delivery mechanisms can yield operational savings. In a model BYOD environment, software can be stored on centralized servers; it does not have to be directly installed on individual devices. This obviates the need for IT to support the installation and upkeep of each device's software inventory. It also makes it possible to streamline support of the application's software patches, upgrades and migrations, including the prospect of near-instant rollback upgrade protection.

What's more, the use of a secured application development methodology and data delivery mechanisms that employ technologies such as HTML5 and PKI encryption can further separate the device from a corporate data footprint. Developing and delivering of applications on a centralized model enables IT to consolidate development efforts and remove the need for regression testing across multiple devices.

Key Benefits of BYOD

- Ease of working outside the office
- Staff have relevant equipment
- Attract and retain top talent (any age)
- Reduce device management costs
- Attract and retain younger workers
- Attract and retain other worker types (such as home-based)
- Reduce training and on-boarding costs
- Enable self-service IT
- Improve business continuity
- Easiest way to handle proliferation of devices
- Speed of on-boarding third-party workers/contractors

The Challenges of an Any-Device Implementation :

For all its advantages, a BYOD strategy also presents some hurdles that should be considered early in the development of a device-agnostic strategy. Data security, of course, is paramount. Security should be baked into every aspect of access to the network, data and applications. Protection of the corporate data through isolation from personal data should also be addressed. Transitioning to a device-agnostic infrastructure will require new skills from network engineers and security teams, as well as up-to-date network access controls. Before a BYOD strategy can be implemented, IT must gain a comprehensive understanding of how these technologies are applied. A fundamental security component of a BYOD infrastructure is the addition of an MDM (mobile device management) solution. These solutions limit or resolve IT policies against traditional mobile devices. They do not address the more strategic considerations necessary to create a BYOD infrastructure, however, and should be considered tactical in nature when not a part of a comprehensive strategy.

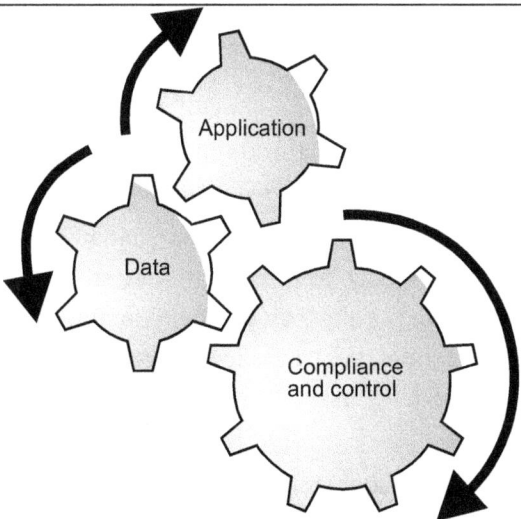

Fig. 6.10 : Challenges for BYOD

The weakest link in mobile device security is often the user. Liability often originates at the top: C-level executives often muscle exceptions to use personal devices, but these leaders pose the greatest risk because they have access to the company's most important information. A BYOD strategy will demand that CIOs implement and enforce a very strong set of policies to govern employee use of devices and access. Policies should be carefully designed to meet the needs of all users while safeguarding the organization's data according to its business model.

Device support should be meticulously designed to meet the needs of users while ensuring that IT is not unduly burdened with hardware and device on-boarding issues. A careful balance between employee satisfaction and access to IT resources is critical. Organizations should involve human resources and legal departments to ensure that the policies are acceptable to employees and also meet requirements for data security and compliance mandates.

Employees who participate in a BYOD program should be required to sign binding agreements before being allowed to access resources using a personal device. Participants must understand that they may be required to relinquish some rights to control of the device, such as requirements to install a mobile device management client, encryption of email or the device itself, and use of strong passwords. A clear understanding of these stipulations should be articulated to the employee to ensure a successful BYOD transition.

At a minimum, BYOD policies should require installation of the organization's security profiles on the equipment, assert the right to wipe the device if it is lost or stolen, and spell out the support and repair policies for the equipment. Employees also should be required to back up personal information stored on the devices because the organization cannot be responsible for loss of personal files should the hardware require a data wipe.

One particularly thorny issue can arise if an organization initiates a legal hold against a BYOD user and IT is required to temporarily confiscate the device to capture its state and data. Similarly, when an employee leaves the company, voluntarily or otherwise, IT should be entitled to legally wipe corporate data and applications from the device. This typically requires up-front permission from the user.

Another challenge for BYOD programs arises from costs associated with use of devices. If, for instance, the company retains management of a smart phone service plan, employees must understand that they will be responsible for costs associated with excessive data use, copious 411 calls or selection of smart phones that are more expensive to use in some circumstances.

Finally, a BYOD strategy will represent a huge cultural shift for most organizations. To ensure that all possible implications are considered, CIOs must involve business leaders, as well as HR, auditors and legal staff, in the earliest phases of developing a BYOD strategy.

QUESTIONS

1. Explain different routing protocols in MANET.
2. How naming and addressing is done for wireless and sensor networks?
3. Explain content based and geographic routing.
4. Explain challenges and design issues for routing in sensor network.
5. Explain different routing protocols in WSNS.
6. Explain received trends in WSN and MANET in short.

IMPORTANT POINTS

FAST ETHERNET AND GIGABIT ETHERNET

- Ethernet is the most widely used local area network protocol.
- Each station on Ethernet network has a unique 48-bit address imprinted on its network interface card (NIC).
- Fast Ethernet has data rate of 100 Mbps.
- In fast Ethernet auto-negotiation allows two devices to negotiate the mode or data rate of operation.
- The fast Ethernet reconciliation sublayer is responsible for passing the data in 4-bit format to Media Independent Interface (MII).
- The fast Ethernet MII is an interface that can be used with both 10-and 100-Mbps interface.
- The fast Ethernet PHY sublayer is responsible for encoding and decoding.
- The common fast Ethernet implementations are 100Base-TX(two pairs of twisted pair cable), 100Base-FX(two fiber optic cables), and 100Base-T4(four pairs of voice-grade, or higher, twisted-pair-cable).
- Gigabit Ethernet has data rate of 1000-Mbps.
- Gigabit Ethernet access methods include half-duplex using traditional CSMA/CD (not common) and Full duplex (common method).
- The Gigabit Ethernet reconciliation sublayer is responsible for sending 8-bit parallel data to the PHY sublayer via a GMII interface.
- The Gigabit Ethernet GMII defines how the reconciliation sublayer is to be connected to the PHY sublayer.
- The Gigabit Ethernet PHY sublayer is responsible for encoding and decoding.
- The common Gigabit Ethernet implementations are 1000Base-SX(two optical fibers and a shortwave laser source), 100Base-LX(two optical fibers and a long-wave laser source), and 100Base-T(four twisted pairs).

WLAN AND BLUETOOTH

- The IEEE 802.11 standard for wireless LANs define two services: Basic service set (BSS) and extended service set (ESS). An ESS consists of two or more BSSs; each BSS must have an access point (AP).
- The physical layer methods used by the wireless LANs include frequency hopping spread spectrum (FHSS), direct sequence spread spectrum (DSSS), orthogonal frequency-division multiplexing (OFDM) and high rate direct sequence spread spectrum (HR-DSSS).

- FHSS is a signal generation method in which repeated sequences of carrier frequencies are used for protection against hackers.
- The wireless LAN access method is CSMA/CD.
- Bluetooth is a wireless LAN technology that connects devices in a small area.
- A Bluetooth network is called as piconet. Multiple piconet forms a scatternet.
- A Bluetooth network consists of one master device and upto seven slave devices.

ATM

- Asynchronous Transfer Mode (ATM) is a cell relay protocol which allows high speed connection in combination with SONET.
- A cell is a small, fixed block (53 bytes) of information.
- The ATM data packet is a cell composed of 53 bytes (5 byte header and 48 byte payload).
- ATM eliminates the varying delay times associated with different-sized packets.
- ATM can handle real time transmission.
- A user-to-network interface (UNI) is a interface between a user and a ATM switch.
- A network-to-network interface (NNI) is a interface between two ATM switches.
- In ATM, connection between two endpoints is accomplished through transmission paths (TPs), Virtual Paths (VPs) and Virtual circuits (VCs).
- In ATM, a combination of virtual path identifier (VPI) and virtual circuit identifier identifies a virtual connection.
- The ATM standard defines three layers :
  a. Application Adaptation Layer (AAL) accepts transmissions from upper layer services and maps them into ATM cells.
  b. ATM layer provides routing, traffic management, switching, and multiplexing services.
  c. Physical layer defines the transmission medium, bit transmission, encoding, and electrical-to-optical transformations.
- The AAL is divided into two sublayers : segmentation and reassembly (SAR) and convergence sublayer (CS).
- There are four different AALs, each for a specific data type :
  a. AAL1 for constant-bit-rate stream.
  b. AAL2 for short packets.
  c. AAL 3 / 4 for conventional packet switching
  d. AAL5 for packets requiring no sequencing and no error control mechanism.

PACKET SWITCHING

- There are two popular approaches to packet switching : datagram approach and virtual circuit approach.
- In datagram approach, each packet is treated independently of all other packets.

IP ADDRESS

- IP address is 32 bit address that uniquely and universally defines a host or router on the internet.
- The portion of IP address that identifies the network is called as the netid.
- There are five classes of IP addresses. Classes A, B and C differ in number of hosts allowed per network. Class D is for multicasting, and class E is reserved.
- The class of the network is easily determined by examination of the first byte.
- Unicast communication is one source in sending a packet to one destination.
- Multicast communication is one source in sending packet to multiple destinations.
- Subnetting divides one large network into several smaller ones.
- Subnetting adds an intermediate level of hierarchy in IP addressing.
- Default masking is the process that extracts the network address from an IP address.
- Supernetting combines several networks into one large one.
- Every computer attached to the internet must know its IP address, the IP address of the router, the IP address of the name server, and its subnet mask (if it is a part of subnet).
- DHCP is a dynamic configuration protocol with two databases.
- The DHCP server issues a lease for an IP address to a client for a specific period of time.
- The IP protocol is a connectionless protocol, every packet is independent and has no relationship to any other packet.
- Packets in the IP layer are called as datagrams.
- A datagram consists of a header (20 to 60 bytes) and data.
- MTU is the maximum number of bytes that data link protocol can encapsulate. MTUs vary from protocol to protocol.
- Fragmentation is the division of the datagram into smaller units to accommodate the MTU of data link protocol.
- Every host or router has a routing table to route IP packets.
- In next-hop routing, instead of a complete list of the stops the packet must make only the address of the next hop is listed in routing table.
- In network specific routing, all hosts on a network share one entry in the routing table.

- The static routing table's entries are updated manually by an administrator.
- Classless addressing requires hierarchical routing to prevent vast routing table.
- IPv6 is the latest version of Internet Protocol. It has 128 bit address space, a revised header format, new options, an allowance for extension, support for resource allocation, and increased security measures.
- IPv6 uses hexadecimal colon notations with abbreviation method available.

ARP, ICMP

- The Address Resolution Protocol (ARP) is a dynamic mapping method that finds a physical (MAC) address for a given IP address.
- An ARP request is broadcast to all devices on the network.
- An ARP reply is unicast to the host requesting the mapping.
- The Internet Control Message Protocol (ICMP) sends five types of error-reporting messages and four pairs of query messages to support the unreliable and connectionless Protocol (IP).
- ICMP messages are encapsulated into IP datagrams.

TCP AND UDP

- These are transport layer protocols that create a process-to-process communication.
- UDP is an unreliable and connectionless protocol that requires little overhead and offers fast delivery.
- In the client-server paradigm, an application program on local host, called the client, needs services from an application program on the remote host, called a server.
- Each application program has a unique port number that distinguishes it from other programs running at the same time on the same machine.
- The client program is assigned a random port number called a ephemeral (temporary) port number.
- The server program is assigned a universal port number called a well known port number.
- The combination of the IP address and the port number, called the socket address, uniquely identifies a process and a host.
- The UDP packet is called a user datagram.
- UDP has no flow control mechanism.
- TCP is a connection-oriented, reliable, stream transport layer protocol in the internet model.
- The unit of data transfer between two devices using TCP software is called a segment; it has 20 to 60 bytes of header, followed by data from the application program.

COMPUTER NETWORK TECHNOLOGY (T.E. I.T.) — IMPORTANT POINTS

- TCP uses sliding window mechanism for flow control.
- Error detection is handled in TCP by the checksum, acknowledgement and time-out.
- Corrupted and lost segments are retransmitted, and duplicate segments are discarded.
- TCP uses four timers- retransmission, persistence, keep-alive and time-waited –- in its operation.
- Connection establishment requires three steps; connection termination normally requires four steps.
- The TCP window size is determined by the receiver.

CONGESTION CONTROL AND QUALITY OF SERVICE

- The average data rate, peak data rate, maximum burst size and effective bandwidth are qualitative values that describe the data flow.
- A data flow can have a constant bit rate, a variable bit rate or traffic that is bursty.
- Congestion control refers to the mechanisms and techniques to control congestion and keep the load below capacity.
- Delay and throughput measure the performance of the network.
- Open-loop congestion control prevents congestion; closed-loop congestion control removes congestion.
- A flow can be characterized by its reliability, delay, jitter and bandwidth.
- Scheduling, traffic shaping, resource reservation and admission control are techniques to improve quality of service.
- FIFO queueing, priority queueing, and weighted fair queueing are scheduling techniques.
- Leaky bucket and token bucket are traffic shaping techniques.
- The Resource Reservation Protocol (RSVP) is a signaling protocol that helps IP create a flow and makes a resource reservation.

CLIENT SERVER MODEL

- In the client server model, the client runs a program to request a service and the server runs a program to provide the service. These two programs communicate with each other.
- One server program can provide services for many client programs.

- Client can be run either iteratively (one at a time) or concurrently (many at a time).
- Servers can handle clients either iteratively (one at a time) or concurrently (many at a time).
- A connectionless iterative server uses UDP as its transport layer protocol and can serve one client at a time.
- A connection-oriented concurrent server uses TCP as its transport layer protocol and can serve many clients at the same time.
- When operating system executes a program, an instance of the program, called a process is created.
- If two application programs, one running on a local system and the other running on remote system, need to communicate with each other, a network program is required.
- The socket interface is a set of declarations, definitions and procedures for writing client-server programs.
- The communication structure needed for socket programming is called a socket.
- A stream socket is used with a connection-oriented protocol such as TCP.
- A datagram socket is used with a connectionless protocol such as UDP.
- A raw socket is used by protocols such as ICMP that directly use the services of IP.

HTTP

- It is the main protocol used to access data on the World Wide Web (WWW).
- The World Wide Web is a repository of information spread all over the world and linked together.
- Browsers interpret and display a Web document.
- A browser consists of a controller, client programs, and interpreters.
- A web document can be classified as static, dynamic and active.
- A static document is one in which the contents are fixed and stored in a server. The client can make no changes in the server document.
- Hypertext Markup Language (HTML) is a language used to create static web pages.
- Any browser can read formatting instructions (tags) embedded in an HTML document.
- A dynamic web document is created by a server only at a browser request.
- The CGI is a standard for creating and handling dynamic web document.

- A CGI program with its embedded CGI interface tags can be written in a language such as C, C++, shell script or Perl.
- The server sends the output of CGI program to the browser.
- The output of a CGI program can be text, graphics, binary data, status code, instructions, or an address of a file.
- An active document is a copy of a program retrieved by the client and run at client side.

MULTIMEDIA

- Audio/video files can be downloaded for future use (streaming stored audio/video) or broadcast to clients over the internet (streaming live audio/video). The internet can also be used for live audio/video interaction.
- Audio/video need to be digitized before being sent over the internet.
- Audio files are compressed through predictive encoding or perceptual encoding.
- Joint Photographic Experts Group (JPEG) is a method to compress pictures and graphics.
- The JPEG process involves blocking, the discrete cosine transform, quantization, and lossless compression.
- Moving Pictures Experts Group (MPEG) is a method to compress video.
- MPEG involves both spatial compression and temporal compression. The former is similar to JPEG, and the latter removes redundant frames.
- We can use a web server, or a media server, or a media server and RSTP to download a streaming audio/video file.
- Real-time data on packet switched network require the preservation of the time relationship between packets of a session.
- Gaps between consecutive packets at a receiver cause a phenomenon called as jitter.
- Jitter can be controlled through the use of timestamps and a well judged choice of playback time.
- A playback buffer holds data until they can be played back.
- A receiver delays playing back real-time data held in the playback buffer until a threshold level is reached.
- Sequence number on real-time data packets provides a form of error control.
- Real-time data are multicast to receivers.

- Real-time traffic sometimes requires a translator to change a high bandwidth signal to a lower quality narrow bandwidth signal.
- A mixer combines signals from different sources into one signal.
- Real-time multimedia traffic requires both UDP and Real Time Transport Protocol (RTP).
- RTP handles timestamping, sequencing and mixing.
- Real Time Transport Control Protocol (RTCP) provides flow control, quality of data control and feedback to the sources.
- Voice over IP is a real-time interactive audio/video application.
- The Session Initiation Protocol (SIP) is an application layer protocol that establishes, manages and terminates multimedia sessions.
- H.323 is an ITU standard that allows a telephone connected to a public telephone network to talk to a computer that has been connected to the internet.

APPENDIX – A

Networking Models

THE OSI MODEL

1. GENERAL :

The International Organization for Standardization (ISO) began developing the *Open Systems Interconnection (OSI)* reference model in 1977. It has since become the most widely accepted model for understanding network communication; once you understand how the *OSI model* works, you can use it to compare network implementations on different systems.

When you want to communicate with another person, you need to have two things in common: a communication language and a communication medium. Computer networks are no different; for communication to take place on a network composed of a variety of different network devices, both the language and medium must be clearly defined. The OSI model (and networking models developed by other organizations) attempts to define rules that cover both the generalities and specifics of networks :

- How network devices contact each other and, if they have different languages, how they communicate with each other.
- Methods by which a device on a network knows when to transmit data and when not to.
- Methods to ensure that network transmissions are received correctly and by the right recipient.
- How the physical transmission media is arranged and connected.
- How to ensure that network devices maintain a proper rate of data flow.
- How bits are represented on the network media.

The OSI model isn't a product. It's just a conceptual framework you can use to better understand the complex interactions taking place among the various devices on a network. It doesn't do anything in the communication process; appropriate software and hardware do the actual work. The OSI model simply defines which tasks need to be done and which protocols will handle those tasks at each of the seven layers of the model. The seven layers are as follows :

- Application   (layer 7)
- Presentation (layer 6)
- Session   (layer 5)
- Transport   (layer 4)
- Network   (layer 3)
- Data-Link   (layer 2)
- Physical   (layer 1)

2. PROTOCOL STACKS

The OSI model splits communication tasks into smaller pieces called subtasks. Protocol implementations are computer processes that handle these subtasks. Specific protocols fulfill subtasks at specific layers of the OSI model. When these protocols are grouped together to complete a whole task, the assemblage of code is called a *protocol stack*.

The stack is just a group of protocols, arranged in layers, that implements an entire communication process. Each layer of the OSI model has a different protocol associated with it. When more than one protocol is needed to complete a communication process, the protocols are grouped together in a stack. An example of a protocol stack is TCP/IP, which is widely used by Unix and the Internet — the TCP and IP protocols are implemented at different OSI layers.

Each layer in the protocol stack receives services from the layer below it and provides services to the layer above it. It can be better explained like this : Layer N uses the services of the layer below it (layer N–1) and provides services to the layer above it (layer N + 1).

For two computers to communicate, the same protocol stacks must be running on each computer. Each layer on both computers' stacks must use compatible protocols in order for the machines to communicate with each other. The computers can have different operating systems and still be able to communicate if they are running the same protocol stacks. For example, a DOS machine running TCP/IP can communicate with a Macintosh machine running TCP/IP.

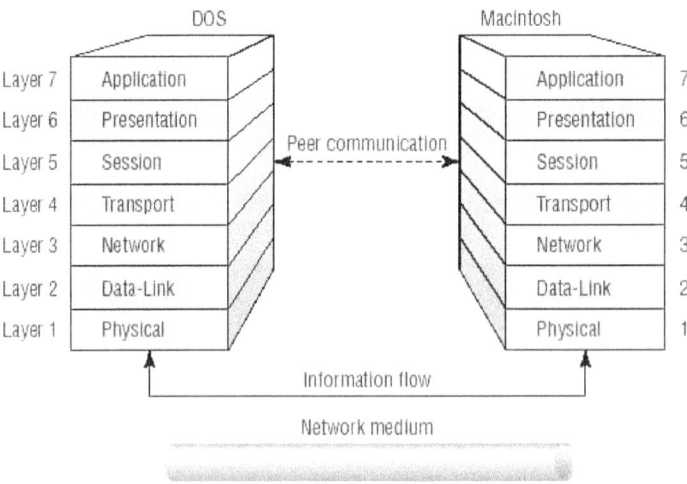

Fig. A1 : Each layer communicates with its counterparts on other network hosts

(i) The Physical Layer :

The Physical layer is responsible for sending bits from one computer to another. Physical layer components don't care what the bits *mean*; their job is to get the bits from point A to point B, using whatever kind of optical, electrical, or wireless connection that connects the points. This level defines physical and electrical details, such as what will represent a 1 or a 0, how many pins a network connector will have, how data will be synchronized, and when the network adapter may or may not transmit the data

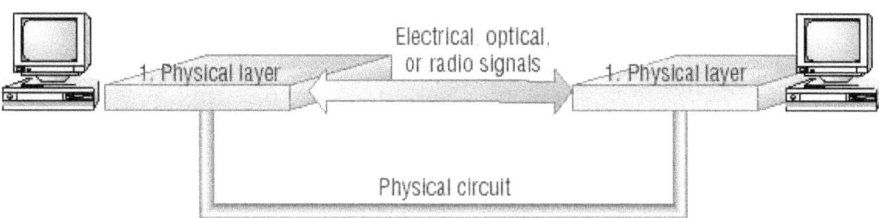

Fig. A2 : The Physical layer makes a physical circuit with electrical, optical, or radio signals

The Physical layer addresses all the minutiae of the actual physical connection between the computer and the network medium, including the following :

- Network connection types, including multipoint and point-to-point connections.
- Physical topologies, or how the network is physically laid out (e.g., bus, star, or ring topologies).
- Which analog and digital signaling methods are used to encode data in the analog and digital signals.
- Bit synchronization, which deals with keeping the sender and receiver in synch as they read and write data.
- Multiplexing, or the process of combining several data channels into one.
- Termination, which prevents signals from reflecting back through the cable and causing signal and packets errors. It also indicates the last node in a network segment.

(ii) The Data-Link Layer :

The Data-Link layer provides for the flow of data over a single physical link from one device to another. It accepts packets from the Network layer and packages the information into data units called frames; these frames are presented to the Physical layer for transmission. The Data-Link layer adds control information, such as frame type, to the data being sent.

This layer also provides for the error-free transfer of frames from one computer to another. A *cyclic redundancy check (CRC)* added to the data frame can detect damaged frames, and the

Data-Link layer in the receiving computer can request that the CRC information be present so that it can check incoming frames for errors. The Data-Link layer can also detect when frames are lost and request that those frames be sent again.

In broadcast networks such as Ethernet, all devices on the LAN receive the data that any device transmits. (Whether a network is broadcast or point-to-point is determined by the network protocols used to transmit data over it.) The Data-Link layer on a particular device is responsible for recognizing frames addressed to that device and throwing the rest away, much as you might sort through your daily mail to separate good stuff from junk.

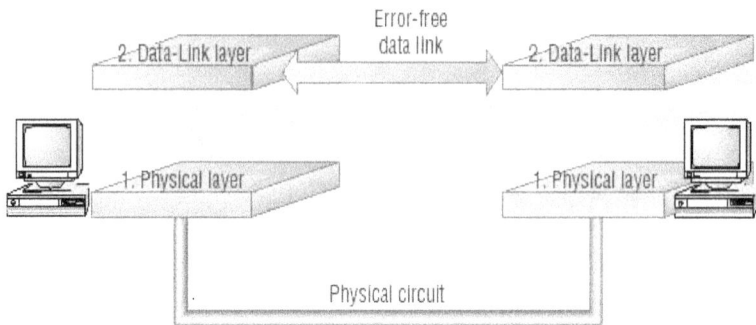

Fig. A3 : The Data-Link layer establishes an error-free link between two devices

The Institute of Electrical and Electronics Engineers (IEEE) developed a protocol specification known as IEEE 802.X. (802.2 is the standard that divides this layer into two sublayers. The MAC layer varies for different network types and is described further in standards 802.3 through 802.5.) As part of that specification (which today we know as Ethernet), the Data-Link layer is split into two sublayers:

- The *Logical Link Control (LLC)* layer establishes and maintains the logical communication links between the communicating devices.
- The *Media Access Control (MAC)* layer acts like an airport control tower—it controls the way multiple devices share the same media channel in the same way that a control tower regulates the flow of air traffic into and out of an airport.

The LLC sublayer provides *Service Access Points (SAPs)* that other computers can refer to and use to transfer information from the LLC sublayer to the upper OSI layers. This is defined in the 802.2 standard.

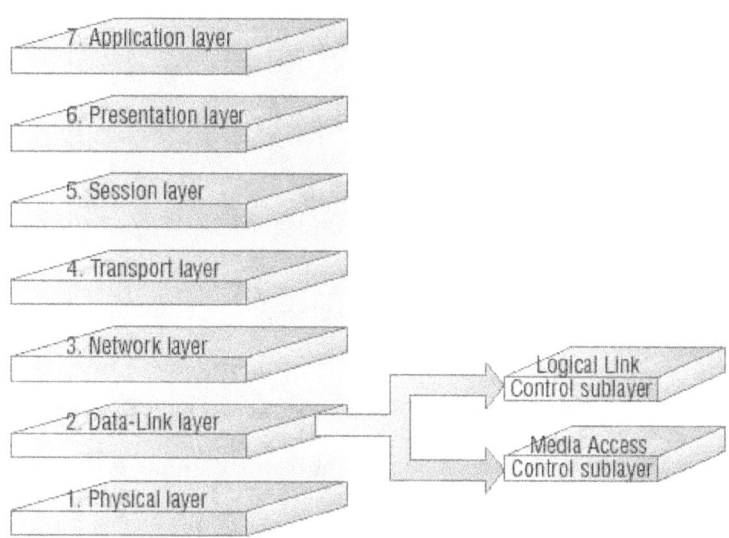

Fig. A4 : The IEEE split the ISO Data-Link layer into the LLC sublayer and the MAC sublayer

The MAC sublayer, the lower of the two sublayers, provides for shared access to the network adapter and communicates directly with network interface cards. Network interface cards have a unique 12-digit hexadecimal MAC address (frequently called the hardware Ethernet address) assigned before they leave the factory where they are made. The LLC sublayer uses MAC addresses to establish logical links between devices on the same LAN.

(iii) The Network Layer :

The Network layer handles moving packets between devices that are more than one link away from each other. It makes routing decisions and forwards packets as necessary to help them travel to their intended destination. In larger networks, there may be intermediate devices and subnetworks between any two end systems. The network layer makes it possible for the Transport layer (and layers above it) to send packets without being concerned with whether the end system is on the same piece of network cable or on the other end of a large wide area network.

To do its job, the Network layer translates logical network addresses into physical machine addresses (MAC addresses, which operate at the Data-Link layer). The Network layer also determines the quality of service (such as the priority of the message) and the route a message will take if there are several ways a message can get to its destination.

The Network layer also may split large packets into smaller chunks if the packet is larger than the largest data frame the Data-Link layer will accept. The network reassembles the chunks into packets at the receiving end. Intermediate systems that perform only routing and relaying functions and do not provide an environment for executing user programs can implement just the first three OSI network layers.

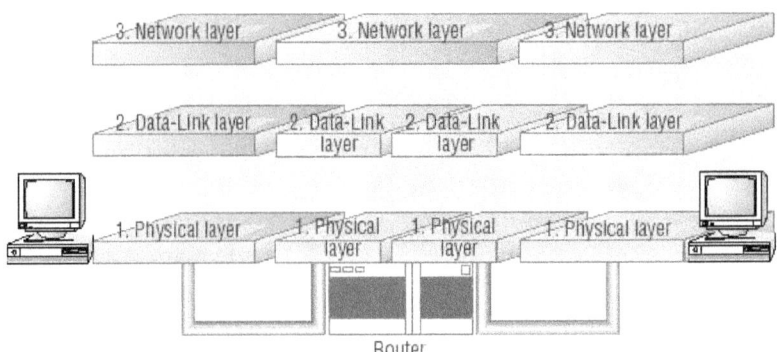

Fig. A5 : The Network layer moves packets across links to their destination

The Network layer performs several important functions that enable data to arrive at its destination. The protocols at this layer may choose a specific route through an internetwork to avoid the excess traffic caused by sending data over networks and segments that don't need access to it. The Network layer serves to support communications between logically separate networks. This layer is concerned with the following :

- Addressing, including logical network addresses and services addresses.
- Circuit, message, and packet switching.
- Route discovery and route selection.
- Connection services, including Network layer flow control, Network layer error control, and packet sequence control.
- Gateway services.

In Windows Server 2000/2003, the various routing services for TCP/IP, AppleTalk, and Internetwork Packet Exchange/Sequenced Packet Exchange (IPX/SPX) perform Network layer services. In addition, the TCP/IP, AppleTalk, and IPX stacks provide routing capacity for those protocols.

(iv) The Transport Layer :

The Transport layer ensures that data is delivered error free, in sequence, and with no losses or duplications. This layer also breaks large messages from the Session layer into smaller packets to be sent to the destination computer and reassembles packets into messages to be presented to the Network layer. The Transport layer typically sends an acknowledgement to the originator for messages received.

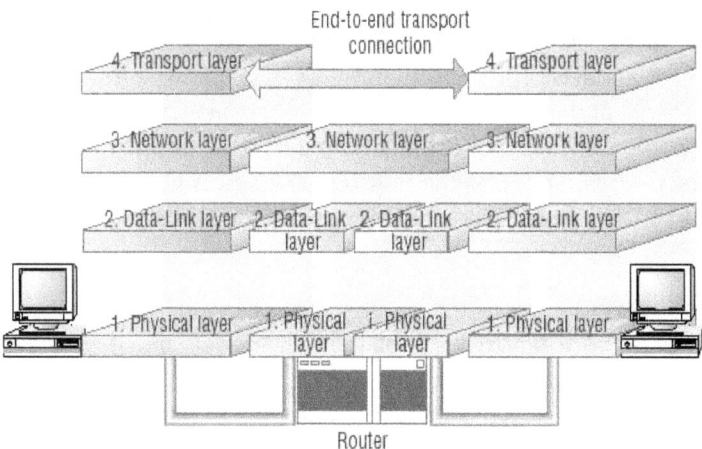

Fig. A6 : The Transport layer provides end-to-end communication with integrity and performance guarantees

(v) The Session Layer :

The Session layer allows applications on separate computers to share a connection called a session. This layer provides services, such as name lookup and security, that allow two programs to find each other and establish the communication link. The Session layer also provides for data synchronization and checkpointing so that in the event of a network failure, only the data sent after the point of failure would need to be resent. This layer also controls the dialog between two processes and determines who can transmit and who can receive at what point during the communication.

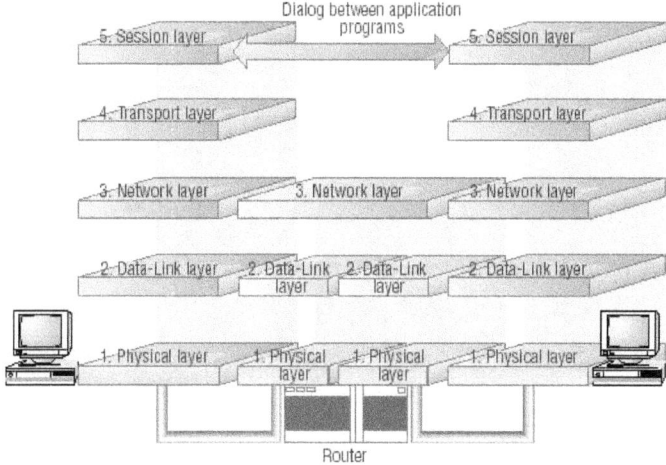

Fig. A7 : The Session layer allows applications to establish communication sessions with each other

(vi) The Presentation Layer :

The Presentation layer translates data between the formats the network requires and the formats the computer expects. The Presentation layer performs protocol conversion; data translation, compression, and encryption; character set conversion; and the interpretation of graphics commands. The network redirector, long a part of Windows networking, operates at this level. The redirector is what makes the files on a file server visible to the client computer. The network redirector also makes remote printers act as though they are attached to the local computer (see Fig. A8).

(vii) The Application Layer :

The Application layer is the topmost layer of the OSI model, and it provides services that directly support user applications, such as database access, e-mail, and file transfers. It also allows applications to communicate with applications on other computers as though they were on the same computer. When a programmer writes an application program that uses network services, this is the layer the application program will access. For example, Internet Explorer uses the Application layer to make its requests for files and web pages; the Application layer then passes those requests down the stack, with each succeeding layer doing its job (see Fig. A9).

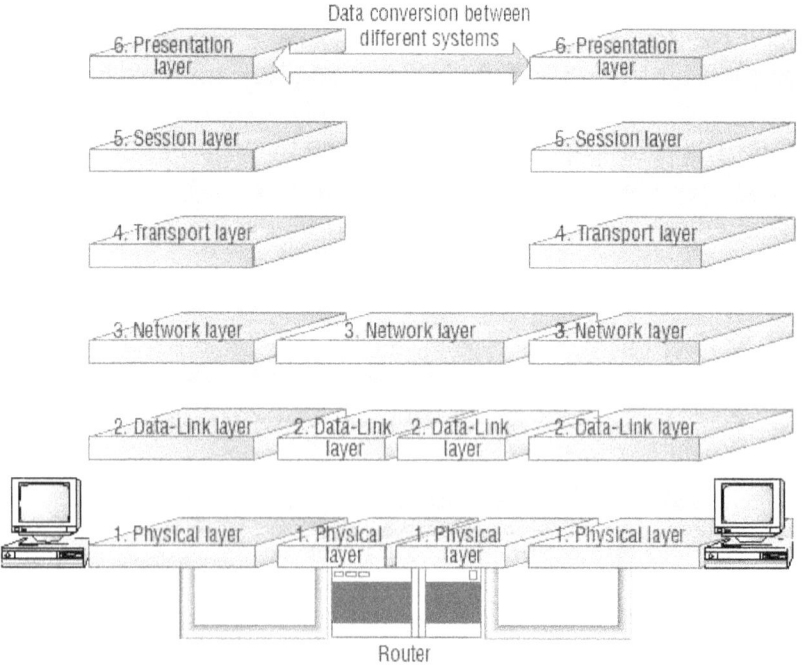

Fig. A8 : The Presentation layer allows applications to establish communication sessions with each other

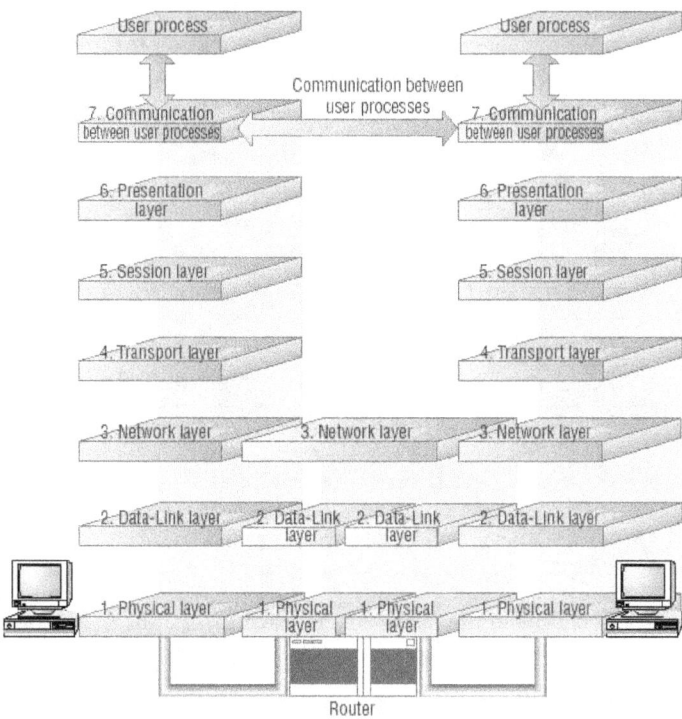

Fig. A9 : The Application layer is where the applications function, using lower levels to get their work done

3. COMMUNICATION BETWEEN STACKS

When a message is sent from one machine to another, it travels down the layers on one machine and then up the layers on the other machine.

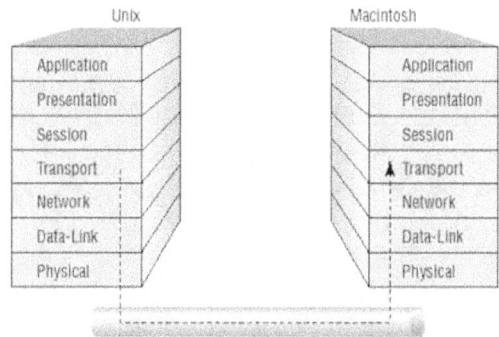

Fig. A10 : Traffic flows down through the stack on one computer and up the stack on the other

As the message travels down the first stack, each layer it passes through (except the Physical layer) adds a header. These headers contain pieces of control information that are read and processed by the corresponding layer on the receiving stack. As the message travels up the stack of the other machine, each layer removes the header added by its peer layer and uses the information it finds to figure out what to do with the message contents.

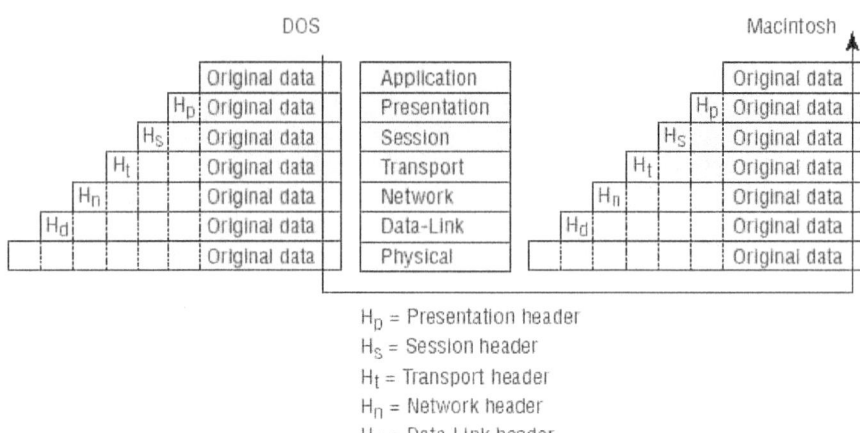

H_p = Presentation header
H_s = Session header
H_t = Transport header
H_n = Network header
H_d = Data-Link header

Fig. A11 : As packets flow up and down the stacks, each layer adds or removes necessary control information (data encapsulation)

As an example, consider the network we are using while writing this book. It's a TCP/IP network containing several Windows 2000, Windows Server 2003, Macintosh, and Windows NT machines, all connected using the TCP/IP protocol. When we mount a share from our Windows Server 2003 file server on the Mac desktop, at layer 7, the Mac Finder requests something from the Windows Server 2003. This request is sent to the Mac's layer 6, which receives the request as a data packet, adds its own header, and passes the packet down to layer 5. At layer 5, the process is repeated, and it continues until the packet makes it to the Physical layer.

The physical layer is responsible for actually moving the bits across the network wiring in the office, so it carries the request packet to a place where the Windows Server 2003 machine can "hear" it. At that point, the request packet begins its journey up the layers on the Windows Server 2003 file server. The header that was put on at the Data-Link layer of the Mac OS is stripped off at the Data-Link layer on the Windows Server 2003 machine. The Windows Data-Link layer driver performs the tasks requested in the header and passes the requests to the next, higher layer. This process is repeated until the Windows Server 2003 file server receives the packet and interprets the request. The Windows Server 2003 would then formulate an appropriate response and send it to the Mac.

4. THE BASICS OF NETWORK PROTOCOLS

Protocols are nothing more than an agreed-upon way in which two objects (people, computers, home appliances, etc.) can exchange information. There are protocols at various levels in the OSI model. In fact, it is the protocols at a particular level in the OSI model that provide that level's functionality. Protocols that work together to provide a layer or layers of the OSI model are known as a protocol stack or protocol suite. The following sections explain how network protocols move data between machines.

HOW PROTOCOLS WORK

A protocol is a set of basic steps that both computers must perform in the right order. For instance, for one computer to send a message to another computer, the first computer must perform the steps given in the following general example :

1. Break the data into small sections called packets.
2. Add addressing information to the packets, identifying the destination computer.
3. Deliver the data to the network card for transmission over the network.

The receiving computer must perform these steps :

1. Accept the data from the network adapter card.
2. Remove the transmitting information that was added by the transmitting computer.
3. Reassemble the packets of data into the original message.

Each computer needs to perform the same steps, in the same way and in the correct order, so that the data will arrive and be reassembled correctly. If one computer uses a protocol with different steps or even the same steps with different parameters (such as different sequencing, timing, or error correction), the two computers won't be able to communicate with each other.

NETWORK PACKETS

Networks primarily send and receive small chunks of data called *packets*. Network protocols construct, modify, and disassemble packets as they move data down the sending stack, across the network, and back up the OSI stack of the receiving computer. Packets have the following components :

- A source address specifying the sending computer
- A destination address specifying where the packet is being sent
- Instructions that tell the computer how to pass the data along
- Reassembly information (if the packet is part of a longer message)
- The data to be transmitted to the remote computer (often called the *packet payload*)
- Error-checking information to ensure that the data arrives intact

These components are assembled into slightly larger chunks; each packet contains three distinct Parts and each part contains some of the components listed previously :

- **Header** A typical header includes an alert signal to indicate that the data is being transmitted,
- source and destination addresses, and clock information to synchronize the transmission.

- **Data** This is the actual data being sent. It can vary (depending on the network type) from 48 bytes to 4 kilobytes.
- **Trailer** The contents of the trailer (or even the existence of a trailer) vary among network types, but it typically includes a CRC. The CRC helps the network determine whether or not a packet has been damaged in transmission.

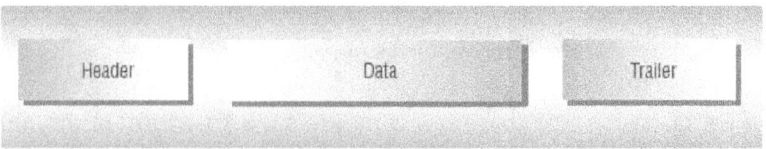

Fig. A12 : A packet consists of a header, the data, and a trailer

OSI Model Summary

OSI Layer	Major Functions
Physical (Layer 1)	Defines the physical structure of the network and the topology.
Data-link (Layer 2)	Provides error detection and correction. Uses two distinct sublayers: the Media Access Control (MAC) and Logical Link Control (LLC) layers. Identifies the method by which media is accessed. Defines hardware addressing through the MAC sublayer.
Network (Layer 3)	Handles the discovery of destination systems and addressing. Provides the mechanism by which data can be passed from one network system to another.
Transport (Layer 4)	Provides connection services between the sending and receiving devices and ensures reliable data delivery. Manages flow control through buffering or windowing. Provides segmentation, error checking, and service identification.
Session (Layer 5)	Synchronizes the data exchange between applications on separate devices.
Presentation (Layer 6)	Translates data from the format used by applications into one that can be transmitted across the network. Handles encryption and decryption of data. Provides compression and decompression functionality. Formats data from the application layer into a format that can be sent over the network.
Application (Layer 7)	Provides access to the network for applications.

TCP/IP PROTOCOL SUITE

- This model was developed before OSI model.
- Due to that the layers of TCP/IP protocol suit do not exactly match with the layers of OSI model.

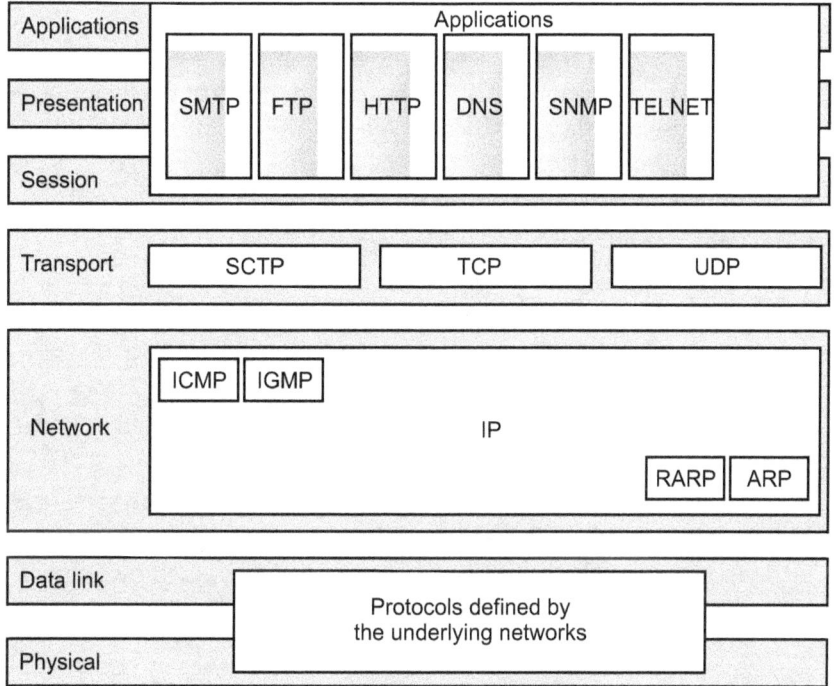

Fig. A13 : TCP/IP and OSI model

- There are four layers in TCP/IP model.
  1) Physical Layer and Data Link Layer (host to network layer)
  2) Network Layer
  3) Transport Layer and
  4) Application Layer
- The first four layers are similar to that of the OSI models first four layers.
- The three topmost layers of OSI model are represented by a single layer in the TCP/IP model. Refer following figure.
- TCP/IP is a hierarchical protocol, where the word hierarchical means that each upper layer level protocol is supported by one or more lower level protocols.
- At Transport layer, TCP/IP defines three protocols : Transmission Control Protocol (TCP), User Datagram Protocol (UDP), and Stream Control Transmission Protocol (SCTP).

- At network layer Internetworking Protocol is the main protocol that has been defined by TCP/IP.
- The layers of TCP/IP are as follows :
- **Physical and Data Link Layers :**
    - TCP/IP does not define any specific protocols at these layers.
    - It supports all standard and proprietary protocols.
- **Network Layer :**
    - At network layer along with Internetworking Protocol, Network layer also uses four more supporting protocols: ARP, RARP, ICMP and IGMP. Which are discussed in short below:
- **IP :**
    1) It is unreliable and connectionless protocol.
    2) It uses best effort service mechanism.
    3) In the best effort mechanism, IP provides no error checking and error tracking. It assumes unreliability of underlying layers and does its best to get transmission through to its destination, but with no guarantees.
    4) IP transports data in terms of IP packets which are also called as IP datagrams.
    5) Each datagram is transported separately.
    6) It is not necessary that all the Datagram's should follow the same route because of this datagram may arrive at the destination in out of order manner.
    7) IP does not keep the track of the routes and has no provision for reordering datagram's once they arrive at the destination host.
- **ARP :**
    1) This protocol plays an important role while mapping the IP address with the MAC address (physical address).
    2) On a typical physical network such as LAN, each device on the link is identified by a physical or station address usually imprinted on the network interface card (NIC).
    3) ARP is used to find physical address of the node when its IP address is known.
- **RARP :**
    1) The Reverse Address Resolution Protocol allows a host to discover its internet address when it knows only its physical address.
    2) It is used when a computer is connected is connected to the network for the first time or when a diskless computer is booted.
- **ICMP :**
    1) This protocol helps to send the datagram problems back to the sender of the datagram

2) It sends the query and error reporting messages.

- **IGMP :**
    1) It is used to facilitate the simultaneous transmission of a message to a group of recipients.

- **Transport Layer :**
    - There are two major protocols in the transport layer
        1. Transmission Control Protocol (TCP)
        2. User Datagram Protocol (UDP)
    - IP is a host-to-host protocol, it means that, it can deliver packet from one physical device to another.
    - While UDP and TCP are called as end-to-end protocols, which are responsible for the delivery of the message from a process (situated at the source machine) to another process (situated at destination machine).
    - A new transport layer protocol Stream Control Transmission Protocol (SCTP) has been devised to answer the needs of some new applications.

- **UDP :**
    1) It is a process-to-process protocol that adds only port addresses, checksum error control, and length information to the data from the upper layer.

- **TCP :**
    1) It is a reliable stream transport protocol.
    2) The term stream in this context means connection-oriented.
    3) At the sender's side, TCP divides a stream of data into smaller units called as segments.
    4) Each segment includes a sequence number for reordering after receipt, together with an acknowledgement number for the segments received.
    5) Segments are carried across the internet inside IP datagram.
    6) At the receiver's side, TCP collects each datagram as it comes in and reorders the transmission based on sequence number.

- **SCTP :**
    1) This protocol contains good features of TCP and UDP.
    2) Stream Control Transmission Protocol provides support for new applications such as IP telephony.

- **Application Layer :**
    - It is like the combination of session, presentation and application layers of the OSI model.
    - It contains many protocols such as FTP, SMTP, HTTP, DNS etc.

COMPUTER NETWORK TECHNOLOGY (T.E. I.T.) APPENDIX A

OSI MODEL Vs TCP/IP MODEL

TCP/IP	OSI
Vertical approach.	Horizontal Approach.
No session layer, its characteristics are provided by transport layer.	Separate session layer.
No presentation layer, characteristics of presentation layer are provided by the application layer.	Presentation layer is present.
It has 4 layers.	It has 7 layers.
It is not easy to replace protocols as technology changes.	Here, protocols are better hidden and can be easily replaced as technology changes.
It does not clearly distinguish between service, interfaces and protocols.	There is a clear distinction between service, interface and protocols.

Problems in TCP/IP model :

1) It does not clearly distinguish between service, interfaces and protocols
2) This model is not general model, it can not describe any protocol stack other than TCP/IP
3) This model does not give separate importance to the physical and data link layer.

WIRELESS TECHNOLOGY :

Wireless devices have become extremely popular because of the mobility they provide. The term wireless network refers to technology that allows two or more computers to communicate using standard network protocols, without network cabling. They are most often referred to as wireless local area networks (WLANs). This technology has produced a number of affordable wireless solutions that are growing in popularity with businesses and schools, or when network wiring is impossible, such as in warehousing or point of sale handheld equipment.

Wireless networking hardware requires the use of technology that handles data transmission over radio frequencies. The most widely used standard is the IEEE 802.11 standard that defines all aspects of Radio Frequency Wireless networking. Currently, the IEEE standards for wireless are 802.11a, 802.11b, and 802.11g. There are plans to implement 802.11e and 802.11i in 2004. Because standards operate on radio frequencies, one of the issues with the current wireless technology is that it is a broadcast signal, so basically it advertises that it is out there, making it easy to pick up.

To connect a wireless network to a wired network, you need some sort of bridge between the wireless and wired network. This can be done either with a hardware access point or a software access point. Hardware access points are available with various types of network interfaces, but typically require extra hardware to be purchased if your networking requirements change. A software access point does not limit the type or number of network interfaces you use; it is only limited by the number of slots or interfaces available in the computer. It may also allow considerable flexibility in providing access to different network types. A software access point may include additional features such as shared Internet access, Web caching, and content filtering.

The 802.11b standard specifies a transfer rate of 11 Mbps, which is sufficient for most broadband connections. As the signal deteriorates, the transfer rate drops dramatically, to 5.5 Mbps, 2 Mbps, and then 1 Mbps, although actual throughput is about half these rates. Optical wireless transmission via light beam is capable of transmitting data at speeds up to 622 Mbps.

There are two kinds of wireless networks, ad-hoc and access points. An ad-hoc, or per to peer wireless network, consists of computers that are equipped with a wireless NIC. Each computer can communicate directly with all of the other wireless enabled computers. They can share files and printers this way, but may not be able to access wired LAN resources.

A wireless network can also use an access point, or base station. In this type of network, the access point acts like a hub, providing connectivity for the wireless computers. It connects the wireless LAN to a wired LAN, allowing wireless computers access to LAN resources. There are two subcategories of access *points* : hardware and software access point. Hardware access points offer comprehensive support of most wireless features, but not all devices may be compatible. Software access points run on a computer equipped with a wireless network interface card as used in an ad-hoc or peer-to-peer wireless network.

Each access point has a specific range in which a wireless connection can be maintained between the client computer and the access point. The actual distance varies depending upon the environment. When pushed to the limits of the range, the performance may drop because the quality of connection deteriorates and the system tries to compensate. Indoor ranges for wireless devices are 150 to 300 feet but may be shorter if the construction of the building interferes with radio transmissions. Although longer ranges are possible, performance will degrade with distance. Outdoor ranges are quoted up to 1000 feet, depending on the environment.

HUBS :

A **hub** is a multiport repeater that retransmits a signal on all ports. When a packet arrives at one port, it is sent to the other ports so that all segments of the LAN can see it. Because it operates at layer 1 of the OSI model, it can connect segments or a network but cannot segment a network. Most hubs come with a minimum of 4 ports but can have as many as 48. There are two basic types of hubs : active and passive. Active hubs are the type described previously in this paragraph. A passive hub simply allows the signal to pass through without any amplification or regeneration. Intelligent or manageable hubs add features to active hubs that enable each port to be configured and the traffic passing through the hub to be monitored. A switching hub is a type of active hub that can read the destination address of packets and forward it to the correct port.

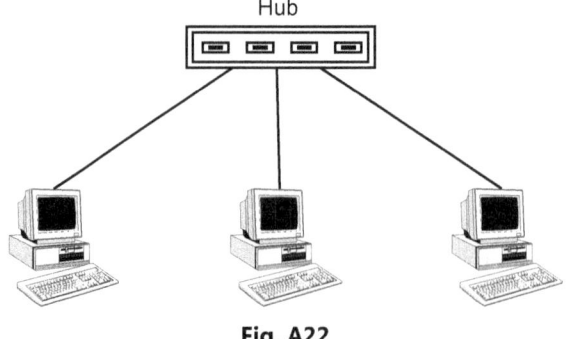

Fig. A22

Most hubs require no configuration, and passive hubs do not even require power. And remember that the devices connected to hubs all share the same bandwidth. In other words, if you have a 10 Mbps hub and three devices are transmitting at the same time, each device gets one third of the bandwidth. (See Fig. A22)

A stackable hub is designed to be connected and stacked on top of another hub, forming an expanding stack. This stackable approach allows equipment to be easily expanded as it grows in size and also reduces clutter.

BRIDGES :

A **bridge** is a device that connects two or more segments of a network to make them one. It could be described as a device that determines whether a message from you to someone else is going to the local area network or to someone on the LAN in the next building. A bridge examines each message, passing on those known to be within the same LAN, and forwarding those known to be on the other connected LANs. It looks similar to a hub but functions at the next layer of the OSI model, the Data Link Layer. Bridges have a single input and a single output port. It stores the MAC address for each device and then analyzes the incoming packets to determine what to do with them as they come through. Basically, it learns all the MAC addresses of the network to construct a database used for forwarding or filtering packets. A bridge can connect two different types of topologies because it does not understand anything above the Data Link layer. It doesn't matter whether one machine is using TCP/IP and another is using International Packet Exchange (IPX) Sequenced Packet Exchange (SPX) because they are only concerned with the MAC addresses and not the protocols. This allows them to move data more rapidly, but it takes longer to transmit because a bridge analyzes each packet.

SWITCHES :

Switches are rapidly becoming more popular than hub when it comes to connecting desktops to the wiring closet. Switches operate at the Data Link layer of the OSI model. Their packet forwarding decisions are based on MAC addresses. That is, a switch simply looks at each packet and determines from a physical address (the MAC address) which device a packet is intended for and then switches it out toward that device.

Switches allow LANs to be segmented, thereby increasing the amount of bandwidth that goes to each device. This means that, unlike a hub, each port on the switch is like a network segment itself. If you have a 10 Mbps switch with three devices connected to it, all three devices can use 10 Mbps of bandwidth. A switch repeats data only to the specified port, whereas a hub sends the data to all ports. In this context, it is said that each segment is a separate collision domain but all segments are in the same broadcast domain. The basic functions of a switch include filtering and forwarding frames, learning media access control (MAC) addresses, and preventing loops.

In wide area networks such as the Internet, the destination address requires them to be looked up in a routing table by a device known as a router. Some newer switches also perform routing functions. These switches are sometimes called IP switches or layer 3 switches.

ROUTERS :

Routers operate at the Network layer of the OSI model. They forward information to its destination on the network or the internet. Routers maintain tables that are checked each time a packet needs to be redirected from one interface to another. The routes may be added manually to the routing table or may be updated automatically using various protocols. Although primarily used to segment traffic, routers have additional useful features. One of the best is its ability to filter packets either by source address, destination address, protocol, or port. A router may create or maintain a table of the available routes and their conditions, and then use this information along with distance and cost algorithms to determine the best route for a given packet. Typically, a packet may travel through a number of network points with routers before arriving at its destination. Routers can also be configured to use strong protocol authentication.

On the internet, a router is a device that determines the next network point to which a packet should be forwarded toward its destination. The router is connected to at least two networks and decides which way to send each information packet based on its current understanding of the state of the networks to which it is connected. A router is located at any gateway, including each internet point of presence. Many times the connection from a router to the internet is through a device called a Channel Service Unit/Data Service Unit (CSU/DSU). The router is then internally connected to a LAN port on a switch. See Fig.A23 for an example of a router.

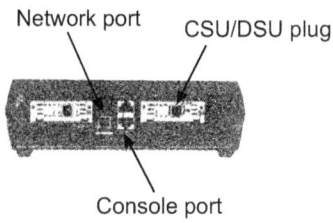

Fig. A23

Now that we have defined cabling and the devices that hook everything together, it's time to look at how to lay out the network. The actual geometric layout of the workstations is important because it will determine the type of cable, access, and protocols used.

www.ingramcontent.com/pod-product-compliance
Lightning Source LLC
Chambersburg PA
CBHW080422230426
43662CB00015B/2190